D1244097

Blaming the Victim
in the Heyday
of Psychoanalysis

EDWARD DOLNICK

Simon & Schuster

Madness
on the
Couch

SIMON & SCHUSTER
Rockefeller Center
1230 Avenue of the Americas
New York, NY 10020

Copyright © 1998 by Edward Dolnick
All rights reserved,
including the right of reproduction
in whole or in part in any form.
SIMON & SCHUSTER and colophon are
registered trademarks of Simon & Schuster Inc.
Designed by Edith Fowler
Manufactured in the United States of America

10   9   8   7   6   5   4   3   2   1

Library of Congress Cataloging-in-Publication Data
Dolnick, Edward, date.
    Madness on the couch : blaming the victim in
the heyday of psychoanalysis / Edward Dolnick.
        p.   cm.
    Includes bibliographical references and index.
    1. Psychoanalysis.   2. Psychiatric errors.
3. Schizophrenia — Treatment — History.
4. Autism — Treatment — History.   5. Obsessive-
compulsive disorder — Treatment — History.
6. Mental illness — Etiology.   I. Title.
RC506.D63   1998
616.89'17'09 — dc21   98-23737   CIP
ISBN 978-1-4165-7794-2   ISBN 1-4165-7794-7

Title page: Melencolia I, etching by Albrecht Dürer, 1514.

To Lynn, and Sam and Ben

Contents

8   CONTENTS

I beseech you, in the bowels of Christ, think it possible you may be mistaken.

—Oliver Cromwell

Prologue:
In Search of El Dorado

I am actually not at all a man of science, not an observer,
not an experimenter, not a thinker. I am by temperament
nothing but a conquistador — an adventurer, if you want it
translated — with all the curiosity, daring, and tenacity
characteristic of a man of this sort.

— SIGMUND FREUD

T HIS IS THE STORY of an expedition in quest of a treasure that had
lain mockingly out of reach throughout human history. Though all their
predecessors had failed, *these* explorers never felt the least premonition that
they had wandered off course. Instead, armed with boundless faith in a
treasure map they kept clutched to their chests, growing bolder and more
eager with each obstacle overcome, they marched along with the swagger of
conquistadores.

Their quarry was not gold but the secrets of the mind, the severely
disturbed mind in particular. Inspired by Freud, an ambitious band of psychiatrists and psychoanalysts planned to confront insanity, and to conquer
it. A less likely band of adventurers would be hard to find, but the swagger
was real. Bookish and sedentary, their battles confined to lecture halls and
medical journals, they nonetheless saw themselves as righteous knights cutting a swath through ranks of jealous enemies and ignorant rivals. One of
mankind's oldest enemies, madness, might soon be vanquished.

Freud, with characteristic boldness, had placed his own discoveries on
a par with those of Copernicus and Darwin. Now his disciples had taken on
a challenge that even their hero had never dared confront. Freud had
cautioned that psychoanalysis had nothing to offer the victims of psychosis.
Until useful medicines came along, he suggested, the best course was to
focus on neurotics rather than psychotics, on the worried well rather than

the profoundly sick. "Psychoanalysis," Freud observed "half jokingly" in 1909, "meets the optimum of favorable conditions where its practice is not needed, i.e., among the healthy."

By the 1950s and '60s, the master's warnings had been drowned in a tumult of excited voices. Psychoanalysts and psychiatrists could cure even schizophrenia, the most feared mental disease of all, they claimed, and they could do it simply *by talking* with their patients. It was a boast of dazzling audacity, based on a simple premise. The idea was that devastating mental illnesses were essentially no different from lesser psychological woes — both had the same roots, and both could be treated in the same way. The adult's illness reflected the child's fantasies and experiences, and "talk therapy" provided access to those crucial buried memories. In keeping with Freud's teachings, psychotherapy was seen as analogous to surgery. The present-day psychologist Lauren Slater summarizes this classical view: "The past is pus. The patient talks about it, her tongue like the surgeon's scalpel that scrapes the wound clean. Dabbed and dried, the poison now drained, the abrasion can begin to heal."

The therapists' guiding belief was that symptoms were symbols. The reason autistic children retreated from human contact into an untouchable zone of silence, for example, was that they had endured repeated rebuffs from their emotionally frigid parents. Heartless parenting had transformed normal, healthy children into numbed and withdrawn automatons. The most frequent culprit, the experts explained, was a "refrigerator mother."

This is a book about those therapists and their treasure hunt. It focuses on three "conditions" (there is dispute over the proper label) — schizophrenia, autism, and obsessive-compulsive disorder — and on one central belief that dominated psychoanalysis in its days of glory. This was the idea that diseases could be deciphered, that they were laden with symbolic messages like short stories by a heavy-handed author. The ranting of a schizophrenic on the street corner, the retreat of an autistic child behind invisible walls, the endless hand-washing of an obsessive-compulsive were not simply acts, but messages. They were, the therapists fervently believed, desperate if inarticulate cries for help. And now, for the first time, those cries could be decoded.

This was a new belief, or at least a new incarnation of an old belief. Mankind had been debating the roots of madness since ancient days. Was insanity a matter of an "imbalance of humors," and therefore to be treated by bloodletting operations and similar adventures in surgery, or were the mad possessed by devils and therefore in need of a priestly exorcism? The two explanations come roughly under the headings of "biology" and "psychology," and the pendulum has cut back and forth at least since Hippocrates.

Sometimes it pauses in its swing, and those pauses can last for centuries. Each time, the prevailing side hails its latest victory as permanent and damns its predecessors as black-hearted ignoramuses. From the Enlightenment until roughly 1900, the dominant view was that mental illness was no more and no less mysterious than any other form of disease. The brain was an organ of the body, and like other organs it could become diseased. Voltaire had put it succinctly: "A lunatic is a sick man whose brain is in bad health, just as the man who has gout is a sick man who has pains in his feet and hands."

Then came Freud. The greatest and most spellbinding of those who claimed the power to see the true face of humanity hidden behind a mask, he made organic theories of disease seem silly and shallow. The pendulum, stuck for so long on "biology" that it had grown rust-covered, suddenly swung back in favor of "psychology." In chapters 1 and 2 we take a close look at Freud. In chapters 3 and 4 we turn to Freud's legions of followers, who applied their mentor's lessons with even more zeal than he himself had shown. Then, beginning in chapter 5, we move to case studies of disease, to close-up looks at psychotherapists engaged in battle with ancient foes.

It is important to note at the outset that my title is metaphoric, not literal. "Madness" is not a medical term but a convenient shorthand. I have used it to embrace three strikingly different conditions, though all three are marked by bizarre behavior that would strike a layman as "mad." I look first at schizophrenia, the most dreaded mental illness; then at autism, thanks to the film *Rain Man* the most familiar member of the grim family of developmental disorders; and finally at obsessive-compulsive disorder, the illness that seems to cry the loudest for psychological interpretation. Authorities today place each into a distinct medical category: schizophrenia is a psychosis, autism a developmental problem, obsessive-compulsive disorder an anxiety disorder. The schizophrenic is the prototypical madman, out of touch with reality, beset by hallucinations, assaulted by mocking voices. The autistic person can appear mad but is in fact "merely" out of reach, living in our world but not sharing it and cut off from the rest of us. The obsessive-compulsive is not mad at all; he is trapped by rituals that he knows are nonsensical but that he is powerless to disobey.

Think of John Hinckley, who is schizophrenic, trying to impress Jodie Foster by shooting the president. Compare Hinckley with Dustin Hoffman's Rain Man (the portrayal of autism was so accurate that the film might have been a documentary). Rain Man was utterly devoid of the desire to impress anyone, or in fact to have anything to do with another person. Then compare either of them with Howard Hughes, the best-known victim of obsessive-compulsive disorder. Hughes spent his last years trapped in his hotel room behind blackout curtains, terrified of germs somehow emitted by the sun, caught in the grip of obsessive rituals that left him as helpless as a tree in the grasp of a strangler fig.

These are crucial differences. It is essential to recognize, though, that psychotherapists in post–World War II America nonetheless saw these three afflictions (and many others) as all of a piece. Equally important, they believed that all three could be *cured* in the same way, by "talk therapy." People tortured by schizophrenia, imprisoned by autism, bedeviled by obsessions and compulsions, could all be delivered from their torment.

These three conditions, it should be pointed out, were far from the only ones to which psychiatrists and psychoanalysts applied their deciphering skills. Indeed, they were only three icebergs in a frigid sea. The same decoding methods applied so assiduously in these three instances were applied with equal fervor to a myriad of illnesses that we might also have considered. Whenever the symptoms of disease included odd behavior (but not only then), psychotherapists were quick to probe the symptoms' meaning. Depression and manic-depression, for example, both drew the most intense rebus-solving scrutiny. So did such conditions as Parkinson's disease.

That fearsome disease, which can end in paralysis and death, is marked by a telltale stiffness. Freud's disciples explained this rigidity as a symbolic renunciation of the world. When therapists turned from Parkinson's disease to catatonia, the victims' statuelike poses inspired even more imaginative diagnoses. The "rigidity" of an arm or leg, the eminent Sándor Ferenczi explained, was "a displaced erection." Stuttering, to turn to another corner of the medical universe, revealed a different message: "If the motor accomplishments of the attempts to speak are carefully observed," one eminent psychoanalyst observed, "the stammerer will be seen in the act of nursing at an illusory nipple." Ulcers told yet another tale: "The critical factor in the development of ulcers is the frustration associated with the wish to receive love."

Most often, as it turns out, the critical factor in the development of ulcers is infection by bacteria that live in the stomach. But ulcers are hardly a grand theme, and when their true nature was revealed around 1990 (when it became clear, as well, that antibiotics provided a cure), psychotherapists handed their ulcer patients to other specialists without great regret. Mental illness was a different matter. Whose province could it be if not therapy's? Who but therapists could unravel the workings of the diseased mind? And so it is to madness we should turn, to see the battle between psychology and biology fought at its fiercest.

It is an age-old battle, and it is not resolved yet. But in the ever-oscillating rivalry between psychology and biology, psychology always has one built-in advantage: it alone offers an escape from the randomness of fate. Biology offers no such consolation. And even if biologists do manage someday to spell out the biochemical details underlying a disease, they will never be able to explain why a particular person has been picked to suffer. Biological "explanations" stop with "it just so happened." That is an unsatisfying answer. It rings with a cold, atheistic bleakness; or, perhaps marginally more satisfying, it evokes the Calvinist doctrine of predestination, which taught that God had, inexplicably, condemned some of His children to burn eternally.

Psychology, in contrast, can make sense of even the worst predicament. Psychotherapists did so by telling a story. Schizophrenia, for example, was caused by parents who bombarded their children with contradictory, Catch-22–style messages and literally drove them mad.

That narrative approach has enormous appeal, for both professionals and the public. Indeed, its appeal long predated Freud, the unchallenged master of psychiatric narrative. When John Keats fell ill with tuberculosis, for example, his contemporaries took his sickness and death as proof of his spirituality — the young poet was too soulful for this brutal world. The last blow was supposedly a particularly vicious attack on Keats's poetry in the *Quarterly Review.*

Humans are, after all, storytelling animals. Especially when confronted by frightening mysteries — death, disease, bad fortune — we weave together explanations as best we can, to serve as a kind of rope bridge across the abyss. Even when the stakes are lower, we cannot seem to keep from telling stories. We peek half-asleep at a pile of blankets kicked onto the floor and cannot help seeing lurking creatures; we look at the night sky and see swans and warriors in the stars; we hear a handful of random facts and devise elaborate conspiracy theories. And when we are confronted with a disease's bizarre symptoms, we set out at once to find their meaning.

It is worth pausing a moment here, before launching into the tale proper, to spell out the boundaries of the territory I want to explore. My focus is on psychotherapy's assault on mental illness in the 1950s and '60s, the heyday of psychoanalysis. There are lessons for us in this story, but my focus is on one special, strange, frenzied era — akin to the California gold rush, perhaps — and not on the overall merits or demerits of psychotherapy. In particular, it is *not* my view that this story of grand ambitions in collision with illnesses as devastating as schizophrenia has a direct bearing on the question of whether "talk therapy" is effective for phobias, anxiety disorders, anorexia, depression, and similar conditions. That question can be resolved only by testing, and countless such tests are underway. Is "talk" alone useful? *Which* talk therapy? For which conditions? What about drugs? What about the combination of drugs *and* talk?

That debate is unresolved, and I intend to bypass it. Nor do I have a vested interest in which side emerges triumphant in the end. On the related question of whether psychotherapy can be useful in coping with run-of-the-mill woes, as opposed to outright illnesses, I can be less tentative. Countless people know firsthand that therapy has helped them cope with a divorce, or a child's death, or a vague but oppressive feeling of inadequacy. There is equally little doubt, I feel sure, about some of the fundamental tenets of psychotherapy. It seems beyond dispute that we act for reasons that we do not understand, that our true motives can differ wildly from our professed ones, that we are at least as much creatures of instinct as of intellect. It seems certain that the unconscious is real (though pinning down that vague notion is a task that has tied serious thinkers in knots) and that our emotions affect our behavior.

But on the other hand, to say that psychotherapy has a place is not to say that it has *every* place. To look to psychotherapy for help in dealing with feelings of misery is one thing; to believe that "talk therapy" can cure a disease like schizophrenia — not merely help in coping with it but actually *cure* it — is a far bolder claim. It is a claim that was made for decades.

The goal of this book is to find why such ideas took hold and what impact they had. Why did psychotherapists harbor such high hopes? What became of their bold dreams? And when it became clear that these cheery doctrines had grim consequences — when, for example, parents were accused of driving their children mad — why did therapists and many of the accused parents themselves *continue* to uphold the new faith?

We begin with Freud, who convinced mankind that the world was a riddle written in code and that he had discovered the codebook.

PART ONE

Freud

A layman will no doubt find it hard to understand how pathological disorders of the body and mind can be eliminated by "mere" words.

—*SIGMUND FREUD*

CHAPTER ONE

The Gospel According to Freud

*[Freud] is extraordinary. Of course he is full of fishy
thinking and his charm and the charm of the subject are
so great that you may easily be fooled. . . . So hold on to
your brains.*

—LUDWIG WITTGENSTEIN

We possess the truth; I am as sure of it as fifteen years ago.

—SIGMUND FREUD

THE MAN WHO CONVINCED two generations of followers that diseases
could be decoded, like hieroglyphics, *looked* conventional enough. Freud
was nearly forty years old, well past the period of flaming youth, before he
embarked on any of the work for which he is known today. He was a
well-respected physician, a securely entrenched member of the middle class
(as securely entrenched, at any rate, as a Jew in anti-Semitic Vienna could
be), and the unchallenged head of a Victorian household that included a
wife, a sister-in-law, and six children. Formal in his speech, meticulous in
his dress, methodical in his habits, Freud hardly seemed a revolutionary.

He was a handsome man, five feet seven and of medium build, with
brown hair, brown eyes, and a neatly trimmed beard. Though he was an
affectionate father, the children were largely the province of his wife —
she also handled such domestic chores as spreading the toothpaste on her
husband's toothbrush — while Freud devoted himself to work. He was a
therapist by trade but not by temperament; his ambition reached beyond
soothing a handful of troubled Viennese. "We do analysis for two reasons,"
he once declared, "—to understand the unconscious and to make a living."

The world-weary tone was characteristic. Freud's true goal was dis-
covering the laws of the mind, and patients were only a means to that end.
Therapy was "not the main or even the essential aim of psychoanalysis," he
explained. "The chief aim of psychoanalysis is to contribute to the science

of psychology and to the world of literature and life in general." When one ex-patient made the mistake of asking Freud to evaluate himself as an analyst, the great man grew testy. "I'm glad you ask," he replied, "because, frankly, I have no great interest in therapeutic problems."

This was no Norman Rockwell doctor with a heart as big as all outdoors and a kind word always at the ready. "In the depths of my heart," Freud once told his great friend Lou Andreas-Salomé, "I can't help being convinced that my dear fellow men, with a few exceptions, are worthless." It was a favorite sentiment. "I have found little that is 'good' about human beings on the whole," Freud declared on another occasion. "In my experience most of them are trash. . . . If we are to talk of ethics, I subscribe to a high ideal from which most of the human beings I have come across depart most lamentably."

Still, there were bills to be paid. Six days a week patients arrived at No. 19 Berggasse, an apartment building in a respectably middle-class Viennese neighborhood. A butcher shop occupied the ground floor, Freud's office and the family apartment the second. Freud took a midday break to walk down the hall and join his family for lunch. He saw patients in a steady stream, the first at nine in the morning and the last perhaps as late as nine at night. He put his patients on the couch, rather than in a chair, so that they did not see *him*. "I cannot put up with being stared at by other people for eight hours a day (or more)," he explained.

Freud sat out of view behind the patient's head, jingling his keys or playing with his watch chain, and jumping in with opinions and interpretations, and even jokes, as they occurred to him. Quite often, one of his beloved dogs was sprawled across the carpet. It was a less austere approach than later Freudians — or even Freud himself, in his advice to others — would deem acceptable. (When Freud's daughter Anna decided that she, too, would become an analyst, Freud bent a far more important rule. He chose to analyze her himself, a father taking on the task of probing such matters as the meaning of his daughter's sexual fantasies.)

In the interest of objectivity, psychoanalysts were not supposed to betray any reactions, neither approval nor disapproval, neither shock nor boredom. "The doctor should be opaque to his patients," Freud decreed, "and, like a mirror, should show them nothing but what is shown to him." The goal was "emotional coldness." "I cannot advise my colleagues too urgently," Freud wrote, "to model themselves during psycho-analytic treatment on the surgeon, who puts aside all his feelings, even his human sympathy, and concentrates his mental forces on the single aim of performing the operation as skillfully as possible."

Nor did Freud look for much more collaboration from his patients than a surgeon would. Analysis was, he said, "a situation in which there is a superior and a subordinate," and there was little doubt about which was which. Freud "was quite dogmatic, and did not like disagreement," an ex-patient recalled. "When I would protest about something, his interpreta-tions, he used the Viennese dialect term, saying: 'You know a *Schmarn* about psychoanalysis.' It's hard to translate the word *Schmarn*, but a vulgar translation would be 'You know shit about analysis.' He said: 'You don't have the right to query my interpretation.' "

Freud made the discovery that he would regard ever after as his greatest in the closing years of the nineteenth century. In the spring of 1900, shortly after the publication of *The Interpretation of Dreams*, he wrote excitedly to a friend. "Do you suppose," he asked, "that someday one will read on a marble tablet on this house: 'Here, on July 24, 1895, the secret of the dream revealed itself to Dr. Sigm. Freud'?"

Freud's faith in his theory never wavered. Nine years later, he told an American lecture audience that "the interpretation of dreams is in fact the royal road to a knowledge of the unconscious; it is the securest foundation of psychoanalysis and the field in which every worker must acquire his convictions and seek his training."

Two decades after that, looking back on *The Interpretation of Dreams* in his old age, Freud still felt the same proprietary pride. "It contains," he wrote, "even according to my present-day judgment, the most valuable of all the discoveries it has been my good fortune to make. Insight such as this falls to one's lot but once in a lifetime."

The secret of dreams was a simple one. The unconscious, Freud said, teems with forbidden desires that we cannot bear to acknowledge. Those wishes appear in dreams, but disguised so that we can endure them. Dreams seem strange and full of gaps and scene shifts because a censor has gotten to the newsstand ahead of us, tearing out incriminating pages, blacking out key sentences, disguising photographs, to preserve our sleep.

Dreams were crucially important to Freud for three linked reasons. First, they were indeed the "royal road" that gave access to the otherwise hidden contents of the unconscious. Second, dreams linked the normal mind and the disturbed one. Since everyone dreams, and yet dreaming is a kind of madness, the thinker who could explain dreams was well on his way to a *universal* theory of mind. The royal road was in fact a bridge. "Do not let us forget," Freud wrote in an essay a few years before his death, "that the same process, the same interplay of forces, which explains the dreams of a normal sleeper, gives us the key to understanding all the phenomena of neurosis and psychosis."

Third, and for us most important, dreams were the ultimate demonstra-tion of the claim that was central to all Freud's thought: nothing was what it seemed, if only one knew how to probe beneath the surface. Not only were dreams "wolves in sheep's clothing," as Freud put it, but so was almost everything else. Gestures, actions, and words all concealed meanings known only to the initiated. As a result, Freud's self-appointed mission to uncover the secret meanings of everyday acts was virtually endless.

Slips of the tongue, accidents, problems coming up with names, even awkward encounters on the sidewalk were all revealed in their true significance. Consider, for example, "the irritating and clumsy process of dodging someone in the street, when for several seconds one steps first to one side and then to the other." That "mask of clumsiness," Freud declared, hid "sexual aims."

Everything was meaningful. Even so homely an activity as squeezing pimples spurred Freud's interpretive labors. Discussing a patient with bad skin, Freud explained that "pressing out the content of the blackheads is clearly to him a substitute for masturbation." Nor was that all. "The cavity which then appears owing to his fault is the female genital."

Nearly every story came back to sex sooner or later. How to explain writer's block, for example? Freud suggested that "writing, which entails making a liquid flow out of a tube," might have taken on "the significance of copulation." What of a reluctance to go outdoors? Perhaps walking had become "a symbolic substitute for stamping upon the body of mother earth." Even intellectual curiosity was nothing but sexuality in disguise. The scientist's "untiring love of asking questions," so reminiscent of a small child's endless questioning, was simply a sublimated version of the child's eagerness to resolve that earliest riddle, "where babies come from."

This was monomania that made Ahab seem like a Sunday fisherman — indeed, Ahab's declaration that "all visible objects are but as pasteboard masks" could have served Freud as a motto—and Freud was relentless. "When a member of my family complains to me of having bitten his tongue, pinched a finger, or the like," he noted, "he does not get the sympathy he hopes for, but instead the question: 'Why did you do that?' "

The question always had an answer. "I believe in external (real) chance, it is true," Freud wrote, "but not in internal (psychical) accidental events." When one of his patients broke her leg, for example, Freud hurried to explain the reason. Shortly before, she had danced at a family gathering, and her husband had rebuked her for carrying on "like a tart." Case closed. "We cannot fail to admire the skill which forced chance to mete out a punishment that fitted the crime so well," Freud wrote. "For it had now been made impossible for her to dance the can-can for quite a long time."

Freud delivered such verdicts with utter certainty, as befitted a man who had unearthed a secret unsuspected by the world at large. At times, he spoke of his ability to decipher everyday actions with something akin to awe, as if psychoanalysis conveyed the powers of the X-ray glasses that used to be advertised in the back pages of comic books: "To the observer of human nature they often betray everything—and at times even more than he cares to know," Freud wrote. "A person who is familiar with their significance may at times feel like King Solomon who, according to oriental legend, under-stood the language of animals."

But Freud was after bigger game than slips of the tongue or falls down the stairs. Disease was the true quarry, and dreams again provided the crucial analogy. Just as dreams appeared random and chaotic but in fact contained hidden meanings, so disease was really a code written on the body. It was a lesson that Freud's disciples would apply zealously long after their mentor's death.

But before considering the disciples, it is worth taking a close look at the master himself. All the tools that would eventually become standard items in the psychoanalytic code-breaker's kit — most notably the ability to unearth even the most deeply buried hidden meaning and a ferocious self-assuredness that refused to consider the possibility of error — were there from the beginning in Freud. Even in the hands of an expert, these were dangerous tools. Freud wielded them with dazzling grace, like a daredevil juggler who nonchalantly tosses snarling chain saws in graceful arcs from hand to hand.

In this chapter and the next, we will watch Freud at work. Then, to peek ahead at the rest of the book, we will look at what happened when a new generation raced to try its own hand at tricks that had seemed so easy from the sidelines.

Freud gave the first extended account of his code-breaking techniques in the case history of a young girl he called Dora. He explained, for example, why she periodically lost her voice and suffered coughing fits. The attacks came and went. So did a certain Herr K., a friend of Dora's father, whose business involved frequent travel. "I asked her what the average length of these attacks had been," Freud wrote. " 'From three to six weeks, perhaps.' How long had Herr K.'s absences lasted? 'Three to six weeks, too,' she was obliged to admit." This was almost too easy. "Her illness," Freud declared, "was therefore a demonstration of her love for K."

Like a magical suitcase that could accommodate any imaginable ob-ject, the code-breaking system was infinitely elastic. Freud conceded, for example, that Dora's bouts of illness turned out not to fit quite as neatly as all that with Herr K.'s travels, but he waved the problem aside. "Later on it no doubt became necessary to obscure the coincidence between her attacks of illness and the absence of the man she secretly loved," he wrote, "lest its regularity should betray her secret."

Another of Dora's symptoms was just as easy to decipher. Along with her coughing and muteness, Dora suffered from dyspnea, or shortness of breath. "Dora's symptomatic acts and certain other signs," Freud said, "gave me good reasons for supposing that the child, whose bedroom had been next door to her parents', had overheard her father in his wife's room at night and had heard him (for he was always short of breath) breathing hard while they had intercourse." The father's panting had become the child's chronic struggling for breath. "In many cases, as in Dora's," Freud wrote, "I have been able to trace back the symptom of dyspnoea or nervous asthma to the same exciting cause — to the patient's having overheard sexual intercourse taking place between adults."

Freud took for granted that Dora's various symptoms — coughing, shortness of breath, episodes of muteness — were hysterical. Why? Because, Freud explained, her father's friend Herr K. had "suddenly clasped the girl to him and pressed a kiss upon her lips. This was surely just the situation to call up a distinct feeling of sexual excitement in a girl of fourteen who had never before been approached. But Dora had at that moment a violent feeling of disgust, tore herself free from the man, and hurried past him to the staircase and from there to the street door."

Freud saw through *that*. "The behavior of this child of fourteen was already entirely and completely hysterical," he declared. "I should without question consider a person hysterical in whom an occasion for sexual excitement elicited feelings that were preponderantly or exclusively unpleasurable." This even though the "child of fourteen" was a virgin who had been grabbed without warning and kissed by a man old enough to be her father, in fact a close friend *of* her father's.

The same focus on sexual symbolism revealed the true meaning of another patient's headache symptoms. In a cryptic passage in a letter to a friend in 1899, Freud provided a shorthand summary of his thinking. "Hysterical headaches rest on an analogy in fantasy which equates the top with the bottom part of the body (hair in both places — cheeks and buttocks — lips and labia — mouth = vagina), so that an attack of migraine can be used to represent a forcible defloration, and yet the entire ailment once again represents a situation of wish fulfillment. The necessary conditions of the sexual become clearer and clearer."

The symbol-decoding approach also explained agoraphobia. A woman's fear of venturing outdoors, Freud explained, derived from "the repression of the intention to take the first man one meets in the street." The ravings of a madman, to take a more dramatic example, were not incoherent howls or even cries of anguish but messages to be deciphered. Even a madman's *acts*, as opposed to his words, were symbolic. In 1908, for example, Freud described an encounter with a young man who had been institutionalized for schizophrenia. "I observed one of his attacks myself," Freud wrote to a colleague, "and it was uncommonly instructive, as it represented an act of coitus, or rather his rage at an act of coitus observed by him (obviously his parents). His spitting is sperm-ejaculation. The whole thing is very transparent."

Once Freud had laid out the rules, his followers leapt into the game. Karl Abraham, a loyal but plodding member of the inner circle, noted that facial tics, for example, resembled grimaces and therefore had "obvious hostile significance." Premature ejaculation, Abraham explained, represented a different sort of symbolic message. "Just in the same way as the small child wets his mother with his urine which he cannot as yet contain, the patient wets his partner in his premature ejaculation, thus making evident that she is a substitute for his mother."

Smith Ely Jelliffe, a prominent American analyst and a Freudian disciple, explained in a 1917 textbook why an elderly schizophrenic woman continually pounded one hand with her other fist. "It was discovered that in her earlier days she had been jilted by a shoemaker. This peculiar action could be seen, in the light of this knowledge, as but the movements of the shoemaker pounding at his last."

This decoding reached its high point in the work of the German psychoanalyst Georg Groddeck. "Illness has a purpose. . . ," Groddeck wrote in 1923. "Whoever breaks an arm has either sinned or wished to commit a sin with that arm, perhaps murder, perhaps theft or masturbation; whoever grows blind desires no more to see, has sinned with his eyes or wishes to sin with them; whoever gets hoarse has a secret and dares not tell it aloud."

Groddeck was an eccentric, a self-described "wild analyst," but he was not an overzealous naïf whose views embarrassed his more sober colleagues. On the contrary, he was an influential thinker who corresponded with Freud, and this passage is from his best-known work, *The Book of the It*. (Freud took the term "id," to designate "the dark, inaccessible part of our personality," from Groddeck's "it.") Groddeck had sent Freud the manuscript of *The Book of the It* to look over before publication. "Groddeck is quite certainly four-fifths right in his belief that organic illness can be traced to the It," Freud wrote to another colleague, "and perhaps in the remaining fifth he is also right." *

"Sickness is also a symbol," Groddeck went on, in the same passage cited above, "a representation of something going on within, a drama staged by the It, by means of which it announces what it could not say with the tongue. In other words, every sickness, whether it be called organic or 'nervous,' and death too, are just as purposeful as playing the piano, striking a match, or crossing one's legs. They are a declaration from the It, clearer, more effective than speech could be."

Nothing if not clear, Groddeck went out of his way to emphasize just how sweeping his views were. "He alone will die who wishes to die, to whom life is intolerable," he declared. Remarkably, Freud himself expressed the same view, and in almost the same words. In 1930, already gravely ill with cancer of the jaw, he observed that "it is possible that death itself may not be a biological necessity. Perhaps we die because we want to die."

---

* It should also be noted, though, that on another occasion Freud rebuked Groddeck for providing exclusively psychological explanations of disease. "Your experiences, after all," Freud wrote, "don't reach beyond the realization that the psychological factors play an unexpectedly

• •

Freud was a complex character—ambitious, combative, charismatic, superstitious, intelligent (as a student, he was perennially first in his class)—and, perhaps, no better a judge of himself than anyone else is. In a letter to a colleague who had just written a book called *Human Motives*, for example, he wrote, "I believe that in a sense of justice and consideration for others, in disliking making others suffer or taking advantage of them, I can measure myself with the best people I have known. I have never done anything mean or malicious."

What, never? Who among us could live up to such a boast? For the notoriously belligerent Freud, a fierce hater with no notion of a statute of limitations, it was a particularly unlikely claim. *Twenty-five years* after he had banished his onetime disciple Alfred Adler for heresy,* for example, Freud exulted at the news that Adler had died of a stroke while attending a scientific meeting in Scotland. "For a Jew-boy out of a Viennese suburb," he snapped, "a death in Aberdeen is an unheard-of career in itself and a proof of how far he had got on. The world really rewarded him richly for his service in having contradicted psychoanalysis."

The pattern of loving friendships ending in vicious feuds or hostile cease-fires repeated itself time and again. Freud broke with his onetime mentor and colleague Josef Breuer, with his intellectual soul mate Wilhelm Fliess, with his handpicked successor Carl Jung. The split with Jung, Freud's beloved "son and heir," was especially painful. When Jung accused Freud of emphasizing sex to the exclusion of all other human motivations, Freud banished his former favorite. "So we are at last rid of them, the brutal, sanctimonious Jung and his disciples . . . ," Freud wrote to a colleague when the deed was done. "All my life I have been looking for friends who would not exploit and then betray me, and now, not far from its natural end, I hope I have found them."

The reasons Freud was so wary of betrayal are outside our scope—we will leave to others the job of psychoanalyzing Freud—but one part of the puzzle lies close at hand. He had indeed found the truth, he was convinced, and he was determined to safeguard it from those who would twist his words and muddle his message. It was a conviction that Freud's followers would take up as their own, and it made for a moral righteousness that left them deaf to criticism. Those who opposed the truth—whether patients or professionals—faced the wrath of the crusader who found an infidel blocking his path. No "adversaries, diluters, and misinterpreters," Freud warned, would be allowed to stand in his way. "In the execution of this duty," Freud's friend

---

important role also in the origin of organic diseases. But are these psychological factors *alone* responsible for the diseases?"
* The use of the word "heresy" might seem a rhetorical excess, but Freud himself referred to Carl Jung and Adler as "the two heretics."

Hanns Sachs declared, "he was untiring and unbending, hard and sharp like steel, a 'good hater' close to the limit of vindictiveness."

The stakes were so high, it cannot be overemphasized, because Freud was possessed of the certain knowledge that he had made a discovery for the ages. "Overtly and without apology," the devoutly Freudian literary critic Lionel Trilling once observed, "Freud hoped to be a genius, having before that avowed his intention of being a hero." Freud spoke of himself not as a mere human being but as a force of history. "I know that I have a destiny to fulfill," he declared. "I cannot escape it and I need not move towards it. I shall await it."

Fame was surely due him, for Freud rated his insights with those of Copernicus and Darwin. Both of those titans of science, Freud liked to explain, had dealt mankind enormous shocks to its self-esteem. Copernicus had demonstrated that the earth was not the center of the universe but a tiny speck in an undistinguished suburb. Darwin had shown that humans were not the pinnacle of creation but animals who still bore ineradicable signs of their animal ancestry. Now Freud had come along and delivered "human megalomania ... its third and most wounding blow." He had proved that humans were blind to their own motives, that "the ego ... is not even master in its own house, but must content itself with scanty information of what is going on unconsciously in its mind."

Nor were Copernicus and Darwin the only greats Freud compared himself with. At one time or another, the Freud scholar John Farrell notes, Freud likened his achievement and daring to that of the most exalted figures in world history and mythology: the biblical Joseph, Moses, Oedipus, Alexander the Great, Hannibal, William the Conqueror, Columbus, Leonardo, Kepler, Cromwell, Danton, Napoleon, Garibaldi, Bismarck, and even Zeus. More impressive still, Freud noted, his triumphs belonged to him alone. Einstein, for example, "had the support of a long series of predecessors from Newton onward, while I have had to hack every step of my way through a tangled jungle alone."

This was a monumental display of self-confidence. More important, this vaunting pride on the part of a single man soon transformed itself into an overwhelming *institutional* pride. Freud placed total faith in his own judgments; the psychoanalysts of the next generations took these same judgments as their own, and took on Freud's utter self-confidence as well.

The source of Freud's confidence was easy to place. Each day brought new confirmations of his views. Take his theory that dreams "invariably and indisputably" represent secret wishes. Support for the theory came, first of all, from patients who agreed with Freud's interpretations of their dreams. But support came also from those who emphatically *rejected* Freud's insights. Freud recounted proudly how he had dealt with one patient whose dream seemed to run counter to his thesis. She was a woman who disliked her mother-in-law and had gone out of her way to make sure that she would not have to spend her summer vacation with her. Then she had a dream that she and her mother-in-law *had* spent their vacation together. "Was not this the sharpest possible contradiction of my theory that in dreams wishes are fulfilled?" Freud asked his readers, with the showmanship of Houdini showing a bewildered audience his handcuffed wrists. Then he proceeded to wriggle free. "No doubt," Freud answered his own question, "and it was only necessary to follow the dream's logical consequence in order to arrive at its interpretation. The dream showed that I was wrong. *Thus it was her wish that I might be wrong, and her dream showed that wish fulfilled."* (Italics in original.)

This was not merely hubris but iron-clad hubris. Not only was it unlikely that the theory could be in error, but it was virtually unthinkable. The Catholic Church talks of "invincible ignorance"; here was invincible arrogance.

It would prove a formidable legacy.

For our purposes, focused as we are on how Freud's descendants treated mental illness, two aspects of Freud's thought are crucial. The first is that diseases can be interpreted like dreams; the second is that psychoanalysts have a unique pipeline to the truth.

To focus so narrowly is to neglect whole fields. Freud took all of human nature as his subject, and we shall have to pass by any number of fundamental Freudian concepts — the Oedipus complex, penis envy, the death instinct, among many others — without pausing to linger. Beyond that, we will not survey the changes in Freud's own thinking during his long life nor the divisions that long ago split psychoanalysis into rival camps. The Freudian banquet is a rich one, and it seems a shame to limit ourselves to two items. But it is not as if we have neglected the main dishes in favor of a few watery appetizers. It is more as if we only had time to consider Leonardo's paintings but not his inventions, or Shakespeare's plays but not his sonnets.

In examining Freud's legacy, we will stick closely to his own words. The most seductive version of the Freudian saga is the one told by its creator. Freud was a gifted artist, and his case histories, in particular, read like short stories. (To his dismay, Freud never won the Nobel Prize, but he did win the Goethe Prize for Literature.) Few rivals could compete with a psychiatric Scheherazade, especially one whose tales dripped with sexuality. Critics might snipe that Freud's theories hardly qualified as science, but most listeners waved aside such objections as the dreariest pedantry. "I'm sick of this deadhouse stuff," the American analyst Smith Ely Jelliffe once whispered to a colleague at a meeting of the American Neurological Association. "I wish a pretty woman would come in and tell a dream."

Freud was a captivating writer with a gift for creating vivid, sometimes jarring, images and analogies. Some were no more than casual remarks, sparks from the creator's anvil. In a letter to a friend, for example, Freud acknowledged that a new theory was not yet fully developed. "Reporting on it now," he wrote, "would be like sending a six-month fetus of a girl to a ball." Dismissing a rival's book on dreams while reluctantly conceding that its author made some good points, Freud snarled, "The pig finds truffles." * The liveliness carried over to his formal writing. Not content to observe that one could learn about his own unconscious only by putting in months on the couch, rather than by reading, for example, Freud dismissed all such shortcuts as akin to the "distribution of menu-cards in a time of famine."

Even his brief remarks were provocative. Consider, for instance, this characteristic explanation of why some people are superstitious: "Superstition is in large part the expectation of trouble; and a person who has harbored frequent evil wishes against others, but has been brought up to be good and has therefore repressed such wishes into the unconscious, will be especially ready to expect punishment for his unconscious wickedness in the form of trouble threatening him from without." Or this, on illness: "We have long observed that every neurosis has as its result, and probably therefore as its purpose, a forcing of the patient out of real life." The key phrase "and probably therefore as its purpose" seems almost an afterthought. It is a masterly touch, for the display of offhand brilliance makes Freud seem all the more dazzling, as if he has riches to spare.

Freud's favorite literary device, though, was not the casual aside but the elaborate set piece, usually cast as an analogy. When it came time to explain the notion of repressed memories to his first American audience, at Clark University in 1909, for example, Freud quickly moved beyond academic language. In London, Freud said, were two monuments. One commemorated Queen Eleanor, who died in the thirteenth century, the other the victims of the Great Fire of 1666. What would we think, Freud asked his listeners, of a pair of modern-day Londoners who burst into tears at the sight of these monuments? "Yet every single hysteric and neurotic behaves like these two impractical Londoners. Not only do they remember painful experiences of the remote past, but they still cling to them emotionally; they cannot get free of the past and for its sake they neglect what is real and immediate."

In the next day's Clark University lecture, Freud explained repression and resistance by means of a still more elaborate analogy:

> Let us suppose that in this lecture-room and among this audience, whose
> exemplary quiet and attentiveness I cannot sufficiently commend, there is

---

* The "pig" was Wilhelm Stekel. He had once described himself as "the apostle of Freud who was my Christ," but then he committed the double sin of siding with Adler and presuming to compare *his* work on dreams with Freud's. Stekel humbly cited the maxim about a dwarf on the shoulders of a giant seeing farther than the giant, but Freud was not appeased. "That may be true," he snarled, "but a louse on the head of an astronomer does not."

nevertheless someone who is causing a disturbance and whose ill-mannered laughter, chattering, and shuffling with his feet are distracting my attention from my task. I have to announce that I cannot proceed with my lecture; and thereupon three or four of you who are strong men stand up and, after a short struggle, put the interrupter outside the door. So now he is "repressed," and I can continue my lecture. But in order that the interruption shall not be repeated, in case the individual who has been expelled should try to enter the room once more, the gentlemen who have put my will into effect place their chairs up against the door and thus establish a "resistance" after the repression has been accomplished. . . .

If you come to think of it, the removal of the interrupter and the posting of the guardians at the door may not mean the end of the story. It may very well be that the individual who has been expelled, and who has now become embittered and reckless, will cause us further trouble. It is true that he is no longer among us; we are free from his presence, from his insulting laughter and his *sotto voce* comments. But in some respects, nevertheless, the repression has been unsuccessful; for now he is making an intolerable exhibition of himself outside the room, and his shouting and banging on the door with his fists interfere with my lecture even more than his bad behavior did before. In these circumstances we could not fail to be delighted if our respected president, Dr. Stanley Hall, should be willing to assume the role of mediator and peacemaker. He would have a talk with the unruly person outside and would then come to us with a request that he should be re-admitted after all: he himself would guarantee that the man would now behave better. On Dr. Hall's authority we decide to lift the repression, and peace and quiet are restored. This presents what is really no bad picture of the physician's task in the psycho-analytic treatment of the neuroses.

Freud's performance at Clark gives a hint of what made him so appealing. There is a feeling that we in the audience have been initiated into a secret society — we are among the elect, entrusted with powers unsuspected by the mass of humanity, able to see behind masks that others fail even to recognize. "He that has eyes to see and ears to hear may convince himself that no mortal can keep a secret," Freud had declared a few years earlier. "If his lips are silent, he chatters with his finger-tips; betrayal oozes out of him at every pore. And thus the task of making conscious the most hidden recesses of the mind is one which it is quite possible to accomplish." For those of us who have been entrusted with the secrets of psychoanalysis (but only for us), the world is stripped of its disguises and revealed in its true light. It was, we shall see, an invitation destined to seduce audiences around the world.

But what was new here? Freud was hardly the first psychiatrist (he was, in fact, a neurologist by training), though that is how many people think of him. Psychiatry had been an established profession since roughly 1800. What was Freud's contribution? What did psychoanalysis add to psychiatry?

These were questions Freud was happy to answer. He began by damning psychiatry as he had found it. It was "purely descriptive," Freud told a lecture audience in 1915, and therefore scarcely "deserve[d] the name of a science." In psychiatry, "nothing is known of the origin, the mechanism or the mutual relations of the symptoms" afflicting patients. Before Freud, psychiatrists had merely pinned labels on patients; Freud saw to the heart of their problems. Psychiatry had never advanced beyond description; now psychoanalysis had come along to provide *insight*.

Conventional psychiatry had never attained "first understanding," Freud declared disdainfully. Neurotic patients of all sorts "go to doctors, by whom people expect nervous disorders . . . to be removed," he continued. "The doctors, too, lay down the categories into which these complaints are divided. They diagnose them, each according to his own standpoint, under different names: neurasthenia, psychasthenia, phobias, obsessional neurosis, hysteria. They examine the organs which produce the symptoms, the heart, the stomach, the bowels, the genitals, and find them healthy. They recommend interruptions in the patient's accustomed mode of life, holidays, strengthening exercises, tonics, and by these means bring about temporary improvements — or no result at all."

Ernest Jones, Freud's early disciple and eventual biographer, was even more emphatic about the shortcomings of psychiatry in comparison with psychoanalysis. Like his master, Jones portrayed pre-Freudian psychiatrists as bumblers hopelessly beyond their depth, like toddlers trying earnestly but futilely to unlock Daddy's car and start the engine. "Such practitioners casually recommend a patient tortured with obsessions to play golf or to go for a sea cruise; more troublesome hysterical patients are immured in nursing-homes, where a hypothetical malnutrition of the brain — more imaginary than the actual trouble from which the patient is suffering — is remedied by the administration of milk and phosphates. When the futility of such methods becomes too evident then the practitioner is only too apt to fall back on moral disapprobation, and abusive words are spoken of the patient's laziness, obstinacy, and general moral turpitude — a mode of treatment not much more effective than the first one."

What *was* more effective, Jones hastened to point out, was Freudian analysis. "Psycho-analysis," he declared, "offers the medical profession just what it lacks — both understanding of these disorders and the power of dealing with them." Nonetheless, Jones went on grumpily, psychiatrists did their best to reject even this double gift. They tended "to resent being told that neurotic disorders can be both understood and cured, since this necessitates the taking of a deal of trouble." Far easier to ignore the patient's complaints or to blame him for his suffering.

It is an appealing story — all was mess and muddle until a singular genius focused his gaze and brought order out of chaos — and, in Freud's and Jones's telling, it has strong echoes of Isaac Newton's great triumph in physics. "Nature and nature's laws lay hid in night / God said 'Let Newton be!' and all was light." So Alexander Pope had declared, and Newton had explained only the inanimate world. Now Freud had come along to explain human nature and to heal the sick as well.

In the eyes of historians less partisan than Freud and Jones, the question of just what was new in Freud is murkier. Dreams had been considered meaningful at least since biblical days, for example, and dream interpretations complete with "Freudian" theories of sexual symbolism predated Freud by decades. The unconscious, too, was well-known territory before Freud. Freud's mentor Josef Breuer, for example, noted early in Freud's career, in 1895, that "it hardly seems necessary any longer to argue in favor of current ideas that are unconscious or subconscious. They are among the commonest facts of everyday life." In Henri Ellenberger's massive and authoritative *Discovery of the Unconscious*, Freud does not even make an appearance in the first four hundred pages.

Both Nietzsche and Schopenhauer, among others, had described the unconscious in ways that strikingly anticipated Freud. Indeed, Freud noted that Nietzsche's "guesses and intuitions often agree in the most astonishing way with the laborious findings of psychoanalysis," and he cited as an example Nietzsche's aphorism: " 'I did this,' says my Memory. 'I cannot have done this,' says my Pride and remains inexorable. In the end — Memory yields." Similarly, he acknowledged, a passage in Schopenhauer "coincides with my concept of repression so completely that once again I owe the chance of making a discovery to my not being well-read."

Nor was it Freud's contribution to open the eyes of the innocent Viennese to the reality and variety of sexual expression. Freud aside, turn-of-the-century Vienna was a city awash in talk of sex. It was, for example, Freud's colleague at the University of Vienna, the psychiatrist Richard von Krafft-Ebing, who had coined the terms "sadism" and "masochism" and published a hugely successful account of sexual abnormalities, *Psychopathia Sexualis*. Novels dealing with sex and popular accounts of such topics as sex in the animal kingdom were everywhere. Vienna did not embrace Freud's ideas, it is true, but it was not because it found them shocking.

Freudian mythology portrays an embattled genius who devised, on his own, an unprecedented picture of the human mind. That is too simple. "The current legend," as Henri Ellenberger summarizes it in his *Discovery of the Unconscious*, ". . . overlooks the work of previous explorers of the unconscious, dreams, and sexual pathology. Much of what is credited to Freud was diffuse current lore, and his role was to crystallize these ideas and give them an original shape."

That was no mean accomplishment. The unconscious, for example, had been probed before Freud but never surveyed with his devotion. Nor had any of his predecessors explored in such depth the crucial notion that man is not merely a rational being but also a social animal subject to unruly passions and drives. Freud did not create something out of nothing, as he sometimes claimed, but he made systematic what had been haphazard, and he brought the prestige of medicine to topics that had been merely literary.

Freud lives on, still an icon of our culture, but his immortality is of a curious sort. On the one hand, he is hailed as the titan who discovered the unconscious and revealed that we are all too often blind to our own motives. This is to praise Freud for "discoveries" he was of two minds about. As often as he claimed them as his own, he disavowed them as common knowledge. Shakespeare and countless other artists, Freud often wrote, had reached such general insights centuries before he came along. On the other hand, Freud did make specific contributions that he regarded as new and invaluable and his alone — the Oedipus complex, penis envy, dreams as wishes, and so on — and here it is the public who has been of two minds. Or more than two. Many psychiatrists, and more laymen, regard such notions as museum pieces. But orthodox Freudians, though only a handful survive, still cling to Freud's ideas. And even those psychoanalysts who reject much of the Freudian edifice do tend to embrace such central tenets as free association and transference.

And so posterity has yet to reach a consensus on Freud. Psychiatrists are divided along fairly predictable party lines, but the attitude of nonprofessionals is more curious. Those notions that the public identifies most closely with Freud, like the unconscious, are the ones he laid least claim to; those ideas that the public has rejected, like penis envy, are the ones Freud saw as uniquely his. As a culture, we continue to honor Freud, but our praise echoes Samuel Johnson's evaluation of a now forgotten work: "Your manuscript is both good and original, but the part that is good is not original, and the part that is original is not good."

For us, it suffices to note that Freud genuinely believed that he had unearthed the key to human behavior. "I have the distinct feeling," he declared, "that I have touched upon one of the great secrets of nature." The faith in a grand theory that tied the entire universe into a tidy package began as Freud's alone. Soon it spread to a group of followers, and then to the followers' followers, and so on, as telltale a sign of ancestry as the Hapsburg jaw. What began as the proud hope of a single bold thinker became a creed that affected countless lives.

CHAPTER TWO

The Power of Conviction

In such a case "No" signifies the desired "Yes."
— SIGMUND FREUD

THE GOSPEL WAS SPREAD by a band of true believers. Fueled by ideological zeal, reinforced by a steady influx of new recruits, racing eagerly along under the Freudian banner, they had neither time nor inclination for second thoughts. If there were warning signs along the way, they roared by them, hurrying and heedless.

This ideological fervor, and all the dangers that accompanied it, had been foreshadowed in Freud himself. But like the early signs of fever, those danger signs had passed unnoticed. Among those warning signals, two should have been especially worrisome. The first was Freud's embrace of sweeping pronouncements. Throughout Freud's work, the words "always," "never," "invariably," "infallibly," recur like drumbeats. The second trouble sign was that, almost compulsively, Freud reduced the spectrum of possible human motivations to a single vivid hue, sex. "Whatever case and whatever symptom we take as our point of departure," Freud declared in an 1896 lecture on hysteria, *"in the end we infallibly come to the field of sexual experience."* (Italics in original.) This was a law of "universal validity," Freud went on in the same lecture, and he summed up his views with a flourish: "At the bottom of every case of hysteria, there are *one or more occurrences of premature sexual experience.*" (Italics in original.)

Throughout his career, Freud changed his mind on issues great and small, but he never moved from this central theme. From first to last, he saw sex under every bed, so to speak. "I can only repeat over and over again — for I never find it otherwise — that sexuality is the key to the problem of the psychoneuroses and of the neuroses in general," he insisted in 1905. "No one who disdains the key will ever be able to unlock the door." In 1906, he put this view even more bluntly. "If the *vita sexualis* is normal," he wrote, "there can be no neurosis."

He made no exceptions. "Every new arrival on this planet is faced by the task of mastering the Oedipus complex," he wrote in 1920. "Anyone who fails to do so falls a victim to neurosis." "It became ever clearer," he repeated in 1924, that the Oedipus complex is "the nucleus of every case of neurosis." It is "the central experience of the years of childhood," he added in 1938, and he noted that "no human individual is spared such traumatic experiences."

The notion that young children not only loved their parents but lusted after them, not only felt angry with them but felt murderous rage, might strike his readers as "unsavory and incredible," Freud acknowledged. But facts were facts. "I can only insist that psychoanalytic experience has put these relations in particular beyond the reach of doubt," he declared, "and has taught us to recognize in them the key to every neurosis."

There was the Freudian signature, an assertion that simultaneously laid down a universal law and revealed a sexual message. In discussing paranoia, to take another example, Freud declared that "the delusion of persecution invariably depends on homosexuality." The topic might change, but not the tone. On women: "All women feel that they have been injured in their infancy and that through no fault of their own they have been slighted and robbed of a part of their body." On boys: "With boys the wish to beget a child from their mother is never absent." On girls: "With girls the wish to have a child by their father is equally constant."

Deep as it was, Freud sometimes put his preoccupation with sexual symbolism to one side. The impulse to proclaim universal, all-embracing laws, on the other hand, was too strong to set aside. "The motive for being ill," he declared, "is, of course, invariably the gaining of some advantage." In explaining the hidden meanings of what are now called Freudian slips, to consider another example, Freud spoke with his customary disdain for alternative interpretations. "Is this the explanation of *all* cases of slips of the tongue?" he asked, using italics to proclaim his boldness. "I am very much inclined to think so, and my reason is that every time one investigates an instance of a slip of the tongue an explanation of this kind is forthcoming."

In similar fashion, all large-animal phobias had a single explanation. "It was the same in every case: where the children concerned were boys, their fear related at bottom to their father and had merely been displaced on to the animal." And all addictions were really a single addiction in disguise. "The insight has dawned on me," Freud wrote, "that masturbation is the one major habit, the 'primary addiction,' and it is only as a substitute and replacement for it that the other addictions—to alcohol, morphine, tobacco, and the like—come into existence."

Freud's penchant for one-size-fits-all explanations was a fundamental part of his mental life, as deeply entrenched as his dislike of religion or his fascination with archeology. Characteristically, he erected even this personal quirk into a universal law. "Mankind," he declared, "has always harbored the longing to be able to open all secrets with a single key." Whether or not it was true of mankind in general, it was surely true of Freud in particular. (Almost as soon as he began treating Dora, the teenaged girl troubled by coughing fits and shortness of breath, Freud wrote that the new case had "smoothly opened to the existing collection of picklocks.") As early as 1907, Josef Breuer, Freud's older colleague and onetime mentor, had warned of the dangers of this relentless single-mindedness. "Freud is a man given to absolute and exclusive formulations," Breuer wrote. "This is a psychical need which, in my opinion, leads to excessive generalization." *

Breuer's caution is especially noteworthy because in years to come psychiatrists would invoke Freud as the patron saint of open-mindedness who had taught them to honor the individuality and complexity of each patient. They portrayed scientists, in contrast, as viewing patients as little more than ambulatory test tubes. In shocked tones, analysts would denounce their scientific rivals as "reductionists," a dirty word intended to convey that biochemists and neurologists and geneticists sought to reduce the depth of the human soul to a few measurements on a graph.

Freud has been made to wear many labels, but it would be deeply misleading to think that he would have allied himself with those who saw scientists as cold-blooded pedants. Freud himself was trained as a scientist, and he prided himself on having a tough-minded, practical, scientific bent. The belief that someday psychology would be established on a solid scientific foundation was a constant throughout his life. He proclaimed that hope in 1895, at the dawn of his career, in a supremely ambitious venture called the *Project for a Scientific Psychology.* The aim, Freud explained in his opening sentence, was "to furnish a psychology that shall be a natural science." The *Project* soon ended in frustration and despair. After half a year of feverish work and frenzied excitement, Freud admitted that "I no longer understand the state of mind in which I hatched the psychology . . . it appears to have been a kind of madness." Still, he continued to endorse the goal, even if he rejected this first attempt at a solution. "The *Project*, or rather its invisible ghost," wrote James Strachey, the editor of the standard English-language edition of Freud's works, "haunts the whole series of Freud's theoretical writings to the very end."

Psychoanalysis *was* a science, Freud insisted, and his discoveries were

---

* Freud's great rival Carl Jung could be equally single-minded and dogmatic, although he saw religion where Freud saw sex. "Among all my patients in the second half of life — that is to say, over thirty-five — there has not been one whose problem in the last resort was not that of finding a religious outlook on life. It is safe to say that every one of them fell ill because he had lost that which the living religions of every age have given to their followers, and none of them has been really healed who did not regain his religious outlook."

laws of nature. Those laws might be explained artfully or clumsily, but they were scientific discoveries and not artistic creations. "You should not for a moment suppose that what I put before you as the psycho-analytic view is a speculative system," he insisted. "It is on the contrary empirical." Even Freud's unrelenting focus on sex originated in his desire to ground psychology in biology. "In the sexual processes," Freud wrote to Jung, "we have the indispensable 'organic foundation' without which a medical man can only feel ill at ease in the life of the psyche."

Similarly, the great virtue of the dream theory, Freud's perennial favorite, was precisely that it snatched dreams from the fuzzy-minded and explained them scientifically. That explanation, it should be noted, was deeply reductionist. Every feature of a dream, no matter how trivial, was deeply significant. Every dream, virtually without exception, stemmed from a wish. Only one method of dream interpretation, the psychoanalytic one, was valid.

Freud's faith in his discoveries was unshakable. Consider, for example, his explanation of shell shock in soldiers who fought in World War I. Here were men suffering terrible emotional distress despite having no physical wounds. Clearly, they counted as neurotic, and yet their woes stemmed from traumas on the battlefield rather than in the nursery. Where did sex — supposedly at the heart of *every* neurosis — come into it? Freud was undaunted. "Mechanical agitation," he explained, referring to the hellish roar and rumble of trench warfare, "must be recognized as one of the sources of sexual excitation."

Even when a fourteen-year-old patient died shortly after he had pronounced her cured, Freud was unfazed:

> The child fell ill of an unmistakable hysteria, which did in fact clear up quickly and radically under my care. After this improvement the child was taken away from me by her parents. She still complained of abdominal pains which had played the chief part in the clinical picture of her hysteria. Two months later she died of sarcoma of the abdominal glands. The hysteria, to which she was at the same time predisposed, used the tumor as a provoking cause, and I, with my attention held by the noisy but harmless manifestations of the hysteria, had perhaps overlooked the first signs of the insidious and incurable disease.

This is remarkable, although the odd phrasing may throw us off momentarily. Freud tells us that a patient came to him complaining of stomach pains and that he diagnosed her as having "unmistakable hysteria." Two months later she was dead of stomach cancer. A lesser man would have questioned his diagnosis. But even though his "radically" cured patient now lay dead, and even though her abdominal pains had continued after her supposed cure, Freud *still* maintained that he was correct in having diagnosed her as suffering from hysteria! It is possible that she suffered from hysteria as well as cancer, of course, but it shows extraordinary self-assurance that Freud simply took that for granted.

If the brute evidence of a teenager lying dead could not convince Freud to change his mind, a mere patient hardly stood a chance. When Freud explained to Dora that she was in love with Herr K. despite her claims to despise him, for example, the feisty eighteen-year-old responded with "a most emphatic negative." Freud scarcely paused for breath. This denial was simply proof that he had been right all along. "The 'No' uttered by a patient after a repressed thought has been presented to his conscious perception for the first time does no more than register the existence of a repression and its severity; it acts, as it were, as a gauge of the repression's strength," he declared. "If this 'No,' instead of being regarded as the expression of an impartial judgment (of which, indeed, the patient is incapable), is ignored, and if work is continued, the first evidence soon begins to appear that in such a case 'No' signifies the desired 'Yes.' "

But Freud also provides countless examples of interpretations that his patients did accept with a "Yes." In those cases, "Yes" signified "Yes," and Freud had confirmation that his interpretations were correct. This seemed a bit pat, even Freud acknowledged, and in another essay he took the trouble to justify his approach:

> "So that's your technique," I hear you say. "When a person who has made a slip of the tongue says something about it that suits you, you pronounce him to be the final authority on the subject. 'He says so himself!' But when what he says doesn't suit your book, then all at once you say he's of no importance — there's no need to believe him."
>
> That is quite true. But I can put a similar case to you in which the same monstrous event occurs. When someone charged with an offense confesses his deed to the judge, the judge believes his confession; but if he denies it, the judge does not believe him. If it were otherwise, there would be no administration of justice, and in spite of occasional errors we must allow that the system works.

This is a tricky bit of rhetoric, for the guiding analogy is by no means indisputable. Is a slip of the tongue something that calls for a "confession"? Is Freud an impartial judge, and is it true that a judge must automatically reject every claim of innocence?* Without answers to such questions, Freud's self-justification looks like an argument but amounts to little more than the familiar taunt "Heads I win, tails you lose."

---

* Freud acknowledged these questions. "Are you a judge, then?" he imagined an interlocutor asking. "And is a person who has made a slip of the tongue brought up before you on a charge? So making a slip of the tongue is an offense, is it?" But having raised the relevant questions, he hurried off without answering them.

• •

In two areas, however, one narrow and one broad, Freud did display unaccustomed caution. Twice he issued warnings to his followers. Twice they ignored him. Both times the consequences were fateful.

To glance ahead, we will see that, at least when it came to major mental illnesses, Freud's disciples did him no honor. They ignored Freud's best qualities — intelligence, far-ranging curiosity, respect for science — and emulated only his worst traits — ideological zealotry, intellectual smugness, the vehement rejection of outside opinions. After Marx, Brezhnev.

The first of Freud's two warnings, the narrow one, had to do with psychoses, as opposed to mere neuroses. These major illnesses, Freud warned, were out of bounds. Unlike psychiatrists of the past, psychoanalysts should concentrate on the neurotic rather than the overtly mad. Schizophrenia, in particular, should be left alone.

There was no mistaking his message. In 1917, for example, Freud claimed that psychoanalysts had cured patients suffering from hysteria and anxiety and obsessional neurosis, but he went on to point out that "there are, however, other forms of illness in which . . . our therapeutic procedure is never successful." In particular, he warned, patients with schizophrenia "remain on the whole unaffected and proof against psychoanalytic therapy."

Freud's only direct experience with schizophrenia was a three-week stint early in his career, at a private mental hospital outside Vienna. All the patients were rich, many were titled, Freud had to make his rounds in silk hat and white gloves, and three weeks was more than enough. "I do not care for these patients," he confessed on a later occasion. ". . . They annoy me . . . I feel them alien to me and to everything human. A peculiar kind of intolerance which undoubtedly disqualifies me as a psychiatrist."

The problem was that these alien patients were beyond reach. "Even we cannot withhold from them something of the reverential awe which peoples of the past felt for the insane," Freud acknowledged. It was this unbridgeable gulf between us and them that accounted for the inability of psychoanalysis to help these unfortunate people. "They reject the doctor, not with hostility but with indifference," Freud noted. ". . . What he says leaves them cold, makes no impression on them; consequently the mechanism of cure which we carry through with other people — the revival of the pathogenic conflict and the overcoming of the resistance due to repression — cannot be operated with them. They remain as they are." Schizophrenics, Freud declared flatly, "are inaccessible to our efforts and cannot be cured by us."

The problem, Freud hastened to note, was *not* that he did not understand schizophrenia. In fact, despite what he acknowledged as his "unfamiliarity with schizophrenia," he understood it perfectly well. Schizophrenia, and paranoia in particular, stemmed from the patient's struggle to deny unruly and unacceptable homosexual feelings. (We will examine Freud's views on schizophrenia in chapter 5.) With its focus on repressed sexual feelings, this was an explanation with a familiar ring.

But explaining a disease was different from treating it. Since schizophrenic patients ignored their psychiatrist's insights and therefore made treatment impossible, the therapist had no choice but to tend to more accommodating patients. "We know that the mechanisms of the psychoses are in essence no different from those of the neuroses," Freud told his devoted follower Marie Bonaparte, "but we do not have at our disposal the quantitative stimulation necessary for changing them. The hope of the future here lies in organic chemistry or the access to it through endocrinology."

This brings us to Freud's second warning. Unlike the first, which was narrow — avoid schizophrenia! — this was a general injunction. Do not presume too much, the supremely self-confident Freud warned. In particular, do not forget that humans are shaped by both heredity and environment and that neither can be ignored. "Do not suppose that we underestimate" the importance of heredity, Freud wrote. "Precisely as therapists we come to realize its power clearly enough. In any case we can do nothing to alter it; we too must take it as something given, which sets a limit to our efforts."

As we have seen, Freud often ignored his own advice. In Dora's case, for example, he compared organic explanations of her cough to "the grain of sand around which an oyster forms its pearl." This was a characteristically Freudian bit of rhetoric. The effect was to give with one hand and take away with the other, simultaneously acknowledging the possibility that Dora's symptoms might have a conventional medical explanation and downplaying that idea in favor of a truer, deeper one.

Still, in comparison with the generation that would follow him, Freud was a model of restraint. In the heredity-versus-environment debate, Freud's post–World War II followers were fiercely proenvironment; they saw talk of heredity as little more than gussied-up racism. This was in large measure a carryover from the Nazis' endorsement of eugenics. But psychoanalysts were suspicious of heredity, even aside from racism, because they saw it as an attempt to reduce psychology to biology. (Freud, as we have seen, *favored* such an attempt.) That approach had been tried, and found wanting, for centuries. The libraries were full of bold but soon-forgotten pronouncements that schizophrenia, say, was caused by abnormal blood vessels or lesions at particular sites in the brain or a toxic excess of one compound or another. In the current debate, the analysts felt sure, the heredity camp remained the province not of thinkers but of second-raters, the domain of modern-day alchemists mumbling formulas and manipulating test tubes and devoid of any guiding theory.

Freud, on the other hand, professed himself to be neutral in the heredity-versus-environment controversy. "Are [neuroses] the inevitable result of a particular constitution or the product of certain detrimental (traumatic) experiences in life?" he asked a lecture audience in 1916. "This dilemma seems to me no more sensible on the whole than another that I might put to you: does a baby come about through being begotten by its father or conceived by its mother?"

That cautious tone was unusual. Freewheeling recklessness was far more Freud's style than professorial moderation. And it was this "boldness" and "genius" that Freud's followers would emulate. Listen, for example, to the famous passages on dream symbolism, which go on for page after page with almost manic exuberance. A cigar was very seldom just a cigar:

> The more striking and for both sexes the more interesting component of the genitals, the male organ, finds symbolic substitutes in the first instance in things that resemble it in shape — things, accordingly, that are long and up-standing, such as *sticks, umbrellas, posts, trees* and so on; further, in objects which share with the thing they represent the characteristic of penetrating into the body and injuring — thus, sharp *weapons* of every kind, *knives, daggers, spears, sabres,* but also fire-arms, *rifles, pistols* and *revolvers* (particularly suitable owing to their shape). In the anxiety dreams of girls, being followed by a man with a knife or a fire-arm plays a large part. This is perhaps the commonest instance of dream-symbolism and you will now be able to translate it easily. [Italics in original.]

Freud was only warming up. Any object more convex than concave, it seemed, could symbolize the male genitals. He rattled off a few examples: water-taps, watering-cans, fountains, hanging lamps, pencils, pen-holders, nail files, hammers, balloons, airplanes, blimps, snakes, fish, hats, overcoats, and cloaks.

Similarly, he noted, the female genitals took symbolic form as "pits, cavities, and hollows," as well as "vessels and bottles, . . . receptacles, boxes, trunks, cases, chests, pockets," not to mention ships, cupboards, stoves, rooms, doors, gates, wood, paper, objects made of wood or paper, snails, mussels, churches, chapels, apples, peaches, fruit in general, woods, bushes, landscapes, jewels, and treasures.

Even such seemingly neutral objects as stairways were stripped of their disguises. We "began to turn our attention to the appearance of steps, staircases and ladders in dreams," Freud wrote, "and were soon in a position to show that staircases (and analogous things) were unquestionably symbols of copulation. It is not hard to discover the basis of the comparison: we come to the top in a series of rhythmical movements and with increasing breathlessness, and then, with a few rapid leaps, we can get to the bottom again. Thus the rhythmical pattern of copulation is reproduced in going upstairs."

This was a game without rules, and many attempts at interpretation were bound to be dubious. In an influential essay on Leonardo da Vinci, for example, Freud explained why the great painter left so many of his projects unfinished. It had to do with his childhood, of course, which would have presented most writers with the problem that Leonardo's early life is almost completely lost to history. Undaunted, Freud deduced the key features of Leonardo's childhood from the known facts of his adult life. In particular, it was plain to Freud (though not to conventional scholars) that Leonardo's father had neglected his young son. From there on, it was smooth sailing. "There is no doubt that the creative artist feels towards his works like a father," Freud noted, and since Leonardo's father had neglected *him*, Leonardo neglected *his* creations. "He created them and then cared no more about them, just as his father had not cared about him."

In 1909, to take a clinical example, Freud published the famous case history of "Little Hans," a boy with a phobia about horses. The boy's mother and father "were both among my closest adherents," Freud noted, and Freud saw Hans himself only a single time. The rest of the time he dealt with the boy's father, who came to Freud with accounts of his conversations with his son and returned home bearing Freud's newest theoretical insights.

To Freud's eye, the case was plain. Here was the Oedipal drama playing itself out in the streets of Vienna. Why was Hans afraid of horses? "The horse must be his father — whom he had good internal reasons for fearing." Those fears were the universal ones, namely that Hans's father would castrate him for lusting after his mother. And why did Hans, in his single meeting with Freud, say that he was particularly frightened "by what horses wear in front of their eyes and by the black round their mouths"? Because the boy's father had a mustache and eyeglasses, which Hans had "directly transposed from his father on to the horses."

Hans's motives in all this were just as plain. "The content of his phobia," Freud went on, "was such as to impose a very great measure of restriction upon his freedom of movement, and that was its purpose. . . . After all, Hans's phobia of horses was an obstacle to his going into the street, and could serve as a means of allowing him to stay at home with his beloved mother. In this way, therefore, his affection for his mother triumphantly achieved its aim. In consequence of his phobia, the lover clung to the object of his love."

This was a more elaborate explanation than the one that Hans himself had suggested. He had been terrified of horses, he told his father, ever since the day he had seen a horse pulling a bus collapse in the street. His mother, who had been with him at the time, seconded Hans's account. And the fearsome black object near a horse's mouth and eyes, Hans said, was not a symbol of his father's mustache and glasses but was in fact the horse's leather muzzle.

For Freud and his followers, no such mundane explanations would do when more elaborate ones could be found. Simple explanations were not signs of common sense but of shallowness. And reluctance to go along with Freud was more than a sign of intellectual weakness; it was an ethical failure as well, an alliance with all those timid and conservative "thinkers" who shut their eyes to unpleasant realities. But skepticism reflected still deeper problems. Psychoanalysis had a hard time making its way in the world not because its arguments were dubious but because its critics were neurotic. "I knew very well of course that anyone may take to flight at his first approach to the unwelcome truths of analysis," Freud wrote. "I had always myself maintained that everyone's understanding of it is limited by his own repressions (or rather, by the resistances which sustain them) so that he cannot go beyond a particular point in his relation to analysis."

This was a brilliant ploy, still in use today. Its effect was to place psychoanalysis above criticism, since to criticize was to flaunt one's neuroses. On the other hand, those who *did* possess the requisite mental health to accept the truths of analysis grew ever stronger in their faith, for they found evidence to back their views everywhere they looked. The influential analyst Sándor Ferenczi, for example, an early member of Freud's inner circle, wrote a paper called "Psychoanalytical Observations on Tic," in which he explained the meaning of tics. Even Freud had suggested that tics represented some sort of organic problem, but Ferenczi dismissed that idea. He cited the case of a patient whose head continually shook back and forth when she greeted anyone or said good-bye. Despite the friendly words she addressed to her visitors, Ferenczi noted, the woman seemed to be shaking her head "no," and "I was obliged to tell her that the shaking of her head was intended to give the lie to the friendly manner or gesture."

"I was obliged to tell her" captures a worldview in a single phrase. Smugness was perhaps the most striking trait of the disease-deciphering psychoanalysts. They were not suggesting but declaring, not proposing explanations but laying down the law. And there was no appealing the court's decision.

No skeptics from outside the psychoanalytic circle, Freud decreed, were fit to comment on his theories. "The whale and the polar bear, it has been said, cannot wage war on each other, for since each is confined to his own element they cannot meet," he wrote. "It is just as impossible for me to argue with workers in the field of psychology or of the neuroses who do not recognize the postulates of psycho-analysis and who look on its results as artefacts."

Only those who had been through the analytic process themselves had a chance of seeing the truth. "How then could I expect to convince you, the Impartial Person, of the correctness of our theories," Freud asked, "when I can only put before you an abbreviated and therefore unintelligible account of them, without confirming them from your own experiences?" Nonbelievers could only be converted, not convinced.

The problem was not only that psychoanalysts and nonanalysts saw the world differently, but that psychoanalysts saw it more deeply. "One cannot properly deny the findings [reached by the psychoanalytic method] . . . so long as one puts it aside and uses only the customary method of questioning patients," Freud wrote. "To do so would be like trying to refute the findings of histological technique by relying upon macroscopic examination."

Eight decades later, psychoanalysts were still making the identical argument, in almost the identical words. "I can't convince anybody that there are microbes in this world unless I apply a light microscope," argued Theodore Shapiro in 1990, by way of dismissing an anti-Freudian theory of dreaming proposed by the psychiatrist Allan Hobson. "I can't tell you anything about the ultrastructure of cells unless I apply an electron microscope," continued Shapiro, who was at that time the editor of the *Journal of the American Psychoanalytic Association.* "How can Hobson say anything about the insights to be derived from dreams if he doesn't apply the psychoanalytic method?"

Not only outside opinions, but also outside evidence, were unwanted. Freud warned explicitly against any attempts to check the accuracy of his case histories. "It may seem tempting to take the easy course of filling up the gaps in a patient's memory by making inquiries from the older members of his family; but I cannot advise too strongly against such a technique.... One invariably regrets having made oneself dependent upon such information; at the same time confidence in the analysis is shaken and a court of appeal is set up over it."

Not only were the recollections of family members disdained, but so were the opinions of the patients themselves. We noted Dora's unavailing protests earlier (where "no" signified "yes"), and that example was only one of many. In a review of the case of Little Hans, for example, Joseph Wolpe and Stanley Rachman noted that "if the enlightenments or interpretations given to Hans are followed by behavioral improvements, then they are automatically accepted as valid. If they are not followed by improvement we are told the patient has not accepted them, and not that they are invalid."

This fancy footwork was part of a dance that every psychoanalyst would master. Patients might improve after therapy—this demonstrated the power of psychoanalysis—or they might not. What was the moral of those failed cases?

As usual, it was Freud who came up with the answer that generations of followers would echo. The moral, Freud declared, was that some patients did not want to be cured. The fault was in the patient, not the treatment. There were patients, Freud explained, who "refuse to give up the punishment of suffering." Even for Freud, this was a tough sell. It was "particularly difficult to convince the patient that this motive lies behind his continuing to be ill," he acknowledged with dismay, for too often the stubborn patient "holds fast to the more obvious explanation that treatment by analysis is not the right remedy for his case."

This notion of infallibility could prove risky, as we shall see when we come to Freud's descendants. For Freud himself, the low point came in the now notorious case of Emma Eckstein. Her story, which has become a battleground for those engaged in combat over Freud's reputation, deserves our consideration because it provides a dramatic demonstration of the depth of Freud's belief that symptoms were symbols.

Eckstein was a young woman, single and attractive, with dark, wavy hair and large, deep-set eyes. She had become a patient of Freud's in the early 1890s. No surviving records tell us just why she sought help, though she apparently had problems walking and suffered from stomach ailments and menstrual pains. In 1895, Freud called Wilhelm Fliess in on the case.

Fliess was an ear, nose, and throat specialist in Berlin. An unimpressive man physically — in years to come an acquaintance would describe him as "very charming and old-fashioned; almost a dwarf with a huge stomach" — he overflowed with ideas. He was Freud's closest friend in the 1890s, indeed the closest friend Freud would *ever* have, and a cherished intellectual ally in the years when Freud was creating psychoanalysis. Freud was "almost reverential" in his devotion to the younger man, in the words of Jeffrey Masson, editor of *The Complete Letters of Sigmund Freud to Wilhelm Fliess.* Many of the letters are as effusive as notes between lovers. "Your praise is nectar and ambrosia for me," Freud wrote in 1894, and he went further in 1896: "How much I owe you: solace, understanding, stimulation in my loneliness, meaning to my life that I gained through you, and finally even health that no one else could have given back to me."

Freud's reference to his restored health was significant. His friend Fliess believed devoutly that such varied symptoms as headaches, cardiac pains, digestive problems, difficulties in childbirth, and menstrual woes all stemmed from the "nasal reflex neurosis." The idea was that the nose, by virtue of mysterious connections with the rest of the body, was somehow the seat of a great number of medical problems. Troubles in certain "genital spots" within the nose, for example, gave rise to painful menstruation and to difficulties in childbirth. (Fliess laid out this aspect of the theory in a work dedicated "to my dear Sigmund" and entitled *The Connections Between the Nose and the Female Sexual Organs.*)

Treatment was, to begin with, a matter of cauterizing the "genital spots" or other sites within the nose or applying cocaine to them. But in time Fliess found that these small-scale strategies were sometimes ineffective. Some cases called for heroic measures.

Emma Eckstein appears to have been the first patient drafted under the new regime. Fliess's plan was to cure her various problems by surgery. His strategy, in this first venture into the operating room, was to cut away part of the turbinate bone, deep in the sinuses. It sounds to modern ears like the most blatant quackery — many skeptics thought so even at the time — but Fliess was a well-regarded physician and his theories had a certain vogue in the 1890s. In any event, Fliess operated on Emma Eckstein in February 1895.

On March 4, Freud wrote to Fliess: "Eckstein's condition is still unsatisfactory: persistent swelling, going up and down 'like an avalanche'; pain, so that morphine cannot be dispensed with; bad nights. . . . the day before yesterday (Saturday) she had a massive hemorrhage." This was worrisome, but worse was to come. On March 8, Freud sat down to write Fliess the bad news. It would "probably upset you as much as it did me," Freud warned, "but I hope you will get over it as quickly as I did."

Then Freud delivered astonishing news. Emma's hemorrhages and swelling had continued; her pain was worse; the operation site had begun to smell foul. Freud had called in two consultants. "There still was moderate bleeding from the nose and mouth; the fetid odor was very bad. [A doctor named] Rosanes cleaned the area surrounding the opening, removed some sticky blood clots, and suddenly pulled at something like a thread, kept on pulling. Before either of us had time to think, at least half a meter of gauze had been removed from the cavity. The next moment came a flood of blood. The patient turned white, her eyes bulged, and she had no pulse. Immediately thereafter, however, he again packed the cavity with fresh iodoform gauze and the hemorrhage stopped. It lasted about half a minute, but this was enough to make the poor creature, whom by then we had lying flat, unrecognizable."

Fliess's letters to Freud are lost—Freud destroyed most or all of them a few years later—and so we cannot be sure how he dealt with the news that he had forgotten surgical gauze in his patient's nose. Freud continued to update him. On March 20: "Poor Eckstein is doing less well. . . . Ten days after the second operation, after a normal course, she suddenly had pain and swelling again, of unknown origin. The following day, a hemorrhage; she was quickly packed. At noon, when they lifted the packing to examine her, renewed hemorrhage, so that she almost died. . . . I have given up hope for the poor girl and am inconsolable that I involved you and created such a distressing affair for you. I also feel very sorry for her; I had become very fond of her."

Freud wrote again, on March 28, this time in a tone that betrayed considerable anxiety. "Dearest Wilhelm," he began, "I know what you want to hear first: *she* is tolerably well; complete subsidence, no fever, no hemorrhage. The packing that was inserted six days ago is still in; we hope to be safe from new surprises." (Italics in original.)

It was not to be. On April 11, Freud launched immediately into the bad news. "Dearest Wilhelm, Gloomy times, unbelievably gloomy. Above all, this Eckstein affair, which is rapidly moving toward a bad ending." Emma had begun bleeding again, and "there was a new, life-threatening hemorrhage which I witnessed. It did not spurt, it surged. . . . Add to this the pain, the morphine, the demoralization caused by the obvious medical helplessness, and the tinge of danger, and you will be able to picture the state the poor girl is in. We do not know what to do." Then, at last, on May

25, good news: "Emma E. is finally doing very well and I have succeeded in once more alleviating her weakness in walking, which also set in again."

Eckstein continued in Freud's care. The next year, in April 1896, Freud wrote Fliess about her yet again. He had, Freud wrote exuberantly, come up with "a completely surprising explanation of Eckstein's hemorrhages — which will give you much pleasure." The young woman had nearly bled to death not because she had endured useless surgery nor because her surgeon had left a ribbon of gauze up her injured nose. On the contrary, Freud explained, her bleeding was symbolic! "Her episodes of bleeding were hyster-ical, were occasioned by *longing*, and probably occurred at the sexually relevant times (the woman, out of resistance, has not yet supplied me with the dates)." (Italics in original.)

Returning to the same theme in another letter a week later, Freud spelled out Emma's motives in a bit more detail. "When she saw how affected I was by her first hemorrhage while she was in the hands of Ro-sanes," he told Fliess, "she experienced this as the realization of an old wish to be loved in her illness, and in spite of the danger during the succeeding hours she felt happy as never before." (This upsurge of joy came at a time, it bears repeating, when Freud had described Emma as a "poor creature," "unrecognizable," and without a detectable pulse.) "Then, in the sanato-rium, she became restless during the night because of an unconscious wish to entice me to go there; since I did not come during the night, she renewed the bleedings, as an unfailing means of rearousing my affection."

Nothing that had happened, neither Emma's near death nor the perma-nent disfigurement of her face, was Freud's fault, or Fliess's. "For me you remain the physician," Freud had reassured his friend soon after the fiasco, "the type of man into whose hands one confidently puts one's life and that of one's family." (In fact, Freud *had* put himself into Fliess's hands, sub-jecting himself to repeated operations on his nose and sinuses to cure an irregular heartbeat. It was presumably these surgeries that Freud had in mind when he expressed gratitude to Fliess for restoring his health.)

In the case of Emma Eckstein, however, someone was clearly at fault. Who could it be? Slightly over a year after the botched operation, Freud wrote Fliess with his final verdict. "[Emma's] story is becoming even clearer; there is no doubt that her hemorrhages were due to wishes."

Such excesses have inspired a number of revisionist historians to exam-ine the tales that Freud spun round his own career. This was no easy task. On several occasions, Freud destroyed the letters and manuscripts he had gathered over the years. In 1885, for example, well before he had achieved any reputation, Freud destroyed fourteen years' worth of accumulated pa-pers. "As for the biographers," he wrote in a letter telling his fiancée what he had done, "let them worry, we have no desire to make it too easy for them."

The letters to Fliess, which document the birth of psychoanalysis (and the story of Emma Eckstein), survive only because one of Freud's greatest admirers bought them from a bookseller and saved them, despite Freud's pleas to burn them.

The revisionists' crucial claim is that Freud's theories derived not from what he learned from his patients, as he claimed, but from his own preconceptions. He got away with it, these skeptics charge, by enlisting his formidable literary skills to obscure the distinction between what his patients told him and what he himself contributed in the process of "interpreting" and "reconstructing" their words. In part, this blurring was inadvertent. It followed from Freud's belief that symptoms carry hidden messages, that Dora's illness, say, *was* tantamount to a declaration of love for Herr K. What looks to a nonanalyst like blatant overreading could appear, to a true believer, as mere translation.

Freud seldom dealt with this issue in detail. In the process of writing up his case histories, he preferred to remove all signs of his labors, like a fox brushing away his footprints with his tail. He was not, he insisted, putting words in his patients' mouths; on the contrary, his task was to reveal what patients were *really* telling him.

On rare occasions, Freud acknowledged the guiding role he played. In the case of Little Hans, for example, he conceded that "it is true that during the analysis Hans had to be told many things that he could not say himself, that he had to be presented with thoughts which he had so far shown no signs of possessing, and that his attention had to be turned in the direction from which his father was expecting something to come."

Early in his career, Freud was even less coy in describing the analyst's task. After having deciphered a patient's symptoms, he wrote in 1898, "we may then boldly demand confirmation of our suspicions from the patient. We must not be led astray by initial denials. If we keep firmly to what we have inferred, we shall in the end conquer every resistance by emphasizing the unshakable nature of our convictions."

This reference to "what we have inferred" was key. It is an innocuous-looking phrase, but it reveals a vital point. Freud wrote as if he were simply passing along what his patients told him. In reality, the process was more complicated. Freud had inferred from his patients' dreams and associations what their words truly meant, and then *he* had told *them* what their unconscious had to say. (Often these "memories" were news to the patients themselves.) "The technique of psychoanalysis," Freud explained, "enables us in the first place to infer from the symptoms what those unconscious phantasies are and then to make them conscious to the patient."

The analyst's role sounds, at first, akin to that of a United Nations translator. In fact, it was an altogether less neutral, more free-form job. Freud sewed together his patient's free associations to form a kind of patchwork quilt, drawing together some ill-fitting pieces here, reworking some unruly

THE POWER OF CONVICTION

bits there, and even adding patches of his own where he deemed it necessary. The quilts are lovely things — they can be admired as art objects — but it is far from clear that Freud played by the rules in crafting them.*

Sorting out such questions has become a cottage industry. An international cast of scholars — the notable names include Frederick Crews, Frank Cioffi, Allen Esterson, Ernest Gellner, Malcolm Macmillan, Frank Sulloway, Peter Swales, and Richard Webster — has produced a shelf of thorough, meticulous books that document the case against Freud in seemingly irrefutable detail. These colleagues in the anti-Freud brigades come from a variety of backgrounds. Cioffi, for example, is a University of Kent philosopher, now retired, Allen Esterson a retired teacher of mathematics, Frank Sulloway an acclaimed historian of science.

Crews, a professor emeritus of English at the University of California, Berkeley, is perhaps the best known. Once a Freud enthusiast himself, he recanted years ago. His "self-deprogramming" has resulted in a series of scathing essays, many of them collected in a 1986 volume called *Skeptical Engagements* and in a 1995 book, *The Memory Wars*. Quiet and professorially tweedy in appearance, Crews is in fact a tenacious combatant. But many of his psychoanalytic rivals portray his disdain for Freud as a symptom calling for diagnosis rather than an argument calling for response. Crews's critique has nothing to do with the quality of Freud's thought, they contend; it is, instead, a transparent proclamation of Oedipal rage against the "father" whose influence Crews is still trying desperately to fight clear of.

---

* By far the most important example, though it is out of our way, has to do with the birth of psychoanalysis. At the dawn of his career, Freud argued strenuously that all neurotic patients had endured sexual abuse during early childhood. In time, he abandoned that theory in favor of a position he maintained ever after. In the new theory as in the old, neurotic symptoms were brought about by sexual secrets boiling and bubbling away in the unconscious. But there was a crucial difference. In Freud's revised view, neurotic patients had not suffered actual abuse at someone else's hands; instead, they themselves had fantasized illicit sexual encounters and then had repressed their memories of that fantasizing. With this momentous shift in emphasis, from trauma inflicted by other people to psychic turmoil arising from within, Freud was well on his way to the Oedipus complex, and psychoanalysis was launched on its now-familiar course.

Why did Freud change his mind? The conventional answer, first put forth by Freud and dutifully repeated through the decades, was that he came to realize that his patients' stories simply did not hold together. Surely sexual abuse could not be so common. Freud had been taken in. A later claim, championed by the psychoanalytic renegade Jeffrey Masson, was that Freud was guilty of moral cowardice. Afraid that his colleagues would ostracize him for publicizing ugly truths about sexually abused children, he betrayed his patients and dismissed their memories as fantasies.

Which version of events is correct? The answer is documented in the works cited in the endnotes, perhaps most compellingly in Allen Esterson's scrupulously thorough *Seductive Mirage*. Esterson demonstrates beyond a reasonable doubt that neither Freud's version nor Masson's could be correct. Freud did not reject his patients' accounts of their abuse, because there were no such accounts! There were, instead, more quilts — Freud composed his case histories by piecing together a patient's memory fragments and assembling them into a narrative, which he then presented as the patient's own. "The question [critics] should have posed to themselves," Frederick Crews has noted, "is not, Were those stories true? but rather, *What* stories?"

Frank Cioffi, a tough-minded, sharp-tongued anti-Freudian, has focused his attention on Freud's style of argument. He contends that Freud was a "pseudo-scientist" and that psychoanalysis, despite its intellectual trappings, is as much a quack theory as astrology.

Other writers have made similar claims, but they have tended to focus on such questions as whether psychoanalysis makes predictions or simply provides after-the-fact "explanations" like those of business writers discussing the previous day's stock market. Cioffi takes a slightly different tack. His complaint is not that Freud avoids predictions — on the contrary, psychoanalysis is knee-deep in predictions, such as that every dream will turn out to represent a wish — but that he makes up the rules for what counts as evidence as he pleases. The mark of a pseudoscience, Cioffi argues, lies not so much in what it asserts but in the way it gathers evidence in support of those assertions.

Cioffi quotes the science writer Martin Gardner on "pyramidology," a silly but once-popular doctrine that claimed that careful measurements of the Great Pyramid reveal various secrets of nature:

> If you set about measuring a complicated structure like the Pyramid, you will quickly have on hand a great abundance of lengths to play with. If you have sufficient patience to juggle them about in various ways, you are certain to come out with many figures which coincide with important figures in the sciences. Since you are bound by no rules, it would be odd indeed if this search for the Pyramid "truths" failed to meet with considerable success.
>
> Take the Pyramid's height, for example. Smyth multiplies it by ten to the ninth power to obtain the distance to the sun. The nine here is purely arbitrary. And if no simple multiple had yielded the distance to the sun, he could try other multiples to see if it gave the distance to the Moon, or the nearest star, or any other scientific figure.

Cioffi argues, devastatingly in my judgment, that Freud played a similar game. Free to choose which features of a patient's story to focus on and which to ignore, free to decide whether a patient's professed loathing of an acquaintance represented hate or its opposite, free to decide whether a horse's muzzle was really a father's mustache, Freud had more than enough leeway to come to any conclusion whatever. "I would often give a whole series of associations to a dream symbol," an ex-patient of Freud's recalled, "and he would wait until he found an association which would fit into his scheme of interpretation and pick it up like a detective at a line-up who waits until he sees his man."

The arguments of Cioffi and his fellow skeptics have met a curious response. The literary world has rolled along unperturbed in its devotion to Freud, like the character in Thurber who declared that "mere proof won't convince me." Much of the psychoanalytic community, on the other hand, has conceded critical elements of the critics' case (just *which* elements varies from analyst to analyst). In any event, many psychoanalysts insist, the debate over Freud misses the central point — Freud was a genius who made great contributions and who also stumbled down some blind alleys.

After all, the argument runs, psychoanalysis has changed over the years. It should certainly not be dismissed by outsiders who foolishly assume that, six decades after Freud's death, analysts continue to parrot his words. "The popular picture of psychoanalysis as a religion of fanatical followers of Freud is far from a true one," observes the journalist Janet Malcolm, herself a psychoanalytic enthusiast. "Most Freudian analysts can take or leave Freud himself. Their interest in his life, and in the early history of psychoanalysis, is minimal, and their sensitivity to slurs on Freud's character is quite dulled."

That kind of casual disdain for the founding father of psychoanalysis is new. In the era to which we now turn, the 1950s and '60s, it would almost have counted as sacrilege. In the decades just after World War II, psychoanalysis was at its peak of prestige. Perched on that peak, like a great statue dominating the valley below, was the figure of Sigmund Freud.

PART TWO

The Heyday
of Psychoanalysis

There has been nothing like this since the
spread of the potato and of maize.

— ERNEST GELLNER

CHAPTER THREE

The High Ground

*In America today, Freud's intellectual influence is greater
than that of any other modern thinker. He presides over
the mass media, the college classroom, the chatter at
parties, the playgrounds of the middle classes.*

—PHILIP RIEFF, 1959

THE THEATER LIGHTS dimmed, and the beam from the projectionist's booth lit up the screen. The film began with a note of explanation: "Our story deals with psychoanalysis, the method by which modern science treats the emotional problems of the sane. The analyst seeks only to induce the patient to talk about his hidden problems, to open the locked doors of his mind. Once the complexes that have been disturbing the patient are uncovered and interpreted, the illness and confusion disappear and the devils of unreason are driven from the human soul."

It was 1945. The movie was Alfred Hitchcock's *Spellbound*, and the title seemed especially apt, for an entire nation was about to fall under the spell of this exotic new science. "I remember seeing Ingrid Bergman in . . ." —here Leon Eisenberg, former chairman of Harvard's psychiatry department, raises his voice and mimics an announcer's grand and rounded tones — *"Spellbound."** Eisenberg beams delightedly at the memory. "Now I didn't really think I was going to be analyzed by Ingrid Bergman," he continues, almost shyly, "but I must say, a lovely, glamorous woman like that . . ."

Eisenberg, today one of psychiatry's grand old men, was an impressionable twenty-three-year-old when he watched Ingrid Bergman unravel the secrets of Gregory Peck's dreams. But Eisenberg was hardly alone in falling under Freud's spell. For the brightest young men and women of the day, psychoanalysis exerted a near-irresistible pull. It was prestigious, it was glam-

---

* The screenplay was by Ben Hecht, who had been fascinated by psychoanalysis for decades. The film's elaborate dream sequence was created by Salvador Dali.

orous, it was intellectually alluring and morally appealing, and, best of all, it offered hope in a field that had always been linked with despair and futility. Indeed, those hopes exceeded Freud's. Psychoanalysis no longer confined itself to "the emotional problems of the sane" but prepared to take on insanity as well. In the years immediately following World War II, from the mid-1940s to the mid-1960s, psychoanalysis was at its peak of power and influence.

Psychoanalysis was a particular area within psychiatry — even at their peak, psychoanalysts accounted for only about 10 percent of all psychiatrists — but the small group dominated the larger field. Every medical school recruited analysts to fill its psychiatry chairs; every academic field, from history to anthropology to politics, made heavy use of psychoanalytic terms and concepts; every biographer stretched his subject on the analyst's couch. Nor were these psychoanalytic insights the exclusive property of writers and scholars. "Millions . . . are daily influenced, often unknowingly, by the penetration of Freudian theory," *Time* reported in a cover story in 1956. Five years later, a sociologist echoed that observation. If little Johnny threw a spitball at Mary, John Seeley complained in the *Atlantic Monthly*, no one saw it as a simple act of mischief. "The possibilities have to be — are joyously — entertained that Johnny is working off aggression, compensating for deeply felt inferiority, asserting his masculinity in ways appropriate to his developmental stage, testing for limits, or, in a characteristic upside-down way, saying to Mary in a circuitous and hence safe way, 'I love you.' "

Across the spectrum of American life, from Hollywood to Harvard and at every stop in between, came enthusiastic accounts of Freud and psychoanalysis. *Scientific American* carried accounts of the Oedipus complex and called Freud a "hero" and "the man who dared look steadily at the dark forces within us." The *Atlantic Monthly* devoted a special section to the "incalculably great" impact of the psychoanalytic "revolution." *Life* produced a five-part series on psychology and psychiatry. *Look* ran a first-person article by Sid Caesar entitled "What Psychoanalysis Did for Me."

For countless parents, the introduction to Freud's ideas came by way of a thick, clearly written book by a young pediatrician named Benjamin Spock. *Baby and Child Care* was an immediate and astonishing success. Published in 1946, it was soon selling at a rate of a million copies a year; today the grand total has reached 40 million. "The theoretical underpinning of the whole book is Freudian," Spock declared years later, but *Baby and Child Care* was hardly a propaganda tract. On the contrary, it was packed with the kind of practical information that a parent needed when faced with a howling and feverish infant at two in the morning. Spock was a fervent admirer of psychoanalysis who was himself analyzed three times during his long life, but he was a pediatrician, not an analyst, and his calm voice and practical manner were his great strengths. All that said, it is nonetheless the case that many passages in Dr. Spock are simply Freud with the jargon boiled off.

In a discussion of children seeing their parents naked, for example, Spock explained the Oedipus complex in the most everyday language. "A boy loves his mother much more than he loves any little girl. He feels much more rivalrous with his father and more in awe of him than he feels towards any boy. So the sight of his mother [undressed] may be a little too stimulating and the chance to compare himself so unfavorably with his father every day may make him feel like doing something violent to his old man."

In medical schools, too, psychoanalysis was at its peak of influence. "From 1945 to 1955," the director of the National Institute of Mental Health declared in a speech in 1975, "it was nearly impossible for a nonpsychoanalyst to become chairman of a department or professor of psychiatry." Of the 89 American psychiatric departments in 1962, according to one study, 52 were headed by psychoanalysts. Of the 17 books most recommended to psychiatric residents, 13 were psychoanalytic. Of 14 graduate programs in psychiatry examined in one 1955 survey, all 14 based their training on psychoanalytic principles. "By the mid-1960s," observed the medical historian Edward Shorter, "psychiatry had come in the mind of the American public to mean psychoanalysis. The seizure of power was virtually complete."

The centennial of Freud's birth, May 6, 1956, marked the symbolic crest of the Freudian deluge. President Eisenhower hailed the great day; three memorial meetings were held in Vienna, and wreaths were laid at the base of Freud's bust at the university there; a group of disciples gathered in Chicago to celebrate their mentor's contributions to literature, the arts, and medicine, and their words were carried simultaneously to New York and London as well. The celebration was international, but the Americans outdid all others in their Freudian fervor. The *New York Times Magazine* commissioned the literary critic Alfred Kazin to assess Freud's influence. "No other system of thought in modern times, except the great religions," Kazin declared, "has been adopted by so many people."

Kazin resisted the temptation to raise Freud to the rank of prophet, but that restraint was unusual. The anthropologist Ashley Montagu, for example, believed that Freud's view of mankind was far too pessimistic, but he hailed Freudian theory as "undoubtedly . . . the most insightful contribution to our understanding of human nature in the history of humanity."

The gushing tone was typical. Between 1953 and 1957, Ernest Jones, an analyst himself and perhaps the most devoted of all Freud's followers, published a hugely acclaimed three-volume biography of Freud that portrayed him as an almost mythic figure. Freud's discoveries, Jones declared, were "the nearest to a miracle that human means can compass." This was not starry-eyed devotion, Jones insisted, but simply the fact of the matter. His own psychoanalysis had scrubbed his vision clean. "Immeasurably great as was my respect for both the personality and achievements of Freud," Jones explained, "my own hero-worshipping propensities had been worked through before I encountered him." (Jones dedicated his biography to Anna Freud, the "true daughter of an immortal sire.")

There is almost no exaggerating the reverence that permeated most discussions of Freud and psychoanalysis. Reviewing the first volume of Jones's biography in the *New Yorker* in 1953, for example, Brendan Gill declared that Freud had "reached out to touch *and perhaps in some measure to save* every other life on earth." (Italics added.)

Why Freud? Why America? Why the fifties? Freud had laid out his crucial ideas in 1900, after all, in the work he considered his masterpiece, *The Interpretation of Dreams*. Why did his influence reach its zenith half a century later and half a world away from Vienna?

The answer begins with the mundane observation that America after World War II was where the psychoanalysts were. The historian Laura Fermi spelled out the grim story in *Illustrious Immigrants*, an account of the intellectual diaspora that accompanied Hitler's rise to power. "European psychoanalysis found itself in the unenviable position of being the only discipline, to my knowledge, that Hitler virtually exterminated in continental Europe," Fermi wrote. The Vienna Psychoanalytic Society, for example, managed to survive until 1937. Formerly the largest psychoanalytic society in Europe, it still numbered sixty-nine members even in that last year; by 1945 only three members of that group were still in Vienna. Of those psychoanalysts who escaped Hitler with their lives, two-thirds ended up in the United States. By the end of World War II, the United States had more psychoanalysts than the rest of the world combined.

But seeding America with psychoanalysts was only part of the story. Why did the transplanted analysts (and their American counterparts) flourish in the United States? Freudian ideas had made their way to America well before World War II, beginning with Freud's Clark University lectures in 1909. For the most part, though, psychoanalysis in its early days was more likely to inspire a *frisson* of naughty delight than a deep allegiance. In Chicago in 1913, for example, Ben Hecht (later of *Front Page* and *Spellbound* fame) wrote a newspaper story about the Viennese import. Hecht's editor was thrilled. Freud's doctrines, he exclaimed with delight, were "much more engrossing than our limerick contest." The new theory had, literally, sex appeal. "Our readers will be thrilled to learn," the editor went on, "that they are all potential lunatics who want to stab their fathers or go to bed with their mothers." *

---

* The Viennese seemed as intrigued as the Americans. Freud wrote his friend Wilhelm Fliess, in 1893, that "the sexual business attracts people who are all stunned and then go away won over after having exclaimed, 'No one has ever asked me about that before!' "

In the Roaring Twenties, when sex was everywhere, so was Freud. "Freudian psychology had flooded the field [of psychiatry] like a full rising tide," one dismayed rival would later complain, "and the rest of us were left submerged like clams buried in the sands at low water." But by the time the Depression hit, most Americans had more pressing concerns. Except in New York and one or two other intellectual outposts, psychoanalysis was yesterday's fad. After only a decade or two in the limelight, Freud was passé. As we shall see, though, psychoanalysis did not vanish but went underground. It emerged, transformed and more popular than ever before, just after World War II.

One major reason for this resurgence was the war itself. The revelation of Nazi horrors had countless effects. One was to taint, for years, the field of genetics. Who would study such topics as the similarities between twins knowing that his predecessor in the field was Dr. Mengele? The result was that, when it came to explaining human behavior, psychoanalysis and other "soft" sciences had the field largely to themselves.

In addition, Hitler's condemnation of psychoanalysis as a Jewish science came to serve as a badge of honor, and Freud's own close acquaintance with the darkest corners of the human heart enhanced his credibility. As early as May 1933, Hitler had consigned Freud's writings and other psychoanalytic texts to a Berlin bonfire. Freud himself barely escaped the Nazis. He remained in Vienna until June 1938, when finally, at age eighty-two and dying of cancer, he fled to London. All four of his sisters perished, in their late seventies, in Nazi death camps.

In a broader sense, the sheer horror of the war made the world more receptive to psychoanalytic insights. When the Allies caught their first glimpse of the Nazi death camps, they recoiled in revulsion and disbelief. The Holocaust plainly demanded a deeper explanation of human motivations than anyone had been able to provide. Faced with irrefutable evidence of a culture gone mad — and not just any culture, but the very one thought to embody Europe's deepest and most civilized values — it was tempting to turn to a theory that emphasized the bestial impulses within us all. Civilization was only a veneer, it seemed, and psychoanalysts claimed to know better than anyone else what bubbled and festered beneath that gleaming surface.

The war contributed to the rise of psychoanalysis in another way. Subject to indescribable and inescapable horrors, soldier after soldier had succumbed to "shell shock" (in modern jargon, posttraumatic stress syndrome). In North Africa, for example, shell shock accounted for up to one-third of all combat casualties. Its victims were plagued by nightmares, crying jags, and recurrent fits of terror. The job of the Army's psychiatrists was to return as many of those men as possible to combat, as quickly as possible.

This they did very well, and to great acclaim. Overall, 60 percent of those soldiers who broke down returned to duty within two to five days. Treatment was a kind of quick and dirty psychoanalysis. "It looks ridiculously simple," a *New York Times* war correspondent reported. "The doctor softly reassures the patient that all is well, that he is safe. It is done in low tones, in constant repetition, until the patient just goes to sleep. And it works. . . . Hypnosis . . . helps the patient talk out his case. When he talks about it enough instead of burying it inside himself, the battle is won."

Psychiatrists and the public drew several lessons from such tales. First, they dramatized the value of psychoanalysis in a way no one could miss. (Similar stories from World War I had made for a postwar surge in the popularity of psychoanalysis then, too.) Second, the shell shock story showed that emotional problems could overwhelm anyone caught in a grim enough predicament. Soldiers, after all, were red-blooded Americans who had entered the military in manifest good health. The breakdowns of these strong young men seemed clear proof that it was the environment an individual found himself in, far more than anything to do with his own constitution, that determined his mental health. This was a powerful idea, with implications far beyond the battlefield. Some psychoanalysts wondered, for example, if weeping, raving schizophrenics might be akin to shell-shock victims themselves, except that their battles were with parents and other domestic enemies rather than with foreign tyrants.

The third wartime lesson was more subtle than the first two but more important as well. The same talk therapy that cured hysterical women in Vienna and neurotic businessmen in New York also cured terrorized soldiers dragged from foxholes in North Africa and Okinawa. That was testimony to the power of psychoanalysis, on the one hand, but also proof that all mental ills were fundamentally the same. And if all *diseases* were the same, then all patients were in a sense all the same, too.

This was a crucial part of the appeal of psychoanalysis. The doctrine that all men are brothers gave psychoanalysts a firm claim to the moral high ground. Older doctrines had implied that the sick were a breed apart. Nineteenth-century psychiatrists had called themselves "alienists," in fact, to indicate that their patients were creatures alienated from the rest of mankind. Psychoanalysts emphatically rejected any such talk of divisions between people. Echoing Freud, they proclaimed that there was no fixed barrier between *us* and *them*. One psychoanalyst after another cited the inspiring words of Terence, the Roman playwright: *"Homo sum; humani nil a me alienum puto."* ("I am human; I hold nothing human alien to me.")

This appeal to our common humanity was immensely attractive, both to the public and to medical students looking to choose a specialty, but it had one curious effect. It inspired many psychoanalysts to believe that almost every conceivable problem, from ennui to madness, came within their purview. From today's vantage point, this looks like wild overreaching, but it was something more subtle than that. Analysts had all been analyzed themselves, and they placed enormous value on the experience. "It helped *them,"* says Mary Coleman, a retired Georgetown University neurologist. "It really did. Psychoanalysis helps normal, high-functioning people, and the more normal and the more high-functioning you are, the more successful it is." The fatal flaw, in Coleman's view, was to assume that what helped a high-functioning psychoanalyst would also help a profoundly sick mental patient. But if there are no boundary lines that divide us from one another, then why not?

This identification of doctor and patient was one of the most engaging features of psychoanalysis. "Psychiatrists before Freud, and the ones around Freud but not in the movement, were often entomologists — butterfly collectors," says Harvard's Leon Eisenberg, himself a psychiatrist but not a psychoanalyst. " 'This patient fits this category; look at these symptoms the patient has.' They would bring the patient in front of a room of students and say something provocative so he'd show his wings or his delusions, or whatever.

"They weren't necessarily cruel," Eisenberg continues, "but they treated patients like things or objects. Whereas the analysts tried to understand and suggested that these were people whose disorders had roots and meanings and history, and they weren't so different from the rest of us. So it led to a certain kind of compassion."

It was a lesson drawn straight from Freud, his admirers declared. Freud's greatness, they insisted, was as much moral as medical. "Freud, even more than Lincoln, might well be called the Great Emancipator," the Princeton philosopher Walter Kaufmann wrote in 1960. "Like no man before him, he lent substance to the notion that all men are brothers. Criminals and madmen are not devils in disguise, but men and women who have problems similar to our own; and there, but for one experience or another, go you and I."

Another factor, besides its moral appeal, was key to the popularity of psychoanalysis. In the United States, the nature-versus-nurture debate had been a high-stakes, high-visibility battleground for decades. In its simplest form, the debate centered on personality and temperament: did one child grow up shy and another outgoing, for example, because of differences in upbringing (nurture) or because of built-in, biological differences (nature)? But the true issues were far broader. The underlying question was whether we were prisoners in genetic handcuffs or free agents able to shape our own destinies. Psychoanalysts, with their emphasis on self-knowledge and their close focus on childhood memories and such matters as weaning and toilet-training, seemed to fall squarely in the "nurture" camp.* As matters played

---

* Freud himself switched sides in the nature-nurture debate. Early in his career, he argued that an adult's neuroses stemmed from childhood abuse, events that came from outside. Freud's focus was on the particular events of an individual's early years and therefore on "nurture." In time, though, when Freud declared that neuroses stemmed from sexual *fantasies*

out, "nurture" was the side to be on, and psychoanalysis found itself in the winner's circle yet again.

In the United States, the nature-nurture debate began in earnest around 1900, with battles over immigration policy. America, one heard incessantly from the "nature" camp, was being swamped by an influx of inferior races, Jews prominent among them. A nation built on the straight, true timbers of northern Europe was now threatened with an infusion of twisted, inferior stock from the least desirable corners of the globe. Nonsense, the "nurture" forces insisted. This was prejudice masquerading as science; no culture was "naturally" better or worse than any other.

Perhaps inevitably, the debate spilled over into anthropology. Who better than an anthropologist to resolve the question of whether behavior was innate or acquired? In 1925, a twenty-three-year-old graduate student named Margaret Mead set sail for Samoa. She would return home with a manuscript that proclaimed the "nurture" case and would become one of the century's most influential books. Mead's graduate adviser was the acclaimed anthropologist Franz Boas. A Columbia professor, Boas was the most prominent of those associated with the "nurture" argument. He believed devoutly that the study of other cultures would prove that human beings were almost infinitely malleable. Culture was a "sculptor" with a remarkably free hand. Such familiar traits as competitiveness and sexual jealousy, ambition, and aggressiveness were not universals but qualities found in some societies and not in others.

At Boas's suggestion, Mead spent her time in Samoa learning about adolescence. It was a clever test case. In western culture, the physical changes of adolescence run hand in hand with emotional Sturm und Drang. Is this adolescent melodrama natural and inevitable, or cultural and variable?

After nine months in Samoa, Mead had the answer. "Adolescence represented no period of crisis or stress," she wrote in *Coming of Age in Samoa*, "but was instead an orderly developing of a set of slowly maturing interests and activities." The gentle Samoans, among the "most peaceful peoples in the world," made "a fine art of sex," which they regarded as "the pastime *par excellence.*" In Samoa, which displayed "the sunniest and easiest attitudes towards sex" that Mead had ever encountered, the anguish and heartache familiar to every American parent of teenagers were unknown. Adolescence

---

rather than actual events, he shifted his emphasis from the outside world to inborn drives. Now he focused on instincts purportedly shared by *every* human being, and therefore part of "nature." "All adults suffer from conflictual sexual impulses, Freud decided, not just those who had been molested as children," in the summary of the psychoanalysts Stephen Mitchell and Margaret Black. "Sexuality does not become problematic only when introduced precociously; there is something in the very nature of human sexuality that is problematic, generating inevitable, universal conflicts."

was, on the contrary, "smooth, untroubled, unstressed," and "perhaps the pleasantest time the Samoan girl will ever know." *

Coming of Age in Samoa was an enormous success and remains a standard text today. It was, as well, a huge endorsement of Freudian doctrine. (The book was subtitled "A Psychological Study of Primitive Youth for Western Civilization.") Mead had found the Samoans free of sexual hang-ups and therefore free of neuroses as well. "Familiarity with sex, and the recognition of a need of a technique to deal with sex as an art," she wrote, "have produced a scheme of personal relations in which there are no neurotic pictures, no frigidity, no impotence, except as the temporary result of severe illness, and the capacity for intercourse only once in a night is counted as senility."

The effect was to link anthropology and psychoanalysis ever more tightly in the public mind, and thereby to identify psychoanalysis ever more closely with "nurture." (The links were personal as well as theoretical. When Mead's daughter, Catherine, was born, in 1939, for example, Mead chose Benjamin Spock as her pediatrician "because he had been psychoanalyzed.")

Even before World War II, the pronurture side was the right one to be on. Among those who set intellectual fashion, to be pronurture was to be in favor of progress and open-mindedness. To be pronature was to be backward-looking and backward-thinking. But with the rise of the Nazis, and their murderous embrace of the "nature" doctrine, the debate was finally over. The doctrine of Aryan supremacy meant that even an assimilated Jew whose ancestors had known no home but Germany for generations was racially inferior, *biologically* tainted, and therefore marked for death. No decent person could stomach such thinking. Since Nazism stood for "nature," the long identification of psychoanalysis with "nurture" gave it invaluable moral stature.

---

* Mead's idyllic picture of life in Samoa has since been demolished root and branch by the anthropologist Derek Freeman, in *Margaret Mead and the Heretic*. So far from being the paradise of free love that Mead described, for example, where "the idea of forceful rape or of any sexual act to which both participants do not give themselves freely is completely foreign," Samoa has an incidence of rape among the highest in the world. Mead, it turns out, was hoaxed by her adolescent informants, as a prank. Freeman even found one of Mead's informants, now an old woman, who told him: "Scientists should take care over the explanations people give them. They should first check and make sure that what they are being told is true, and not just a joke."

CHAPTER FOUR

Hope and Glory

*The nature of men can be transformed with the nurture
and dispersion of love.*

—KARL MENNINGER

THE INTELLECTUAL APPEAL of psychoanalysis was every bit as deep as its moral appeal. From early on, from the days of Thomas Mann and Walter Lippmann, the theory had won over many of the best and the brightest. In post–World War II America, that intellectual pull was stronger than ever, in large measure because psychoanalysis was a theory almost without rivals. Academic psychology was not up to much, with its mazes and its research on conditioned reflexes; it seemed, to many an ambitious young man and woman, to be a fine field for those who wanted to study rats and pigeons. And for the clinically minded, conventional psychiatry seemed scarcely more enticing. It offered neurotic patients a grab bag of rest cures and platitudes and the more seriously ill the option of such dubious and dangerous procedures as "shock therapy."

"In those days, what did you have in the way of medical treatments in psychiatry?" asks Leon Eisenberg. "Well, there was electric shock, for one," he says, answering his own question. "The point is, you were giving an empirical treatment, you didn't know why the hell it worked, and it didn't work predictably. Sometimes it worked like a *charm*, I mean, my God, it was a *miracle* to watch"—Eisenberg, a dynamic storyteller, is as astonished at the memory of the long-gone patient he has conjured up as if he were here before him—"and then at other times a patient would get shocked and shocked and shocked and . . . nothing."

Eisenberg runs through a list of other treatments of forty years ago, and then he summarizes the past state of affairs with a plaintive wail. "There was *nothing you could do,*" he cries, "except watch and give humane care. *That's* why psychoanalysis looked so good. Psychoanalysis offered explanations. They weren't verifiable," Eisenberg laughs, "but they gave some kind of meaning to human encounters."

The brain, too, was still a dark continent. Even today, it jealously hides its secrets. The problem is complexity compounded by inaccessibility. The brain contains between 20 billion and 100 billion nerve cells. Each one is in simultaneous communication with upward of 10,000 others; each sends between two and a hundred messages every second, ceaselessly, day and night. How this electrified mound of gray-white Jell-O lights up into consciousness no one even claims to understand. In the 1950s, these mysteries were barely approachable. Neurochemistry and similar fields were in their infancy, and PET scans and other brain-mapping techniques were science fiction fantasies. To have tried to take on the brain scientifically would have been to probe the Pacific with pail and shovel.

That left the field clear. If you were smart and ambitious in the 1950s and '60s, and if you had visions of healing your fellow man, psychoanalysis was the place to be. Allan Hobson, a Harvard psychiatrist who began a residency in psychiatry in 1960, recalls the heady excitement of those days in a breathless whisper. "The reason why twenty-five people from my medical-school class went into psychiatry," he says, eyebrows shooting skyward, hands chopping the air, *twenty-five people in a class of one hundred twenty-five,* where today it would be more like three or four, was because we all thought that psychoanalysis was the greatest thing since sliced bread. We were completely hooked."

Donald Klein, a renowned Columbia University psychiatrist of about the same vintage as Hobson, puts it simply. "I wanted to be a psychoanalyst because it was the most interesting game in town," he says, "and because the analysts were the most interesting people in town."

Freud himself still accounted for part of that glamour. Long after his death, his work was as captivating as ever. Hobson was a "Freud idolater" in college, for example, and he wrote his honors thesis on Freud and Dostoevsky. Better still, by the fifties Freud's insights had been taken up and amplified by a host of others, and analysts could boast a list of accomplishments that stretched across decades. Following Freud's lead, they had created a grand and sweeping theory that not only laid bare the true nature of neuroses and psychoses but also explained the meaning of dreams, the origins of warfare, the reasons men gambled and drank, the sources of religious belief, the cause of homosexuality. They had discovered a system of universal laws that could explain the world and perhaps even reshape it.

Young and idealistic students fell in droves, as in an earlier day they might have gone in for socialism or communism. "In medical school," Hobson recalls, "I think people didn't critically examine the texts to see what the evidence was for any of the claims." He continues almost wistfully, as if recalling a love affair from long ago. "The theory is just so lovely, it really is a beautiful piece of work, no question about it. And everybody wanted to believe it, like a religion really."

In contrast with the grand structure that was psychoanalysis, conventional psychiatry seemed cobbled together and arbitrary, destined to repel anyone with a taste for intellectual elegance. Worse still, it seemed only to skitter along the surface, dealing with symptoms but never moving beyond them to the disease itself. In the analysts' view this was akin to putting rouge on a patient's cheeks and then claiming to have treated her measles; *they*, in contrast, were explorers of the depths and not mere custodians of the surface.

For patients and therapists alike, this was immensely winning. "Freud held out the hope of radical cure, at least in his early writings," says Donald Klein. "By releasing the repressed, or getting rid of some sort of unconscious conflict, you would not only be relieved of your symptoms but you'd be *cured!* And that, of course, was extremely appealing to everybody — the idea that there'd be a whole new you!

"To this day that's a major issue, in terms of the appeal of psychoanalysis," Klein continues. "If you tell a patient, 'Look, I think you're depressed, we'll give you an antidepressant,' he'll say, 'Well, how long do I have to take it?' And we have to say, 'Well, we're not quite sure, most people take it for about a year, and some people, as a matter of fact, they never get off medication.' We give them all the analogies to diabetes and so forth, but people don't want to hear that. 'Oh, my God,' they say, 'medication all my life!' Whereas if they're told, 'We've got a method that if you do it our way, you're cured once and for all,' then that's terrific!"

The method was at least as much art as science, but no one worried much about that. The reason was that those who became psychoanalysts were a self-selected group, leaning more to art than science in the first place. Those more inclined to study the contents of a test tube than the meaning of a dream had already gone elsewhere. Psychoanalysis lured hordes of bright students with a literary bent and a fondness for symbolism; it failed to draw as many scientific-minded skeptics.

The result was that psychoanalytic papers tended to blur the distinction between proof and anecdote. Medicine in general was late to see the need for control groups and double-blind trials and sophisticated statistical methods, psychiatry was later still, and psychoanalysis later even than that. This sequence makes sense, for it is easier to make comparisons in conventional medicine than in psychiatry or psychoanalysis. There is no question about what it means to give a thousand pneumonia patients the same antibiotic; it is harder to define what it means to give a thousand depressed patients the same psychotherapy. In the 1950s and '60s, though, few analysts bothered with such matters. As we will see, that oversight would have considerable consequences.

•   •

Psychoanalysis seemed to have vanished in the Depression, as we have noted. In fact, it had simply taken itself in for repairs. It reemerged after about a decade in a new and improved version better suited to American tastes. This psychoanalytic variant was called "psychosomatic medicine." It sought to explore the links between emotions and health. More important, it served as a kind of inadvertent Trojan horse — by putting less emphasis on sex and more on physiology, it insinuated psychoanalysis into mainstream medicine.

The new field had ancient roots. From medicine's earliest days, physicians (and lay observers) had suggested that those with particular temperaments were prone to particular afflictions. The flip side, that certain temperaments *protected* against illness, was thought to hold as well. In England, during the sixteenth and seventeenth centuries, for example, it was commonly believed that "the happy man would not get plague." In our day the best-known example of a supposed link between temperament and disease is the "Type A" personality. The term was coined in the 1950s by two San Francisco cardiologists who noticed that the chairs in their waiting room always seemed to wear out along the front edge first. The explanation, they realized, was that their patients were literally on the edge of their seats.* This appeared to be a clear warning that character was destiny. To be aggressive, ambitious, hard-driving, it seemed, was to be a heart attack waiting (impatiently) to happen.

Unlike psychoanalysis, which took as a starting point notions that seem outlandish — every young girl feels defective because she lacks her brother's glorious adornment — psychosomatic medicine made intuitive sense. Everyone knows that our emotions affect our bodies; no one who has ever blushed could deny it. Evolution has designed us so that joy, lust, terror all come accompanied by a familiar cascade of bodily changes. In emergencies, for example, our hearts pump faster and harder, our muscles demand an extra supply of blood, our platelets become stickier so that we are less likely to bleed to death if an attacker takes a bite out of us. It is a fine system for someone running from a lion. It is easy to imagine, though, that if a person is in a *chronic* state of panic — if he trips the emergency alarm every time a deadline looms or a client backs out of a deal — then that unrelenting internal turmoil might eventually prove hazardous.

That vague but plausible notion was associated with two names in particular. The first was Franz Alexander. A crew-cut hulk of a man and a renowned German psychoanalyst, Alexander was bold and ambitious —

---

* It was an upholsterer, and not the cardiologists, who pointed out the strange way the waiting room chairs had worn out. The cardiologists ignored his remark and only recalled it four or five years later when their own research seemed to show a link between heart disease and impatience.

Freud himself had predicted that he would do great things — and he burst onto the American scene in 1930 trumpeting his goal of putting "psychoanalysis on the map." He was fiercely self-assured, driven by the knowledge that, as he put it, "in the main, *you* were right and the *world* was wrong." (Italics in original.)

The other great figure in psychosomatic medicine was a Columbia University physician named Helen Flanders Dunbar. Her first influential book was *Emotions and Bodily Changes*, published in 1935. An overview rather than a work of original scholarship, it seemed to combine the best of two worlds by uniting the Freudian notion that symptoms carried symbolic messages with a more conventional medical focus on the biochemical changes involved in disease.

Dunbar was a psychoanalyst, a Dante scholar, a theologian, and, in the curious phrase of the medical historian Nathan Hale, "an engaging and energetic hunchback." She spelled out her theories in an endless series of talks and popular books and articles. The crucial notion was that most people fall ill by choice and not by happenstance. "They asked for it," Dunbar explained in a 1947 book called *Mind and Body*, and she compared people who fell sick with children who went outdoors without a jacket and then came down with a fever. "They have asked for it," Dunbar insisted, "and in the hidden recesses of their minds have even made a blueprint of the disease they want. They select symptoms in much the same way that healthy people select clothes, choosing carefully for style, fit, and the effect upon others. Yet many do not know they have done it."

The fundamental point was that illness was a choice. "Men, women and children turn to pain or discomfort only because of the inadequacy of their own (or their parents') personalities." Why choose to be sick? That was easy. Many patients were "seeking compensation for the neglect or severity they may have suffered in childhood." Still others were " 'spoiled brats' who find in the sickbed the only substitute available at their age for the pampering which they enjoyed as children." Dunbar's cure was as straightforward as the diagnosis. "The sufferers lose their symptoms," she explained, "when their personality difficulties are remedied, that is, when they are helped to become the kind of people they have the capacity to be."

Dunbar took almost the entire medical world as her stage. She explained heart disease and diabetes, asthma and hay fever, ulcers and migraines. She had come to these far-ranging conclusions by way of a comparatively narrow question. What were the emotional factors, Dunbar had wanted to know, that accounted for heart disease and diabetes? For five years, she had studied all the patients admitted to a large New York City hospital. In order to find what was distinctive about cardiovascular and diabetic patients, she needed to compare them with a group of healthy people. But people outside the hospital were unwilling to take the time to participate in Dunbar's studies. Where could she find a captive audience of normal people?

The answer, she realized, was right before her. By studying hospitalized accident victims, she could probe a cross section of society to her heart's content. But the great surprise, and the turning point in Dunbar's career, was her realization that most accidents were not "accidental" at all. (This also marked the end of Dunbar's attempts to find "control groups" to validate her comparisons.) "Only about ten to twenty percent of all these injuries, fatal or otherwise, are caused by really accidental accidents," she reported. "The rest are linked to the personality of the victim." Though patients believed "they [were] the victims of pure bad luck or divine punishment, in reality they have been struck down by their own emotional conflicts."

This was an assertion, not a demonstration, and Dunbar never explained how she had unearthed this "reality." Nonetheless, she was off. Beginning with the premise that emotional conflicts were the key to *accidents*, apparently the most random of afflictions, it was hardly a leap to conclude that emotional troubles were the key to illnesses in general. Dunbar set to work zealously compiling lists of personality traits associated with different illnesses: allergy victims, for example, "have had a strong sexual curiosity and temptation — not necessarily a strong sexual desire — and they tend to be afraid of it." Those with skin diseases shared "a deep-seated emotional conflict between desire for affection and a fear of being hurt if they seek it."

Lumping together enormous numbers of people, Dunbar's lists of personality traits sounded oddly like the Chinese horoscopes that describe the traits shared by all those born in the Year of the Dog. Diabetics, for example, a group numbering in the millions in the United States alone, were distinguished by "a strong emotional conflict between resentment of parents and docile submission to them. . . . Among the men especially there is a history of domination by the mother with strong ties of affection and dependence." The role of the emotions was especially clear, Dunbar believed, in children who suffered from allergies and asthma and rashes. The key was "smother love," a kind of suffocating fussiness seen in overbearing mothers. Take children with eczema, for example: "Smother love has enveloped them so completely that, in a sense, their body is covered by it, and the skin is the part most immediately affected."

Dunbar and Alexander had widespread support in spreading the psychosomatic creed. In 1948, for example, two researchers published a study in the *New York State Journal of Medicine* that summarized twenty years of research. The conclusion, Eli Moschowitz and Mata Roudin announced with impressive mathematical precision, was that "constitution times psychologic trauma gives hyperkinesis, which results in psychosomatic disease." In an enthusiastic account, *Time* provided a translation: "Mental or emotional shock makes certain organs overactive; the patient's personality determines which organs will be affected. The kind of personality, rather than the kind of shock, is the key." Victims of high blood pressure "live intensely and desperately." They were intolerant, anxious, fearful of the future. Those with stomach ulcers, in contrast, were "lean and hungry," sullen and aggressive. People with intestinal troubles were "soft and weak-willed," submissive, dependent, and afraid of crowds.

In 1950, Alexander published his most celebrated work, a tome called *Psychosomatic Medicine.* It featured lists of personality traits like Dunbar's, together with elaborate diagrams bursting with arrows and feedback loops and bearing such labels as "infantile dependency" and "inferiority feelings" and "gastric hypersecretion." It was this volume that the unmarried nightclub singer Adelaide lugged onstage in *Guys and Dolls,* also in 1950, when she distilled psychosomatic wisdom into a single classic song. "In other words," she sang, after perusing Alexander's text, "just from waiting around for that plain little band of gold, / A person can develop a cold." *

Alexander was less lyrical than Adelaide, but his own explanations of disease were on the same lines. He moved far beyond colds and devoted particular attention to asthma:

> We are now ready to answer the question of why and how such a repressed desire for the mother should produce a spasm of the bronchioles, which is the physiological basis of the asthma attacks. On the basis of a psychoanalytic case study, the theory was advanced by E. Weiss that the asthma attack represents a suppressed cry for the mother. . . . This view has been further substantiated by the fact that most asthma patients spontaneously report that it is difficult for them to cry. . . . That suppression of crying leads to respiratory difficulties can be observed in the case of the child who tries to control his urge to cry or tries, after a prolonged period of futile attempts, to stop crying. The characteristic dyspnea and wheezing which appears strongly resembles an attack of asthma.

Other researchers produced similar insights, and newspapers and magazines hurried to relay the discoveries. In 1953, for example, *Time* reported matter-of-factly that "girls who do not get along with their fathers are likely to grow up sexually frigid, and when they marry they are candidates for indigestion and gallstones." Free of internal doubts of their own and nearly free of outside attacks by others, the psychosomaticists grew ever bolder. They progressed, in the words of the historian Nathan Hale, from "caution" to "confidence" to "certainty."

---

* Adelaide may have had it right. In December 1996, Sheldon Cohen, a psychologist at Carnegie Mellon University in Pittsburgh, reported to an audience at a National Institutes of Health conference that he had found that people who suffered "enduring social conflicts" of a month or more were twice as vulnerable to colds as people not under such stress.

By the 1950s, psychoanalysis was running at flood tide. Even in its original, Freudian guise, the theory had been powerful enough to sweep away its rivals. It had subsided in the thirties, but now it had risen again more powerfully than before. This time it had adapted itself to the American terrain, and it had absorbed the force of two rushing tributaries besides. One was the morally alluring notion that all men are brothers, the other the intellectually seductive idea that psychoanalysis was all-embracing. And great as this accumulated power was in appearance, it was even greater in reality. For psychoanalysis was a theory without a significant rival to divert its energy, and all its force was channeled in a single direction.

It was easy to lose one's bearings, and far more cautious figures than Flanders Dunbar and Franz Alexander were caught up in the excitement. Take Seymour Kety. A renowned scientist, Kety was one of the most visible of those working toward a biological explanation of mental illness. In 1951, Kety was named the first scientific director of the fledgling National Institute of Mental Health. As head of a group studying mental illness, Kety was told, he really should have firsthand knowledge of the most formidable tool in the psychiatrist's arsenal — he himself should be psychoanalyzed, at government expense. This was in itself a striking demonstration of the prestige of psychoanalysis, but Kety was ambivalent. He went home to think things over. The government would pick up the tab for the analysis, after all.

"If they said they'd take your appendix out for free, would you let them?" his wife demanded.

This was, Kety agreed later, a good question. Nonetheless, he went ahead with the analysis. He did not attain much in the way of insight into his own character, he would recall, although he thought well of his analyst, the renowned Edith Weigert. But the experience moved Kety to write — and eventually publish, in the journal *Science* — a remarkable mini-essay that he called "The True Nature of a Book."

It was written in the form of a parable and formed part of a larger essay. Kety began by asking the reader to imagine a community of intelligent, civilized creatures who have never seen books. (They have devised other ways to transmit knowledge.) One day a million books appear out of nowhere, magically. The Laboratory of Anatomy has first crack at these strange objects. They take fanatic pains to describe the books precisely, but they pay no particular attention to the "black surface markings" within them. Next come the chemists. They burn a few pages to measure how much heat is given off, and they perform a chemical analysis to learn what the books are made of. They discover traces of carbon, Kety slyly informs us, but the chemists dismiss those smudges as "impurities" and never recognize the ink that is a book's essential feature.

Kety continues. Molecular biologists, physiologists, and physicists all miss the point in various elaborate ways. (The physicists, for example, write complex equations to describe the way the pages move when the book is shaken.) "Finally, the book is brought in desperation to the psychoanalyst in the hope that he will be able to read it." And so he does, succeeding where his narrow-minded scientific rivals had failed.

Nothing could have been further from his intention, Kety concluded his fable, than "to deny the tremendous importance and the major contributions which biochemistry and biophysics and the biologic sciences generally have achieved." Having denied precisely that, Kety went on to wrap his tale up in a moral: "We do not always get closer to the truth as we slice and homogenize and isolate."

The sentiment itself is not so remarkable. Similar ideas were standard features of Romantic poetry ("I do not know, I do not seek to know / How all the formulae for beauty go"). The message was also commonplace among psychoanalysts, who tended to view scientists much as the English upper class viewed those who sullied their hands in trade. But bear in mind that this tale came not from a science-wary poet or psychoanalyst but from a renowned scientist whose explicit mission was to get closer to the truth by slicing, homogenizing, and isolating.

And any number of Kety's contemporaries, themselves researchers who took pride in their tough-mindedness, fell under the same spell. "I blush to admit," wrote Jerome Kagan, the eminent Harvard psychologist, "that I repeated to my first class in child psychology what I had been taught as a graduate student. I said with certainty that some children found it difficult to learn to read because they interpreted the act of reading as aggressive behavior toward their parents."

Looking back on such episodes, people talk with the chagrin of middle-aged professionals queried about drunken high jinks in their student days. (Kety himself quickly rejected his own parable and went on to enjoy a long, celebrated scientific career. At age eighty he could still be found at work each day, at the National Institute of Mental Health.) In bursts of mental contagion that no one has ever explained, levelheaded men and women occasionally succumb to giddy excitement — over the stock market, say, or a million-dollar lottery prize. The excitement feeds on itself, growing ever more frenzied as the number of people caught up in it grows. In Holland in the 1600s, to cite the classic example, "tulip mania" struck like a tornado and sober family men traded their life savings for a single tulip bulb.

In its heyday, psychoanalysis seemed to cast a similar spell. "What I'm trying to tell you," says Allan Hobson, the Harvard psychiatrist, "is that everybody was in it at least up to their waist, and some people were in way over their head."

Of all the features that made psychoanalysis alluring, one outweighed all the others. The key was that psychoanalysis offered hope, and hope that far transcended the field of medicine. In the 1950s, the psychiatrist Robert Coles recalled with only mild exaggeration, "we were taught or led to believe . . . that some combination of ten years of psychoanalysis and a little liberal juggling of the economy, and by golly, heaven would be right around the corner." In America, the land of the new beginning and the self-made man, there were no limits to what psychoanalysis might do.

Allan Hobson thinks that hope was highest, and psychoanalysis was at its peak, in 1960. "Kennedy had just been elected president," he recalls, "the most effective and articulate liberal politician the United States has ever seen, and there was a kind of national messianism in the air." Hobson is a trim man with wispy, white hair and a long, thin nose rearranged by muggers decades ago. He is a lively talker who shouts in anger and squeaks in disbelief and waves his hands as if trying to lift himself into the air. He recalls the glory days of psychoanalysis not as a cynic who observed the drama from the sidelines but as someone caught in the floodwaters himself.

"They passed a mental health bill, without opposition. There were going to be mental health clinics all over the country" — Hobson is incredulous now, and his voice has risen to an almost inaudible peep — *"it was going to solve the problem of poverty!* The reason why all these people were poor was that they hadn't been analyzed. I kid you not. It was sold to Congress on that basis. If everyone had a chance to be psychoanalyzed, they'd all be red-blooded Americans."

That America took to psychoanalysis more enthusiastically than any other nation, and that Americans singled out hopefulness as its most appealing feature, was doubly ironic. For Freud was a deeply pessimistic thinker and one who, for good measure, detested the United States. "America is a mistake," he once wrote. "A gigantic mistake, it is true, but none the less a mistake."

In part, Freud's dislike of the United States was simply snobbery, the disdain of the European sophisticate for his nouveau riche country cousin. His 1909 trip, to deliver his lectures at Clark, was his only visit to the New World. That invitation marked Freud's first official recognition ("As I stepped onto the platform at Worcester," he wrote later, ". . . it seemed like the realization of some incredible daydream"), but even that honor failed to soothe him. Nor had he succumbed to the excitement of seeing his first movie, or visiting Chinatown or Coney Island or Niagara Falls. The wretched American food was too rich to digest, Freud would complain ever after, and his time in America had even managed somehow to destroy his handwriting.

But Freud's anti-Americanism — an "obsession," according to one biographer — ran deeper. The real issue seems to have been fear that Americans, in their shallowness and magpie impatience and perpetual lust for quick fixes, would eagerly take up his doctrines but would misunderstand and mangle them. It was a fear that showed a certain gift for prophecy.

The true mismatch between Freud and the United States had to do not with cuisine but with optimism and pessimism. Freud did talk occasionally of bold cures and butterflylike transformations, it is true, but more often he struck a darker note. At the dawn of his career, in 1893, he famously noted that the aim of psychoanalysis was merely the transforming of "hysterical misery into common unhappiness." At the end of his career, in 1937, he still proclaimed the same message. "The difference between a person who has not been analyzed and the behavior of a person after he has been analyzed," Freud wrote, "is not so thorough-going as we aim at making it and as we expect and maintain it to be."

And when it came to mankind in general, as opposed to patients in particular, Freud's vision was as bleak as anything in Hobbes: "Men are not gentle, friendly creatures who want to be loved, and who at the most can defend themselves if they are attacked . . . ," he wrote in *Civilization and Its Discontents*. "Their neighbor is for them not only a potential helper or sexual object, but also someone who tempts them to satisfy their aggressiveness on him, to exploit his capacity for work without compensation, to use him sexually without his consent, to seize his possessions, to humiliate him, to cause him pain, to torture and to kill him. *Homo homini lupus*. [Man is a wolf to man.]"

This harsh truth, Freud insisted, was indisputable. Man is "a savage beast to whom consideration towards his own kind is something alien. Anyone who calls to mind the atrocities committed during the racial migrations or the invasions of the Huns, or by the people known as Mongols under Jenghiz Khan and Tamerlane, or at the capture of Jerusalem by the pious crusaders, or even, indeed, the horrors of the recent World War — anyone who calls these things to mind will have to bow humbly before the truth of this view."

The crucial, horrifying point was that there was no solution — no fundamental improvement was possible, for the problem was not society's structure but man's nature. "The mental constitution of humanity" and not the actions of particular individuals, Freud had declared during World War I, was the cause of "the excess of brutality, cruelty, and mendacity which is now allowed to spread itself over the civilized world." Our built-in drives, "born afresh with every child," included "those of incest, cannibalism, and lust for killing."

The result is that mankind is trapped: humans can live only within society, for only society's restraints can tame our sexual and aggressive instincts, but to live in society is to sacrifice and subdue one's deepest passions and impulses. Man cannot live without society, and he cannot live as he would like *within* society. *Civilization and Its Discontents*, for all its majesty, is a book-length gloss on the familiar text, "Damned if you do, damned if you don't."

"Life, as we find it, is too hard for us," Freud emphasized. "It brings us too many pains, disappointments, and impossible tasks." A few sentences later, he noted bluntly, as if to end any talk that somewhere there might be an exit door, "The intention that man should be 'happy' is not contained in the plan of 'Creation.' " It would seem hard to create a message less suited to the country whose founding document proclaims an inalienable right to the pursuit of happiness.

And yet Freud's worldview was even blacker than this. Every living creature, he insisted, harbored what he dubbed a death instinct. "In 1920," wrote Freud's psychoanalytic colleague and biographer Fritz Wittels, "Freud astonished us with the discovery that there is in everything living, in addition to the pleasure principle which, since the days of Hellenic culture, has been called Eros, another principle: What lives, wants to die again. Originating in dust, it wants to be dust again. Not only the life-drive is in them, but the *death-drive* as well." (Italics in original.)

When these grim theories reached America, they were transformed, astonishingly, into a doctrine of hope. The change was made, as Freud had feared, by watering down his message until it reached the point of inoffensive blandness. The dilution was performed with the most bravado, almost as if it were a magic trick, by Karl Menninger, a devout admirer of Freud and the emblem of American psychiatry in the 1950s and '60s.

Along with his father and brother, Menninger ran the renowned Menninger Clinic in Topeka, Kansas. Menninger was a fiery, autocratic, impatient man whose personal life was a muddle — among other complications, he and his brother went through long, angry stretches where they ran their clinic together but refused to speak to one another — but his public image was as the embodiment of the wise and gentle healer. He is immortalized in that role in a tableau on medicine, in a stained-glass window of the Washington Cathedral. There, on a clear day in the nation's capital, the visitor can see Karl, his father Charles, and his brother Will, glowing in the sunlight.

In a speech at the annual meeting of the American Psychiatric Association in 1959, Menninger spelled out Freud's message. His talk was titled "Hope." Freud's central theme, Menninger began, was the biblical message "Ye shall know the truth and the truth shall make you free." Then Menninger added his own twist to the tale. "For this emancipating truth Freud searched not in physics or chemistry or biology, but in the tabooed land of the emotions. From the Pandora chest of man's mind, full of harmful and unlovely things to be released upon a protesting world, there turned up — last of all — Hope."

Having somehow found hope, a task that had stymied Freud, Menninger was home free. That home seemed considerably more like Norman Vincent Peale's America than Sigmund Freud's Vienna. "Freud's great courage led him to look honestly at the evil in man's nature," Menninger declared. "But he persisted in his researches to the bottom of the chest, and he discerned that potentially love is stronger than hate, that for all its core of malignancy, the nature of men can be transformed with the nurture and dispersion of love."

Menninger was fond of proclaiming that he himself was "more Freudian than Freud," and he remained devoted even after a pilgrimage to Vienna turned into a fiasco when Freud snubbed his American visitor. For Menninger, no praise of Freud could be too great. He was "a man whose intrepidity and originality of thought, whose intuitive brilliance, whose fruitful adventures into the unknown" put him on a par with Plato and Galileo. Freud was a "genius" whose character was marked by "indefatigable patience and unflinching courage" and "ineffable modesty and gentleness and essential sweetness." A man without peers, Freud had "discovered psychology," and "no one in the field of psychology ever attained to a fraction of his stature."

Possessed of the certain knowledge that in Freud he had found an unfailing guide to the mysteries of the human psyche and equipped with rose-colored spectacles never seen in Vienna, Menninger worked tirelessly to spread his version of the gospel. He began by criticizing his predecessors, even Freud, for having had insufficient faith in the powers of psychoanalysis. "The old point of view assumed that most mental illness was progressive and refractory," he scolded in *The Vital Balance*, his 1963 manifesto. "The new point of view is that most mental illness serves its purpose and disappears, and does so more rapidly and completely when skillfully understood and dealt with."

The skillful treatment Menninger had in mind was psychoanalysis, and not even madness could dent his optimism. "We know there is a possibility for human beings to lose their moorings," Menninger wrote breezily, "to become confused and disturbed. Usually this condition disappears more or less promptly; sometimes it grows worse." There was, really, no great mystery. "At the risk of tiring the reader," he declared, "we venture to repeat the formula: stresses accumulate beyond the powers of the habitual coping devices of the individual to manage smoothly."

Whence this bland and overflowing confidence? Part of it *did* derive from Freud, although Menninger's tendency to paint a smiley face on his hero would have earned him only the great man's contempt. Where Menninger represented Freud accurately was in his faith in the almost magical healing power of words. "Words are the essential tool of mental treatment," Freud had written in 1905. "A layman will no doubt find it hard to understand how pathological disorders of the body and mind can be eliminated by 'mere' words. He will feel that he is being asked to believe in magic. And he will not be so very wrong."

But Menninger's faith in words exceeded even Freud's, for Menninger saw no reason to set limits as to which "pathological disorders" psychoanalysis could treat. Psychiatry had taken a wrong turn, Menninger believed, at the very beginning of its modern era, in the 1890s. The great psychiatric pioneer Emil Kraepelin had devoted his energies to labeling his patients. All very neat, Menninger implied, but what good did it do? "Our concern now," he declared impatiently in *The Vital Balance*, "is not so much what to call something as what to do about it."

The plain words hid a radical message. In psychiatry, Menninger insisted, diagnosing a disease was *not* the first step in treating a patient, as physicians in other fields had long assumed. The reason was simple: diagnosis was irrelevant because diseases were not truly different from one another. "We tend today to think of all mental illness as being essentially the same in quality, although differing quantitatively and in external appearance," Menninger declared. Take patients who seemed to have quite different problems — a despondent man contemplating suicide, for instance; a woman overwhelmed by panic attacks if she dared to venture outdoors; and a schizophrenic man convinced there was a wolf living within him and devouring him from the inside out. To Menninger, all were variations on a single theme.

That theme was anxiety, the true root of all evil. "The assumption was that *all* psychopathology was due to anxiety," recalls Donald Klein, the Columbia University psychiatrist. "If you had a little anxiety, you were nervous. If you had moderate anxiety, you were neurotic. If you had so much anxiety that your ego crumbled and you lost contact with reality, then you were psychotic."

It made for a tidy theory. Other scientists had yearned to find a single, unifying explanation that would tie together all the mysteries of the cosmos — Einstein spent more than three decades searching for a unified field theory — but psychiatrists had found *their* Holy Grail. Anxiety was the culprit; psychoanalysis was the cure. "For Menninger," in Klein's succinct summary, "there was one disease and one treatment."

"Gone forever is the notion that the mentally ill person is an exception," Menninger declared. "It is now accepted that most people have some degree of mental illness at some time, and many of them have a degree of mental illness most of the time." This certainly seemed like a denial of Freud's efforts to impose a boundary line between neuroses and psychoses. But like the Bible, Freud's works contained passages that could be cited in support of almost any position. He had, indeed, written often of the futility of trying to psychoanalyze schizophrenic patients. Menninger and his followers preferred a different remark, from "Analysis Terminable and Interminable." "Every normal person, in fact, is only normal on the average," Freud wrote in that 1937 essay. "His ego approximates to that of the psychotic in some part or other and to a greater or lesser extent."

It was an enticing belief, partly because it seemed humane and partly because it seemed to fit with our commonsense picture of mental illness. "The idea of continuity between what went on in normal people's lives and what went on in psychopathology was enormously appealing," says Donald Klein. "People said, '*I'm* concerned about sex and sexual taboos and those sorts of things. I can see that somebody who's *very* concerned about them might feel much worse than I do.' "

Americans took that ball and ran with it. They lived, after all, in a nation whose guiding myths were tales of nearly total transformation. Anything was possible; with enough gumption anyone could grow up to become president. That was an old story. The new twist was to adapt the traditional rags-to-riches saga by converting it from an economic fable to a psychological one. The message of American psychoanalysis was not that anyone could grow rich but that anyone could overcome his past and become a new person, healthy and free. It was as if the oddest of odd couples, Horatio Alger and Sigmund Freud, had joined forces.

Mental health was only the beginning. "It would be superficial simply to say that Freud invented a cure for neurosis," the psychoanalyst Abram Kardiner declared in 1957. "To say only that would do Freud a great injustice! Freud did much more than that. . . . He brought into the world a new definition of human fate, because he placed in the hands of man the means with which to alter impediments which were previously considered irremediable. 'You need not be the victim of your own past,' said Freud, 'or of your own environment.' "

In their faith in psychoanalysis, Kardiner and Menninger spoke for an era. Many analysts were convinced that, like heroes in a fairy tale, they had been vouchsafed a gift of matchless power. In public, they tried to refrain from crowing over their good fortune. Among their own, though, there was no need to be coy. In a panel discussion on schizophrenia at an American Psychoanalytic Association meeting, for example, one participant spelled out those features that set psychoanalysis above any would-be rivals:

> Its special strengths derive from its unique access to the patient's inner experiences, his fears and hopes, dreams and fantasies, his prides and his shames, both those he can consciously grasp and those that conceal their influences beyond the reaches of awareness. . . . *Our interpretive work has forced us quite correctly to undervalue other sources of information*, like extra-analytic reports, laboratory examinations, biochemical and physical studies, information about learning, memory, coordination, sociological data, reports from employers, family members, and so on. . . . No other discipline has been able to plumb the depths of inner experiences, to explore with such sensitivity our most intimate feelings and behaviors, and to give to them meaning and significance. [Italics added.]

The only question was where to use so formidable a tool. The answer seemed clear. Psychoanalysis was "the most powerful of all psychotherapeutic instruments," declared Leo Stone, the eminent analyst, and "it is basically a greater error to use it for trivial or incipient or reactive illnesses . . . than for serious chronic illnesses." Armed with a sledgehammer, why use it only to drive carpet tacks?

And so the stage was set. Armed with moral authority and intellectual fervor and brandishing a mighty weapon, psychoanalysts were poised to do great deeds. What greater challenge than madness? Its victims had suffered, helpless and obscure, throughout the ages. Now came the possibility that these poor, imprisoned souls could at last be rescued. "For us," the child psychoanalyst Beata Rank declared in a lecture on treating the "feeble-minded or psychotic" child, "he offers a challenge similar to that recounted in myths and legends where the hero (now therapist) conquers monsters and dragons and undoes the curse bestowed by evil spirits, thereby freeing the beautiful prince or princess."

Of all those monsters, the most feared was the best known. Formidable, immovable, unfathomable, it had long snatched its victims as it chose. This scourge was schizophrenia. The analysts were determined to vanquish it at last.

PART THREE

Schizophrenia

Healing schizophrenia establishes one in his own eyes as having reached the pinnacle of competency—of power and authority—of doing something which even Freud and Jung could not do.

—Arthur Burton

CHAPTER FIVE

The Mother of the "Schizophrenogenic Mother"

We think of a schizophrenic as a person who has had serious traumatic experiences in early infancy at a time when his ego and its ability to examine reality were not yet developed.

— *FRIEDA FROMM-REICHMANN*

A<small>T NIGHT</small>, when the mental hospital grew quiet, the tormentors emerged. They were plain as day to their victim — plain as devils, really — but he alone could see or hear them. Night after night, he leapt from his bed, terrified, pleading for mercy in a mélange of English, French, German, and Hebrew, scrambling atop the bureau in a frenzied attempt at escape, retreating from there to the desk, to the chair, to the bed again, to the bureau, all the time jabbering in a torment of fear. Trailing behind him, struggling to make her own way across the furniture, was the slower, clumsier figure of a tiny middle-aged woman. She was Frieda Fromm-Reichmann, one of America's most renowned psychiatrists. *She* did not see any phantoms, she tried to reassure her patient as she, too, switched from language to language, but if and when she caught sight of them, she would do her best to protect him.

In the battle against schizophrenia, Fromm-Reichmann was in the front lines. She made an unlikely warrior. Only four feet ten, plump, down-to-earth, she looked like a grandmother sent over from central casting. A German Jewish refugee, she had come to the United States in 1935. There she spent her career at Chestnut Lodge, a renowned private mental hospital in the suburbs of Washington, D.C., devoted to the psychoanalytic treatment of psychotic patients. She had originally been hired for two months, as a summer replacement, but those two months stretched to twenty-two years, ending only with Fromm-Reichmann's death from a stroke in 1957.

By that time, she was known throughout the psychiatric community as a wise and kindly therapist. But she was more than that. For venturing to take on madness in its most virulent form, and for emerging victorious, the diminutive Fromm-Reichmann had earned a towering reputation. The psychiatrist Robert Coles, himself a moral exemplar for a later generation, spoke for his peers when he lauded her as a "hero." The best-selling novel *I Never Promised You a Rose Garden*, published in 1964, spread her reputation to the general public. Written by a former patient, Joanne Greenberg, it portrayed Fromm-Reichmann as the savior who had delivered her from schizophrenia. Fromm-Reichmann was "Clara Fried," remarkable in equal measure for her brilliance and her empathy. "After you know her for a while," one of the novel's bedazzled psychiatrists remarks, "you'll find out that with little Clara Fried, brains are only the beginning."

But Fromm-Reichmann left a complex legacy. On the one hand, she confronted schizophrenia head-on—as we have noted, even Freud had blinked when he looked at schizophrenia—but indomitability was only half the story. Equally important, she introduced an essential new element into the schizophrenia picture. This new element was blame, and it would come to dominate the canvas.

Schizophrenia was *not* an organic condition, Fromm-Reichmann argued, despite the contrary views of the nineteenth century's most eminent psychiatrists. Nor did she devote a great deal of time to Freud's speculations on the psychological origins of schizophrenia, though she dutifully paid them homage. Fromm-Reichmann's view was simpler, and it would soon become gospel, passed along and embellished by a series of distinguished disciples over the course of the 1950s and '60s. The message was that schizophrenia was man-made. To be precise, it was *woman*-made. A schizophrenic was shaped by human hands, as much a product of human craft as a reed basket or a clay pot. In the case of schizophrenia, Fromm-Reichmann proclaimed, those shaping hands belonged to mother.

From her medical school days, Fromm-Reichmann had found herself drawn to treating schizophrenics. Unflappable and unafraid, she insisted on seeing patients alone, even the paranoid and violent ones. To bring along an aide for protection, she insisted, would be disrespectful to her patients. Successful treatment was not a matter of adhering to particular techniques or doctrines, she believed, and she disdained "technical rules." What was crucial was "the basic attitude of the individual therapist toward psychotic persons. If he meets them as strange creatures of another world whose productions are not understandable to 'normal' beings, he cannot treat them. If he realizes, however, that the difference between himself and the psychotic is only one of degree and not of kind, he will know better how to meet him."

Madness could be understood just as dreams could be, but virtuoso displays of intellectual acrobatics were not Fromm-Reichmann's style. A schizophrenic patient who was "aloof, detached, and uncommunicative," for example, might simply be "protecting himself from additional fear and potential hostility." *"It is certainly not an intellectual comprehension of the schizophrenic but the sympathetic understanding and skillful handling of the patient's and physician's mutual relationship that are the decisive therapeutic factors,"* she declared. (Italics in original.)

It was a philosophy that was easier to espouse than to enact. It took eighteen months, for example, before one patient at Chestnut Lodge would stop shouting, "You dirty little stinking bitch" and "You damned German Jew; go back to your Kaiser!" and "I wish you had crashed in that plane you took!" Fromm-Reichmann was not one to posture, and she told such stories not to portray herself as noble or long-suffering but in passing, on the way to some other point. In trying to sort out her own "irrational" fear of one patient, for example, she noted that "it is true that she threatened repeatedly to hit me or to throw stones at me," but she also pointed out that the threats had never materialized. Indeed, "very little actually happened except for a few slaps in my face."

Her fellow therapists marveled at the imperturbability of this "well-brought-up, refined, upper-middle-class, German Jewish lady," as one of them described her, no matter the behavior that confronted her. "One day, during a therapeutic hour, as this patient (mute, as usual) was sitting with Dr. Fromm-Reichmann in her office," a colleague recalled, "she noticed that he was fingering his genitals with one hand that was crammed deep into the pocket of his trousers. It was also plain to her that he had an erection. She pondered this situation for a moment, then said to him, 'If it will make you feel any better, please go ahead.' Whereupon the young man unzipped his fly and proceeded to masturbate, while Dr. Fromm-Reichmann sat quietly across from him, her eyes down, her hands clasped in her lap."

Fromm-Reichmann would "sit in a patient's urine with him to show there was no difference between them," another colleague recalled. "Or a patient would give his feces as a gift, and she would take them."

Small wonder that those psychiatrists willing to take on schizophrenia were more often hailed by their peers than emulated. Schizophrenic patients were hard to reach, quite likely poor and disheveled, and perhaps violent. Treatment was likely to be prolonged, difficult, and, worst of all, unsuccessful. What psychiatrist would not prefer a succession of grateful ladies and gentlemen in business attire, who kept their appointments, paid their bills, and eventually moved along?

But to think of schizophrenia as simply a difficult disease is to understate the point woefully. It is relatively common, more prevalent than Alzheimer's disease or multiple sclerosis, and its horrors moved even the experts to shake their heads in awe. They rattled off the bare facts easily enough —

schizophrenia affected about one person in a hundred; it tended to strike between ages seventeen and twenty-five; it afflicted men and women in equal numbers, although men fell ill at a younger age — but even in austere medical journals, they sometimes interrupted their measured prose with a more heartfelt passage.

"Schizophrenia is the cancer of psychiatry," one authority declared, and its victims were "in truly terrible trouble." Another called the disease an "awesome holocaust" that left in its wake a trail of "tragic human debris."

It is a holocaust that we, safe at home, can scarcely imagine. In truth, the challenge is even greater than it first appears. Illness is a foreign country, it has been observed, and we read travelers' tales of their journeys there with mingled fear and fascination. But mental illness is unlike cancer or heart disease or many other afflictions, since it directly affects the way its victims perceive the world. The result is that the very people who know madness best — the natives of this strange land, so to speak — may scarcely be able to describe it in terms the rest of us can grasp.

On the other hand, we cannot do without such guidance. We can imagine ourselves paralyzed or blind or deaf, perhaps, but almost by definition we cannot think clearly about what it would mean to think chaotically. How to imagine being caught in seething white water if all we have ever known is a gently burbling stream?

And so we turn to the natives. Listen to Carol North, for example, in a passage from *Welcome, Silence,* her memoir of schizophrenia. One day North happened to see a piece of glass from a broken Coke bottle:

> There was a message here. I was supposed to use the glass edge to rip away the flesh of my feet to get a view of the machines inside, which would provide a parallel view into the workings of the Other Dimensions. . . . Although the connection was subtle, I was astute; I could see the master plan here. . . .
>
> Eagerly I sat down and began to carve into the top of my foot with a piece of green glass. It wasn't easy, because the glass was so rough. I was surprised at the toughness of my skin. I made several gouges, not even slicing through the long tendons running the length of the top of my foot. A few drops of blood oozed forth, then the wounds just sort of lay there doing nothing. I poked around in them with my finger, trying to get beneath the skin edges to probe into the machinery inside, but the skin was tenacious and hung tightly to my underlying flesh. I pulled the wounds as far open as they would stretch, but I couldn't see any machines inside. The humming stopped. I had missed my chance.

That strange tone, that "juxtaposition of lunacy and sanity," in the words of the psychiatrists Paul Wender and Donald Klein, is telltale. A person brain-damaged in a car crash, say, might be damaged across the board. In contrast, the schizophrenic's mind is a hodgepodge, a surrealist painting that mixes the most bizarre hallucinations and delusions with the most everyday of images. A schizophrenic might believe that he sees dragons climbing out of the walls and yet be able to read the morning newspaper.

Even a lifetime of familiarity does not tame the onlooker's sense of eeriness. "My son is crazy and he's not crazy," says Irma Cardozo-Freeman, a professor of literature and folklore at Ohio State University and the mother of a fifty-year-old schizophrenic. "I can't explain it. He can sit down and write an essay without an irrational thought in it, and yet he's irrational. Not always, but most of the time. He thinks Mick Jagger and Miles Davis talk to him through the radio. Sometimes," she concludes wearily, "I think my son is possessed."

Poignantly, there may be stretches of insight and self-awareness. I recall one schizophrenic man, first diagnosed at age eleven and forty-seven at the time I met him during one recent winter. He lived alone in a single room, the thermostat set to eighty, his mattress in the center of the room and surrounded by teetering stacks of newspapers and books and mounds of dirty clothes. He was able to function on his own — indeed, he was quite bright — but he lurched from topic to topic and spoke in a peculiar singsong, some words long and drawn out and then whole phrases rattled-off-at-high-speed-and-squeezed-into-a-single-breath. "A psychiatrist told me once," he recounted as matter-of-factly as if he were commenting on the weather, "that I would always come across like a phonograph record that someone had left lying in the sun."

Despite the odds, there are many firsthand accounts of insanity. The best are vivid and compelling, though the mere act of providing an understandable description imposes an artificial order, just as a dream recounted to someone else never has the sweep and taken-for-granted strangeness of the original.

The dream analogy is almost unavoidable. Like elements in a dream landscape, for instance, mundane fragments of a schizophrenic's world can suddenly take on a hypnotic vividness. "Environmental stimuli constantly bombarded my senses with unrelenting, nearly unbearable intensity," Carol North recalled. "I spent hours marveling at the texture of the bricks on the buildings, at the intricate moving patterns of the moonlight on the river, at the folds of bark on trees, at designs dancing over the ballroom carpet in the [student] Union, even at the fine weave in my jeans. These were no ordinary designs and patterns; they were pregnant with meaning."

A recovered schizophrenic named Norma MacDonald recounted a similar sensory bombardment. "The walk of a stranger on the street could be a 'sign' to me which I must interpret. Every face in the windows of a passing streetcar would be engraved on my mind, all of them concentrating on me and trying to pass me some sort of message." Often the messages were more overt. Carol North had been tormented by strange voices since she was six years old. She believed that everyone heard voices; no one talked about them, she assumed, because voices, like bodily functions, were private. In time, North's voices became almost incessant, "chattering away nonsensically, like people at a cocktail party in the next room." Later still, by the time North was seventeen, the voices were issuing her orders to kill herself.

Voices are a mark of schizophrenia, but they are only a part of the pain the disease inflicts. Patients are haunted by delusions — false beliefs, like the conviction that the CIA is tracking one's every move — and by hallucinations — voices, for one thing, as well as imaginary but utterly convincing nightmare mirages. "I could find no rest," a patient named Renée complained, "for horrible images assailed me, so vivid that I experienced actual physical sensation. I cannot say that I really saw images; they did not represent anything. Rather I felt them. It seemed that my mouth was full of birds which I crunched between my teeth, and their feathers, their blood and broken bones were choking me. Or I saw people whom I had entombed in milk bottles, putrefying, and I was consuming their rotten cadavers. Or I was devouring the head of a cat which meanwhile gnawed at my vitals. It was ghastly, intolerable."

Almost in passing, as if it was scarcely worthy of singling out, Carol North described feeling "my skin turning gray and starting to slide off my forearms right there in the psychiatrist's office," and "molten blobs of thoughts [that] slipped off my skin and splatted onto the carpet in neat little paths."

Look at a particular patient struck by schizophrenia and there is no dodging questions about where this strange disease came from. Why had it appeared when it did? Had it been lurking somewhere, unrecognized?

Now consider not an individual patient but the history of the disease itself, and the same baffling questions arise. Did schizophrenia suddenly appear, or has it plagued mankind from the beginning? Look in the Bible and in Hippocrates and in dozens of other ancient texts and you find vivid descriptions of leprosy and epilepsy and a host of other illnesses. Where is schizophrenia? Today it is one of the most widespread mental illnesses, present in every culture in the world. Could a disease with such devastating and flamboyant symptoms really have been overlooked? And if it did suddenly appear out of nowhere, why then? Why there?

The historical record is dotted with tantalizing, but equivocal, descriptions of diseases that sound as if they might have been schizophrenia. One sixth-century writer describes a woman who believed that she truly held the fate of the world in her hands — unless she kept her fingers rigid, she feared, the world would be destroyed. In about the year 1000, the Persian physician Avicenna described a young prince who had become convinced he was a cow and begged to be killed "so that a good stew may be made from my flesh." In France in the fourteenth century, King Charles VI (Charles the Mad) suffered from the delusion that his legs were made of glass and that they might break at any moment.*

Strangely, there are no undisputed accounts of schizophrenia until the nineteenth century. Then, suddenly, there were *two* accounts in the same year, 1809, one by an English asylum-keeper and the other by a French physician. These early observers were especially struck by the disease's early onset, in adolescence. "In the interval between puberty and manhood," wrote John Haslam, superintendent of London's Bethlehem Hospital (the word "bedlam" comes from "Bethlem"), "I have painfully witnessed this hopeless and degrading change, which in a short time has transformed the most promising and vigorous intellect into a slavering and bloated idiot." New or not, this disease suddenly seemed to be everywhere. It became a scourge, and the embodiment of insanity.

Frieda Fromm-Reichmann seemed an unlikely authority on such a daunting disease, but she was more formidable than she looked. Despite her grandmotherly facade, she was a zealous and highly disciplined worker, fueled by endless cigarettes and countless cups of coffee. The sense of duty had been implanted early. Fromm-Reichmann had been raised in a stern household, the oldest of three daughters, and the declared favorite of an imperious, never-to-be-crossed mother. The children grew up quiet, well mannered, neat, conscientious. Expectations were high; rebellion was unthinkable. "We had a wonderful, carefree childhood," the third daughter, Anna, recalled in her old age. "We were allowed to learn anything we wanted."

Frieda, her mother's perfect child, excelled from the start, in her lessons and later at the University of Königsberg, where she was one of only a few female students among hundreds of males. Though she devoted her life to an enterprise that Freud had deemed impossible, she insisted that she was no rebel. No disciple of Freud was more devout than she was, Fromm-Reichmann maintained, and she delighted in proclaiming Freud's trailblazing genius. With schizophrenia, it was not so much that Freud had gone astray as that he had, for once, sold psychoanalysis short.

The great man's mistake was understandable, in Fromm-Reichmann's eyes. After all, nearly all his patients had been merely neurotic rather than psychotic. Freud had declared that schizophrenia was untreatable essentially

---

* A favorite topic for historical debate was the mental health of Jesus Christ. Early in this century especially, one treatise after another purported to show that Jesus was schizophrenic. Weren't delusions of grandeur one of the hallmarks of the disease? What about hearing voices, and not just any voice but the voice of God? That debate reached its climax in 1913, with a magisterial rebuttal in the form of a doctoral thesis entitled *The Psychiatric Study of Jesus*. The author was the not-yet-famous Albert Schweitzer.

because the patient was too disturbed to establish a working relationship with the therapist. Here was the key error, and Fromm-Reichmann spelled out the intellectual mistake that had led Freud astray.

He had noted, correctly, that schizophrenics were "withdrawn, detached, and sometimes aggressively hostile," but he had misunderstood what he had seen. This retreat into a private world was not a primary, defining feature of schizophrenia. Instead, it was "a secondary result of very early serious warping of their relationships with the people significant in their environment in infancy and childhood."

This was a message that carried enormous hope — contrary to Freud, schizophrenic patients were not beyond help. The withdrawal from reality was only a symptom, a kind of mental wound. Schizophrenics had been hurt by the world, but they had come into it intact. The damage had come later.

And so it could be undone. The key was a therapist with the patience and stamina to undo the patient's lifelong "warping." Identification between patient and therapist *was* possible. In an account of her own therapeutic successes at Chestnut Lodge, Frieda Fromm-Reichmann put the essential point in italics: *"The schizophrenic has, above all, to be cured of the wounds and frustrations of his life before we can expect him to recover."* The analyst Edith Weigert (who had analyzed Seymour Kety, the scientific director of the National Institute of Mental Health) described Fromm-Reichmann's technique in a bit more detail. She made it sound routine. Perched in her rocking chair and looking her patient squarely in the face, Fromm-Reichmann sat and listened, without judgment, without prejudice, without preconceptions. "Sooner or later the schizophrenic patient experienced that he was no longer alone, that here was a human being who understood, who did not turn away in estrangement or disgust," Weigert wrote. "This rare moment of discovery — unpredictable and unforeseen, like a gift of grace — sometimes became a turning point in the patient's life. The gates of human fellowship were opened — and thereby the slow way to recovery was opened also."

This was a claim that was easy to assert but difficult to demonstrate. Fromm-Reichmann and Weigert and other psychotherapists talked blithely of cures and recovery, but they provided no evidence to back those claims. This is especially troubling because schizophrenia is a slippery disease. The problems begin at the beginning, with diagnosis. Even today, schizophrenia can be diagnosed only on the basis of symptoms — hallucinations, delusions, severe apathy, and so on — rather than on the basis of a blood test or a brain scan or any other objective measure that yields an indisputable label. The diagnosis is still made as it was a century ago, essentially by checking off boxes on a form.

As a result, psychiatrists can disagree on whether a given patient is schizophrenic in the first place. Solomon Snyder, one of the most renowned of present-day psychiatrists, declares emphatically that even Fromm-Reichmann's prize patient, the author of *I Never Promised You a Rose Garden*, was not schizophrenic at all. "Anyone who has ever worked with schizophrenics for even a few weeks," Snyder insists, "knows that neither Vonnegut [Mark Vonnegut, author of *The Eden Express*, a first-person account of madness] nor Deborah in *Rose Garden* was schizophrenic."

More confusing still, schizophrenia follows an unpredictable course. Even in the early years of this century, when there were essentially no treatments of any sort for schizophrenia, the rule of thumb was that one-third of all patients recovered, one-third improved, and one-third did not improve. This should have been an observation that made every psychiatrist cautious about making bold claims. Its plain meaning was that anecdotes and case histories were not enough. *Any* therapy that anyone dreamed up would be able to claim some successes.*

Fromm-Reichmann claimed that her approach to therapy derived from Freud's, but it was not quite so. As we have seen, Freud almost never dealt with schizophrenic patients. In spite of his amateur standing, however, he believed he had seen to the heart of the disease, thanks to an extraordinary patient he had never met. Daniel Paul Schreber was a German judge who spent thirteen years of his life in mental hospitals. The second and longest hospitalization began when Schreber was fifty-one and stretched nearly nine years, from 1893 until 1902. During those nine years, Schreber kept meticulous notes, and in 1903 he published a first-person narrative called *Memoirs of My Nervous Illness.*

Schreber's "nervous illness" would be called paranoid schizophrenia today, and he told a remarkable, if barely comprehensible, tale. Schreber was assaulted by voices and other hallucinations and plagued by delusions —he spoke with the sun, he was tormented by vampires, his body was gradually being transformed into a woman's. For years, he believed, God had directed a series of "rays" toward him; the rays had produced an endless number of painful effects that Schreber called "miracles." He had grown accustomed to this bizarre assault, he wrote, but "even now the miracles which I experience hourly are still of a nature to frighten every other human being to death."

The aim of the book was to invite qualified scientists to examine Schreber so that they could see for themselves that his body was in fact changing itself from male to female. "What other people think are delusions and hallucinations," Schreber explained, were real changes, unprecedented in the course of human history and proof that God's powers were even greater than had been previously understood. Telling his story, Schreber

---

* Few psychiatrists had the skeptical cast of mind of Anatole France, who was shown a stack of discarded crutches at Lourdes and supposedly observed, "What—no wooden legs?"

believed, would spread these new religious truths and would "in the highest degree act fruitfully and as a blessing to mankind."

Freud read Schreber's book in 1910 and published an essay on his case the following year. This was Freud's first report on a hospitalized mental patient. His argument was complex and, characteristically, explained not only Schreber's case but that of every (male) paranoiac. How to account for the paranoid schizophrenic's belief that the world is conspiring against him? That obsessive fear stems from the patient's unconscious homosexuality. Unable to acknowledge the proposition "I love him," the paranoiac protests too much and insists instead, "I *hate* him." This proposition, in turn, is unacceptable, because it forces the patient to see himself as poisoned by hate, and so it is transformed by one final twist into *"He* hates *me." Voilà!*

Fromm-Reichmann hailed Freud's insights, but in fact her approach to schizophrenia came closer to that of her friend and mentor Harry Stack Sullivan. Celebrated in the 1920s and '30s as one of America's best psychiatrists, Sullivan is nearly forgotten today. He was an odd character — a college dropout, an alcoholic, a big spender who skipped out on his father's funeral to avoid being stuck with the bill. He could be "as tender as a pat of butter," one bemused colleague recalled, "or as maliciously attacking as an enraged cobra."

Sullivan was a tall, thin, melancholy figure, "a lonely person from his earliest childhood," in the words of one of the speakers at his memorial service. Perhaps as a result, his psychological theories took as their central theme the hazards of dealing with other people. Where Freud had concentrated on conflicts *within* the individual, Sullivan emphasized the interactions *between* his patient and other people. "The individual is simply not the unit to study," in one commentator's summary of Sullivan's views, for the same reason that "an animal in a cage rather than its natural habitat" is not the right subject for a student of wildlife.

Sullivan may have suffered bouts of schizophrenia himself — he claimed this experience as the source of his insight into the disease — but some biographers suspect he invented these stories. At any rate, he put his theories into practice beginning in 1929, at Baltimore's Sheppard and Enoch Pratt Hospital. There he organized a six-bed ward for young male schizophrenics, sealed off from the rest of the hospital.

Sullivan chose the patients from among the hospital's population of schizophrenics, chose the six aides who dealt with them, and then gave this select staff detailed instructions on how to deal with their charges. The idea, simple verging on banal, was that the patients had fallen ill because of *bad* relationships with others and could therefore be restored to health by *good* relationships. The key was in choosing aides who were sensitive, kind, friendly, and, above all, trustworthy. This down-to-earth, optimistic, can-do strategy, with its emphasis on coping in the present rather than on resurrecting the past, Sullivan declared, was characteristically "American."

The results were extraordinary. Sullivan claimed that about 80 percent of his patients had improved, though he was vague about defining "improvement." (This was not necessarily evasiveness. Sullivan's prose was *always* obscure and often impenetrable. "Intimacy," he declared, in one representative passage, "is that type of situation involving two people which permits validation of all components of personal worth.")

Sullivan had begun his therapeutic career by deciding which bits of Freudian furniture to chuck overboard and which to hang on to. In treating schizophrenics, even many of the basics were unceremoniously rejected. Though he believed that dreams were akin to psychoses, he deemed dream analysis too risky for patients with such a flimsy attachment to the real world. To ask for free associations from a patient who heard werewolves talking to him was to throw gasoline on a fire.

Nor did other classical Freudian techniques seem useful to Sullivan. The therapist could not sit out of view in near-total silence, for example, content to reflect his patient's remarks back to him. (Fromm-Reichmann sat next to her patients, not behind them like Freud, so that they *could* see one another.) The fifty-minute hour, too, was abandoned as too restrictive. The therapist might be obliged to engage her patient for hours at a time. Making matters still more difficult, these deeply disturbed people, unlike neurotics, did not see their therapist as an ally. Having fled the world in favor of a self-created one, they resisted all efforts to bring them back. "Like the animal in the woods fleeing before a predatory foe," the psychiatrist John Rosen declared in a 1952 essay, "the patient fights with all the skill of his instincts."

Therapy sessions were frequently unrewarding, resembling nothing so much as bleak scenes from Beckett. Schizophrenic speech was a "word salad," with recognizable bits tossed together any old way. Or schizophrenics talked "ragtime," careening at high speed through some idiosyncratic encyclopedia. Sometimes they did not talk at all. "In working with these patients," one of Fromm-Reichmann's colleagues explained, "the therapist eventually gets to do some at least private mulling over of the possible meanings of a belch, or the passage of flatus, not only because he is reduced to this for lack of anything else to analyze, but also because he learns that even these animal-like sounds constitute forms of communication in which, from time to time, quite different things are being said, long before the patient can . . . say them in words."

Fromm-Reichmann herself did not go quite so far in interpreting her patients' words and silences. She did insist, however, on the value of the "symptoms as symbols" approach. For four years, while still in Europe, she and her then husband, Erich Fromm, had run a private psychoanalytic hospital where they had worked closely with Georg Groddeck, perhaps the greatest advocate of the disease-deciphering school. Fromm-Reichmann remained a devoted admirer of Groddeck throughout her life. He had "a profound influence on her thinking and work with psychotics," one colleague noted, and she insisted that her students study Groddeck's writings and be prepared to discuss them. Fromm-Reichmann dedicated her only book, *Principles of Intensive Psychotherapy,* to her four "teachers," the German psychiatrist Kurt Goldstein and Freud, Sullivan, and Groddeck.

Well before Frieda Fromm-Reichmann came along, psychiatrists had made sporadic attempts to pin the blame for schizophrenia on something that had gone wrong in the family. In 1934, for example, one group of investigators reported that "in a series of 45 unselected [i.e., random] cases maternal over-protection or rejection was present in sixty percent of the cases." But the studies were hard to credit. Most involved tiny numbers or unrepresentative populations, and all were marred by vagueness and an almost total lack of methodological rigor. One 1936 study focused on kings and found that twice as many insane as sane kings had lost their fathers early in life. In 1940, a psychoanalyst reported on *four* female schizophrenics she had treated. All four suffered, she said, from having had cold, sadistic mothers and soft, indifferent fathers who were merely "imitation" parents.

Then, in 1948, the parent-blaming idea surfaced again. This time it came with a celebrity endorsement. Writing in *Psychiatry,* a journal founded by Harry Stack Sullivan, Frieda Fromm-Reichmann published a paper called "Notes on the Development of Treatment of Schizophrenics by Psychoanalytic Psychotherapy." She began with her familiar claim that, contrary to Freud, schizophrenics could be treated by talk therapy. Then, almost in passing, in one short phrase tacked on the end of a long sentence, Fromm-Reichmann coined a phrase that would reverberate for a quarter-century.

"The schizophrenic is painfully distrustful and resentful of other people," she wrote, "due to the severe early warp and rejection he encountered in important people of his infancy and childhood, as a rule, mainly in a schizophrenogenic mother." That phrase "schizophrenogenic mother" — literally, schizophrenia-producing mother — would be taken up as the drumbeat accompanying psychiatrists into battle against the enemy. For decades, it would sound in the ears of parents who felt that *they* were the enemy.

Less than a year later, with people's ears perked up, *Psychiatry* carried an article amplifying Fromm-Reichmann's remark. Here bad mothers would not be dismissed in a phrase. This time they would be poked and prodded at leisure.

The new paper, written in awkward English by a Viennese-educated psychiatrist named Trude Tietze, bore the innocuous title "A Study of Mothers of Schizophrenic Patients." Unlike Freud, who had focused all his attention on the schizophrenic himself, Tietze drew back and took a broader look. With that new perspective, everything fell into place. What suddenly appeared, Tietze realized, was not simply an individual with problems of his own but an individual caught up in a family beset with problems.

It was a paper with a tremendous influence, and it merits a close look. Tietze, at Baltimore's Johns Hopkins Hospital, had interviewed the mothers of twenty-five adult, hospitalized schizophrenics. They were, Tietze made clear at once, a *very* peculiar bunch. "All the mothers were tense and anxious people who tried to conceal their anxiety, some with more success than others. They described themselves as 'nervous,' 'high-strung,' 'shaking inside,' and 'always anticipating impending disaster.' " None had ever been hospitalized for mental illness or even seen a psychiatrist, but "all of the mothers were fundamentally insecure people, who could feel relatively secure only if they could control the situation."

Despite their similarities, Tietze wrote, the mothers differed in key ways, especially in their dealings with Tietze herself. Five of the women "openly tried to dominate the situation by over-demanding behavior. They remained superficially friendly and polite but were very hostile and resented the psychiatrist." The larger group, seventeen mothers, "appeared docile and submissive, smiling, yet not laughing, their fleeting smile often changing to a frozen grimace." But Tietze soon realized that they, too, resisted her questioning. "Their friendliness and effervescence were superficial and they tended to hide their anxiety and keep the interviewer at arm's length."

Here, barely into her paper, Tietze adopted an adversarial tone that grew steadily more marked as she went along. She seemed especially irritated by the larger, eager-to-please group. The mothers apparently did not know they were acting strangely — "they seemed quite unaware of their own hostility and of the unconscious motivation of their behavior" — but Tietze was determined not to be taken in by their performance. "Once their superficial smiling front was broken through," she wrote, "one was appalled by the emotional emptiness one found. There was a lack of genuine warmth."

To demonstrate this two-facedness, Tietze rattled off a long list of particulars. "These mothers 'cooperated' to the letter with the psychiatrist; they kept their appointments, snow, rain, or hail. They were always on time, always apologetic of taking so much of the doctor's time, always profusely thanking at the end of the interview. They tried in every possible way to ingratiate themselves and to make the best possible impression on the doctors. They acted like 'model patients.' " But Tietze saw through their little game. "They went, however, only through the motions — of themselves they gave little."

Tietze's indictment continued:

They tended to become solicitous about the interviewer whenever an opportunity presented itself. They frequently commented on the hard life of a psychiatrist; if it was raining and they did not see rubbers or an umbrella in the office, they expressed their concern lest the doctor catch a cold.

Every holiday was remembered with a sweet little card, and they frequently placed little notes or presents on the doctor's desk. They never directly asked for any favors; they would ask exactly how long they should visit their children and would carry out any suggestion to the letter, thus often reducing advice to absurdity. Their attitude was: "You are the doctor and you know best."

It does not seem an outlandish attitude for mothers whose children were victims of an overwhelming and mysterious disease, but Tietze would have none of it. "They did not seem to be aware of the burden and responsibility they put on the physician," she complained. "By their seeming surrender in what looked like a dependent relationship they dominated the situation in a subtle way and put the psychiatrist under some strain."

Her irritation grew plainer. These mothers, supposedly so eager to help, seemed not to grasp what Tietze was after. "It was impossible to obtain accurate data in regard to onset and completion of toilet training of their children," Tietze reported. "The prevailing reaction of the mothers to this question was a mixture of amazement and irritation." Nor were they forthcoming about their own private lives. "The majority of mothers were reluctant to discuss their sex life with the psychiatrist," Tietze observed.

When the mothers *did* volunteer personal information, Tietze refused to take at face value what sounded remarkably like maternal devotion. "The children were uniformly described as 'placid, lovable, cuddling babies,' " she acknowledged, but in the same sentence she explained away this behavior: the babies' "helplessness and complete dependency on their mothers seemed to have been a source of considerable gratification."

Even the way these women had responded to their child's illness struck Tietze as misguided. "The acute onset of the psychosis came as an unexpected shock to the mothers, who suddenly felt that they had lost their children," she wrote. "They felt defeated and utterly frustrated and made frantic attempts to retrieve their children. Five mothers spontaneously stated that they would rather see their schizophrenic children dead than insane."

Another observer might have seen that maternal shock and despair as predictable. These were, after all, parents whose once-healthy children were in the chronic ward of a mental hospital where they would likely live out their lives, victims of a disease that had descended without warning. Death, these parents may have felt, would at least have ended their child's suffering.

Tietze took a different view. The key to the children's illness was their mothers' "rejection." These "sick" women had never had an instinctive rapport with their sons and daughters. "It is this intuition or empathy with the child that appears to be missing or inadequately developed in the relationship of the mothers here under discussion to their schizophrenic children," she wrote.

That lack was crucial. Now Tietze explained why she had focused so much attention on the mothers' attempts to control their interviews with her. Such manipulativeness was not simply irritating; it was literally maddening. "It is the subtly dominating mother who appears to be particularly dangerous to the child," Tietze reported. "Her methods of control are subtle and therefore do not provoke open rebellion as undisguised domination may. The children exposed to this form of subtle domination under the disguise of maternal love and sacrifice are deprived of any outlet of their aggressive impulses."

By scrutinizing her twenty-five subjects, Tietze believed she had found a universal pattern. "All schizophrenic patients who were in good enough contact to reality and who formed a reasonably good relationship with their psychiatrist expressed a feeling of rejection by their mothers."

It was an extraordinary paper, and it had an extraordinary impact. Almost immediately, it was hailed as "the most thorough-going research into the nature of parent-child relationships in schizophrenia," and even after a decade it remained "perhaps [the] best known" of what was by then a flood of articles on schizophrenogenic mothers.

Nonetheless, a close reading makes clear that this was an intellectually shabby performance. Tietze never acknowledged, let alone sorted out, a crucial chicken-and-egg question—were these children schizophrenic because their mothers were overanxious and overbearing, or were the mothers frantic and jumpy because their children were schizophrenic?

In addition, though she took every opportunity to hammer home her view that rejection by the mother was at the heart of schizophrenia, Tietze dismissed seemingly contradictory evidence without discussion. She wondered, for example, if children who became schizophrenic had been welcome additions to the family. She found, presumably to her surprise, that "definitely unwanted siblings of the schizophrenic patient, who himself was planned and wanted, turned out to be the best adjusted members of the family." That odd finding, which might well have brought matters to a screeching halt, turned out not to merit even a raised eyebrow. Tietze was on to other matters in the very next sentence.

The paper's most serious weakness was another sin of omission. Tietze carried out her study without a "control" group—a comparison group of mothers that would have let her sort out whether the strange behavior she saw was something peculiar to those who had raised schizophrenic children. "In order to arrive at valid conclusions," she acknowledged blithely, "it would be necessary to compare the twenty-five mothers of this series with a control group consisting of mothers who have never produced a schizophrenic child." Necessary or not, Tietze plowed ahead. "To obtain such a control group," she noted simply, "met with insurmountable difficulties."

She decided to make a different comparison. Working from the assumption that bad mothers produced mentally ill children, Tietze tried to sort out what made some mothers more dangerous than others. She looked at her twenty-five women and divided them into two groups. Group A consisted of all those mothers whose healthy children outnumbered their schizophrenic children. These mothers, perhaps, had *some* redeeming qualities. Group B was a grimmer bunch. It was made up of all those mothers whose only child was schizophrenic, or who had one schizophrenic child and one healthy one. (Two of the twenty-five mothers had two schizophrenic children; those two women were in Group B.)

That odd comparison, the only one that Tietze undertook, "revealed no significant quantitative or qualitative differences" between the two groups of mothers. The question why some children became schizophrenic and others "escaped" their fate, Tietze acknowledged, "remains still open."

Tietze had not been a major figure in psychiatry, and she did not become one. But the snowball she threw started an avalanche. Within a year or two, the idea of the "bad mother" had become a commonplace that scarcely required demonstration. A 1951 paper on male schizophrenics, in the *American Journal of Psychiatry*, captured the matter-of-fact tone. "There is a common belief in the field of mental hygiene," the authors declared in the paper's first sentence, "that mothers of schizophrenic boys are 'overprotective, oversolicitous, domineering, overanxious, and/or rejecting.'" So unremarkable was this observation that it did not even rate a footnote. In two years, an untested claim had become something that "everyone knew."

Psychiatrists rushed to endorse the new insight, delighted that someone had finally unraveled the greatest riddle confronting them. Psychiatry had finally found a way to help schizophrenics — since the disease was caused by parental misdeeds, it could be treated by helping patients come to terms with their upbringing. But this was a discovery with theoretical implications at least as great as the practical ones. For everyone recognized that talk therapy was too expensive, too difficult, and too slow a treatment to transform the lives of the nation's 1 million–plus schizophrenics.

The excitement was that the thing could be done at all, not that it could be done on a mass scale. If a meticulous craftsman had succeeded, after years of labor, in building an antigravity machine, it would have been churlish to ask how much it would cost to put one in every garage. Psychoanalysis had built its antigravity machine.

Where medicine had been baffled for more than a century, where even the greatest names in psychiatry's pantheon had thrown up their hands in bewilderment, Freud's descendants had proved triumphant. Psychoanalysis had done the undoable. This was not merely good news for a particular group of patients; it was good news for psychoanalysis, a validation of this modern therapy in its confrontation with an implacable foe.

Paper after paper spelled out the new doctrines. One could read lists of the traits of the schizophrenogenic mother. She was "guileful and potentially deceitful," "self-indulgent," "irritable," "sarcastic and cynical," "ostentatious," and "exhibitionistic." She was "characterized by a thorough-going Machiavellianism which is employed in the service of a rather unlikable egocentricity. Other people, and this includes her child, seemingly exist only to serve her own ends and are consequently manipulated and exploited—or ignored."

The vogue lasted for decades. In a survey of the medical literature produced between the late 1940s and the early '70s, the psychiatrist John Neill counted more than seventy-five papers on schizophrenogenic mothers, as well as numerous books and book chapters. The idea that mothers produced schizophrenia in their children enjoyed "enormous popularity," Neill wrote, and was "standard practice" on both sides of the Atlantic. Over the course of the same decades Neill found only two cautionary articles, both by the same author.

Not surprisingly, parents were not as taken by the new theories as the psychiatrists were. In Tietze's 1949 paper, for example, she had noted that when the project began, "the immediate response of all [the] mothers was one of curiosity, optimism, and appreciation of the interest taken in their children and themselves." But the mothers soon had their hackles up. "Their enthusiasm . . . waned when the meaning of interpersonal relationship and its implication dawned on them."

Tietze paid little heed. She had *expected* mothers to try to wriggle out from under the burden of blame. Who would rush to embrace the painful truth that she had caused her child's illness? The sicker the child, Tietze found, the harder the mother fought to resist the truth. "Those mothers whose children had been irretrievably withdrawn for years and who had little hope for recovery," she wrote, "were reluctant to accept the importance of environmental influences and preferred to believe in constitution and heredity as etiologic factors."

There was little difference, Tietze's tone implied, between such a misguided mother and a toddler who "preferred to believe" in Santa Claus or the Easter Bunny. But not all psychiatrists were as dismissive as Tietze. There *was* a risk, a few writers acknowledged, that what began as devotion to patients could become an attack on parents. That would be unfortunate, everyone agreed—after all, these parents had been done wrong by *their* parents, and so on up the line—so there was no point in assigning blame.

But if it was a mistake, they went on, it was a natural, understandable, forgivable one. To side with patients against the parents who had victimized them, Fromm-Reichmann's protégé Don Jackson observed, was a "warmly human error."

Ironically, it was Fromm-Reichmann's undeniable warmth that gave the notion of the schizophrenogenic mother much of its staying power. Modest, wise, experienced, Fromm-Reichmann was as far from mean-spirited as a person could be. Her aim was to relieve pain, not to score ideological points or hand down indictments. If even *she* saw parents as culprits, it was hard to imagine that they were not guilty as charged.

CHAPTER SIX

Dr. Yin and Dr. Yang

I felt as though I were losing my mind.
— DR. HAROLD SEARLES

I'm a psychiatrist and I know how to cure.
— DR. JOHN ROSEN

A FULL HISTORY OF SCHIZOPHRENIA and talk therapy would fill a long book, but we can condense the tale by freezing the picture at intervals, strobe-style, and focusing on a handful of the most acclaimed and most accomplished figures. A more or less clear trajectory emerges. Frieda Fromm-Reichmann soon came to seem almost quaint. Each of her successors in turn painted the mothers of schizophrenic children in an ever more malevolent light, and each devoted increasing amounts of time to unearthing the hidden meaning of schizophrenic symptoms.

Closest to Fromm-Reichmann, perhaps, was one of her most renowned successors at Chestnut Lodge, Harold Searles. In the 1950s and '60s, Searles was "probably the most widely read and respected authority [on schizophrenia] in the world," one colleague reported. Searles was thoughtful and charismatic, a lecturer so dazzling that three decades later a listener could still recall his performances. "He would interview patients in the gym at the Mass Mental Health Center," recalls the psychiatrist Allan Hobson, who had heard Searles speak at Harvard, "and there would be three hundred of us crowded in there watching. This was brilliant, theatric stuff," Hobson remembers. "It was like Charcot in the Salpêtrière," he adds, evoking the nineteenth-century psychiatric giant whose lecture-demonstrations had dazzled the young Freud.

Nor was showmanship Searles's only gift. Another therapist, Jacqueline Dryfoos, saw Searles interview a schizophrenic patient twenty-five years ago. In all the intervening time, she says, she has never seen anyone who seemed to radiate such calm, caring, nurturing warmth. "You just wanted to crawl into his lap and cuddle up and let him take care of you," Dryfoos recalls.

The hallmark of Searles's style was his intensely personal tone. He was "ruthlessly honest," one colleague observed, and, what was even rarer, he was as relentless in probing his own inadequacies as in dissecting the weaknesses of others. He confessed in print to posturing and preening and loathing his patients and lusting after them and flailing about to hide his confusion and panic. His besetting sin, he believed, was "obnoxious condescension." One patient finally rebuked him for ending each therapy session by saying good-bye in a self-satisfied tone that implied, in Searles's words, "that the healing Christ would be stooping to dispense this succour to the poor sufferer again on the morrow."

It was characteristic of Searles to have inspired the exchange, and also to have recorded it in such loving and self-lacerating detail. Others might cite Latin maxims to remind readers that no human behavior was beyond their ken. Searles, on the other hand, described *himself* falling into a schizophrenialike confusion. He began one essay on the world as it appears to a schizophrenic, for example, by describing in vivid detail his own "anxiety, confusion, and despair" whenever he had to write a paper. He would collect anecdotes, ransack the library, put in weeks of work, and still feel "threatened with overwhelming panic" at trying to make sense of those unsorted and incoherent gobs of data.

It might seem a glib comparison — it is a long way from writer's block to hallucinations of devouring a cat's head — but Searles insisted on the analogy. His terror, he maintained, was exactly parallel to that of a schizophrenic who has no way to organize and sift the chaos that surrounds him. "He has no reliable way of knowing whether that which he is perceiving is part of an inner, fantasy world, or part of an outer, real world; whether it is something which exists in present or past or future time; whether it is alive or unalive, human or nonhuman."

If writing a paper threw Searles into a panic, it was no surprise that working with deeply out-of-touch schizophrenics was almost overwhelmingly stressful. Searles often felt "violently hateful" toward a particular patient, for example, and was "shocked on many occasions at the vividness of my fantasies of smashing in her skull." At other points with the same woman, Searles felt "deeply moved" and "guilty" and "profoundly helpless" and "profoundly grateful" as well as prey to "murderous rage." He was, he acknowledged, a long way from Freud's detached observer. "I had become, in a sense, deeply immersed in the patient's illness," Searles confessed, so much so that he began to fear that in all his relationships he was "basically evil and basically destructive."

These were immensely difficult patients. Over the course of fourteen years, from 1951 through 1964, Searles treated eighteen schizophrenic patients in individual therapy sessions, in four 50-minute "hours" a week in his office or the patient's hospital room. Treatment could last from a few months to fourteen years, and Searles's patient load regularly included six schizophrenics at a time.

Those bare figures only hint at the difficulties Searles faced. Therapy was a marathon, and the course ran across miles of broken glass. For most patients, so-called talk therapy began with months of silence. Hour after hour, week after week, Searles and his patient sat in a room, together physically but apart in any sense that mattered, two people in parallel worlds. Finding a human connection seemed almost impossible. "At the end of each of the maddeningly silent sessions [with one schizophrenic patient]," Searles recalled, "I would constrain my fury and scorn towards him and politely say, as he started towards the door, 'So long, Mr. Bryant—I'll see you tomorrow,' to which he would mutter a furious reply, 'Go to hell, you son of a bitch!' "

Most psychiatrists would have left the story there, as yet another instance of how hard it was to deal with ungrateful patients. As usual, Searles went a step further. "After this had happened several times," he wrote, "it dawned on me that he was very accurately expressing the covert message contained in my 'polite' parting comment to him."

For patients who were not silent, matters were harder still. One paranoid woman used to scream that Searles had cut off his own hands and replaced them with the hands of the patient's long-dead grandmother. Searles's head, she believed, was not really his but the transplanted head of some person from her past. The same woman, Searles said, "once declared to me, with chilling conviction, her certainty that I was a machine sent to kill her; and, at another time, that I was a woman who had killed my husband and was likewise about to kill her."

Inevitably, one consequence of working with such hard-to-reach patients was to make the therapist doubt himself. Searles often succumbed, he confessed, to feelings of "overwhelming and deeply discouraging" bewilderment. He seemed perpetually to be staggering under a weight too heavy to manage, with no finish line in sight where he could set it down. Worse still, Searles's patients proclaimed his inadequacies to the world. One woman, for example, embarrassed him by her inappropriately childish dress, an "advertisement" that proclaimed just how little help Searles had been to her. Colleagues could be just as threatening. Nurses, for example, often reported that patients were doing well on the ward. His response to such "glowing reports," Searles admitted, was "jealousy and guilt." If patients were doing so well when they were away from their therapist, what use was he? The good news simply provided Searles with "confirmation of his own lack of therapeutic worth."

In a kind of tic of self-revelation, Searles told one such story after another. One patient inspired only "cold annoyance," despite her "racking sobs and streaming cheeks." Another asked questions "at a moment when I had withdrawn into sullen resentment or rage." That kind of sulking combat could go on indefinitely. *For years,* Searles wrote, he and one schizophrenic woman spent whole sessions "in mutually vindictive comments and non-verbal torture operations."

Nonetheless, Searles claimed an impressive cure rate. Of his eighteen schizophrenic patients, he described thirteen as remarkably improved (though seven of the thirteen remained hospitalized), one as considerably improved, two as slightly improved, and one as unchanged; one of the eighteen committed suicide.

When it came to explaining where schizophrenia came from, Searles was almost as personal as when discussing his approach to therapy. One of his patients, for example, was "a physically attractive and often very seductive" woman. A paranoid schizophrenic, she would "stroll about the room or pose herself on her bed, in an extremely short-skirted dancing costume, in a sexually inflaming way." She spoke hardly a word about sex, however; she talked almost exclusively about "theology, philosophy, and international politics." The conflict between the two messages tormented Searles — he was sure that the sexual teasing was real, but he could not help wondering if it could possibly be a figment of his imagination. Balancing the two messages was "such a strain," he wrote, "that I felt as though I were losing my mind."

From this personal anecdote to an explanation of schizophrenia in general was but a small step. Think of *his* confusion in the face of a mixed message, Searles suggested, and then imagine a child raised in a home where the parents' signals were perpetually in conflict. Suddenly, schizophrenia seemed an almost predictable outcome.

Growing up intact, Searles argued, was not something that happened automatically. Becoming a person was difficult, dicey business, and it required steady and dependable guides. "Ambiguous and unpredictably shifting family roles make it impossible for the child to build up reliable and consistent pictures of the world around him," Searles wrote in 1967, and the effect was to render reality "either inscrutable or kaleidoscopic, or both."

Unpredictability was the great hazard. "What is traumatic," Searles explained, "is not a total lack of love coming from [the mother], which would be easier to endure." The problem is that the mother's love for her child is "expressed capriciously" and is "unexpectedly and suddenly replaced by rejection." Abandonment would be easier. "If one is left chronically on one's own, one can make do," Searles continued. "But to be caught up, unpredictably, in an intensely warm relatedness, and then as unpredictably to find oneself psychologically utterly alone, constitutes a deep assault upon one's personal integration." Trapped in a household with inconsistent and unreliable parents, the child can never build a stable identity. Instead, he finds himself dazed and damaged in the midst of unpredictability and chaos, trapped permanently in an earthquake zone.

Armed with this theory, the mysterious symptoms of schizophrenia became decipherable. They were desperate attempts to ward off anxiety, "unconscious defenses against intolerable emotional conflicts." Why, for example, does a paranoid person believe that everyone is plotting against him? As a defense against his deepest fear, the almost unthinkable realization that he is so insignificant that he is beneath notice. Or, if a person was unable to confront a particular emotion, he might recast his story so that some persecutor was responsible for the unacceptable feeling. Searles described one paranoid man, for instance, who, rather than confront his grief, insisted that "his streaming tear glands were controlled by some weirdly mysterious agency outside himself." Another patient, this one unable to acknowledge her sexual feelings, claimed that she was "repeatedly raped by some eerie and invisible outside agency."

Why were the defenses so roundabout? Why spin such elaborate tales? For two related reasons, Searles argued. First, schizophrenics were beset by conflicts that they could not or would not acknowledge. One woman, for example, "unaware of her murderous rage as such, experienced instead a hallucination of a line of exploding teeth marching endlessly up one wall of her room, across the ceiling, and down the other side."

Second, schizophrenics had regressed in their thinking to childhood or infancy, an era when their understanding of what was real and what was delusion, what was literal and what was metaphoric, was still unformed. One patient who felt embarrassed, for example, "felt a literal, rather than a figurative, sensation of sinking through the floor." Patients in awe of Searles literally saw him as a giant, he said; those who felt contempt saw him as a midget.

The schizophrenic's world was a bewildering kaleidoscope of reality and hallucination, past and present, memory and perception. Faced with such chaos, the patient's strange beliefs served an essential role. They brought structure and simplicity to "a world which is as bewilderingly complex as the adult world is to a little child." Schizophrenia and its delusions, in Searles's presentation, were attempts to find pattern and predictability in what appeared at first as overwhelming disarray.

The analogy between the schizophrenic's worldview and the child's, like the one between writer's block and a schizophrenic's panic, seems a stretch. The adult world may seem puzzling (or boring) to a small child, but is it terrifying? Is the small child's world truly peopled with images of melting skin and exploding teeth? In attempting to link the schizophrenic's world with the familiar one, Searles had drained schizophrenia of the bizarreness that was its defining feature.

• •

For Searles, understanding his patients meant deciphering their hidden messages. Words, gestures, and postures all carried layers of secret meaning. "One patient's drooping shoulders, stubble of beard, and tramplike mode of dress vividly convey his feeling of not-belonging, and his reproach to those about him for not making him a part of their society." Another patient's "freakish demeanor and her mouthing of confused and half-inaudible sentences serve, eventually, to tell her therapist graphically how grotesque in appearance, and unintelligible in speech, *she* perceives *him* to be." (Italics added.)

The world was soaked in symbolism. Searles was quick to detect sexual messages, but most of his interpretations were not stereotypically Freudian. Indeed, many were so strange that it is hard to imagine that anyone else could have come up with them. One patient caught Searles's eye, for example, and then pressed her hand to her belly. "It feels as though there's a crazy shit in here that's going to the left," she told him. This was, Searles explained, "a much-disguised way" of expressing the following "unconscious feeling and idea: 'I feel that my crazy shit of a therapist, who has just come into this room, is becoming a Communist.'"

Another patient, who had the odd habit of saluting everyone he encountered, reserved for Searles a salute with "a defiant, contemptuous little additional jerk to it, after his hand has snapped up to his brow, a jerk which clearly conveys something translatable in words as, 'Up your ass, you stuffed shirt!'" The patient, evidently a Marcel Marceau of silent eloquence, could pass along other messages as well. "At other moments," Searles continued, "the salute conveys equally strong feelings of fondness, genuine respect, and a pleading for help."

Occasionally, one of Searles's patients tried to slip the decoder ring onto her own finger. Ordinarily the most patient of men, Searles would have none of it. One patient, he noted dismissively, "felt that my accidental dropping of an ash-tray was my way of telling her that I was going to drop her."

Like Fromm-Reichmann, Searles believed that anxiety lay at the root of schizophrenia. Like Fromm-Reichmann, too, he attributed that anxiety to the inadvertent misdeeds of schizophrenogenic mothers. At the beginning of his career, Searles recalled later, parent-bashing had been in vogue. In the early fifties, the staff at Chestnut Lodge gathered twice a week to discuss their patients. "The therapists — including myself — presenting these cases often tended to paint a totally, or almost totally, black picture of the patient's childhood family relationships," Searles noted. "The feeling-atmosphere of the presentation was one of blame of the parents more than anything else."

Searles never rejected that point of view but, characteristically, he did present it in an idiosyncratic way. "There is a great deal of literature on this subject," he noted in 1958, "the bulk of it in agreement as to the predominantly and basically hateful nature of the relationship in question." His own view, he emphasized in an essay called "Positive Feelings in the Relationship Between the Schizophrenic and His Mother," was a "sharp departure" from that conventional wisdom.

But if it began as a departure, it became a round-trip. Like most journeys, Searles's antiblaming argument proceeded in several stages. He began by arguing that mothers and later-to-become-schizophrenic children only *appeared* to hate one another. What looked like "intense, mutual hostility," Searles contended, was in fact the "unconscious, mutual denial of these deeply repressed positive feelings." Mother and child really loved one another — they just weren't able to show it.

Then came the second stage of the argument. The reason the child's mother failed to express her love was that, in her own childhood, "her expressions of love [had] rendered her mother anxious and psychologically withdrawn." Thus trained to fear love, the girl had grown into a woman who saw herself "as a being unworthy of being loved and devoid of genuine love to offer to other persons, including her children."

So unworthy was she that she pushed her child away. Searles gave examples to prove his point. One mother, Searles reported, almost always referred to her daughter by her married name, "Mrs. Matthews." Another, ostensibly telling Searles that her son had not won a prize at his high school graduation, inadvertently revealed her true feelings: "He wasn't anything." Stymied by emotional indifference, the children of such parents suffered psychic wounds. One schizophrenic woman told Searles that she had long felt like a "snow man in a glass," an untouchable figure in a paperweight world; another reported that she had believed for years that she was a robot and not a human being.

By the end of this "Positive Feelings" paper, Searles had arrived back at the starting line. Schizophrenia was once again a disease caused by "the mother's failing the child." The source of that failure was not malice or callousness but the mother's own deep-seated problems (which stemmed from *her* mother's failings). As we have seen, Searles was not alone in this "understanding" view of how mothers failed their children, but he was the first to label his critique a defense.

Searles was still blaming parents, but more in sorrow than in anger. To parents, it must have seemed a subtle distinction.

No psychiatrist could have been less like Harold Searles than John Rosen. Where Searles was patient, empathetic, and plagued by doubt, Rosen was fierce, forceful, and violent. The trend we began to see as we moved from Fromm-Reichmann to Searles — an increased emphasis on the mother's role in creating schizophrenia, an increased tendency to see the symptoms of schizophrenia as symbols — reached its high point in Rosen, who flared (and then plummeted to earth) as unmissably as a Fourth of July rocket.

Rosen was one of the best known and most controversial figures in psychiatry in the 1950s and '60s. He claimed to cure even the most desperately ill patients, schizophrenics prominent among them, and he numbered Rockefellers, Annenbergs, and Lindberghs among his clients. "You're speaking about one of the greats, you know," Barbara Stuart, a Rosen patient and the wife of the chairman of the board of Quaker Oats, once told a newspaper interviewer. "People come to him right from the padded cell."

Rosen was an astonishing figure, as we shall see, and it is important to begin by noting that he was a major figure as well. A Philadelphia psychiatrist and a faculty member at Temple University Medical School, Rosen came to wide notice in the early 1950s when he announced his discovery of a new form of psychotherapy. He called it "direct analysis," to indicate that he spoke "directly to the [patient's] unconscious." Rosen's admirers addressed him in awestruck tones. "He was always spoken of in wonder by those who saw what he accomplished," wrote Raymond Corsini, the editor of a thousand-page volume called *Handbook of Innovative Psychotherapies*, in a preface to an essay by Rosen. "When I began this book I wrote to him, never really expecting him to accept my invitation to contribute. The reader is now in for a thrilling experience." In 1968, Rosen was lionized in an acclaimed novel called *Savage Sleep*. Explicitly based on Rosen, it told the story of "an inspired young doctor [who entered] into a world where no sane man has ever dared venture before." In 1971, the American Academy of Psychotherapy named Rosen its Man of the Year.

The theory behind direct analysis, Rosen contended, came straight from Freud. Practice was another matter. Freud had described his role as lifting the veils from men's eyes so that they could see the truth; Rosen's approach was to grab his patients by the shoulders and shake the nonsense out of them. He would vanquish schizophrenia by showing his patients that he was more powerful than their disease. "Sometimes," he said, by way of explaining his technique, "when I have the patient pinned to the floor, I say, *'I can castrate you. I can kill you, I can eat you. I can do whatever I want to you, but I am not going to do it.'* " (Italics in original.)

Patients, Rosen said, found this behavior reassuring. "The patient gets the feeling of having met a master who could do anything he wanted to him by virtue of his physical strength but will not do it because he loves him," he wrote. "The patient is usually relieved from anxiety, feels safe, and is much closer to reality."

Rosen's approach to therapy was marked, in his words, by "forcefulness, closeness, and lack of formality." These were euphemisms. One way of "confronting the patient with reality," for example, Rosen explained, was "to call his bluff dramatically in regard to some delusion and then point out the absurdity of his behavior." One patient "whined endlessly that he was going to be cut up into little pieces and fed to the tigers. When I could stand no more of this, I walked into his room with a big knife, saying, 'All right, if you're so anxious to be cut up, I'll cut you up.' "

Rosen claimed that his therapy worked wonders. He had treated thirty-seven schizophrenic patients, he reported in one of his earliest and most celebrated papers, and he had cured all thirty-seven. This was unprecedented. Most psychiatrists fled schizophrenic patients; some, like Searles, labored with them over the course of years. Now along came Rosen. He took on schizophrenic patients, some of whom had been in mental hospitals for decades, and sent them home, cured, in a matter of weeks or months!

Rosen was perfectly open about his use of threats and bullying. Such stratagems were not scandals unearthed by critics but tactics proclaimed by Rosen himself. Psychiatrists from across the nation gathered to hear Rosen lecture and to observe his therapy sessions. Some were dismayed. More were dazzled. Jule Eisenbud, a prominent psychiatrist, compared Rosen's skills with an athletic superstar's: "It looks very easy, just as it looks easy when Tilden plays tennis!"

The theory of "direct analysis" rested on two pillars: mothers caused schizophrenia, and insanity was, literally, a kind of perpetual nightmare. Rosen preached both doctrines to his fellow psychiatrists with nearly the intensity he used in treating his patients. Where many psychiatrists were tentative and guarded in their judgments, Rosen seemed out to convert his audiences by bludgeoning them into submission. In a 1953 paper with the hard-to-miss title "The Perverse Mother," he spelled out the first of his core beliefs in his opening sentence: "A schizophrenic is always one who is reared by a woman who suffers from a perversion of the maternal instinct."

The fiery tone was characteristic; so was the absolute certainty, the flat assertion that schizophrenia always had the same cause. Rosen was not pushing a theory, his tone implied, but simply stating a fact. It was a fact, moreover, that was immune to contradictory evidence. The mother of a schizophrenic child *must* be malevolent, Rosen argued, even if there was no sign of her evil nature. He told of one mother, for example, who "begged and pleaded" for help with her schizophrenic daughter. "Her apparent sincerity was unquestionable," Rosen observed, "and it would seem that if giving her life could save her daughter, she would consent. Is it possible that such a woman failed to give her daughter the necessary love in infancy?"

Having raised the key question, Rosen brushed it aside. "I myself cannot consciously discern the non-loving qualities in this mother," he admitted. "Neither could anyone else. I don't doubt, however, that her daughter did, but how she did and what they were remains to be revealed through a searching analysis of this schizophrenic girl."

Armed with this theory of the unloving mother, everything fell into place. "Now," for example, "the deeper explanation of the phenomenon of paranoid ideas" became clear. The key was that the patient was not *imagining* messages but was *remembering* them from infancy. Infants, Rosen pointed out, communicate with their mothers nonverbally. Paranoiacs believe they are receiving messages outside the usual channels of communication, *as they truly had when they were infants,* and the threatening voices in their head simply recap the messages from "a parent who, unable to love, responded with feelings or affects that amounted to, 'Be still. Be quiet. Be dead.' "

But why, then, did schizophrenia appear in adolescence or later, rather than in infancy? Rosen had an answer to that question, too. Like the Leaning Tower of Pisa, a child raised by an unloving mother was "built on a shallow, uneven foundation" and was therefore permanently vulnerable and shaky. As that unsteady child grew older, each critical stage of development — puberty, the move out of the parents' house, marriage, the birth of children, parenthood — would bring new stresses and pressures. Eventually, "the whole Tower of Pisa reaches a certain height, and then, no longer able to withstand the pull allegorically represented as the force of gravity, the whole psychologic structure crumbles back to what it started from, a shaky foundation."

With the same boldness with which he explained the cause of schizophrenia, Rosen went on to explain its cure. Since the disease was caused by terrible mothering, the cure was good mothering. But where would the poor patient, now grown, find a good mother to provide the nurturing he had never had?

Rosen's answer was simplicity itself. His "governing principle," he declared, was that *the therapist* "must be the idealized mother who now has the responsibility of bringing the patient up all over again. This duty must be undertaken because the patient has been forced, under heavy psychic threat, to become again for the most part an infant."

The therapist would have to become "the ever-giving, ever-protecting maternal figure" the patient had never known, and there could be no shortcuts, no faking. "Only if the therapist is able to provide love and protection, only if he can convince the patient that he really understands his needs and is prepared to satisfy them, will the patient dare to wake up" from his ongoing nightmare. In practice, Rosen was as far from maternal as one can imagine — what mother threatens to cut her children into pieces? — but he never acknowledged the contradiction between his preaching and his practice.

His nurturing duties were all-consuming. In treating one married patient in her late twenties, for example, Rosen "tended her, fed her, treated her like a baby for nine months." For the first two of those months, he spent ten hours a day with her; for the following seven months, he spent four hours a day. Soon after, she was well.

The key was convincing the patient that he had a determined and insightful ally. Then he would "gain the sense that he is no longer alone; he is understood. Somebody is trying to understand, somebody is trying to help. Somebody will give him what he cannot get by himself." The therapist's task was "to let the sufferer know that his mumbo jumbo signals, like those used by the infant, are being understood." With each new message unraveled, "the psychosis begins to loosen its grip and reality begins to seep in and show itself."

And just how was the therapist to decipher schizophrenic mumbo jumbo? That was the easy part, and it brings us to the second of Rosen's two core beliefs: Freud's landmark work on the meaning of dreams was "self-evidently" the key to the meaning of madness as well. Sometimes Rosen preferred to quote Jung. "Let the dreamer walk about and act as though he were awake," Jung had declared in 1903, when he was still a follower of Freud, "and we have at once the clinical picture of dementia praecox," as schizophrenia was then known.

All that was needed, Rosen maintained, was to take Jung's remark literally. "What is the psychosis," Rosen demanded, "but an interminable nightmare in which the wishes are so well disguised that the psychotic does not awaken? Why not then awaken the psychotic by unmasking the real content of his psychosis? Once the psychosis is stripped of its disguises, will not this dreamer too awaken?"

So every gesture, every mannerism, had to be unraveled, "every symptom, each remark, every symbol must be untwisted, clear down to its earliest ontogenetic and even philogenetic roots in the unconscious. Only when the symptom is so clearly unmasked to the patient that it will no longer serve its purpose, will he be able to relinquish it for a more sensible way of handling his instinctual drives."

Rosen in pursuit of a symbol was formidable to behold. "There always is meaning in the productions," he maintained. "The baby never cries without a reason." Echoing Freud and then surpassing him, Rosen emphasized that literally everything had a symbolic meaning. "Anything from a stomach rumble to an elaborate fantasy may be the material for interpretation," he declared.

But there was one crucial difference between a neurotic patient's dreams and a schizophrenic's ongoing nightmare. A dreamer's problems could be unraveled at leisure. Interpretations could be mulled over, hinted at, explored in the most tentative and gingerly fashion. In schizophrenia, the stakes were far higher. "One must, therefore, take certain liberties which psychoanalytic technique ordinarily forbids," Rosen wrote. "The therapist becomes the surgeon confronted with the need for heroic surgery."

Rosen reveled in the role. What he proclaimed to be symbol-decoding became instead a frontal assault on the patient's fantasies. Rosen described one young woman, for example, who carried a pillow around with her; she rocked it, read to it, referred to it as her son Stevie. Rosen would have none of it. "I grabbed the pillow and banged it on the floor, saying, *'See, that can't be a baby. I threw it on the floor with all my might and it didn't cry.'* " (Italics in original.)

His behavior might look extreme, Rosen conceded, but there was method in it. His performance with the pillow, for example, was an appeal "to that tiny portion of the ego that is in contact with reality." Rosen's refusal to play along with the patient, he argued, "acted as a wedge in the patient's psychosis and very often induced the patient to renounce some of his delusions and hallucinations."

One favorite trick was to undermine a patient's delusions by "boring from within." The procedure could be elaborate, with Rosen as producer and director in what was truly a theater of the absurd. One of his patients, for example, was a paranoid man who believed that he was wanted by the FBI for burning down the shrine of Ste. Anne de Beaupré. Rosen enlisted various staffers in a drama: two played FBI agents, complete with identification, and brandishing a list of criminals wanted for arson. Rosen began by encouraging his patient to tell his story.

Then, just at the point when the man confessed to arson, Rosen interrupted. "You're a damn liar," he screamed. "You think by your cheap trick you can get your name in the papers. You can't get away with that with me. You know damn well that *I* burned down Ste. Anne de Beaupré." Then another doctor in on the scheme began to shout that *Rosen* was lying; *he* was the one who had burned down the shrine.

The "FBI agents" announced that all three men — the patient, the other doctor, and Rosen — were under arrest. "What's your name? And your name? And your name?" they demanded. "Get out the list, Joe," one agent said. "Are these guys on the list?" They checked intently, while the three suspects looked on nervously. None of the names was on the list. The agents left, muttering in disgust. "A bunch of cheap publicity hounds," they snarled as they stalked off.

Rosen claimed that this minidrama helped shock his patient to his senses. "Over the next five weeks, the delusional system evaporated completely, and in its place was a timid, frightened man, facing reality and being considered for discharge on a convalescent status."

Such trickery was necessary, Rosen explained, because patients resisted any attempts at help. Schizophrenia was not a disease as much as a strategy, a desperate attempt at coping with the terrors of life. "So far as the patient is concerned," Rosen wrote, "it is not simply something that happens to him; it is the way he must live in order to survive. The purpose behind schizophrenic behavior is to control in some magical way those aspects of the environment, external as well as internal, that are too oppressive for the patient to face as they really are."

To show his fellow psychiatrists precisely how to deal with these desperate and wily patients, Rosen published several transcripts of his interviews. They were, according to one admirer, the first verbatim psychiatric transcripts ever published. Presumably, they represent therapy sessions that Rosen was especially pleased with.

One long interview was with a sixteen-year-old schizophrenic girl named Mary. Rosen prefaced the scene with a sentence of background:

On October 21, the eighth day, Mary knew that she was sick, but she thought she had polio and that I was a dentist.

MARY: So who got the polio, dentist? I got to suffer. She just waked me up. I can't help it.
ROSEN: *Stop talking crazy.*
M: It don't sound crazy yet.
R: *Yes, it does.* [Patient mumbles.] *You're still crazy.*
M: No.
R: *You don't even know who I am.*
M: A dentist.
R: *No, I'm not a dentist.*
M: I know you.
R: *What is your name, please?*
M: [Gives correct name.] She's a genius. I have polio. How do you cure that?
R: *You wish you did have polio. You would rather have polio than realize what your real trouble is.*
M: No, but I was sick. How do you get over this?
R: *I am a psychiatrist.*
M: Are you sure you're Jewish — the way you talk?
R: *I said that I was a psychiatrist.*
M: And I said, God himself told it to me.
R: *What did your father tell you?*
M: Nothing. I was born a Jew.
R: *Who cares?*
M: So you're probably the crazy one.
R: *No, you're the crazy one.*
M: I know. How do you go about curing it?
R: *Well, I'm a psychiatrist and I know how to cure.*
M: How do you do it?
R: *By talking.*
M: Go ahead and talk.
R: *I'm trying to find out what made you crazy.* [Patient giggles.] *I think your mother did it.*
M: I was nervous all the time.
R: *I know. I don't think your mother cared for you.*
M: How do you know?
R: *I know your mother.*

Soon after, on November 6, Rosen provided damning evidence that the patient's mother had no interest in her. "I called Mary's attention to the fact that in the three weeks that she was in the hospital her mother had not come to see her once," Rosen wrote. "The patient fainted dead away."

Then, in the next sentence, Rosen added an astonishing P.S.: "I should say, in all fairness, that the mother had been acting on my orders. Perhaps a harsh procedure but not as harsh as schizophrenia. My purpose was to focus the patient's attention on the pathogenic lack of love rather than to allow her to be confused by the mother's loving attitudes."

Rosen's transcript picked up on November 7, the next day:

R: *What made you faint yesterday?*
M: I don't know. I just didn't feel good.
R: *What was it? What was in your mind the moment you started to get faint?*
M: I got dizzy. I don't know.
R: *Do you know where you are and what's been happening?*
M: Yes. [She mentions the name of the hospital.]
R: *What is this hospital for?*
M: For mental and nervous cases?
R: *Why are you here?*
M: To get better.
R: *What's the matter with you?*
M: Nothing. I don't know. I was just sick.
R: *What is the sickness? Don't hesitate to tell me.*
M: I don't know.
R: *What is your sickness?*
M: I was nervous. I was upset. I don't know.
R: *I don't like a liar.*
M: No, I don't lie. Why should I lie to you?
R: *Because you want to hide the fact that you were crazy.*
M: So? Well, I'd rather not tell it to anybody.
R: *Well, you can tell it to me. Don't lie to me again, Mary.*
M: My mother didn't come.
R: *She will come.*
M: Why didn't she come during the week?
R: *That's why you became crazy — on account of your mother.*
M: I don't know. I am very stupid.
R: *No, it's not your fault. It's her fault.*
M: She was probably very busy out there. We live in Brooklyn.
R: *I don't like this business of your trying to make believe. During the insanity you went on an imaginary journey.*
M: I went to a hospital.
R: *I don't mean really. I mean in the imagination. You felt you were all over the world.*
M: I was an Indian queen.

R: *If you were the queen, you were married to the king. That way, in your imagination, you could be married to your father. The father is always king.*

M: I love him. I just wanted — It was a sad day.

R: *The truth hurts.*

Five days later, Rosen sent Mary home. He had cured her, he reported proudly, and he had done it in "four weeks to the day."

Today, Rosen's name is hardly known, and direct analysis is no more. The story of the demise of direct analysis is straightforward — schizophrenia follows a waxing and waning course, and it eventually became undeniable that Rosen's claimed cures were, at best, only random and fleeting improvements unrelated to direct analysis. The evidence was available early on, but no one heeded it for years. Rosen's Man of the Year award, for example, came in 1971, and the *Handbook of Innovative Psychotherapies* that spoke so glowingly of him was published in 1981.

As early as 1958, though, the psychiatrist William Horwitz had managed to track down nineteen patients of a group of thirty-seven Rosen claimed to have cured. Seven of those nineteen, it turned out, had not been diagnosed as schizophrenic in the first place; of the twelve who were indeed schizophrenic, all twelve had later been readmitted to mental hospitals at one time or another, some of them several times. None had recovered. A second study, in 1966, came to a similar conclusion, and was similarly ignored. Despite these alarm bells, and despite Rosen's much-publicized accounts of his brutal methods, it was years before anyone denounced "direct analysis" as a dangerous fraud.

Rosen's downfall, in contrast with that of his theory, was a dramatic affair. None of his psychiatric colleagues ever reprimanded him publicly for threatening his patients — on the contrary, as we have seen, they heaped praise on him for his daring and innovativeness — but eventually some of his patients accused him of mistreating them. Rosen's peers missed the danger signals because they accepted his justification of his rough tactics. In 1960, for example, O. Spurgeon English, the head of the psychiatry department at Temple University (and therefore Rosen's department head), published an article explaining direct analysis and praising Rosen's "almost uncanny insight." (Horwitz's debunking article had appeared two years earlier.) Rosen, wrote English, "critically attacks the patient's insane behavior and thinking. The patient is never allowed, for a single day, to relax comfortably and complacently, surrounding himself with delusional thinking or immature behavior. Dr. Rosen tirelessly seeks to make him uncomfortable and dissatisfied with it and the patient must perforce adopt conventional thinking and behavior to escape the therapist's wrath, criticism, or sarcasm."

Sometimes, it turned out, there was no escape. The most notorious example involved a young woman, Sally Zinman, a thirty-three-year-old college instructor and the daughter of a banker friend of Rosen's. Zinman woke up one day in October 1970 not knowing her own name. Her father turned her over to Rosen. His treatment, according to accounts Zinman would later give, involved beatings and two months locked in a "dungeon," a bare, windowless room equipped only with a mattress and a bucket for a toilet. Other such stories surfaced. In 1981, for example, Rosen paid $100,000 to settle a case involving the death of a schizophrenic woman, Claudia Ehrmann, who had been under his care. According to prosecutors in the case, Ehrmann died when two of Rosen's attendants tried to force her to speak. One held her by the legs and the other punched or kneed her. (Rosen was not present at the time of the death.) Ehrmann died, the autopsy noted, of "blunt force injuries of the abdomen."

On March 29, 1983, faced with the prospect of charges of sixty-seven violations of the Pennsylvania Medical Practices Act and thirty-five violations of rules of the State Board of Medical Education, Rosen gave up his license to practice medicine.

CHAPTER SEVEN

From Bad Mothers
to Bad Families

We now know that the patient's family of origin is always severely disturbed.

— THEODORE LIDZ

IN 1956, WHILE SEARLES AND ROSEN were wrestling with demons on the East Coast, a new idea came out of the West. It hit the world of schizophrenia "like a bombshell," in the words of the Swiss psychiatrist Luc Ciompi. The explosion burst "a dam of rigid views about this mysterious disorder and loosed a flood of publications" that continued to flow two decades later. New though it was, this breakthrough idea shared two key features with its predecessors — it blamed parents for their child's schizophrenia, and it saw the symptoms of the disease as symbols that could be deciphered.

The bombshell was an idea called the "double bind." Like a Catch-22 — Joseph Heller's novel had been published the year before — a double bind was essentially a "damned if you do, damned if you don't" predicament. Gregory Bateson, the father of the idea, introduced it in an essay called "Toward a Theory of Schizophrenia" in a characteristically eccentric way.

Imagine a Zen master, Bateson wrote, who tells his pupil, "If you say this stick is real, I will hit you. If you say it is not real, I will hit you. If you don't say anything, I will hit you." Lest anyone miss the point, Bateson hurried to spell out the moral. "We feel that the schizophrenic finds himself continually in the same situation as the pupil, but he achieves something like disorientation rather than enlightenment."

The double bind was the brainchild of the most unlikely of outsiders, an anthropologist rather than a psychiatrist, a medical innocent, in fact, who had never treated a sore throat, let alone a case of schizophrenia. Gregory Bateson was a gawky, unmade bed of a man, six feet five and with "more limbs and height than he knew what to do with." The soles of his shoes flapped, his hair flew every which way, his pants were dotted with holes. "His *car* had termites, it really did," one awed colleague recalled. A male acquaintance called Bateson "the most physically unattractive man I've ever known," but women disagreed. More than one left her husband for him, and several others came close. One was Margaret Mead; she and Bateson married in Singapore, in 1936. It was Bateson's first marriage, Mead's third.

Bateson was a member of a distinguished English academic family (his father, an eminent scientist and the inventor of the word "genetics," named him Gregory in honor of Gregor Mendel). He was twenty-one, he would say later, before he met anyone without a graduate degree. Despite his pedigree, Bateson himself spent his life on the fringes of academia rather than at its center. Though at one time or another he held visiting professorships at Harvard, Stanford, and the University of California at Santa Cruz, for example, he was never a permanent member of any faculty. He subsisted as a kind of intellectual vagabond, on a precarious series of grants coaxed from bewildered and bemused foundations by his magical conversation. Depending on who was making the judgment, Bateson was either a genius or "a prince of the muddleheaded."

He had begun academic life as a zoologist — his first publication was on red-legged partridges and why, sometimes, certain feathers on their back were striped like belly feathers — but he later switched to anthropology. A passage in Margaret Mead's autobiography shows how varied Bateson's interests remained, and how hard they were to categorize: "As the war engulfed us," she wrote, "Gregory turned to other interests and never came back to this kind of field work. Instead, he has preferred to generate small stretches of data, based on tape recordings and films of interviews with schizophrenics and observations of octopuses in tanks, otters at the zoo, or dolphins in captivity."

A dazzling talker, in the space of a brief conversation he might drop references to Norbert Wiener, to Bertrand Russell, to Einstein and Pythagoras and Freud, to Lewis Carroll, to paddling a canoe in New Guinea, to Zen masters and enlightenment. "Gregory's students used to complain to him that they did not know what his courses were *about,*" his daughter, the anthropologist Catherine Bateson, wrote. "There were dolphins in them, but they were not about dolphins; there were New Guinea rituals and schizophrenics and alcoholics and Balinese child rearing, woven together with quotations from Blake or Jung or Samuel Butler and the challenges to students to look at a crab or a shell and say how they recognized it as produced by organic growth."

It was not only students who were confused. Jay Haley and John Weakland worked with Bateson "forty hours a week for ten years," Haley recalls, and the two spent much of that time "trying to figure out what we were investigating." "At least once a week, at meetings over coffee in the morning,"

Weakland adds, "we would raise that question — 'Gregory, what is this project all about?' "

As best as anyone but Bateson could understand, it had something to do with communication and its hazards. Bateson had talked the Rockefeller Foundation into a grant on "The Role of Paradoxes and Abstraction in Human Communication," in which he pondered such logical puzzles as the assertion of Epimenides the Cretan that "all Cretans are liars." (The point of the dolphin and otter and octopus studies was apparently to see if animal communication gave some insight into human communication.) Bateson moved from such logical puzzles to schizophrenia for two reasons. First, schizophrenia seemed an intriguing field of study for anyone interested in communication and how it could go wrong. Second, foundations found the idea of contributing to a breakthrough in understanding schizophrenia more enticing than the prospect of helping to unravel Greek riddles. "There was money in it," Jay Haley notes curtly.

In time, Bateson came to prefer to explain double binds with an example not from the Buddha but from *Mary Poppins.* Bateson often read audiences the passage where Mary Poppins, the nanny, has brought her wards Jane and Michael to the shop run by Mrs. Corry and her daughters, Fannie and Annie:

> "I suppose, my dear" — she turned to Mary Poppins, whom she appeared to know very well — "I suppose you've come for some gingerbread?"
>
> "That's right, Mrs. Corry," said Mary Poppins politely.
>
> "Good. Have Fannie and Annie given you any?" She looked at Jane and Michael as she said this.
>
> "No, Mother," said Miss Fannie meekly.
>
> "We were just going to, Mother," began Miss Annie in a frightened whisper.
>
> At that Mrs. Corry drew herself up to her full height and regarded her gigantic daughters furiously. Then she said in a soft, fierce, terrifying voice:
>
> "Just going to? Oh, *indeed!* That is very interesting. And who, may I ask, Annie, gave you permission to give away my gingerbread?"
>
> "Nobody, Mother. And I didn't give it away. I only thought . . ."
>
> "You only thought! That is *very kind* of you. But I will thank you not to think. *I* can do all the thinking that is necessary here!" said Mrs. Corry in her soft, terrible voice. Then she burst into a harsh cackle of laughter. "Look at her! Just look at her! Cowardly-custard! Crybaby!" she shrieked, pointing her knotty finger at her daughter.
>
> Jane and Michael turned away and saw a large tear coursing down Miss Annie's huge, sad face, and they did not like to say anything, for, in spite of her tininess, Mrs. Corry made them feel rather small and frightened.

If a person spent his whole life trapped in such double binds, Bateson argued, schizophrenia was almost to be expected. Searles had said similar things, but Bateson draped the old ideas in glamorous new words replete with philosophical and mathematical allusions. As Bateson portrayed it, the problem was not simply with people who were inconstant and untrustworthy. The confusion cut deeper, all the way to the heart of language and communication. A victim of perpetual double binds "would not know what kind of message a message was," Bateson argued. "If a person said to him, 'What would you like to do today?' he would be unable to judge accurately by the context or by the tone of voice or gesture whether he was being condemned for what he did yesterday, or being offered a sexual invitation, or just what was meant."

The recourse available to an ordinary person — asking what the other person meant — would be unavailable to a schizophrenic, simply because he could not see the double binds that engulfed him. Instead, he would remain perpetually baffled and frustrated, like a prisoner trapped inside one of M.C. Escher's impossible landscapes.

Bateson figured there were three possible responses for someone caught up in double binds. First, he might assume that every message concealed a secret meaning. "If he chooses this alternative, he will be continually searching for meanings behind what people say and behind chance occurrences in the environment, and he will be characteristically suspicious and defiant."

Second, he might "give up trying to discriminate between levels of message and treat all messages as unimportant or to be laughed at." Third, he might try to ignore the messages altogether. "Then he would find it necessary to see and hear less and less of what went on around him, and do his utmost to avoid provoking a response in his environment. He would try to detach his interest from the external world and concentrate on his own internal processes and, therefore, give the appearance of being a withdrawn, perhaps mute, individual."

So there were three responses to double binds: suspicion, dismissal, and withdrawal. And lo and behold, every medical textbook described three main forms of schizophrenia: paranoia, marked by suspiciousness; hebephrenia, marked by a giggling dismissal of the world; and catatonia, marked by withdrawal.

Psychiatrists embraced the theory at once. It was intellectually respectable and intuitively appealing, it was catchy, and it smacked of real life rather than of dusty theory. Examples turned up everywhere one looked. In medieval Europe, for example, Jews had been consigned to various money-lending trades and then abused for having taken up such despised occupations. What was that but a double bind? A psychiatrist chanced on a perfect illustration in a novel: "A little boy complained to his mother, 'Daddy hit me.' His father came in and said, 'Are you telling another of your lies? Do you want me to hit you again?' " *

Looked at in the light of double bind theory, even familiar observations seemed to yield new information. Psychologists, for instance, had spent years studying the behavior of rats in cages where half the floor was electrified. Following Pavlov, they began by asking how long it took a rat to learn to scurry to the floor's safe half.

One variant of the standard setup was well known to yield an unsurprising result: if *both* halves of the floor were electrified, leaving the rat no refuge, it panicked. It ran around randomly, perhaps, or raced back and forth frantically or cowered pitiably in a corner. Now the light dawned. "The person caught in the [double bind] dilemma resembles in a manner of speaking a rat in a two-chambered cage, both sections of which have been wired to receive constant electric shocks," explained the psychiatrist Luc Ciompi. The double bind theory suggested, said Ciompi, that in the desperation of a terrorized rat lay hidden "the explanation for the pathological behavior patterns of schizophrenics."

But the greatest appeal of Bateson's theory was that it opened up entirely new territory to explore. Freud had looked at schizophrenia as a problem in the individual's development; somehow the patient had failed to steer a safe course along the rocky coast of childhood. Fromm-Reichmann and her followers had added another element to the picture: the child had not simply veered off course. On the contrary, his schizophrenogenic mother had propelled him toward disaster.

Now came the double bind theory, which pinned the blame for schizophrenia not on the mother's attitudes toward her child but on the family's style of communication. Attention shifted from the mother to the family, and from past abuses to present-day interactions.

Bateson took for granted that the mothers of schizophrenic children were "hostile" and "anxious" and "unloving," but his real point was deeper. To be schizophrenic, in Bateson's view, was to be caught in an ongoing linguistic snarl, a tangled web of contradictory and impossible-to-resolve messages. The patron saint of the new theory, it often seemed, was not Sigmund Freud but Lewis Carroll.

Indeed, *Alice in Wonderland* and *Through the Looking-Glass* were favorite texts of Bateson's. He was especially fond of Carroll's "bread-and-butterfly," a curious creature whose wings were thin slices of bread and butter and whose head was a lump of sugar. Its only food, Alice was informed, was "weak tea with cream in it."

---

* The theory also calls to mind the old joke that Dan Greenburg tells in *How to Be a Jewish Mother*. "Give your son Marvin two sportshirts as a present. The first time he wears one of them, look at him sadly and say in your Basic Tone of Voice: 'The other one you didn't like?' "

So the bread-and-butterfly was doomed: if it lowered its sugar-head into the tea to eat, its head dissolved; if it kept its head out of the tea, it starved. Heads you lose; tails you lose.

It seems a curiously abstract and bookish approach to a disease as grim and manifestly real as schizophrenia. And indeed, the enormously influential double bind theory was based not on a large number of observations of schizophrenic patients and their families, or even on a small number, but on no observations at all.

Bateson acknowledged that he had come up with his theory first and only learned about schizophrenia later. "The theoretical possibility of double bind situations stimulated us to look for such communication sequences in the schizophrenic patient and in his family situation," he wrote in his original paper on the double bind. Jay Haley, one of Bateson's coauthors on that first paper and to this day a devoted admirer, has since added some flesh to those bare bones. "Bateson put in the grant that schizophrenia was caused by parents punishing their child for expecting punishment," Haley reminisced in 1990. "When the kid does something wrong, they punish him. The next time, the kid cringes when they come near and they get indignant, because they don't like that impression. So they punish him for expecting them to punish him.

"We got the grant, two years, to study this and document it," Haley continues. "And we said to Gregory, 'How do you know this happens?' And he said, 'It happens.' . . . We went up to the Sierras and we rented a cabin, and the three of us spent two full days in that cabin arguing, and laying out the two years of work we had ahead of us on this grant and trying to find out what on earth he was talking about. And I remember, at some point when we said, 'How do you know the parents punish the kid for expecting punishment?' he said, 'That's the sort of thing that has to happen, or he wouldn't have a confusion in his communication and learning.' And we said, *'the sort of thing?'* And from then on it was easy. We chatted about all the different possibilities of that sort of thing, and that was where the double bind came from."

Depending on one's perspective, this was either a remarkable leap of intuition or a curious inversion of the usual order of business. Perhaps fittingly, it seems to echo Bateson's beloved Red Queen and her declaration, "Sentence first — verdict afterwards."

The double bind hypothesis, Bateson conceded, had "not been statistically tested." Nonetheless, he went on to propose that "the family situation[s] of the schizophrenic" had three "general characteristics" in common.

First, the mother of a child destined for schizophrenia would become "anxious and withdraw if the child responded to her as a loving mother." This was one-half of the double bind. Second, the mother could not accept her own "feelings of anxiety and hostility toward the child" and therefore tried to cover them up so that her child *would* "respond to her as a loving mother." This was the double bind's second half. Then came the slamming of the exit door: no one else in the family—such as a strong father—was capable of providing a way out of the impasse.

"If the mother begins to feel affectionate and close to her child," Bateson explained, "she begins to feel endangered and must withdraw from him; but she cannot accept this hostile act and to deny it must simulate affection and closeness with her child." So the child is caught. To see through his mother's deception would be to "face the fact that she both doesn't want him and is deceiving him by her loving behavior." And to accept her play-acting would be to "deceive himself about his own internal state."

This was a harsh choice—the child could deny himself a loving mother, or he could deny his own perceptions. Either way, he lost out. In Bateson's summary: *"The child is punished for discriminating accurately what she is expressing, and he is punished for discriminating inaccurately— he is caught in a double bind."* (Italics in original.)

Under the literary trappings, this was a profoundly harsh theory. Don Jackson, a psychiatrist and a coauthor of the double bind paper, put the case more plainly than Bateson himself had. Just as malaria was a mosquito-borne disease, Jackson suggested, so was schizophrenia "a family-borne disease."

Bateson preferred a gentler, more ironic tone. He liked to illustrate the double bind theory with a story about a young schizophrenic man, in fairly good shape after a breakdown, whose mother visited him in the hospital. "He was glad to see her and impulsively put his arm around her shoulders, whereupon she stiffened. He withdrew his arm and she asked, 'Don't you love me any more?' He then blushed and she said, 'Dear, you must not be so easily embarrassed and afraid of your feelings.' "

That way, Bateson made clear, madness lay. Psychiatrists rushed to agree. It had been plain even before Bateson that parents *caused* schizophrenia, but no one knew precisely what they had done wrong. Now came Bateson to provide explanation where there had been only description. It was as if an astronomer had explained to a bewildered audience *why* the sun rises in the east and sets in the west. No psychiatrist after Bateson would dare to discuss schizophrenia without emphasizing the central importance of the double bind.

Of all the psychiatrists who believed that schizophrenia could be treated by talking, perhaps the most important was Yale's Theodore Lidz. He was not an imposing figure—he was a man of medium height and middling intellect, an adequate lecturer but not a compelling one, a clear writer by academic standards but not an inspiring one—but in the debate over schizophrenia, Lidz played an absolutely central role.

The great names in the field had more flair. There were Fromm-Reichmann and Searles, selflessly laboring through the years at Chestnut

Lodge; and Rosen, grabbing patients by the neck and dragging them out of madness; and Bateson, spinning clever tales in his academic aerie. In comparison, Lidz was a party-liner, a conventional thinker. In a May Day parade in the Soviet Union, he would have been one of the beribboned generals in the reviewing stand. But his importance transcended that of the others, for he was backed by Yale's authoritative name and by his own position as chairman of the Department of Psychiatry. More important, Lidz alone had moved from anecdotes to data. Other psychiatrists, gifted though they might have been, were healers, not scientists. Others had described individual schizophrenic patients; Lidz had pinned down the disease itself.

He would repeat that message, with the persistence and intensity of a battering ram, in paper after paper, year after year, decade after decade, notably in the fifties and sixties but continuing into the seventies and eighties. Feisty, combative, dogmatic, and above all utterly certain he was in the right, Lidz never wavered. He managed to imbue even the passive voice required in medical articles with a note of grandeur and inevitability, as if all of previous history had been but a preparation for his arrival. "Eventually," he wrote in 1957, "a research group undertook intensive explorations of the lives of the families in which schizophrenic patients were raised."

He never tried to sugarcoat his message. These are the facts, his tone implied, now live with them. "We now know that the patient's family of origin is always severely disturbed," he declared in 1978, and he took pains to emphasize that he meant every word. "Though it is hazardous to say 'always,' I know no reason not to do so. Those who disagree with the 'always' have not studied the patients' families intensively."

Lidz had. For twelve years, from 1952 to 1964, he and his colleagues at the Yale Psychiatric Institute scrutinized seventeen schizophrenic patients and their families. For the rest of his long career, Lidz continued to till the same tiny field. In an endless series of books and articles and lectures, all based on the same seventeen upper-middle-class New England families, he explained what was "always" true about "all" schizophrenics and their families.

Read the papers and the same few parents turn up time and again, like soldiers in a stage army. In 1955, for example, Lidz described a man he called Mr. Grau, who was "constantly critical of his wife and oblivious to her feelings." In 1957, Mr. Grau was back: "Mr. Grau was paranoically bitter against all Catholics, not an unusual situation, but here the paranoid bigotry focused upon his wife who was a devout Catholic." In 1964, Mrs. Grau had her turn in the spotlight. She was "an unusually vague, rambling, and scattered person who could talk a great deal and leave the listener puzzled as to whether she had said anything. . . . She created the erroneous impression of being feeble-minded."

Lidz built on the work of Fromm-Reichmann, Bateson, and others, but he went further than they had. Like his colleagues, he began with a devout belief that schizophrenics were the victims of bad mothering. Several of the women in his study, for instance, "needed and used a son to compensate for their own sense of emptiness and worthlessness as a woman." Others were "typical 'schizophrenogenic' mothers" who were miserable with their "frustrated lives," and still others were "aloof, hostile, or overtly rejecting" in their relationships with their sick children.

But Lidz broadened the attack: the *fathers* of his patients were no prizes, either. "The fathers were as pathological as the mothers," he wrote, "and often the more serious disturbing influence in the family." They were jealous of their own children and resentful of any closeness between mother and child. If they had sons, they were hopeless as role models. "Few of the fathers in our study presented masculine images for their sons to incorporate that were even vaguely satisfactory."

But Lidz moved beyond his peers in a more fundamental way. He made explicit a point that the others had only implied or passed over lightly. Schizophrenia was not a "disease or an illness" but a "personality disorder." It was not something that a person *had*, like tuberculosis, not an invader "that has inserted itself into a person and possessed him, depriving him of reason." Instead, it was merely "one of the potential fates to which man is subject."

A person could *be* schizophrenic, just as he could be shy, but to say "he *has* schizophrenia" would be as silly as to say "he has shyness." In conversation, Lidz often broke his own rule, but his point was far more than a tomato-tomahto quibble. By arguing that schizophrenia was an example of development gone awry, and not a disease, he was claiming it for psychotherapy and warning away any would-be poachers from biochemistry or neurology or any other rival specialty.

In the course of growing up, Lidz argued, a person could veer off course. If he could neither face the world nor change it, there was still an alternative. He could escape from it. "When the path into the future is barred," Lidz wrote, "and even regression is blocked because the persons upon whom one would depend cannot be trusted, there is still a way. One can simply alter his perception of his own needs and motivations and those of others. He can abandon causal logic, change the meanings of events, retreat to the period of childhood when reality gave way before the fantasy of his wish, and regain a type of omnipotence and self-sufficiency. In short, he can become schizophrenic."

Not everyone could take this escape route. It was only a way out, Lidz argued, for those whose families had left them so damaged and confused that their links with reality were little more than a silky thread.

Lidz was not one of those, like Georg Groddeck, who saw all illness as psychological. He liked to point out that he had begun his medical career by studying brain injuries and brain diseases. "I came to understand organic brain disorders quite well," he recalled impatiently in a 1995 interview. "I wrote my first paper on a man with a right prefrontal tumor. By the time I started seeing schizophrenic patients, I knew that this had *nothing* to do with the organic disorders I had been studying."

The proof was that schizophrenics, despite their hallucinations and delusions and jumbled speech, were intellectually intact. Lidz had been a serious bridge player, he recalled, but he was no match for one of his schizophrenic patients. So where *did* the bizarre behavior come from, if not from a disordered brain? Not a modest man, Lidz acknowledged nonetheless that this was a mystery that almost solved itself. All he had had to do, even in his first encounter with schizophrenics and their families, was open his eyes.

"After spending an hour with the parents or sometimes with only one of them," Lidz wrote, "I found myself feeling mixed up if not actually somewhat ill." The implication was obvious: "If I became mixed up after spending an hour or two with these parents, what would it be like to be raised by them?"

"Talking to the parents of schizophrenic patients was a real chore," Lidz recalled in 1995, his voice growing animated and anguished three decades after the fact. "And that held for *all* schizophrenic patients. We had no trouble relating to parents of depressed patients or neurotic patients, but when it came to schizophrenic patients, we sometimes almost went crazy trying to get them to understand or do what we thought had to be done."

Even in his published papers, where there was time to weigh his words, Lidz's impatience and frustration bubbled through. "Psychiatrists have not been able to avoid mothers of schizophrenic patients," he complained in a typical passage from a 1955 paper, and he noted that the mothers' odd ways made "a lasting impression upon the psychiatrists whom they harass." One woman, Mrs. Benjamin, "spoke incessantly and said very little, and even less that was pertinent to the situation." A certain Mrs. Newcomb, "in one of her most insightful statements," pointed out that her husband "didn't get as annoyed with my talk as most men."

Often, Lidz moved from boredom to barely restrained indignation. He described, for example, an "impervious" mother named Mrs. Ubanque, who listened blankly to her schizophrenic daughter as she "freely poured out her feelings to her parents and in heart-rending fashion told them of her bewilderment and pleaded for their understanding and help." Finally, "during the height of her daughter's pleas, Mrs. Ubanque offhandedly turned to one of the psychiatrists, tugged at the waist of her dress and blandly remarked, 'My dress is getting tight. I suppose I should go on a diet.'"

It did not take a trained eye to see that something was profoundly wrong with the parents of schizophrenics. "We have had medical students observe family therapy sessions," Lidz told an interviewer in 1972, "and their response has been, 'My God, I couldn't live in that family for a week, there is something so malignant.'"

Even people utterly innocent of medicine saw the same thing. Lidz remembered vividly a conversation he had had decades before with a man who had come to visit his nephew in the hospital. The younger man was schizophrenic, the victim of a breakdown shortly after his graduation from college.

Lidz had launched into his standard patter: "We don't know much about this condition, we're just starting to understand, I can't really tell you the outcome, it's going to be pretty tough." His visitor interrupted. "I didn't come to *ask* you why he's schizophrenic," he said impatiently. "I came to *tell* you why."

The explanation, in short, was that the young man's life with his parents had been "absolutely chaotic." Lidz would spend the rest of his career elaborating on his visitor's insight. But the crucial idea was there at the outset, and it scarcely changed through the years: schizophrenics were made, not born. "*That* stuck with me," Lidz recalled recently, as he looked back at his career from the vantage point of his eighty-five years.

When Lidz began looking at schizophrenia, he found the same message everywhere he turned. "We wanted to know what was wrong with the parents," he explained. "A better question would have been, what was *right* with them?" No matter where he looked, Lidz found that the parents of schizophrenics had failed their children. "In each aspect of the family life which we examined," he fretted, "something was seriously amiss."

He rattled off an A-to-Z of trouble spots. There were problems in the parents' personalities, in their relationship with one another, in their relationship with their child, in the family's verbal communication, in its nonverbal communication, and on and on. Furthermore, Lidz noted, it was not simply that some of these families were troubled in some of these areas. On the contrary, "each of the families was disturbed in virtually all of these respects."

So Lidz changed course. If *everything* was wrong, there was little hope of pinpointing a specific problem that made the difference. Lidz continued to believe that children who became schizophrenic had suffered at the hands of their parents. But perhaps it would be more useful to focus on what the families had neglected to do than on what they had done wrong.

"We began to consider the possibility," Lidz wrote in 1964, "that schizophrenia might be a deficiency disease." As with eighteenth-century British sailors suffering from scurvy, the key to the puzzle might be identifying what was missing. What schizophrenics lacked, according to Lidz, was the "nurturance" and "guidance" that reasonable parents provided their children.

That much was familiar. But Lidz went on to emphasize another devastating lack in schizophrenic families, which he gave the awkward name "enculturation." Put simply, these strange parents failed to teach their children what counted as acceptable behavior in our culture.

Instead, the parents presided over a tiny, peculiar, private kingdom with its own rites and traditions. The schizophrenic child grew up in a closed court ruled by an eccentric and ineffectual king and queen. Life at home was "training in irrationality." Small wonder that the child was utterly unprepared for the world outside his front door.

But learning other people's ways was the least of the child's problems. The larger task, which his parents also undermined, was acquiring a sense of self. Indeed, the parents behaved as if they were conspiring to undermine that goal. They partook of private rituals, used language in strange and idiosyncratic ways, and sent conflicting signals.

Worst of all, the parents insisted that the child discard his own views and perceive the world through their eyes. This "brainwashing," Lidz said, began "in infancy." The outcome, predictably and tragically, was to prevent "the child's achievement of a firm identity."

"We now realize," Lidz declared magisterially in a 1978 summary of his views, "that the family in which the schizophrenic patient grows up has failed abysmally to provide these requisites for the child's integrated personality development." In an interview in 1995, he put the same point more compactly, and with his characteristic cocksureness. "I'd like to see," he growled, "the schizophrenic patient who grew up in a family that was okay."

Families were not simply bad, but bad in predictable and systematic ways. Lidz dubbed the two most common patterns "schism" and "skew." Schismatic families were torn in two by blatant parental conflict; skewed families were damaged more subtly but just as deeply, "skewed" toward one deeply disturbed parent whose behavior the other spouse accepted as normal. Schismatic parents were openly at war; skewed parents were silent conspirators.

The striking feature of the skewed family was the schizophrenogenic mother, who managed the neat trick of being at the same time "extremely intrusive into her child's life" and "impervious to the child's needs." She was "overprotective and engulfing," constantly sending her children the message that leaving her would kill her. The father misbehaved less dramatically but was assuredly no help. "Ineffectual in the home and usually disdained by the mother," he "behaved like another child" or became "intensely rivalrous with his son for his wife's affection and attention."

Lidz's reference to a son was hardly accidental. Skewed families, he believed, tended to produce schizophrenic sons rather than daughters. Schismatic families tended to produce schizophrenic daughters. Schismatic parents were overtly hostile toward one another, each seeking to enlist the child in the perpetual battle with the other spouse. These mothers were less formidable characters, with what little self-confidence they might have had "undermined by the constant derogation" of their spouses. The husbands, in turn, were "dominating," "narrowly grandiose," "sometimes paranoidally rigid and suspicious."

The child in such schisms was caught in an impossible dilemma. To please one parent was to earn the contempt of the other; to try to please both of these irreconcilable adults was to act as scapegoat and sacrifice oneself.

The therapist's duty in such cases was clear. "My tendency has been to get the patient to recognize, especially younger patients, that his parents are not omnipotent or omniscient," Lidz told an interviewer in 1972, "and that he can provide his own protection, that he has to stop seeing through their eyes and filling their needs and begin to direct his energies towards his own life rather than to theirs."

He amplified the point, less formally, in 1995. "We don't do it by just saying, 'Hey, you know, your mother is crazy!' " he laughed. "What we do is raise doubt, saying, 'Well, it's possible,' or, 'There are other ways of looking at it.' "

That approach, which applied far beyond schizophrenia, fit nicely with Freud's dictum that the truth shall set you free. But Lidz saw himself as having moved beyond Freud, although he freely acknowledged that Freud's influence on him had been "very great" and even noted that he "would never have become a psychiatrist without having read Freud as a young man."

Lidz saw his own relentless emphasis on the family as his central contribution to psychiatry. Freud had focused so closely on the individual, Lidz believed, that he had neglected the family that had shaped him. This was not strictly true — Lidz acknowledged that the Oedipus complex, for example, was intelligible only as a theory about both the child and his parents — but he insisted that "nevertheless, Freud kept family relationships peripheral in his theories." *

In another way, too, Lidz saw himself as having moved beyond Freud. He himself was a scientist, searching for patterns in patients followed for many years, exploring hypotheses, sifting the data dispassionately. Freud, genius though he was, had been a freelancer and an artist rather than a sober and systematic investigator.

To a considerable degree, it was a self-serving picture. If Lidz's work was science, it was deeply flawed science. In essence, Lidz had peeked at the answer section at the end of the book: he knew from the start that the parents he was interviewing had raised a schizophrenic child. Inevitably,

* After comparing psychoanalysis to surgery in his *Introductory Lectures on Psychoanalysis,* Freud went on, "Ask yourselves now how many of these operations would turn out successfully if they had to take place in the presence of all the members of the patient's family, who would stick their noses into the field of the operation and exclaim aloud at every incision."

that knowledge biased his judgment. Making matters still murkier, Lidz's picture of his patients' childhoods relied on the recollections of those patients and their parents twenty years after the fact.

It was a setup fraught with risk. But Lidz never bothered with controls, the most elementary precaution in science, and he never seemed to understand why anyone would have expected it. "There was no sense in having normal controls because it was obvious that these were such aberrant families," he snapped, when pressed in 1995.

On every question about his science, Lidz was equally curt and dismissive. Why was it reasonable to generalize about one of the most widespread of all mental illnesses from a dozen-and-a-half instances? Because "intensive studies of a few people were better than superficial studies of lots of people." How did he know that these parents had been strange before their children fell ill and not *because* they had fallen ill? Because "we went back far enough to feel that they were peculiar or difficult people before they ever married." Why was it, if parents were to blame, that the brothers and sisters of the schizophrenic child were healthy? "They're not. We wrote a paper on the siblings, and fewer siblings are okay than anybody thought."

Unfazed and imperturbable, Lidz even shrugged off questions about his integrity. Why had he not informed his seventeen subjects and their families that they were the subjects of a research program? Why had he written about them without permission? Because in his first papers on schizophrenia he had tried telling patients they were part of a study, "and it made for trouble, so we decided not to tell."

Lidz had taken on similar questions in print and brushed them aside there, too, with his characteristic self-assuredness. "Whatever the shortcomings," he declared in 1960, "there is reason to believe that the studies have yielded the most comprehensive and intimate pictures of any families yet studied for any purpose."

To the end of his long life, Lidz never gave an inch. At eighty-five, still making his way to his Yale office every day, the former department chairman maintained the aura of a deposed king. Despite the cane and hearing aid, despite the recent death of his wife (a double blow, for she had been not only helpmate but professional colleague), he remained alert and fierce and at his post. The phone seldom rang, visitors rarely called, but those who ventured into Room 610 in the Yale psychiatry building heard the old familiar refrain.

Lidz knew his views were deeply out of favor — in the struggle to reveal schizophrenia's secrets, neurologists armed with PET scanners and molecular geneticists wielding DNA probes had long since banished talk therapists — but he had seen other fads come and go. He consoled himself with the melancholy wisdom that psychiatry had lost its way before and had eventually regained its bearings.

In his silent and dusty office, Theodore Lidz, the unrepentant, waited out his lonely exile.

Almost as soon as Theodore Lidz began publishing his accounts of his seventeen families, other psychiatrists hurried to publish their own versions of the new gospel. The effect was twofold. First, the family-blaming doctrines reached a newer, wider audience. Second and more important, the new theories rose in status. No longer associated with a single research group, they became general knowledge, the common coin of every up-to-date psychiatrist. What "everyone knows" proved far more compelling than what one person asserted.

Perhaps the most influential of the new missionaries was the psychoanalyst Silvano Arieti. In his *Interpretation of Schizophrenia*, published in 1955, and, four years later, in the huge and authoritative *American Handbook of Psychiatry*, which he edited, Arieti painted the new picture of schizophrenia clearly and concisely. The material itself was familiar. What was new was Arieti's impersonal, matter-of-fact presentation. This, it seemed, was description, not polemic. Arieti was merely describing a disease, much as one might say that pneumonia is characterized by chills and fever and a cough. The zealot pounding his pulpit had given way to the academic methodically listing his points on the lecture-hall blackboard. "Although it is the mother who contributes mostly in producing the conditions which we are going to describe," Arieti noted in one typical passage, "we usually find in the history of schizophrenia that both parents have failed the child, often for different reasons. Frequently the combination is as follows: A domineering, nagging, and hostile mother, who gives the child no chance to assert himself, is married to a dependent, weak man, too weak to help the child. A father who does not dare protect the child because of the fear of losing his wife's sexual favors, or simply because he is not able to oppose her strong personality, is just as crippling to the child as the mother is."

Whatever his methodological shortcomings, Lidz had reported the observations that his theories were based on. Arieti bypassed that step. Now facts were delivered from on high, pristine and gleaming and unsullied by human hands. It made for a neat, even a compelling, presentation. Arieti wrote clearly and revealed none of the quirkiness of Searles or the crankiness of Rosen. The tone was quiet, assured, commonsensical, as down-to-earth as Dr. Spock. One could almost forget that Arieti was writing about schizophrenia: "The child wants to be approved; his self-esteem is built up by the approval he receives. If the parents have a warm, loving, respectful and sympathetic attitude toward the child, he will develop the same attitude toward himself and later on toward others."

If, on the other hand, the parents fail to nurture their child, he will grow up anxious and afraid. "Each child has to be disapproved at times; but if he meets an atmosphere of constant scolding, criticism, nagging, he will grow up with the conviction that there is something bad in him, that he is worthless. This inner feeling of worthlessness may accompany him throughout life and may be reinforced, even by minor failures."

For Theodore Lidz, schizophrenia was not a disease but a desperate attempt at coping with an almost impossible predicament. R. D. Laing, the Scottish guru and psychoanalyst, took Lidz's argument a giant step further. The schizophrenic was not so much victim as visionary. "Madness need not be all breakdown," he declared in 1964. "It may also be breakthrough. It is potentially liberation and renewal as well as enslavement and existential death."

Laing was a small, birdlike figure with dark eyes, long wavy hair, and an intense, charismatic speaking style. Enormously influential on both sides of the Atlantic, he preached the new doctrine in forums of every sort — in books that sold millions of copies and were a fixture in every college dormitory room, in controversial talks to professional audiences, in college tours that were more like rock concerts than academic lectures. To be out of one's mind was the ultimate in being open to experience. In a world of doomsday weapons perpetually at the ready, Laing proclaimed, what passed for sanity was in fact madness and madness was in truth a deeper form of insight.

In the psychedelic sixties, this was a hugely popular message. Madness was chic, and Laing was at the crest of the wave. Bumper stickers proclaimed I'M MAD ABOUT R. D. LAING; an ad in the back of the *Village Voice* in 1971 sought like-minded partners for "two chicks who dig Coltrane, The Dead and R. D. Laing." Schizophrenia was painted as a voyage of discovery, an exploration, and the schizophrenic as a hero who deserved "no less respect than the often no less lost explorers of the Renaissance." Someday men and women would look back and "see that what we call 'schizophrenia' was one of the forms in which, often through quite ordinary people, the light began to break through the cracks in our all-too-closed minds."

Despite its tie-dyed trappings, though, Laing's message was essentially a variant of the one we have encountered throughout these chapters. For Laing, as for Lidz and Bateson, schizophrenia was a performance to be decoded rather than an illness. For Laing, as for the others, the family was the culprit. For Laing and the others, case histories were the path to knowledge, and "controls" were irrelevant or unnecessary. Once again, symptoms were symbols, and parents were villains. A new messenger carried an old message. Laing was Lidz in love beads, with the difference that Laing downplayed talk of cures as coercive and manipulative.

Though Laing was a classically trained psychoanalyst, he was always unorthodox. He had been put off by the austerity of his own analysis, between 1956 and 1960. Charles Rycroft, Laing's analyst, "never opened the door for me," Laing recalled years later. "He sat in his chair, rang a bell downstairs, and when the bell rang I—like a trained rat—went upstairs, opened his door, he stood up from his chair, I lay down on his couch and he sat down out of sight and *that was it!* The second after fifty minutes he would say 'time's up,' and I would get up, walk to the door, turn around and say 'good-day,' shut the door and walk out. Five times a week, for fifty minutes."

Laing repudiated such techniques in favor of a less structured, less formal atmosphere of "civilized courtesy." His private patients were free to sit or pace if they chose, rather than lie on the couch. They called Laing "Ronnie," not "Dr. Laing." He offered advice, much of it quite down-to-earth and having nothing to do with arcane issues of analytic doctrine. One woman, for example, came for treatment because for years her father had beaten her. "I said, 'I mean *you* haven't got a problem,' " Laing told her. ". . . Don't go back in that house, that's the end of it, right?"

Despite his rejection of many Freudian precepts, Laing always retained enormous respect for Freud's insights. "Freud was a hero," Laing wrote in 1960 in *The Divided Self.* "He descended to the 'Underworld' and met there stark terrors. He carried with him his theory as a Medusa's head which turned these terrors to stone. We who follow Freud have the benefit of the knowledge he brought back with him and conveyed to us."

In particular, Laing clung to his faith in Freud's deciphering approach. (He was especially devoted to Freud's acquaintance Georg Groddeck, the fervent believer in symptoms as symbols. Laing said that he had read Groddeck's *Book of the It* at least a dozen times.) In one characteristic passage in *The Divided Self,* Laing discussed a patient, Julie, who "in her psychosis called herself Mrs. Taylor." What could she mean, Laing asked, and he immediately answered his own question. "It means 'I'm tailor-made.' 'I'm a tailored maid; I was made, fed, clothed, and tailored.' " This, Laing maintained, was Julie's pithy and acute summary of her own predicament. "It gives in a nutshell the gist of the reproaches she was making against her mother when she was fifteen and sixteen."

In a book published in 1977, nearly two decades after his work with Julie, Laing showed an abiding fondness for such decoding. His six-year-old daughter, he wrote in *Conversations with Adam and Natasha,* had asked her mother, "Can God kill himself?" Laing went on to discuss her question with an old friend, Monty, presumably a psychoanalyst himself. " 'There is an incredibly close relationship between sex and death,' " Monty had told Laing. " 'I will tell you what the question is saying. She is asking, "Does God masturbate?" ' "

"And that is, 'Does daddy masturbate?' " Laing had replied.

" 'Precisely,' " Monty had continued. " 'She wishes to know whether you do it without mummy, whether you need mummy: whether she can do it with you instead of mummy.' "

• •

Schizophrenia could be understood only by taking the symbol-unraveling approach. (Laing preferred to talk of "persons diagnosed as schizophrenic," to emphasize that he viewed "schizophrenia" as a label and not a disease.)* The symptoms of schizophrenia were so difficult to understand, Laing insisted, because the schizophrenic was trying desperately to fend off a world he saw as bent on his destruction. "A good deal of schizophrenia is simply nonsense, red-herring speech, prolonged filibustering to throw dangerous people off the scent, to create boredom and futility in others. The schizophrenic is often making a fool of himself and the doctor. He is playing at being mad."

What some psychiatrists dismissed as nonsense and "word salad" was to Laing a kind of high-stakes performance art, an improvised act of intellectual bravado designed to hold the world at bay. In *The Politics of Experience*, for example, in 1967, Laing quoted two schizophrenic men engaged in a seemingly impenetrable dialogue. Laing offered no translation of his own. On the contrary, his point was that the dialogue's inaccessibility *proved* just how cagey the two speakers were. "To regard the gambits of Smith and Jones as due *primarily* to some psychological deficit," Laing wrote, "is rather like supposing that a man doing a handstand on a bicycle on a tightrope one hundred feet up with no safety net is suffering from an inability to stand on his own two feet. We may well ask why these people have to be, often brilliantly, so devious, so elusive, so adept at making themselves unremittingly incomprehensible." (Italics in original.)

Schizophrenics were artists whose obscurity was willful. The messages they were at such pains to camouflage had to do with their families. "To the best of my knowledge," Laing wrote, *"no* schizophrenic has been studied whose disturbed pattern of communication has not been shown to be a reflection of, and reaction to, the disturbed and disturbing pattern characterizing his or her family of origin." (Italics in original.)

"Without exception the experience and behavior that gets labeled schizophrenic is *a special strategy that a person invents in order to live in an unlivable situation,"* Laing continued. "In his life situation the person has come to feel he is in an untenable position. He cannot make a move, or make no move, without being beset by contradictory and paradoxical pressures and demands, pushes and pulls, both internally from himself, and externally from those around him. He is, as it were, in a position of checkmate." (Italics in original.)

---

* The notion that "madness" is simply a label applied by the powerful to the powerless predates Laing by centuries. In the 1600s, for example, the poet Nathaniel Lee was committed to Bethlehem. "They said I was mad, and I said they were mad," Lee declared. "Damn them, they outvoted me."

Here we see two themes united. The first is the finger-pointing and family-blaming of Fromm-Reichmann and Freud's other successors; the second, the tendency to make universal, sweeping pronouncements like those of Freud himself.

Laing did downplay the malevolence of mothers in particular, but the main effect was simply to distribute blame more widely. "One might do better to think of schizophrenogenic families, rather than too exclusively of schizophrenogenic mothers," he wrote. So many families were schizophrenia-producing, he wrote in 1967, that a British child was ten times as likely to end up in a mental hospital as in a university. "We are driving our children mad more effectively than we are genuinely educating them," he declared.

It is perhaps worth noting that when it came to dangerously unstable parents, Laing spoke from experience. His own mother, Amelia, was poised precariously on the borderline where eccentricity shades into madness. She was beautiful, intelligent, dishonest, and extravagantly resentful and suspicious of other people, not least her own son. When Laing was five, she burned up his favorite toy, a wooden horse, on the grounds that he had grown too attached to it. When he was an adult, he returned home from service in the army to find that his mother had burned all his papers and destroyed his piano with an ax. Later still, when Laing was about forty, she fashioned a small "Ronald doll" that she would stick with pins in the express hope of inducing a heart attack in her son. When Amelia herself finally died, Laing, then fifty-nine, said that his biggest regret in life was that he had not hurt her more.

But Laing's view of the harm wreaked by families was based on observations of his patients, not his parents. He arrived early at the position he would maintain ever after. Ironically, his path to a harsh indictment of parents was by way of an experiment in the kind and humane treatment of their offspring. In 1953, as a young psychiatrist in his first civilian job after his stint in the British Army, Laing convinced his superiors to allow him to try an experiment with twelve intractable schizophrenic patients. These were women kept in an overcrowded ward, deprived of every personal possession down to and including underwear and cosmetics, and only rarely seen by doctors.

Laing changed all that. He set aside a clean, bright room for these dozen patients, furnished it with magazines and even a stove so that they could make their own tea and cookies, and staffed it with two nurses who provided a good deal of individual care. The Rumpus Room, so-called, was open Monday to Friday, nine to five. After eighteen months in this new setting, all twelve patients had improved so much that they were discharged.

One year later all twelve were back in the mental hospital. Why? Laing's colleagues proposed a straightforward explanation. The women suffered from an incurable disease; it followed a waning and waxing course, so temporary improvements were possible, but it was likely that any improvement would be short-lived. Laing's view was different. If the patients had fallen ill when they left the hospital, it was because something had *made* them ill.

What that something was, Laing had no doubt. The patients had returned to their families, and they had fallen back into their schizophrenic ways. The connection could hardly have been plainer. Who could fail to see that families were the source of the problem?

Through the sixties and into the seventies, Laing continued to spread that message. Its content was not far different from that of his fellow psychiatrists, but he reached a new audience. Other psychiatrists spoke to one another; Laing reached them, too, as well as an enormous audience of students and intellectuals. The message they all imbibed was that schizophrenia was a stance, not a disease — it represented a heroic (if perhaps confused) rejection of a corrupt society.

And then, sometime in the mid-1970s, it all collapsed. Done in by drugs and drink and the whim of intellectual fashion, Laing was suddenly old news. His fall was fast and painful. In November 1983, for example, he showed up drunk and stoned for a lecture to the Oxford Psycho-Analytic Forum. He came onstage to rapturous applause, walked up and down in silence for several minutes, began to speak, and then interrupted himself to tug at a tooth that was bothering him. After a prolonged and silent struggle, he wiggled the tooth free, declared the lecture over, and left the stage for the nearest pub.

He died only a few years later, in 1989, at the age of sixty-two, of a heart attack on a tennis court in Saint-Tropez. He left behind ten children (by five women) and a body of work that had once lit up the sky like a comet but then vanished, out of sight and out of memory, as if it had never been.

In Laing's case, the man outlived the name. But long before his death, Laing's parent-blaming views of schizophrenia and the related views of his fellow psychiatrists had percolated their way into the culture. In a kind of trickle-down, the message made its way out of such temples of psychoanalysis as Yale and Chestnut Lodge and Laing's base in London and into the American hinterlands. Parents across the country found themselves accused of crimes they had no idea they had committed. In Durham, North Carolina, in 1965, for example, a woman named Nancy Ashmore sought help when her fifteen-year-old daughter "went to pieces."

She tells her story today in a sad, slow voice and a thick southern accent. Each word seems to require a physical effort, as if she is on the brink of exhaustion. "The doctor said to me, 'Well, Mrs. Ashmore, if you'd gone to a psychiatrist and gotten *yourself* well, Elaine never would have had to be hospitalized,' " she recalls.

"Well, that was just like a death blow. He said that not once but three times, and I just had a terrible time living with it and trying to think, 'God, if I did this to her, what am I doing to the other children?' "

CHAPTER EIGHT

Ice Picks and Electroshocks

*Surgeons now think no more of operating on the brain
than they do of removing an appendix.*
— *editorial*, New York Times, *1949*

P SYCHOANALYSTS HAD NEVER had an exclusive claim to the treatment of mental illness, but they had long dismissed their biologically minded rivals with a sneer. The great insight that had put Freud and his followers on a new path, they believed, was the decision to focus on the workings of the mind rather than the brain. To try to treat mental illness by poking and probing the brain was a primitive approach, one that was as futile in modern times as it had been in ancient days when surgeons drilled holes in their patients' skulls so that demons could escape.

In large measure, this disdain was justified. The two best-known and most-used physical therapies for mental illness in the first half of this century were electroshock and lobotomy, the lightning bolt and the ice pick. Both approaches were a compound of high hopes and deep frustration; neither had any rationale beyond the most rudimentary, and both seemed more akin to brutal, futile assaults on the patient than to medicine. The essential point is that these treatments were the reigning alternatives to psychoanalysis. *It* looked good in large measure because the alternatives were so bad. There was a secondary effect, as well. When antipsychotic drugs eventually came along, they were oftentimes effective in easing symptoms, but analysts dismissed them nonetheless, because they took for granted that the supposed "advances" were the same old horrors decked out in presentable new outfits.

In the analysts' eyes, biological treatments for madness were merely the newest verse of an ancient song. In the heyday of talk therapy, no psychoanalytic text was complete without a long, mocking, Rabelaisian paragraph detailing the half-baked cures that physicians through the centuries had inflicted on their patients. Karl Menninger's contribution was typical. Menninger depicted the history of pre-Freudian psychiatry in particular, and of medicine in general, as little more than a compendium of error. Each nostrum and surgical procedure was more misguided than the last, and yet physicians never learned from their follies. What were a physician's options when confronted with an illness he did not understand? "He may bleed, he may physic, he may poultice, he may trepan," Menninger wrote. "He may prescribe goat gallstones or powdered unicorn horn or the ancient elixir of theriac, of marvelous renown. Mattioli, too, is powerful; it contains 230 ingredients. Or usnea, listed in our official pharmacopoeia until the nineteenth century and carried in all apothecary shops. It consisted of moss scraped from the skull of a hanged criminal. Or crocodile feces or the powdered lungs of a fox."

Other psychiatrists brought the argument up to date, especially as it pertained to schizophrenia. "Researchers have examined every possible spot of the body of the schizophrenic patient, from top to bottom, from the hair to the sexual glands, in a relentless attempt to find clues which would reveal the organic nature of this condition," Silvano Arieti scoffed in 1955.

The scientists had searched, and they had failed. Now it was the therapists' turn. And, they proclaimed, they had succeeded royally. "In contrast to the persistently negative results obtained by pursuing various 'organic' hypotheses," Yale's Theodore Lidz declared in 1967, "investigators who have carefully explored the family settings in which schizophrenic patients grew up have not been lost in a parched land." Unlike the legions of scientists wandering uselessly in the desert, Lidz went on, he and his fellow talk therapists had been "inundated by significant material."

Lidz and his psychologically inclined colleagues based their view of schizophrenia on pronouncements of Freud's, modified according to taste. Biochemists and geneticists traced *their* intellectual ancestry back to Freud's great rival, Emil Kraepelin. In America today, Kraepelin's name is scarcely known. But "in every country except the United States," the psychiatrist Nancy Andreasen has observed, "Kraepelin, not Freud, is regarded as the founding father of modern psychiatry."

The two men were exact contemporaries — both were born in 1856 — but they had little else in common. Kraepelin was as reluctant to speculate as Freud was eager, as inclined to biological explanations as Freud was to psychological ones, as much an establishment insider as Freud was a resentful outsider. Kraepelin was, as well, a workaholic, a teetotaler, and a notorious cold fish. "If I had died on the trip," recalled one junior colleague who had fallen ill while accompanying his mentor to the United States, "Kraepelin would probably have collected my ashes in a cigar box and brought them home to my wife with the words, 'He was a real disappointment to me.'"

Near the turn of the century, Kraepelin had gathered a team of all-stars around him at the university psychiatry clinic in Heidelberg. Unlike Freud, they focused on the brain rather than the mind. A young researcher named Aloys Alzheimer, for example, was the first to recognize the telltale tangles of brain cells that mark what is now known as Alzheimer's disease. Kraepelin himself labored diligently to test the theory that mental diseases had physical roots. In an attempt to see if heredity played a role in insanity, for instance, he collected painstaking family records from the patients who crowded into his hospital. To test whether mental illness was somehow caused by the stresses of European urban life, he traveled to Singapore to examine patients there. He found that the climate was different, the food was different, the way of life was different, but the symptoms of the mental patients were the same.

Such studies reinforced Kraepelin's skepticism about psychological explanations of schizophrenia. But although he believed that the disease arose from faulty brain structure and chemistry, he conceded that proof was a long way off. In 1913, in a bleak passage in the last edition of his celebrated textbook on schizophrenia, he acknowledged that its causes remained shrouded in "impenetrable darkness."

The failure to find a biological explanation for schizophrenia was all the more galling because the late nineteenth century had seen a host of advances in understanding the brain and its workings. These breakthroughs inspired a sense of confidence bordering on smugness. "It is difficult to exaggerate the neurologists' sense of expectancy, their faith that within the foreseeable future every puzzle would be solved at last," wrote Nathan Hale, the medical historian. (Fifty years later, as we have seen, that faith had turned to ashes, as the brain revealed seemingly endless layers of complexity.)

That early optimism stemmed from a series of discoveries about the geography of the brain. By studying patients carefully while they were alive — by observing stroke victims who had lost the ability to speak, for example — and then by examining their brains postmortem in search of telltale lesions, neurologists had begun to compile rudimentary brain maps. It became clear that the brain's two halves had different roles, for example, and that even nearby regions in the same hemisphere might be specialized to carry out different tasks. These specializations were surprisingly subtle. In 1861, for instance, the French surgeon Paul Broca found that damage to a particular region of the brain could leave a person unable to speak but able to understand other people's speech; in 1876, the German neurologist Carl Wernicke pinpointed another area where damage left a victim able to speak but *un*able to understand others. (The picture has grown ever more complex. Modern-day neurologists have shown, for example, that a second language learned early in life is stored in a different place in the brain than a second language learned later on. They have found patients who can provide definitions of inanimate objects ["lighthouse"] but not of animals ["pig"], and others who can recognize ordinary objects but not familiar faces. They may fail to recognize even their own face, seen in a mirror!)

The nineteenth century's breakthroughs in neurology were only part of the story. At roughly the same time, medicine took another giant step into the modern world. Louis Pasteur and Robert Koch, among others, made the monumental discovery that "germs" caused disease. One dreaded disease after another—anthrax, rabies, tuberculosis, cholera, gonorrhea, leprosy, among others—yielded up its secrets to scientists at their microscopes, and "vapors" and "humors" were banished at last.

The roster of triumphs extended to mental illnesses as well. In psychiatry, the greatest success of all involved a victory so complete that today almost all signs of the battle have vanished. At the end of the nineteenth century, one of the most common and most dreaded diseases was paresis, or general paralysis of the insane. Invariably fatal, it left its victims both demented and paralyzed; they died in convulsions. Paresis had been known at least since the early 1800s, but by the century's end it was suddenly everywhere. Asylums overflowed with these "paretic" patients. Most were middle-aged men, notable not only for their numbers and their suffering but for the strangeness of their symptoms. Mania was an early danger signal; one Frankfurt professor bought ten cars and a hundred wristwatches in a single day.

For decades, doctors had speculated wildly about the disease's origins. Wilhelm Griesinger, the eminent German psychiatrist, put the blame on high living, and on bad cigars in particular. Others suspected complications from syphilis, but that view was unpopular. Many victims of paresis insisted they had never had syphilis, and even those who admitted having once had the disease pointed out that they had made complete recoveries decades before. The telltale sores on their penis had healed in a few days and never returned, and they had never had another symptom. In any event, what connection could there be between long-healed sores and paralytic insanity?

In 1884, Richard von Krafft-Ebing, the Viennese psychiatrist, finally resolved the debate. He knew that syphilis struck only once; once healed, a victim could be sure that no matter how reckless his behavior he would never again endure a second batch of penile sores. In a display of recklessness of his own, Krafft-Ebing scraped the sores of a group of newly infected syphilitic men and injected the material into nine paretic patients.

All nine insisted they had never had syphilis. But all nine remained free of sores. Von Krafft-Ebing had won the day: whatever caused syphilis must somehow cause general paralysis years later. In time, the organism that caused syphilis, the spirochete *Treponema pallidum*, was identified. The presumption was that *Treponema*, lingering undetected in the body for decades, eventually went on to destroy the brain. In 1905, supposition became fact: *Treponema* was identified, postmortem, in brain tissue taken from paresis victims. In 1910 came a "magic bullet" called Salvarsan, the first treatment for syphilis.*

This defanging of a vicious mental illness was an astonishing success. It was hard not to think that it would be the first of a string of triumphs for the "organic" approach to psychological illness. Schizophrenia, in particular, was the next target on every scientist's list.

During the years of these biological advances, Freud (who was himself an accomplished neurologist) had been on a different track. By following the meanderings of a patient's stream of consciousness rather than by staring at brain cells through a microscope, Freud insisted, he had arrived at insights denied to Kraepelin.† But any turn-of-the-century gambler would have discounted Freud's bold talk. Rattling off medicine's roll call of victories in battle, our gambler would have happily put his money on Kraepelin.

Fifty years later, all bets were off, especially when it came to schizophrenia. By the time of World War II, scientists had worked for half a century to understand schizophrenia, biologically minded psychiatrists and neurologists had tried one treatment after another, and none of them had anything to show for their labor. The "organic" camp was in disarray.

As the best scientists admitted, every attempt to pin schizophrenia down scientifically had begun with exuberant hopes and ended in dismal failure. Despite decades of searching, no one had found brain lesions that marked schizophrenia nor microorganisms like those that caused paresis. There had been only a long series of false alarms, most of them from ambitious but second-rate scientists. "There was a series of papers and of great claims," the biochemist Seymour Kety recalled in a recent interview. "People were going after the Nobel Prize, because anybody who discovered the biochemical basis of schizophrenia was going to get one." There were top-flight scientists working on schizophrenia in the 1950s, Kety among them, but they kept

---

* In 1917, the Viennese psychiatrist Julius Wagner-Jauregg announced another physical cure for paresis. He had noticed that psychotic patients who contracted fevers sometimes became lucid. He decided to induce fever intentionally. In June 1917, Wagner-Jauregg watched as blood was drawn from an ex-soldier suffering from malaria and injected into the arm of a young man with advanced paresis. (Malaria was favored as a source of fever because it could be controlled, with quinine.) The patient contracted malaria. In December, six months after his malaria treatment, he was discharged, his insanity apparently dispelled! Other paretic patients made similar recoveries. In 1927, Wagner-Jauregg became the first psychiatrist to win the Nobel Prize. The hope, never realized, was that the fever treatment would also work as a treatment for forms of insanity other than paresis.

† Kraepelin could hardly contain his indignation. "Here we meet everywhere the characteristic fundamental features of the Freudian trend of investigation," he complained in 1919, "the representation of arbitrary assumptions and conjectures as assured facts, which are used without hesitation for building up of always new castles in the air towering ever higher, and the tendency to generalization beyond measure from single observations. . . . As I am accustomed to walk on the sure foundations of direct experience my Philistine conscience of natural science stumbles at every step on objections, considerations, and doubts, over which the lightly soaring power of imagination of Freud's disciples carries them without difficulty."

their voices down. It was plain to serious researchers that they had miles to go, and they focused their efforts on basic research rather than on imminent breakthroughs.

In 1959, Kety, at that time chief of the laboratory of clinical science at the National Institute of Mental Health, surveyed the field in the journal *Science*. His article was a landmark that left no doubt about how little was known about schizophrenia. Kety recounted a series of studies that were poorly conceived, poorly carried out, and much ballyhooed. One researcher, for example, had trumpeted his discovery of especially high levels of certain compounds in the urine of schizophrenics; no such compounds turned up in the controls' urine. Here, at last, was the telltale physical marker that lay at the heart of schizophrenia!

A researcher in Kety's lab had taken a closer look. The telltale substances, it turned out, were compounds found in coffee. The schizophrenics, hospitalized and subsisting on an institutional diet, drank countless cups of coffee every day. The controls, as it happened, were Seventh-Day Adventists, whose religion forbade coffee. The findings had nothing whatever to do with schizophrenia.

Kety reported a number of such fiascoes, though always in the most measured tones. His point was a simple one. Schizophrenia was terribly complicated — perhaps, like cancer, it was not a single entity but a family of diseases — and understanding it would require more care and better science. This was emphatically *not* the message that Kety's psychoanalytic rivals took away from his paper. They saw Kety's exhortation to his fellow scientists to redouble their efforts as a confession of impotence. If even the high priest of biology had thrown up his hands in despair, they asked, who could deny that schizophrenia was rightfully the province of the psychoanalysts?

The scientists' failure to *understand* schizophrenia was only half the story. The failure of conventional, brain-based medicine to *treat* it was the other half. It was not for want of trying. Psychiatrists and neurosurgeons had fired every weapon in their arsenal, but madness mocked their every approach. They responded, in the words of the neurologist Macdonald Critchley, "as in frustration one kicks or thumps into action a faulty radio."

At one time or another virtually any proposed remedy for madness had been deemed worth trying. One psychiatrist notes, for example, that Charles Darwin's grandfather Erasmus, a highly regarded physician, devised "a chair in which agitated psychotic patients were strapped down and then whirled around rapidly. The treatment was considered complete when blood emerged from their ears." In our own century, castration, vasectomies, high doses of oxygen or carbon dioxide, heated "mummy bags" to induce fevers and refrigerated ones to produce chills, and injections of horses' blood all had their day.

These treatments soon gave way to "shock" and to lobotomy. This grim history is well told in Elliot Valenstein's groundbreaking and indispensable *Great and Desperate Cures.* Valenstein unearthed a host of original documents, and all later accounts, including this one, follow in his footsteps.

Thanks to *One Flew Over the Cuckoo's Nest* and countless other movies, we think of "electroshock" when we hear the words "shock therapy." But the story of shock therapy began, in 1933, with a nonelectrified version. Manfred Sakel was a Viennese doctor working in a sanatorium for well-heeled drug addicts. One of Sakel's patients happened to be diabetic. He accidentally gave her an overdose of insulin and found, when she awoke from her coma, that she seemed to have lost her craving for morphine. Sakel concluded that he had found a cure for drug addiction. Soon he administered another accidental overdose of insulin, this one to an addict who happened to be psychotic. When this patient regained consciousness, he, too, seemed improved.

Sakel began to treat schizophrenics by intentionally giving them overdoses of insulin to induce comas. In a flurry of publications beginning in 1933, he claimed an almost universal success rate. By the end of the decade, insulin-coma therapy for schizophrenia had been taken up around the world.

It was a harrowing procedure. "This method," according to one *proponent,* "is to give a patient large doses of insulin to lower the amount of sugar in his blood, thus producing a state of mental confusion and excitement. For an hour or more, perhaps, he lies in a semi-conscious state, twitching, jerking, and perhaps talking incoherently, until a deep coma supervenes. When using this treatment for the relief of schizophrenia, the psychiatrist may keep the patient in coma for half an hour. Sugar is then administered by means of a stomach-tube or intravenous injection, and he quickly wakes up." A typical course of treatment might involve dozens of comas over the course of weeks or months.

In the meantime, a Hungarian psychiatrist named Ladislas von Meduna had devised a shock therapy of his own. Meduna believed that, in autopsies, he could tell the brains of schizophrenic patients from those of epileptics. The two diseases, he decided, were "antagonistic." Where there was one, there could not be the other.

From that starting point, Meduna's path was clear. He could *treat* schizophrenia by *inducing* epilepticlike convulsions in schizophrenic patients. "With faint hope and trembling desire," Meduna set to work. The best convulsions came, he soon found, from injections of a compound called Metrazol. Like Sakel, Meduna leapt into print with claims of an astonishing cure rate. And like insulin-coma therapy, Metrazol convulsion therapy was soon in routine use around the world as a treatment for schizophrenia.

In 1938, a third variant of shock therapy came into use, this one discovered by the Italians Ugo Cerletti and Lucio Bini. This was electro-shock. Electrodes were attached to the sides of the patient's head, a switch was thrown, and the patient went into convulsions. (Bini had experimented on hogs at a slaughterhouse in Rome to find a safe dosage of electricity.) Electroshock soon outdistanced Metrazol. It was easier to administer, and it produced convulsions that were not quite as violent — patients were less likely to fracture their arms and legs and spines. (Electroshock, now called electroconvulsive therapy, is still in use and still controversial. It is a last-resort treatment for depression, used in the neighborhood of 100,000 times annually in the United States. According to the American Psychiatric Associ-ation, 80 percent of those who undergo electroconvulsive therapy improve, in comparison with 60 to 70 percent of those who take antidepressants.)

At the same time that his colleagues were contemplating different ways to induce coma and convulsions, an ambitious Portuguese neurologist was planning a more direct assault on madness, and on history. Egas Moniz was an aristocrat, a scholar, a member of Parliament, a diplomat who hoped someday to become prime minister, and a medical pioneer who had devised a celebrated technique for X-raying the brain.

In 1928 and again in 1933, Moniz had been briefly considered for the Nobel Prize in medicine. He had fallen short. Now, at age sixty-one and bitter that his day was fast disappearing, he happened to attend a remarkable lecture at the Second International Congress of Neurology, in London. The talk described the effects of frontal-lobe surgery on two chimpanzees, Becky and Lucy. The chimps' intellectual performance had plummeted after sur-gery, the speaker reported, but he added one curious observation: Before her surgery, Becky had been bad-tempered. When she could not remember which of two cups contained food, for example, she threw a tantrum. After surgery, however, Becky could make mistake after mistake and still seem almost cheerful.

Moniz rose to ask the speaker a question. If surgery on a chimp had had such a dramatic effect, he wondered, "why would it not be feasible to relieve anxiety states in man by surgical means?" On November 12, 1935, three months after his return from London to the University of Lisbon, Moniz watched as his assistant Almeida Lima drilled two holes into the shaven skull of a sixty-three-year-old woman afflicted with long-standing depression and paranoia. (Moniz did not carry out the operation himself because he suffered from gout that at times left his hands almost useless.) Operating "blind," the assistant inserted a hypodermic needle through one hole and then the other and injected alcohol into the frontal lobes of his patient's brain.

Over the course of the next several weeks, Moniz supervised seven similar operations. The eighth time, he tried something new. This time he had Lima use a knifelike instrument rather than an alcohol injection. The "leucotome" looked something like a knitting needle with a small wire semicircle mounted along one side, near the needle's tip. The wire loop did the actual cutting as Lima spun the needle in his fingers. Lima inserted the leucotome through a hole drilled in the top of his patient's skull and then tunneled through the nerve fibers in his way. The theory behind this procedure could hardly have been simpler. Moniz reasoned that mental illness was the result of "fixed thoughts" that had somehow become "stabilized" in particular nerve pathways in the frontal lobes and that needed to be cut out. He called the surgery his "core operation" because of its similarity to coring an apple.

In 1936, Moniz published eight articles describing his new procedure; in 1937, six articles and a book. He claimed remarkable results, although he provided no details. After his first twenty operations, for example, Moniz reported seven cures, seven patients who had improved, and six who had neither improved nor worsened.

One of Moniz's articles happened to catch the eye of an American neurologist named Walter Freeman. A professor at George Washington University, Freeman was cocky, combative, controversial, a showman and a self-promoter whose ambitions were as grand as those of Moniz. As soon as he had finished reading, Freeman sent off to Moniz's supply house for a set of leucotomes of his own. With a week's practice on brains from the morgue, he was ready to set to work.

Freeman quickly became the greatest American advocate of lobotomy as a cure for mental illness. By 1942, he and his colleague James Watts had published a book called *Psychosurgery*, detailing their accomplishments. The two men were cochairmen of George Washington University's Department of Neurology and Neurological Surgery, and their book made an enormous splash. "Some three hundred people in the U.S. have had their psychoses surgically removed, Dr. Freeman revealed last week," *Time* reported in November 1942, and it went on to note that "a score of U.S. surgeons are now using the revolutionary new technique."

Time ran a photo of Freeman and Watts at work, one on either side of a patient stretched out on an operating table. The article explained that "Drs. Freeman and Watts drill a small hole in the temple on each side of the patient's head where two skull bones meet. Surgeon Watts then inserts a dull knife into the brain, makes a fan-shaped incision upward through the prefrontal lobe, then downward a few minutes later. He then repeats the incisions on the other side of the brain." *Time* relegated one disquieting observation to a parenthesis: "In two operations they have cut cerebral arteries. Both patients died."

That somber note was rare. In the popular press, this blind assault on the brain was treated almost casually. *Time* was, if anything, more restrained than most. "The patient is given only a local anesthetic at the temples — the brain itself is insensitive," it noted, "and the doctors encourage him to talk, sing or recite poems and prayers while the operation is in progress. As his lobes are sliced, he becomes drowsier, more confused and incoherent. When his replies to questions show that his mind is thoroughly disoriented, the doctors know they have cut deep enough into his brain."

This was not merely driving without a map but barreling down the road with the windshield painted black. Freeman told a story about asking a patient, "What's going through your mind now?" The patient had replied, "A knife."

But Freeman and Watts insisted that their results justified their jauntiness. Of their 136 cases, they said, 98 were greatly improved, 23 somewhat improved, and only 12 were failures. (*Time* reported these numbers without checking the arithmetic. Freeman and Watts neglected to point out that the total added up to 133, not 136, because 3 patients had died on the operating table.) These lobotomy patients had spent years in mental hospitals, and now they were nearly all back at home or at work.

Surgery did change a patient's personality, Freeman and Watts conceded, but they implied that patients welcomed many of the changes. "The freedom from painful self-consciousness, and also from preoccupation with former conflicts, repressions, frustrations and the like, and the associated elevation in mood, renders life particularly agreeable to them and they enjoy it to the fullest."

Soon, though, Freeman would modify his views. Though lobotomized patients appeared to do well immediately following their operations, their improvement was short-lived. The trouble, Freeman decided, was that many patients had been too far gone to help. He had been wrong to call lobotomy a last resort; he realized now that it had to be used before it was too late.

That called for a new approach to surgery. Old-style lobotomies required a neurosurgeon and, afterward, extensive nursing care. By 1945, Freeman had decided to take up a quicker, easier technique pioneered by an Italian psychiatrist. He described the procedure in an excited letter to his son:

I have also been trying out a sort of half-way stage between electroshock and prefrontal lobotomy on some of the patients. This consists of knocking them out with a shock and while they are under the "anesthetic" thrusting an ice pick up between the eyeball and the eyelid through the roof of the orbit actually into the lateral cut by swinging the thing from side to side. I have done two patients on both sides and another on one side without running into any complications, except a very black eye in one case. There may be trouble later on but it seemed fairly easy, although definitely a disagreeable thing to watch. It remains to be seen how these cases hold up, but so far they have shown considerable relief of their symptoms, and only some of the minor behavior difficulties that follow lobotomy. They can even get up and go home within an hour or so.

Surgery via ice pick had two key selling points. Since the brain was entered by way of the eye socket rather than through holes drilled in the skull, these "transorbital lobotomies" presented no need for a neurosurgeon's expertise. Any psychiatrist with a steady hand and a strong nerve could carry out the procedure himself. Nor was there any need for the expense of an operating suite. The psychiatrist needed only an ordinary room and a closed door.

Freeman, who was not a surgeon, carried out many of the operations himself in his second-floor office in downtown Washington. When his partner, Watts, entered Freeman's office one day, Elliot Valenstein reports, "he saw Freeman leaning over an unconscious patient slumped in a chair with an ice pick sticking out from above his eye. Freeman looked up and, without any hesitation, asked Watts to hold the ice pick so that he could photograph the patient."

Watts, a neurosurgeon, was outraged at his neurologist colleague's casual approach to surgery. The two men parted ways, but Freeman continued on his own as zealously as ever. By September 1952, he was the star of yet another *Time* magazine story. (This time the caption under his photo read, "Icepicks in the eye sockets.") The news angle was that Freeman had just returned from a quick jaunt through West Virginia's mental hospitals, where he had treated patients with "anxiety neuroses, . . . irrational fears, morbid thoughts, hallucinations," and "suicidal depression."

All the patients received the same treatment. "Strapped to an operating table, they got three quick jolts of electricity," *Time* reported, "enough to start violent, involuntary convulsions before they lapsed into anesthetic coma. Next a thin, icepick-like leucotome was inserted under each eyelid, hammered home through the eye socket and into the brain. Carefully manipulating the two icepicks, the doctor severed the connection between thalamus and frontal lobes in the patient's brain. The entire operation took only ten minutes."

Freeman had supervised or performed two hundred of these lobotomies in two weeks. "It is safer to operate than to wait," he declared, and he forecast that within six months half of his West Virginia patients would have improved enough to be sent home.

The years from 1949 to 1952 marked the height of the lobotomy era. In each of those years about 5,000 lobotomies were carried out, about one-third of them of the ice pick variety. (The end came, as we shall see, not in revulsion but because a new treatment — antipsychotic drugs — came along.) The symbolic peak came in October 1949, when the Nobel Prize committee announced its awards. The Nobel Prize in medicine went to Portugal's Egas Moniz.

The *New York Times* hailed the choice in an effusive editorial. Because of the hope that lobotomies offered, the *Times* observed, "hypochondriacs no longer thought they were going to die, would-be suicides found life acceptable, sufferers from persecution complex forgot the machinations of imaginary conspirators." Surgeons, the *Times* proclaimed, "now think no more of operations on the brain than they do of removing an appendix."

Perhaps they should have thought a bit more. The problem was not that surgeons dared to perform lobotomies. Surgery is no career for the fainthearted (brain surgery remains "a crude business" even today, one neurosurgeon observes, much like attempting "to repair a computer with a chain saw"), and operations that look brutal may in fact be lifesaving. But there is a difference between bold action where there is no alternative — think of doctors on Civil War battlefields hacking off arms and legs — and recklessness. Lobotomies grew common though their effectiveness was never proved.* When the surgeons' bold claims were finally examined closely, the talk of cures dried up. Nearly all the early lobotomy studies were carried out without the use of untreated "controls," for example, so no one knew how the fate of lobotomized patients compared with that of patients left alone. Nor was it clear how surgeons chose patients for lobotomies — if their patients were not as sick as others, as some skeptics suggested, it would be difficult to draw valid conclusions.

Some patients did become calmer and easier to manage, but they did not seem cured so much as deadened. "His soul appears to be destroyed," one English woman said in 1947, describing her husband. "He is not the man I once knew." And schizophrenics in particular, even Moniz and Freeman came to believe, did *not* benefit from lobotomies. Despite such second thoughts, *Time* noted blithely in a 1951 survey article on lobotomy that "schizophrenics are the usual subjects, largely because nothing else seems to help them much."

* Today, in a tiny number of cases, brain surgery is still used to treat mental illness. For some patients with intractable depression or manic depression or obsessive-compulsive disorder, neurosurgeons perform an operation called a cingulotomy, in which they cut a lesion in the cingulate gyrus. According to proponents of this surgery, roughly one-fourth of these desperately ill patients improve. No one knows why.

CHAPTER NINE

The Tide Turns

*To have forgotten that schizophrenia is a brain disease will
go down as one of the great aberrations of twentieth-
century medicine.*

—*editorial,* Journal of Neurology, Neurosurgery and
Psychiatry, *1990*

OR DECADES, PSYCHOANALYSTS HAD reacted with horror to the whole
business of shocking the brain and cutting into it. The "organic" approach
to schizophrenia, they felt certain, was dangerous and misguided. And so,
when a breakthrough came, it arrived utterly without warning.

And it was not only one breakthrough but three independent ones —
antipsychotic drugs, which tamed schizophrenia's most frightening symptoms; genetic studies, which served as a kind of gubernatorial pardon for
schizophrenogenic mothers; and direct comparisons of psychotherapy with
other treatments, which found "talk therapy" powerless to cure schizophrenia. In the early 1950s, psychoanalysis seemed to be the only approach to
schizophrenia that had a chance. By the late 1960s, the notion of talking to
schizophrenia seemed like a strange and hopeless venture.

The first breakthrough came in 1949, in France, where a surgeon
named Henri Laborit was casting about for a way to keep his patients' blood
pressure from falling when they were under anesthesia. Laborit wondered
about antihistamines, mysterious compounds discovered only a few years
before by an Italian scientist, Daniel Bovet. The discovery would soon earn
Bovet a Nobel Prize, and it already had both businessmen and scientists
abuzz. Histamine is a substance that occurs naturally in our bodies and
accounts for the red eyes and runny nose and other miseries of allergy. The
market for substances that countered those effects would be enormous.
Allergy sufferers would be eager and lifelong customers, and, better still, so
would everyone who caught cold — weren't their symptoms the same? Drug
companies were giddy with dreams of riches.

Scientists and doctors, too, were consumed with curiosity about antihistamines. Laborit was only one of many researchers who had picked up the scent. His question was a practical one — since it was known that an injection of histamine lowered blood pressure, and since a drop in blood pressure was a hazard of surgery, could it be that antihistamines might prevent that drop?

The answer, alas, turned out to be no. But to his surprise, Laborit saw something he had not been watching for: he noticed that the surgical patients he had given an antihistamine seemed less tense than other patients. Both before they went under anesthesia and after they came out of it, they were calm but not groggy. Laborit suggested to two Parisian psychiatrists that they might try giving *their* patients an antihistamine. Perhaps those patients, too, would feel less anxious.

Jean Delay and Pierre Deniker tested manic patients, depressed ones, neurotics, and schizophrenics of every stripe. By 1952, the results were clear. For schizophrenics in particular, a modified antihistamine named chlorpromazine, or Thorazine, did seem to ease anxiety, and it did so without fogging the mind.

But that was the least of it. The crucial and absolutely unexpected news was that this new drug seemed to tame or turn off the delusions and hallucinations that were the hallmark of schizophrenia. For the first time, the dungeon that was schizophrenia had been pierced by a shaft of light.*

The news raced around the world. In Lexington, Kentucky, in 1954, for example, Donald Klein was a young psychiatrist helping to supervise a hundred-bed ward of chronic patients. Most were World War I veterans, and many had been hospitalized as long as thirty years. "Most of them had spent their days sitting around on benches all those years, staring at the walls," Klein remembers.

With no very high hopes, Klein and his colleagues set out to test the new French drug. They gave patients what was, by today's standards, a minute dose, and sat back and waited. Within a few weeks, Klein recalled recently, with astonishment undimmed by the passing of forty years, "a couple of patients *just woke up!* They had been mute, catatonic, unrespon-

---

* The discovery of many of the major drugs in psychiatry was a matter of serendipity. The first antidepressant, for example, was discovered by physicians trying to treat tuberculosis. Well before their TB symptoms responded, some patients reported feelings of euphoria. The story of lithium, used around the globe to treat manic-depression, is even odder. Its effectiveness against mania was discovered in 1949 by John Cade, an Australian who was by his own description "an unknown psychiatrist, working alone in a small chronic hospital with no research training, primitive techniques, and negligible equipment." On the theory that mania was caused by a toxin manufactured by the body itself, Cade began injecting guinea pigs with urine from manic patients. The guinea pigs died, and Cade tried instead to inject them with components of urine rather than the urine itself. To make uric acid soluble so that he could inject it, Cade mixed it with lithium. As a control, he also tried injecting the guinea pigs with lithium alone. To his astonishment, he found that he could now pick up a guinea pig, ordinarily one of the most skittish of creatures, and place it on its back, where it lay still and gazed docilely upward.

sive, and one of them came up to me in the hall and said, 'Doc, when am I getting out of here?' "

That first patient was "Rip van Winkle," awakened after a sleep of three decades, Klein would write later. "He didn't know where he was, or how he had gotten there, or what had happened for the past thirty years. He knew nothing about the Depression, World War II, penicillin, or the atomic bomb. He didn't know that he had been in a hospital or that he was in Kentucky. He had spent thirty years essentially out of contact with reality."

And then, almost like that, he had returned to the world. Klein, today a professor at Columbia and a major figure in American psychiatry, is not an effusive man. Smart, impatient, sarcastic, down-to-earth, he is not given to hyperbole. But his experience in Kentucky, he declares unequivocally, was "a medical miracle."

Drugs had been used in psychiatry for decades, but they were little more than the chemical counterparts of a hammer blow to the head. The startling difference with Thorazine was that it seemed to work without stunning the patient into submission. His hallucinations and delusions vanished or dwindled, and he remained alert. "The big change," says Harvard psychiatrist Allan Hobson, "was that the antipsychotic effects were in high proportion to the sedating effects. Before, you really had to turn the lights out to stop that stuff."

And the Thorazine story had a deeper meaning. Not only did it promise hope to patients, which in itself was a giant step forward, but it also provided a vital clue to the nature of the disease they suffered from. The crucial point was simple to state — the same drug that could utterly transform a schizophrenic patient had vastly less impact on a healthy person. Why was that important? Because it provided a hard-to-miss hint that the brain of a person with schizophrenia was different from the brain of a healthy person. Donald Klein explained:

> Some medication has the same effect on everyone. Gelusil, for example, seems to lower stomach acidity in everyone, whether their stomach is sick or not. The effect of such a drug is like a rheostat. It pushes things up and down regardless of the patient. Aspirin, on the other hand, acts like a thermostat. It lowers a fever temperature, but it does not bring the temperature down below normal. And if someone has a normal temperature, it does not lower it. The same thing is true of digitalis. It normalizes a deranged heartbeat, but nothing happens when it is given to a person with a normal heart.
>
> The anti-psychotics act in the same thermostatic manner. They have an enormous effect on the mentally ill. But if they are given to a normal person, nothing happens. Prolixin is one hundred times more powerful than chlorpromazine as an anti-psychotic, but they both have the same effect — slight sedation — on a person who is not psychotic.

And not only did Thorazine work specifically, but it also worked quickly. "You could see it *the next day,*" cries Harvard's Allan Hobson, his voice a squeak of amazement. "These people would become relatively calm. They'd be in a seclusion room, nude, smearing feces on the wall and racing around talking ragtime, and the next day" — he drops into a stage whisper — *"they were better."* Hobson pauses, as if to make sure that he has made his point. From the whisper, he segues into a roar. "It was dramatic as hell!" he bellows.

Hobson and Klein, it should be noted, were hardly pharmaceutical zealots. At this early stage in their careers, both men were sympathetic to psychoanalysis and the "talking cure." Hobson was a devout admirer of Freud, and Klein went on to become a psychoanalyst even after his experience with Rip van Winkle in Kentucky.

Some psychoanalysts staggered under this blow — we will discuss the analysts' response in detail later in this chapter — but many more seemed unfazed by it. As it turned out, they would not have much time to ponder their response. A second blow followed quickly on the first. This one had to do not with drugs but with genetics.

From the beginning, it had been clear that schizophrenia runs in families. But so do many things — wealth and poverty, red hair, the ability to speak Chinese, heart disease. The problem was in teasing heredity apart from environment. Parents pass on half their genes to their children, after all, but they also help to create the environment that those children grow up in. If a family is plagued by schizophrenia, does one blame bad genes or a bad environment?

The situation is even murkier than it first appears. With a few diseases — with Huntington's chorea, for example, which killed Woody Guthrie — there is no ambiguity. If you carry the gene, you are 100 percent certain to fall victim to the disease. How you live your life is beside the point. Drink a bottle of Scotch a day or join a monastery and renounce all worldly vice, and your fate is unchanged. But with most ailments — heart disease, for one — bad genes make for higher risk, but they are not an immutable death sentence. A man may inherit genes that predispose him to a heart attack, but if he sticks with carrots instead of steaks, he may live to a healthy old age.

In the case of schizophrenia, a closer look at the figures shows how tantalizing the mystery is. In the general population, about one person in a hundred is schizophrenic. But the numbers rise dramatically if you look at the blood relatives of someone with schizophrenia. The first cousin of a schizophrenic has a 2 percent chance of becoming schizophrenic sometime during her life; for aunts and uncles the chance is 4 percent; for siblings, 9 percent; for the child of a schizophrenic parent, 13 percent.

Most of those figures were painstakingly compiled by geneticists out to prove the power of heredity. And, indeed, the figures fell neatly in line with genetic predictions — the more genes someone shared with a schizophrenic, the higher the person's odds of becoming schizophrenic.

But these concordance rates, as they are called, begged the key question, because people who shared genes presumably shared much else as well. Rather than resolve the heredity-versus-environment question, in fact, these statistics served instead to heighten the battle by providing ammunition to both camps.

Consider twins, for example. Twins can be fraternal or identical. Fraternal twins share half their genes, on average, like any siblings. Identical twins have identical genes. If one fraternal twin is schizophrenic, the odds are 17 percent that the other twin is schizophrenic, too. But if one identical twin is schizophrenic, the odds that the other twin is schizophrenic are 48 percent.

"Aha!" cry both sides at once, as they each grab for the same piece of evidence. "Don't you see?" the geneticists demand. "Identical twins are more alike genetically than fraternal twins, and their risk of schizophrenia is greater, just as we predicted." *"Of course* identical twins are at higher risk than fraternal twins," the environmentalists reply. "The parents talked to them alike and dressed them alike and treated them alike in every way you can imagine. And besides, schizophrenia is a disease that has to do with a person's sense of identity, so naturally you'd expect that identical twins would be at special risk."

Both sides did agree on one fundamental point. If one identical twin has schizophrenia, there is nearly a 50 percent chance that the other twin is schizophrenic, too. That risk is *fifty* times higher than for a person picked at random. But high though that risk is, it might seem as if it should be higher still. If schizophrenia is genetic, and if identical twins have identical genes, why isn't the concordance rate 100 percent? *

The explanation, everyone agreed, had to be that even if schizophrenia was a genetic disease, it was not *only* a genetic disease. To become schizophrenic, a person needed more than bad genes; he needed some contribution from the environment. Perhaps that contribution was a viral infection in infancy; perhaps it was too much of a particular vitamin in the diet, or too little; perhaps it was exposure to a pesticide, or to radiation, or to toxins in the water. Or perhaps it was a bad mother.

---

* A prizewinning study by the geneticists Irving Gottesman and Aksel Bertelsen highlighted a similar riddle. If one identical twin was schizophrenic and the other was not, the two researchers found, the children of the healthy twin were as likely to be schizophrenic as the children of the schizophrenic twin. This seemed a clear sign, on the one hand, that schizophrenia was somehow transmitted genetically. But on the other hand, if schizophrenia was in the genes, why wasn't the healthy twin affected? (The answer, it seems, is that the healthy twin, although genetically vulnerable to schizophrenia, had the good fortune never to encounter whatever it

That was certainly a possibility, everyone acknowledged. On the other hand, it was hardly a sure thing. If you looked at diabetes, for example, the concordance rates were similar to those for schizophrenia. In particular, if one identical twin had diabetes, the chance that the other twin had it, too, was again about 50 percent, rather than 100 percent. And no one blamed diabetes on malicious parents.

How to untangle nature from nurture?

The first person to find a way out of the impasse was a stubborn young medical resident named Leonard Heston. In 1962, Heston was thirty-one, a newly minted psychiatrist working at a state mental hospital in Oregon. One of his first patients was a paranoid schizophrenic. The man's brother was a paranoid schizophrenic, too, and so was his father!

Heston dove into the medical literature and presented the case at grand rounds. He knew the conventional explanation of schizophrenia — there was, at this point, scarcely an alternative — but Heston argued that bad genes, rather than bad parenting, were the key. "I just met with a *swarm* of criticism," Heston recalls. " 'My gosh, you've missed the point, this awful mother must have caused this illness in her husband *and* two of her sons.' They all *knew* how schizophrenia was caused, and what caused it, and so therefore I had to be wrong."

Heston, on the other hand, knew the mother. "I'd gotten to know her as she was fighting her way through this. She wasn't perfect, but she had done a wonderful job, considering the amount of illness in her family, and that's what got me interested. With all this sickness and disruption around her, she tried to keep a normal life. She'd have a big Thanksgiving dinner for the family, that kind of thing.

"She was in her late fifties at that time, and she worked two jobs, cleaning rooms in a motel and working in canneries during the summertime. She was basically the sole support of the family. Two of the sons were living at home, the third one was in a state hospital and had been there for years and years, and the husband was in and out of the state hospital.

"And there was one normal son, that was another thing. If she was so bad, how was it that there was one normal son? And why was it that the schizophrenia in the father and in the sons appeared so similar in its expression? So putting all that together, I just could not imagine that this woman could have caused this illness. There had to be something else — there had to be something genetic."

But how to prove it? The key, Heston realized, was literally to separate nature from nurture. He came up with the idea of looking at children who

is that triggers the disease. Similarly, a person predisposed to heart disease might remain healthy if he avoided smoking and fatty foods.)

had been adopted in infancy, so that their genes came from one set of parents and their home environment from another. Beneath the scientific trappings, the question was age-old. From fairy tales through *The Prince and the Pauper* and beyond, authors had told stories of infants whisked away from one home and raised in another. Who would they grow up to be?

In a musty room at the state mental hospital, Heston found decades' worth of old medical records. Every so often, female patients at the hospital had had babies. Heston combed through the records, looking for schizophrenic mothers who had given their babies up for adoption years before.

Eventually, he found the names of forty-seven schizophrenic women who had become pregnant and given their babies up for adoption. The hospital had a strict policy that babies did not stay in the hospital with the mother — if no family member came forward within three days to take the baby, the infant was put up for adoption. Then, for purposes of comparison, Heston found a matching group of fifty children whose mothers had *not* been mentally ill. The children in this control group were adopted, too, in case adoption itself somehow led to schizophrenia.

At last, the schizophrenia debate had moved from talk to careful experiments, complete with controls and clear-cut predictions. If schizophrenia was partly genetic, then children born to schizophrenic mothers and given up for adoption should have been at higher risk than children born to healthy mothers and given up for adoption. But if schizophrenia truly was caused by bad parenting, the two groups of children should have been at equal risk.

Armed with his bright idea, all that remained was for Heston to track down the adoptees, who had long since grown to adulthood and, presumably, scattered across the country. "I applied to NIH for a grant," he recalls, "and they just laughed at me." Heston mimics a dismissive chuckle: " 'No, no, you can't do that. Nobody could ever locate these people.' "

Heston went ahead anyway, the fledgling psychiatrist working away as an amateur detective. Starting with a list of the adoptive parents' names and their once-upon-a-time addresses, Heston began by combing through veterans' records and driver's licenses. (He had learned "a lot of tricks for locating people" from a friend who had a job repossessing cars.) At night at the hospital, when he was on call, Heston sat up making phone calls on the free telephone line.

"Oregon at that time was still pretty small-town," Heston explains. "You could nearly always locate someone in a small town. I'd just call the police or the librarian or somebody like that and ask for an old resident. Or if it was a larger city, ask the police if they had a city directory at hand and to give me the telephone number of the next-door house to the old address I had, and then I'd call and ask who had lived in the neighborhood for a long time.

"Sometimes I lucked out and the next-door neighbors were the ones who had lived there a long time. But there was nearly always *someone*, and they'd say, 'Oh yes, I remember that family, they were very nice, and so-and-so married so-and-so, and so-and-so died, and they moved to Santa Rosa, California, and I got a Christmas card from them a couple of years ago.' You get that kind of story, and then you go to Santa Rosa."

To get to Santa Rosa, Heston tapped the resources of yet another friend. This one ran an office of a national car-rental company. "He'd let me go pick up cars in different places and bring them back, free of charge, so that's what I did. I went to Cleveland and Baltimore and two or three times to Canada and several times to California. One time, I brought back a great big old Cadillac from California."

Heston traveled to fourteen states in all. Within a year, he had tracked down all but five of his ninety-seven adoptees and compiled detailed dossiers on each one. Nearly all the subjects knew they had been adopted; hardly any knew anything about their birth parents. Heston administered interviews, personality tests, IQ tests, and psychological profiles. A second psychiatrist evaluated the dossiers "blind," not knowing whether an adoptee was in the control group or the schizophrenic-mother group.

Then they broke the code. In the years since the infants had been adopted, a total of five had become schizophrenic. Of those five, every one had had a schizophrenic mother. The chance that the results were coincidence was a bit less than one in forty.

The conclusion seemed plain. Before Heston came along, geneticists had established that a child born to a schizophrenic mother had about a one-in-ten chance of being schizophrenic herself. Now Heston had looked at children born to schizophrenic mothers but raised by parents who had passed an adoption agency's screening tests and were presumably "normal." And *their* risk of schizophrenia was one in ten, as if they had never left home. The simplest explanation was that the children of schizophrenic mothers carried danger with them, wherever they went.

For the psychoanalysts, this was more unwelcome news, but they did their best to shrug it off. They found it hard to believe that mothers could be as innocent as Heston had found. What about those first few days in the hospital while the mothers still had their babies with them? "I'd run into an objection," Heston recalls, "where people would say, 'Well, my goodness, we didn't think that schizophrenia could be caused by three days' contact, but evidently it can.' "

At the same time that Heston was carrying out his lone-wolf study, a team of eminent and well-funded scientists at the National Institute of Mental Health was putting together a far more elaborate venture. Heston was first, but he was a solo explorer; the new team was a full-scale expeditionary force, a flotilla of seagoing vessels in comparison with a lone canoe.

The NIMH effort grew out of the frustrating, fascinating work of David

Rosenthal, a clinical psychologist. Rosenthal had found something un-thinkably rare — a set of identical quadruplets, then in their mid-twenties, and all of them schizophrenic. Surely, close study of the Genain sisters and their parents, would help to untangle the heredity-environment knot. On first hearing the quadruplets' story, Rosenthal took for granted that genes would tell the tale. As he recalled later, he could "hardly help but wonder what further proof of a genetic etiology anyone would want to have." But as time passed and Rosenthal and his colleagues delved into Genain family history, it became undeniable that Mr. and Mrs. Genain were strange ducks indeed. Maybe parents *were* the culprits.

For three years, all four Genain sisters lived at the National Institute of Mental Health; for long stretches, their parents lived there, too, while psychiatrists, psychologists, and assorted others poked and prodded their six research subjects. The NIMH team measured brain waves and reaction times, analyzed handwriting samples, administered inkblot tests. In the end, they produced a thick book but no solution to the mystery of schizophrenia. In particular, the heredity-versus-environment question remained as vexing as ever. Were the quadruplets schizophrenic because they shared the same genes, or because they had shared the same upbringing?

Solving that riddle, Rosenthal acknowledged, would require a different approach. He and his biochemist colleague Seymour Kety soon came up with a straightforward but fantastically labor-intensive plan. It would involve not the close-up study of four patients but the statistical analysis of an entire nation's roster of schizophrenics.

The massive NIMH venture grew, in part, out of a homely observation by Kety, one of the team's leaders. He and his wife, as it happened, had two adopted children. "I'd noticed an interesting characteristic of the parents of adopted children, and we caught ourselves doing it, too," Kety recalls, a bit sheepishly. "If the kid does something that you're proud of, you say, 'See, that's the effect of a good environment.' And if he does things that you're not so proud of, then you say, 'Well, it's in the genes.'" Adopted children, Kety realized, were a kind of natural experiment in unraveling nature and nurture.

The Kety-Rosenthal strategy was the reverse of Heston's. Heston had begun with schizophrenic mothers and looked at what became of the chil-dren they gave up for adoption; Kety and Rosenthal began with adoptees who had grown up to become schizophrenic adults and then looked back at their parents and siblings.

Now, everyone agreed that schizophrenia ran in families. The point was that adoptees had *two* families — the adoptive one that had raised them and the biological one that had given them up. So each schizophrenic adoptee had two sets of relatives.

Kety and Rosenthal made a straightforward prediction. If "nature" was the reason that schizophrenia ran in families, then one would expect to see trouble in the *biological* relatives of the schizophrenic adoptees. And if "nurture" was the reason that schizophrenia ran in families, then one would expect trouble in the *adoptive* relatives, the ones who had raised a schizophrenic child.

Testing that prediction took half-a-dozen years and repeated trips across the ocean. Kety, who spent the 1961 academic year as a professor of psychiatry at Johns Hopkins, devised the protocol as he commuted back and forth to Baltimore from his home in the suburbs of Washington, D.C. The key was finding a large enough sample of people who had been adopted and had become schizophrenic. More than that, researchers would need somehow to track down *two* sets of relatives and then evaluate the mental health of all those relatives.

American records, it quickly became clear, were not up to the task. Denmark provided the answer. One agency of the Danish government had detailed information on every adoption in the country going back to the 1920s — name, birth date, and address of each biological and adoptive parent, as well as information on the adoptive parents' address, income, and occupation. Another register contained a record, from 1924 on, of each Danish citizen's address from birth to death. Still another agency, this one dating from World War I, contained the record of every Dane who had been admitted to a hospital for a psychiatric disorder. In return for a promise of confidentiality, Kety and Rosenthal and their colleagues were given carte blanche.

They set to work combing through more than two decades' worth of adoption records from Copenhagen and its environs, an area that included roughly one-quarter the population of Denmark. (In a follow-up study, Kety would go on to study the entire country.) The researchers put in place an elaborate system of safeguards, for there were countless dangers to avoid. Could it be, for example, that adoptive families were wealthier, and therefore healthier, than biological families? Or might the adoptive families be healthier because adoption agencies had screened out the odd birds? Such possibilities would have to be taken into account before valid comparisons could be made. Similarly, the psychiatrists themselves might be biased. Since a diagnosis of schizophrenia is a judgment call, they might find only what they expected to find. The remedy was to impose a cumbersome new set of "blinding" procedures so that the psychiatrist deciding whether a given person was schizophrenic or not had no clues to that person's family background.

When the results finally came in, they seemed clear enough to justify all the trouble. Schizophrenia was concentrated in the biological relatives, although they had never spent time with the child they had given up for adoption. The adoptive relatives, the ones who had lived day in and day out with a person who became schizophrenic, showed only the same rate of schizophrenia as the population at large.

If you looked not only at schizophrenia but at the broader category called "schizophrenia spectrum disorders," the same pattern held. The rate of these schizophrenialike disorders among the biological relatives was 21 percent, among the adoptive relatives only 5 percent. (These findings also provided still another possible explanation of the observation that schizophrenics had strange parents. First had come the theory of Theodore Lidz and many others that parents with psychological troubles of their own gave birth to healthy children and then literally drove them mad. Back had come a countertheory: perhaps the parents were in fact normal and only appeared strange because of the lifelong stress and misery of dealing with a mad child. Now came a third possibility: if schizophrenia was a genetic disease, perhaps some parents seemed odd because they had a little of what their children had a lot of. "Thank you, Ted Lidz," says Paul Wender, today a psychiatrist at the University of Utah and in the 1960s a junior colleague of Kety's on the adoption studies. "You've shown us that the parents are gene carriers.")

These were dramatic findings — they made it hard to deny that schizophrenia was, at least in good measure, a genetic disease — and they swayed many observers. But no findings could have been conclusive, and many psychoanalysts remained unconvinced. Perhaps a bad mother could not cause schizophrenia in just any child. But what about a genetically vulnerable one: mightn't she just topple him right off the edge?

Kety and Rosenthal had not put an end to the debate, but their findings did shift the balance profoundly. The cause of schizophrenia remained a mystery, but it now seemed clear that schizophrenia ran in families because it was genetic, not because the families had done anything wrong. It was still possible that bad families caused the disease, at least in those who were genetically predisposed, but that was no longer an article of faith. Now it was a claim that required proof.

In time, in the genetic counterpart of a composer's theme and variations, researchers would explore countless versions of the adoption story. (Kety's nationwide study confirmed the findings of the Copenhagen-based one.) They looked, for example, at children born to schizophrenic parents and raised by those same parents. How did they compare with children born to schizophrenic parents but given up for adoption? As it turned out, both groups of children faced the same risk of schizophrenia — their risk was higher than most people's (because they had a schizophrenic parent), but there was no *extra* risk in living day in and day out with a schizophrenic parent.

Yet another variation on the adoption theme yielded the same result. This time researchers looked at children who had been born to nonschizophrenic parents but adopted by schizophrenic parents. (These parents had passed the adoption agencies' screening either by a fluke or because they had not yet developed schizophrenia at the time they adopted their children.) Were these children at increased risk of schizophrenia? Again, no. (They did tend to tell investigators, "You can't believe what a crazy home I was raised in.")

All these studies seemed to preach the same moral: schizophrenia was, in part, a genetic disease, and it was *not* caused by strange or erratic ways of parenting.

While the psychoanalysts were mustering a response to this latest round of attacks, they suffered a third hit. It was the simplest, and perhaps the most damaging, of the blows they weathered.

The setup was straightforward. In the mid-sixties, a well-regarded psychiatrist at UCLA, Philip May, randomly assigned 228 schizophrenic patients at the Camarillo State Hospital in California to one of five treatment groups: one group received only psychotherapy; one only drugs; one psychotherapy plus drugs; one electroshock; and one, the control group, only standard patient care. Patients were evaluated after treatment of six months to a year. (In later follow-up studies, May tracked down the patients three, four, and five years after his initial study.)

May's Schizophrenia Research Project was large in scale, sophisticated, and carefully conceived and carried out. In the ideologically charged world of psychiatry, this was as close as one could come to a neutral comparison. May published his findings in a series of papers over the years. The first of these publications, a book called *Treatment of Schizophrenia: A Comparative Study of Five Treatment Methods*, made the biggest splash. It was published in 1968, the same year that Kety and Rosenthal announced the results of their adoption studies.

May's key finding was that schizophrenic patients treated by drugs only or by the combination of drugs and psychotherapy fared the best; there was almost no difference between those two groups. The electroshock patients improved somewhat. The patients who did worst were those treated only by psychotherapy and those in the "control" group, who were not treated at all; these two groups, too, fared almost identically.

What did it all mean? Drugs, May concluded, were "undoubtedly the single treatment of choice at the present time — the only question is whether there is anything to be gained by giving individual psychotherapy as well." Psychotherapy without drugs, on the other hand, was "expensive and ineffective." So if psychotherapy was useful at all, it was not as a treatment in itself but merely as an adjunct to medication.

For the analysts, this was devastating news. (In a foreword to May's book, the psychiatrist Milton Greenblatt talked of May's "startling" and "traumatic" findings.) May expressed himself in properly flat scientific prose — he found "the effect of psychotherapy was nonsignificant" — but every reader could draw the conclusion for herself. For schizophrenic patients, it seemed, psychotherapy was beside the point.

In time, matters would grow even worse. Other schizophrenia studies looked at intensive psychoanalysis, as opposed to talk therapies that provided support and empathy but steered away from deep interpretations. Psychoanalysis, they concluded, was not merely ineffective but could in fact be harmful. For these damaged and profoundly out-of-touch patients, according to one survey, "overly aggressive treatments [were] analogous to pouring boiling oil into the wounds."

Psychoanalysts treating schizophrenia had been hit with three punishing blows in succession. The unexpected effectiveness of drugs, the adoption studies, and the treatment comparisons all pointed in the same direction — a person with schizophrenia had a brain disease; he was not on a spiritual journey or coping in an eccentric way with insufferable parents. His disease, moreover, was not one that could be talked away.

How did the analysts respond? Amazingly, and to the dismay of their critics, they lunged ahead seemingly as formidable as ever, like a grizzly bear that takes a bullet in the shoulder, the leg, *the chest!* and still continues to advance.

The antischizophrenia drugs that struck some observers as literally miraculous, for example, scarcely seemed worthy of notice to many others. Analysts waved off drugs as "chemical straitjackets" that subdued patients, muffling symptoms but not truly dealing with them. "Only a person can heal a person," Karl Menninger declared, unperturbed. The search for quick-fix miracles was, in any event, an old story. Every veteran psychoanalyst could tell stories of hopes falsely raised and quickly dashed; lobotomies and shock treatments had been greeted with fanfare not long before. Now came drugs, fool's gold in a different package but fool's gold all the same.

This disdain for medication was not simply a reflex prejudice. Even today the workings of antipsychotic drugs are poorly understood. At the time they were discovered, when no one had the least notion of how or why they worked, it was all the more natural to be suspicious. Nor did the unexpected effectiveness of drugs automatically put an end to the view that schizophrenia was caused by bad mothering. Think of a bullying boss whose yelling gives his subordinates headaches; aspirin might make their pain go away, but that says nothing about the *source* of their distress, the boss. And despite the talk of miracles, it was clear from the start that, at best, drugs relieved symptoms. They certainly did not cure.

For about 25 percent of schizophrenic patients, even today, drugs seem to help scarcely at all. For perhaps 5 percent of patients, they make matters worse. And they can have devastating side effects. The most feared is a twitching, jerking, tongue-wagging puppet dance called tardive dyskinesia. It is associated with long-term drug treatment, but it can continue even after a person stops taking medication, and no treatment is known.

•   •

But the analysts had a philosophical objection to drugs that ran deeper than their practical objections. The key to therapy, they believed, was "transference," the establishment of a relationship between patient and therapist. "We were told we should *not* give patients medication because it would interfere with the transference," recalls Allan Hobson, who began his psychiatric career in 1960. "If we really wanted them to get well, we had to leave their transference capabilities untainted by chemicals. The idea was that psychoanalysis was the treatment of choice, and drugs were actually counterproductive." (May's findings would later undermine this argument.)

As a measure of the depth of the antidrug hostility, consider Hobson's experience with a twenty-three-year-old psychotic named Bertal. When Hobson arrived at Harvard, on July 1, 1960, Bertal was his first patient. He lived at home with his mother, and she had brought him to the hospital; he had been hospitalized twice before. Bertal was hostile, anxious, almost silent. He was ill, Hobson's mentors told him, because of his mother's overprotectiveness. "We thought she was the problem," Hobson recalls. "I'm embarrassed to admit it, it sounds so preposterous, but we thought *she* was the pathogen."

Though drugs had been available since the early 1950s, Hobson was told not to give Bertal medication even during his worst episodes, for fear of hampering his ability to enter into a therapeutic dialogue. It was difficult advice to apply. One day shortly after he was admitted to the hospital, for example, Bertal was hallucinating about dive-bombers and the end of the world. Hobson, in the meantime, was trying to coax Bertal into his office so they could talk about his mother. Terrified that enemy planes were about to strafe him, Bertal raced out of the hospital and into the street and then crawled under a parked car to hide. Hobson chased behind him and sprawled out along the curbstone so that he could talk to his cowering patient. There he did his best to carry out a sidewalk psychoanalysis.

A few days later, during another hallucination, Bertal mistook a senior psychoanalyst for an enemy of some sort and punched him. It was deemed time to try medication. Soon Bertal was on Thorazine and able to sit calmly in Hobson's office, engaged in quiet, rational conversation about his relationship with his mother.

For psychiatric novices like Hobson, such experiences helped to dispel their infatuation with psychoanalysis. Older, more experienced therapists were more immune to doubt. Nor did the adoption studies dent their confidence.

Leonard Heston, the young psychiatrist who carried out the first adoption study, was a barely known novice, and easy to ignore, but Seymour Kety, too, was deeply suspect. For one thing, he was not even a psychiatrist, let alone a psychoanalyst. Worse still, his adoption studies involved nameless, faceless patients rather than individual, compelling case histories. His papers were thick with statistical arcana, standard deviations and degrees of freedom and chi squares, and utterly without reference to psychoanalytic doctrines. Psychiatrists like Yale's Lidz, an archrival of Kety's for many years, were indignant. *They* dealt with schizophrenic patients every day of their lives; Kety would not recognize a schizophrenic if he materialized from one of his countless charts and bit him. How dare this outsider presume to pronounce on their field?

The adoption studies, in fact, were triply suspect. They were associated with Kety, who was resented as an interloper; they relied on statistical arguments, which raised the specter of numerical hanky-panky; and they reflected a branch of medical research notorious for its sordid past. It was not only that with Nazism a relatively recent memory it was hard to hear the word "genetics" without thinking of "eugenics"; it was also that students of schizophrenia had special reason to be wary of genetic arguments. The first statistics on schizophrenia and heredity had been compiled by Ernst Rüdin, a pioneer in psychiatric genetics and a prominent figure in Nazi Germany. Rüdin had served on Hitler's Task Force of Heredity Experts, headed by Heinrich Himmler, which had formulated the 1933 laws mandating sterilization for those who were retarded, schizophrenic, or epileptic, among other conditions. He was, Robert Jay Lifton noted in *The Nazi Doctors,* "the predominant medical presence in the Nazi sterilization program," and in a special issue of his medical journal celebrating ten years of Nazi rule, he had praised Hitler for his "decisive . . . path-breaking step toward making racial hygiene a fact among the German people . . . and inhibiting the propagation of the congenitally ill and inferior." No one lumped Kety, a Jew born in Philadelphia, with Rüdin and his ilk, but it was no surprise that any talk of schizophrenia and genetics met an icy reception.

May's study comparing psychotherapy with other schizophrenia treatments was angrily rejected as well, though May was hardly an antipsychoanalytic zealot. Of the thirteen psychiatrists May assembled for his groundbreaking study, nine were psychoanalysts (one of the nine, Genevieve May, was May's wife). A key part of the study, the selection of "typical" schizophrenic patients, was carried out by two psychoanalysts.

But the criticism one heard again and again was that May had leapt to the wrong conclusion. Perhaps it was true that the psychotherapists he had watched had failed to do their patients much good. The correct conclusion, analysts bitterly insisted, was not that psychotherapy was the wrong treatment for schizophrenia but that May had chosen the wrong psychotherapists.

Later studies would attempt to resolve that question by examining the success rates of psychoanalytic stars as opposed to run-of-the-mill therapists. Stars or journeymen, the result turned out the same: psychotherapy was ineffectual; schizophrenia was a mountain that talk could not budge. *Still* the psychoanalysts stuck with their beliefs. Perhaps the stars weren't all they were reputed to be?

•   •

That pattern recurred time and again. No finding ever struck the analysts as decisive; they were able to show that even results that seemed utterly contrary to psychoanalytic theory turned out, once looked at in the proper light, to be confirmations of established doctrine. In 1962, for example, two psychiatrists studying the mothers of schizophrenic children reported a curious finding. These mothers, supposedly a cold and distant bunch, were more likely than a comparison group of mothers to have breast-fed their children. How could that be?

The explanation, according to Annemargret Osterkamp and David Sands, was that breast-feeding, in this case, was not a sign of closeness between mother and child. On the contrary, the mothers' eagerness to breast-feed their infants suggested "a need to deny negative feelings towards the children." This finding, the authors noted, was "consistent with a number of current concepts about psychopathology and early parent-child relationships" and supported the widespread belief that "schizophrenia has its roots in disturbed early interpersonal activities." It was true, the authors conceded, that birth complications had been more common among the schizophrenic children than the neurotic ones, but that, too, was easily explained. "It is likely that the birth difficulties often represent physical manifestations of the mothers' unconscious negative attitudes towards the children."

We all hang on to cherished beliefs in the face of contrary evidence. "He's really a good boy; he's just going through a phase," we say, or "She'll come back. I'm sure of it." Even in science and medicine, where objectivity supposedly prevails, the same pattern holds. Despite what the textbooks say about how new findings instantly render old beliefs obsolete, researchers cling to their pet theories with iron grips. One prominent exponent of the schizophrenogenic mother theory noted, for example, that many parents of schizophrenic children appeared quite normal. His response was not to question his theory but to marvel at the "subtle malignancy" of some parents.

But whether they recognized it or not, the psychoanalysts' day was done. With all their drawbacks, antipsychotic drugs meant that at least something could be done to help schizophrenics. Psychotherapists talked boldly of cures, but no one else could see them. Nor did the therapists' theories look any better than their treatments. The "schizophrenogenic mother," for example, had dominated the schizophrenia skyline like some malevolent Statue of Liberty. Now she had disappeared, or at least hidden herself so cunningly that the swarms of researchers studying adopted families had missed her.

Even the double bind theory, once hailed as a breakthrough in every analytic paper, had faded away. The problem, appropriately, was paradoxical: double binds were both too common and too rare. The very abundance of examples had been part of the appeal in the first place (Groucho Marx's not wanting to belong to a club that would be willing to have him as a member; young men and women being turned down for entry-level jobs because they lacked experience), but it should have been a danger signal. If double binds were everywhere, and double binds caused schizophrenia, how could schizophrenia be so rare?

On the other hand, common as they were, double binds were like policemen — they never seemed to be around when you needed them. A problem that "has plagued therapists and researchers alike," one of Bateson's successors acknowledged two decades after the theory's unveiling, "is that double binds are hard to find in the 'real' world . . . they are hard to locate and to identify as enduring patterns." When therapists studied dialogues between schizophrenic patients and their parents, no two observers could even agree on whether or not particular exchanges were in fact double binds, let alone agree on what their impact might be.

The inevitable result was that as the medical parade marched along, the analysts remained behind, true to their old beliefs. This was hardly a surprise. Pride, habit, and obstinacy all conspire to make researchers wary of challenges to their established views. They may go so far as to tinker with an old model, and in time it may become almost unrecognizable, but rarely will it be abandoned outright.* A scientist or therapist who has devoted a lifetime to a particular doctrine is unlikely to toss it casually aside; she is more likely to spend her days trying to salvage matters with a tune-up here, a new part there, perhaps a jury-rigged repair.

This is true even in the "hardest" of hard sciences, where the data are presumably the least open to interpretation. It was all the more true for the analysts, who tended to see themselves more as artists than as scientists. In time, old theories do give way to new — the schizophrenogenic mother is no more, for the reasons we have discussed above — but the transition is slow and difficult. "A new scientific truth does not triumph by convincing its opponents and making them see the light," the great physicist Max Planck once noted, "but rather because its opponents eventually die, and a new generation grows up that is familiar with it."

* The writer Jessica Mathews described an encounter with a student in a college biology class who proposed to show that plants exposed to prayer grow faster than plants that are not prayed over. Under Mathews's supervision, the student set up a careful experiment. It revealed no difference between plants in the prayed-over group and a control group. The student's conclusion? His prayers had not been heard because he had not been in a state of grace.

PART FOUR

Autism

The precipitating factor in infantile autism is the parent's wish that his child should not exist.

—BRUNO BETTELHEIM

CHAPTER TEN

A Mystery Proclaimed

*There have come to our attention· a number of children
whose condition differs . . . from anything reported so far.*

— LEO KANNER

FOR BRUNO BETTELHEIM, the knock on the door came in May of 1938. Bettelheim was thirty-four, an intellectual, a Jew, an aspiring psychoanalyst in the birthplace of psychoanalysis, Vienna. Hitler had just taken over Austria.

At first, it was unclear just what the arrest meant; though Bettelheim's passport was confiscated, he was not immediately imprisoned. That came soon enough. Within a few weeks, he and 700 or 800 other Jews and political opponents of the Nazi regime were shoved onto a train out of Vienna. Their destination, they would learn, was the concentration camp at Dachau.

After a night and a day of travel, amid nearly constant beatings, the train reached Dachau, near Munich. Almost every prisoner had been injured, and at least twenty had been killed. Bettelheim had been bayoneted and clubbed over the head and was bleeding badly. For him and most of his fellow prisoners, he wrote later, these first uprooted days were "the worst torture they would be exposed to, either physically or psychologically."

Bettelheim seemed fated to be one of the first to perish. An upper-middle-class intellectual in thick glasses, a married man who had taken over the family business on his father's death, he had been snatched out of the only world he had ever known. But brutal as the initiation into camp life was, Bettelheim held up better than he might have expected. "Most of all," he recalled later, "I felt pleased with myself because the tortures had not driven me out of my mind nor changed either my ability to think or my general point of view."

Bettelheim survived six months in Dachau and another six months in Buchenwald. By that time, he had shrunk to 86 pounds from his original 150. Then, for reasons that were never explained, he was told he was about to be released. His prison garb was traded for civilian clothes and his family was told to expect him. Suddenly, the SS announced that there would be no release. Bettelheim was flung back into the pit. In time, word came of a second release. A second time he was given new clothes; a second time his family prepared for him; a second time the SS canceled the release. Finally, word came of a third release. This one was for real.

For the rest of his long life, he would be tortured by the memory of the killings and suicides and humiliations he had witnessed. Plagued by nightmares and tormented by guilt for having survived when so many had died, he nonetheless continued to insist that he had gained something from his torment. What he had learned, he believed, was how humans react when they are trapped in "extreme situations," whenever they are helpless in the face of cruel and arbitrary power.

Like his colleagues who treated schizophrenics, Bettelheim went on to deal with people weighed down by overwhelming burdens. He and his peers knew what was happening in schizophrenia — Bettelheim was well informed on the psychology-versus-biology debate — but that was a ruckus taking place backstage. His focus was on a different disorder, rarer and perhaps stranger, called autism. In the decades to come, Bettelheim would argue that his wartime experiences provided the crucial clue to understanding this new-found affliction. It was a belief that would change the landscape for years to come.

In April 1943, an Austrian-born psychiatrist named Leo Kanner had startled his peers with a declaration that, among its other effects, helped to shape the course of Bruno Bettelheim's life. Kanner and Bettelheim shared a nationality and an interest in emotionally disturbed children. Apart from that, the two men had almost nothing in common. Kanner was modest and down-to-earth, a shrewd and gentle man perpetually wreathed in cigar smoke, "a pied piper whom no child can resist," as a colleague put it. Bettelheim was bad-tempered and fiercely judgmental. (He once wrote an essay taking Anne Frank and her family to task for hiding together, when splitting up would have been more prudent.) Even Kanner's rivals spoke fondly of him; even Bettelheim's colleagues stepped warily around him.

Of the two, Bettelheim is far better known. His story has recently been told in detail, for example, in Richard Pollak's book *The Creation of Dr. B.* Kanner has received far less notice. This is partly because he was a quieter character, and partly because Bettelheim worked harder (and more success-fully) at winning a mass audience. While Kanner spoke mainly to his fellow professionals, Bettelheim turned up everywhere, in newspapers and maga-zines, on radio and television. In the public mind, Bettelheim spoke for child psychiatry; in the eyes of his fellow psychiatrists, Kanner was by far the more important figure.

Kanner changed the face of psychiatry, and laid out the territory that Bettelheim would spend the rest of his life exploring, with a bold paper published in 1943 in a now-defunct medical journal called *The Nervous Child.* His goal, simply put, was to prove that there was something new under the sun. From his opening sentence, he made sure that no one could miss his point.

"Since 1938," he began his now-classic paper, "there have come to our attention a number of children whose condition differs so markedly and uniquely from anything reported so far, that each case merits — and, I hope, will eventually receive — a detailed consideration of its fascinating peculiarities." In clear and jargon-free prose, without a single footnote, Kanner went on to describe eight boys and three girls who suffered from a previously undescribed and baffling disorder. Kanner named it "autism," from the Greek for "self," for the strangest quality of these strange children was that they seemed to be utterly without interest in other people.

Kanner's judgment carried weight. In the melancholy knowledge of how a child's development can go awry, he was a match for anyone in the world. He had founded the Johns Hopkins Children's Psychiatric Clinic in 1930. Over the years, he had seen countless disturbed and disabled children. Autism, he felt sure, was something new. Charles, for example, was a four-year-old who had been brought to Kanner's clinic by his bewildered mother. "The thing that upsets me most," she said, "is that I can't reach my baby." The child seemed perfectly healthy, physically, and he was certainly bright. "When he was one-and-a-half, he could discriminate between eighteen symphonies," his mother recalled in notes she put together for Kanner. "He recognized the composer as soon as the first movement started. He would say 'Beethoven.' "

On the other hand, *something* was off, though it was hard to pinpoint the problem. "At about the same age," the mother went on, "he began to spin toys and lids of bottles and jars by the hour. . . . He would watch it and get severely excited and jump up and down in ecstasy. Now he is interested in reflecting light from mirrors and catching reflections. When he is interested in a thing, you cannot change it. He would pay no attention to me and show no recognition of me if I enter the room."

Of all the symptoms, this remoteness seemed the most frightening. "The most impressive thing," Charles's mother observed, "is his detachment and his inaccessibility. He walks as if he is in a shadow, lives in a world of his own where he cannot be reached."

In this brilliant first paper on autism — after half a century still the best introduction to the subject — Kanner highlighted virtually every symptom that later researchers would see as telltale. There was the endless spinning; the parroting of other people's words; the hours spent on such "projects" as opening a door and closing it and opening it again; the fury if toys or books or blocks happened not to be arranged in some special and mysterious order.

More impressive still, Kanner managed not to be distracted by some crucial-sounding *differences* between his patients. Three of his autistic children didn't speak at all, for example, while the others displayed an "astounding vocabulary" and rattled off poems and lists of the presidents and even lullabies in foreign languages. But none of the children used language in the ordinary way, as a means of communication. Some appeared severely retarded, and others displayed formidable memories and other Rain Man–like gifts.

In the end, Kanner decided that Charles's mother had it right. The symptom that towered above all the others was the sense of aloneness. These were children isolated behind invisible but nonetheless unbreachable prison walls. "Every one of the children," Kanner reported, "upon entering the office immediately went after blocks, toys, or other objects, without paying the least attention to the persons present. It would be wrong to say that they were not aware of the presence of persons. But the people, so long as they left the child alone, figured in about the same manner as did the desk, the bookshelf, or the filing cabinet."

As best anyone could tell, these autistic patients cared as little about members of their own family as they did about Kanner and the other strangers who worked with him. Even as infants, they had never shown the least sign of anticipation when a parent moved to pick them up, not a smile or a burble or a beaming eye. Looking for a cuddle from their child, mothers and fathers were left trying to hug "a sack of flour."

The children remained impassive as they grew older. Kanner tried hard to keep his tone objective, but a note of eeriness kept creeping in. "The father or mother or both may have been away for an hour or a month," he wrote. "At their homecoming, there is no indication that the child has been even aware of their absence."

In hindsight, autism seems to have been floating around, unrecognized, for centuries. One early case, conspicuous not least because it is well documented, is especially tantalizing. In 1800 in Paris, society was all atwitter about the discovery of "the wild boy of Aveyron." He had been found wandering naked in the forest one winter day, hunting for food. The child looked to be about twelve, but he might as well have dropped from another planet: unable to speak, unresponsive to questioners, unable even to hint at who he was or where he had come from, he was utterly alone in the world.

At a time when *the* great topic of the day was the effect of society on "natural man," the discovery of this mysterious boy seemed heaven-sent. In every salon and café, Paris debated whether this was a brute in human form, or an innocent child of nature, or an outcast whom society had tossed on its refuse heap. Newspapers carried the latest odds on whether "Victor," as he had been named, would ever learn civilized ways.

A physician named Itard took Victor into his home. (Their story is told in Truffaut's *Wild Child*.) The silent boy spent hours a day wrapped head to toe in a blanket, rocking back and forth. Despite five years of hard and patient labor, Itard never could teach his pupil to speak. And yet Victor had pockets of ability that were surprising in someone who in many ways appeared severely retarded. He learned some sign language, for example, and he took great care with such everyday household rituals as setting the table or preparing a simple pot of beans.

So he was capable of learning. Disconcertingly, though, Victor seemed barely aware of other people. "I am dismayed to see the natural man so egotistical," reported one of his first observers.

But was this egotism or was it a failure to connect with anyone else? To anyone who has read Kanner's accounts of children who treated their parents as objects rather than as people, Victor's behavior sounds uncannily familiar. Victor had "no sense of gratitude toward the man who feeds him," one dismayed contemporary reported, "but takes the food as he would take it from the ground."

Listen to clinical tales of autism even today and the researchers' astonishment shines through. One doctor recalls a story of an autistic girl, a bright twelve-year-old, who reported to him that "Joanie is making a funny noise." It turned out that Joanie was weeping bitterly. The sound had registered, but not its meaning.

Another doctor asked an autistic teenager whose mother had died of cancer how he was doing. The boy was a "high-functioning" fifteen-year-old with a form of autism called Asperger syndrome. "Oh, I am all right," he replied, in the oddly formal diction sometimes seen in autism. "You see, I have Asperger syndrome, which makes me less vulnerable to the loss of loved ones than are most people."

Among autistic people who speak — half are mute throughout their lives — that flat, robotic tone is characteristic. Another autistic young man, this one a twelve-year-old, happened to see a booklet on Asperger syndrome on his doctor's desk. He skimmed it and saw that he himself seemed to fit the description but showed no emotional reaction to the news. "Now I can tell my classmates why I pace the school-yard briskly ten times up and down each break all the year round," he declared.

Kanner had singled out two defining traits of autism. Emotional aloofness was the first. The second, which was just as strange, was an "obsessive desire for the maintenance of sameness." No change in routine could be tolerated — let a single magazine in a haphazard stack be in a different position than yesterday, or one toy block in a jumble of blocks be turned at a slightly different angle than it had been left, and the autistic child might fall into a panic.

Parents became hostage to their child's unyielding rages. One mother compiled a list of unexpected changes that might trigger "disaster": a new arrangement of furniture, the sun not shining, a traffic light not working, a car that would not start. An autistic four-year-old named Ian wept uncontrollably if his parents deviated in the smallest detail from their usual route on a drive, or if they served him square crackers rather than round ones, or six pieces of tofu rather than seven.

In San Diego, one mother quickly learned that her autistic son would scream inconsolably unless she wore a particular dress, gray and white with pink flowers. In desperation, she ordered several identical versions for herself and one in a different size for her mother, who sometimes came to help, and another for her mother-in-law. Her son seemed not to care *who* wore the dress, so long as it was the right dress.

There is virtually no exaggerating the insistence on routine. Ian has watched the tape of *Charlotte's Web* some 1,500 times, his parents replacing each version as it wears out. A UCLA psychiatrist, Kenneth Colby, recalls language experiments in which he provided autistic children with typewriters. "A normal kid would sit down and type 'abc' or '12345,' " Colby says. "An autistic child would push the 'x' key, and he would sit there and push that key all day, every day, for three weeks at a time."

Autistic children do play, after a fashion, but the fashion is not the usual one. Dolls and stuffed animals hold little appeal; a flashlight, or an empty spool of thread, or a bucket of nuts and bolts might be far more enticing. "When we'd bring our [autistic] son to Grandma's house," the psychologist Bernard Rimland recalls, "she'd open the door and he'd run right past her to the closet where she kept the vacuum cleaner. He'd play with the vacuum cleaner for a couple of hours, and then when we'd leave he'd run by her again, never having said hello to her at all."

Such accounts share an uncanny resemblance. One mother remembers her autistic daughter, at nine months old, sitting in a sandbox in a New York City playground, oblivious to the running and shouting all around her. She sat amid the tumult, pouring sand through her fingers, spellbound, for an hour and a half. An autistic woman named Temple Grandin described an almost identical scene from *her* childhood. "I could sit for hours on the beach watching sand dribbling through my fingers," she recalled. "I'd study each individual grain of sand as it flowed between my fingers. Each grain was different, and I was like a scientist studying the grains under a microscope. As I scrutinized their shapes and contours, I went into a trance which cut me off from the sights and sounds around me."

Case histories from a continent away and two centuries ago strike the identical notes. Victor, the wild boy of Aveyron, was fascinated by "a ray of sun reflected upon a mirror in his room and turning about on the ceiling, [or] a glass of water let fall drop by drop from a certain height upon his finger tips when he was in the bath." Such entertainments were enough, an observer noted, "to divert and delight this child of nature almost to the point of ecstasy."

In 1951, eight years after Kanner's landmark paper, a Dutch psychiatrist, D. Arn. van Krevelen, remained dubious about the existence of this new affliction. He had yet to see an autistic child himself, and none had ever been described in the European literature. Then an autistic girl was brought in. She was "as much like those described by Kanner," an astonished van Krevelen reported, "as one raindrop is like another."

Parents were baffled and terrified. What in the world was going on with their children? They looked perfectly normal, after all, with none of the telltale stigmata of brain damage or retardation. Many seemed not only unimpaired but positively beautiful. And while some autistic children came into the world kicking and screaming, others had seemed bright and friendly, even precocious, until around the time of their first birthday. Then their ties to the world began to fray. Or, more precisely, their ties to the people in that world. Though a handful of sand could retain its fascination indefinitely, human beings seemed to go unnoticed. Parents reported that their autistic children might ignore visitors altogether or perhaps climb across their backs or crawl over their heads. When she brought her son to the beach, one mother said, he would walk straight to his destination even if his journey carried him across newspapers or hands or feet or torsos. He made no effort to swerve onto people, but he also made no effort to avoid them.

This obliviousness to people was so marked that Kanner was able to use it as an informal diagnostic test. If he stuck a normal child with a pin, the child would whirl around to see who had poked him. An autistic child never seemed to connect the pin with the person who held it; he would ignore Kanner and look at the pin itself, or he would look at the hand that held it. Again and again, parents made a similar observation. Their autistic children often treated them as if they were tools and not human beings — a child might grab his mother's hand (without looking at her face) and put it on a doorknob or a water faucet.

Even after years of living in the same household, this painful "shunning" persisted. Another mother could recall only a single occasion when her autistic daughter had seemed glad to see her. On a particular Friday afternoon, "her face had lit up when she'd seen me, and she'd taken off toward me at a run," she remembered years later. The little girl was five years old. "I was so thrilled I had stood there transfixed with my arms out, thinking, 'She loves me.' But she had stopped when she was five feet away, shutting off, and she had never repeated the behavior."

A woman named Ruth Sullivan tells a similar story. The fifth of her seven children, Joseph, is autistic. Now thirty-six years old, Joseph was one of Dustin Hoffman's models for *Rain Man*. The movie stuck faithfully to the facts of autism, Sullivan says. The feats that seem most incredible — Raymond's memorizing the telephone book, or recognizing at a glance that a box contained 246 matches, or multiplying 1,739 by 5,826 in his head as quickly as someone else could punch the numbers into a calculator — are all taken from life. In only one instance, says Sullivan, did Hollywood stretch the truth. "The one scene I had the most trouble with," she says, "was probably the one that most people had the least trouble with—when the girl kissed him in the elevator." To picture Raymond enduring the intimacy of even a single gentle kiss, Sullivan says, was almost unimaginable.

Why? Why do these people act as if they have no emotional ties to the rest of the human race?

Temple Grandin, a professor at Colorado State University and a celebrated figure in the world of autism, has probed that question herself in two strange and compelling autobiographies. She can understand "simple, strong, universal" emotions, Grandin says, but she can't imagine what it would be like to love another person. Subtle feelings are even more elusive. Grandin has never known what it is to feel embarrassed or shy, for example, and the countless social cues that pass between people leave her at a loss. She describes herself as "an anthropologist on Mars," always trying to guess the mysterious codes of the puzzling creatures she lives among.

Her diagnosis is simple. "The emotion circuit's not hooked up—that's what's wrong."

Temple Grandin has a Ph.D. in animal science. Her specialty is the design of feedlots and slaughterhouses. Her approach to the world could hardly differ more from that of Leo Kanner. Kanner's explanation of autism was far less mechanical, and far more influential.

In his first paper on autism, however, he stuck remarkably close to a "just the facts, ma'am" presentation. Only at the very end of the thirty-four-page article did he venture a few steps beyond the observable. "It is not easy to evaluate the fact that all of our patients have come of highly intelligent parents," he wrote, and he noted one other "prominent" fact.

"In the whole group," Kanner wrote, "there are very few really warm-hearted fathers and mothers." Instead, parents and other relatives tended to be "strongly preoccupied with abstractions of a scientific, literary, or artistic nature, and limited in genuine interest in people. Even some of the happiest marriages are rather cold and formal affairs. Three of the marriages were dismal failures. The question arises whether or to what extent this fact has contributed to the condition of the children."

These first mentions of warm hearts and cold marriages sounded almost casual. Soon such remarks would become the pivot of the entire autism debate.

But in this first paper, Kanner was not yet ready for explanations, and we can see him debating with himself. A minute before, he had hinted that autistic children were aloof because their parents were standoffish. No sooner had he blurted it out than he took it back. "The children of our group," he noted, "have all shown their extreme aloneness from the very beginning of life." How could parents be to blame for a condition that had always been present?

Now he had convinced himself. As if to prevent any possibility of further wavering, Kanner repeated the point in more emphatic form and in a place that no one could miss. The final paragraph of this first, landmark paper began with a flat declaration: "We must, then, assume that these children have come into the world with innate inability" to form emotional ties with other people, "just as other children come into the world with innate physical or intellectual handicaps."

That was in 1943. By 1949, Kanner had reversed course. The about-face would be crucial for an entire generation of parents.

In his first paper, Kanner's sample of autistic children had numbered eleven. In the next six years, he added more than fifty new cases to his tally, and other psychiatrists added case histories of their own. With this wealth of new material, Kanner saw that he had blundered badly. The true explanation of autism was now at hand, and it was obvious. How had he missed it?

In a new paper, he spelled out the latest message in unequivocal tones. "The parents' behavior toward the children must be seen to be fully appreciated," Kanner wrote. "Maternal lack of genuine warmth is often conspicuous in the first visit to the clinic. As they come up the stairs, the child trails forlornly behind the mother, who does not bother to look back. The mother accepts the invitation to sit down in the waiting room, while the child sits, stands, or wanders about at a distance. Neither makes a move toward the other."

Kanner noted, for instance, that a patient named Donald had "sat down next to his mother on the sofa. She kept moving away from him as though she could not bear the physical proximity. When Donald moved along with her, she finally told him coldly to go and sit on a chair."

Fathers fared no better. "Many of the fathers hardly know their autistic children," Kanner reported. He claimed to be speaking literally. Kanner asked one father if he would recognize any of his children if they passed him on a busy street. He thought for a moment and then replied, with "unemotional objectivity," that, no, he was not sure that he would.

The parents weren't harsh, Kanner conceded, but they were inept, utterly at a loss as to what children want. "The children were, as modern phraseology usually has it, 'planned and wanted.' Yet the parents did not seem to know what to do with the children when they had them. They lacked the warmth which the babies needed." Fathers cared only about their work, and mothers were hovering and oversolicitous rather than loving and kind. "They were anxious to do a good job, and this meant mechanized service of the kind which is rendered by an overconscientious gasoline station attendant."

Having described the parents — and no one had a sharper clinical eye — Kanner moved briefly and matter-of-factly to the obvious follow-up, the impact on children of such maladroit parents. Not a melodramatic man, he allowed himself a single rhetorical flourish, one last change on the theme of the parents' failure of "warmheartedness": "Most of the patients were exposed from the beginning to parental coldness, obsessiveness, and a mechanical type of attention to material needs only. They were the objects of observation and experiment conducted with an eye on . . . performance rather than with genuine warmth and enjoyment. They were kept neatly in refrigerators which did not defrost. Their withdrawal seems to be an act of turning away from such a situation to seek comfort in solitude."

It is hard to imagine a theory that could have been sent into the world with more bona fides than this picture of "refrigerator" parents who rejected their own children. Leo Kanner was a world-renowned physician acclaimed as the "father of child psychiatry"; he was director of child psychiatry at Johns Hopkins Hospital; and he had literally written the book in his field, an enormous and authoritative text called simply *Child Psychiatry.* He had discovered autism and named it, and now he had explained it.

The explanation would soon make its way — suitably modified by others — out of the medical journals and into the popular culture. Against the wave of books and magazine articles preaching the new gospel, what chance did a mere mother have?

February 12, 1967, was a Sunday, and Sundays were generally good days in Bill and Annabel Stehli's household. It was free time, a chance for the young couple to put their mundane worries to one side and do nothing more strenuous than settle down with the newspaper.

Their problems, their friends assured them, weren't far different from anyone else's. Bill was a stockbroker who longed to chuck it all and become an artist; Annabel was a writer with few credits but grand ambitions. Bill was handsome and dashing, a good dancer and an elegant dresser. Annabel was tall and thin, a mile-a-minute talker, an amateur actress, a self-described "nouveau pauvre" member of an old family fallen on hard times. The young couple lived in Brooklyn Heights, in an apartment that would be nice if they could manage to fix it up. They had two children, both girls. It was the younger one they worried about.

Georgie was two, and she had always been a good baby — unnaturally good, it sometimes seemed — but when she was still only a month old, her mother had become "absolutely certain" that something was profoundly wrong.

"I couldn't get her to smile," Annabel recalled. "I tried to chalk everything up to her prematurity, thinking she'd catch up, but I was afraid she was retarded, and was baffled by how she didn't seem to care whether or not she was held, fussed over, sung to, or cooed at. She acted detached, as if she lived in her own world, as content as a goldfish. I thought it was crazy, but I felt snubbed by her. I felt rejected by my own baby."

At any rate, nothing out of the ordinary had happened *this* day. Bill

Stehli had settled in with the Sunday *New York Times* business section. Annabel picked up the *Times Magazine* and flipped to a column called "Parent and Child." Each week a different expert chose a topic to discuss. "Our studies concentrate on autistic children," Annabel read, "youngsters who have totally shut themselves off from all relations with others and who have the potential for good or even superior intelligence."

Annabel Stehli had never heard of autism or the article's author, a psychologist named Bruno Bettelheim. But he wrote as if he knew everything about *her.* "Our work demonstrates how important it is that from birth on the child gets responses from the environment that encourage his spontaneous moves toward the world," Bettelheim declared. "He should not be ignored or overpowered." The stakes were high. "Things may go terribly wrong if the world is experienced as basically frustrating too soon."

Too shaken to share the article with her husband, Annabel put the magazine away. She felt, she said later, "as though I were being accused of a crime I didn't even know I'd committed."

Two weeks later, she came across a review in the *Times* of Bettelheim's latest book, an account of autism called *The Empty Fortress.* "Foremost among the handful of psychiatrists and psychologists who have dedicated themselves to unraveling the puzzle of autistic behavior," it read, "is Bruno Bettelheim. No brief review can do justice to his wisdom or his compassion."

By summer, Annabel had worked up the nerve to take *The Empty Fortress* out of the library. It was time to learn something about autism. Three decades later, sitting in a handsome living room in suburban Connecticut, she recalls the scene precisely. "I can tell you everything about that day," she says quietly. "We lived in a duplex in Brooklyn Heights, the living room walls were light yellow with white woodwork, it was a cheery day with the sun pouring in the windows, and this evil tome was sitting there on the dining room table, giving off radiation. If I'd been a Geiger counter, I would have been making a *lot* of noise."

Timidly approaching the book, she flipped it open at random. Autism is "a defense against unbearable anxiety," she read. "The source of this anxiety is not an organic impairment, but the child's evaluation of the conditions of his life as being utterly destructive."

"It was just a terrifying thing for me," Stehli recalls today, "because here was someone who was assassinating my character, and my sense was that most people agreed with him. I couldn't read most of it. It was too painful. But I got the picture. It was probably like a Jew in Germany in 1936 reading something by Hitler about what Jews are like."

A Jew in Germany would have had the tiny consolation of knowing at least that the slurs directed at her were false. Stehli was not so self-assured. Could Bettelheim's charges be true? "I thought he might be right. I was sure I had taken advantage of the fact that Georgie was such a 'good' baby and could entertain herself so easily, and I had left her too much to her own devices." Horrified and bewildered, Stehli tried to think it through. "Could it be that I had within me such awesome power as to be able to create a condition as dire as autism? What was I, a kind of maternal witch?"

Georgie's behavior grew more disturbing through that summer and fall. In nursery school, she sat immobile, not caring whether she was on a teacher's lap or on the floor. At home, she stood in a corner, always the same one, eyes rolled back in her head, arms pinned to her sides, spinning in endless circles.

In the meantime, life had fallen apart in an almost unbelievable way. Georgie's five-year-old sister had been diagnosed with leukemia and had been given a year to live. Bill Stehli had fallen in love with a close friend's wife and had left his family for her. Now Annabel Stehli had an appointment with a New York psychiatrist named Derek Small, to find out once and for all what Georgie's problem was.

The answer was quick in coming. "There is no question in my mind that your daughter is disturbed," Small said. "She is an autistic child, and she is also retarded." Annabel protested in disbelief; Small ignored the interruption. "She is obviously retarded and low-functioning, and a great deal of it is due to the fact that you" — he looked straight at Annabel — "have avoided contact with her."

"The words 'avoided contact,'" Stehli would say later, "hit me like bullets, but I tried to fight on. Actually, I would have preferred bullets."

CHAPTER ELEVEN

The Buchenwald Connection

My reactions to events . . . were strongly influenced by the experience of having been at the mercy of others who believed they knew how I should live — or rather that I should not live.

— BRUNO BETTELHEIM

BRUNO BETTELHEIM had fled Europe in 1939 and headed for the United States, where he soon landed at the University of Chicago. There he taught courses on psychology and education and, more important, served as head of a university-run experimental school for emotionally disturbed children.

It was called the Orthogenic School (the name, which predated Bettelheim, reflected a focus on child development and came from two Greek words, *orthos* meaning "straight" and *genos* meaning "origin"). In the early 1950s, the school enrolled its first autistic children. Their numbers would grow over the years, but they always remained a small minority. *The Empty Fortress*, published in 1967, was Bettelheim's third book on the school and its work. It was his breakthrough work, the book that put him on the map as the best-known authority on autism.

A captivating storyteller — this alone set him apart from most of his peers — Bettelheim had been proclaiming his view of autism for years. In 1959, for example, he had written a remarkable essay for the *American Journal of Sociology* on "feral children." These supposed "wild children" were solitary creatures of the forest. According to legend and folklore, they raised themselves, like the wild boy of Aveyron, or were raised by wolves, like Romulus and Remus. Such tales have ancient roots, but the topic had been revived in the 1940s when two mute, terrified, violent "wolf girls" were reportedly discovered in India.

Bettelheim had no patience for such talk. These were not half-wild creatures, he insisted, but autistic children whose parents had abandoned them. Their strange, animal-like behavior was "the result of the inhumanity of some persons, usually their parents, and not the result, as has been imagined, of the humanity of animals, such as wolves." The true story was not that wolves can act like parents but that parents can act like wolves.

Bettelheim had published a second article on autism in 1959, this one in *Scientific American,* and it brought his views to a wider and more influential audience. This was a much-acclaimed account of a nine-year-old named Joey, a "mechanical boy" who believed that he himself was a machine who was run by other machines. Before eating, for example, Joey would plug an imaginary wire into an imaginary outlet so that the current could power his digestion.

Other articles in the same issue of the magazine dealt with such topics as radiation belts and earthquake waves. Bettelheim's case history of "a child who had been robbed of his humanity," presented with his customary flair, stood out from this austere fare like a fairy tale in a chemistry textbook. It was a fairy tale with a moral. "I have never seen a child really accepted and loved by his parents who developed childhood schizophrenia [as autism was sometimes called]," Bettelheim declared.

Autism had been Bettelheim's great interest even before he realized what he was seeing. Between 1932 and 1938, long before Kanner's landmark paper, Bettelheim and his wife had brought an autistic little girl, supposedly "a 'hopeless' case," into their home to live. But it was only at Chicago, in the mid-fifties, that Bettelheim grasped the true meaning of autism.

It was the arrival of a ten-year-old girl named Anna at the experimental school that opened his eyes. She was wild, uncontrollable. Neighbors had had to call the police to keep Anna from harming their children. Even institutions could not hold her. In one psychiatric hospital, she had spent her days crouched in a comer of a maximum-security room, naked because she tore off her clothes, screaming and beating the walls.

She had been born in Poland during World War II, in the grimmest of circumstances. Her parents were Jews trying to hide from the Nazis in a small, earthen cellar beneath the home of a sympathetic farmer. In this cellar, Anna was conceived and born to ill-matched parents who could barely abide one another. On several occasions, the Germans searched the farmhouse, and once they fired shots into it, but they never found the huddled family cowering beneath the trapdoor. Anna and her parents survived the war, and Anna was diagnosed as autistic by a doctor in a displaced persons camp.

Though Anna had never experienced the concentration camps, her story brought Bettelheim's own wartime ordeal sharply to mind. He realized, finally, the bond that linked the two major experiences of his life, his year at Dachau and Buchenwald and his work with emotionally disturbed children. "I had been unable fully to cope with either of these two experiences in isolation," he wrote. "In time, as I saw their interconnection, I could make better sense of them."

The interconnection he saw would transform the way psychiatrists thought about autism. Leo Kanner had chastised parents like Annabel and Bill Stehli as "refrigerator" mothers and "undemonstrative" fathers. Bruno Bettelheim was about to make those descriptions seem like love pats.

"The youngster who develops childhood schizophrenia," Bettelheim declared, "seems to feel about himself and his life exactly as the concentration camp prisoner felt about his: deprived of hope, and totally at the mercy of destructive irrational forces bent on using him for their goals, irrespective of his."

Suddenly, the autistic child's mysterious symptoms were not so mysterious. Wasn't the solitary, withdrawn child in just the same situation as the prisoner whose only hope for survival was to vanish into the background, to avoid eye contact, to disappear into a private world of fantasy? Self-effacement was a prisoner's best strategy, after all, and what was autism but self-effacement taken to the extreme?

If anything, Bettelheim went on, prisoners at the mercy of SS guards were *better* off than autistic children in their parents' home, because the prisoners had at least known a different way of life. "The difference between the plight of prisoners in a concentration camp and the conditions which lead to autism and schizophrenia in children is, of course, that the child has never had a previous chance to develop much of a personality."

That "of course" was characteristic, and devastating. Who could dispute a figure who spoke with such authority? Who could muster credentials to match Dachau and Buchenwald and two decades of daily experience with profoundly disturbed children?

The Empty Fortress was rapturously received. Critics praised Bettelheim for his insight and lauded him for his devotion in giving years of his life to these most difficult and least grateful of patients. The psychiatrist Robert Coles, widely admired for his own civic conscience, caught the prevailing mood in an essay on Bettelheim entitled "A Hero of Our Time." Bettelheim had "taken on the hardest imaginable challenges," Coles wrote, "and done so with almost fierce pride." Even so, Coles acknowledged, those efforts might nonetheless prove futile, for "the child's parents may pose a hopeless obstacle, or the child may have arrived too late [at the Orthogenic School], already so old that no one and nothing can make enough difference to undo what years of extreme and unforgiving self-centeredness have established."

The book embedded Bettelheim's version of autism in the minds of enlightened readers everywhere. It was Bettelheim's magnum opus, his summary of years of watching and thinking. Always forthright to the point of brutality, he took special pains to insure that there was no mistaking his

Freud, about 1914, in a photo taken by one of his sons. Freud was in his fifties and at the height of his powers. A. W. Freud et al. / Mark Paterson & Associates

Frieda Fromm-Reichmann was one of America's best-loved psychiatrists. Wise, kind, and grandmotherly, she was also the first to use the term "schizophrenogenic mother." The phrase, literally "schizophrenia-producing mother," served as an indictment of a generation of parents. CPC Health Corporation, Chestnut Lodge Hospital Library

Gregory Bateson. An anthropologist (and Margaret Mead's third husband), Bateson also ventured into far distant intellectual fields. He devised the influential "double bind" theory of schizophrenia, which argued that parents drove their children mad by habitually speaking to them in self-contradictory "damned if you do, damned if you don't" riddles. Courtesy Lois C. Bateson

Theodore Lidz, Yale psychiatrist. Lidz was perhaps the most prominent and the most dogmatic of those who attributed schizophrenia to bad parenting. "We now know that the patient's family of origin is always severely disturbed," he declared.
Courtesy Theodore Lidz

R. D. Laing. The British psychiatrist had the charisma of a rock star. He dazzled his audiences in the sixties with the message that schizophrenia could be "break-through" as well as "breakdown." The schizophrenic was a voyager on a heroic journey of discovery. © Kirk Tougas

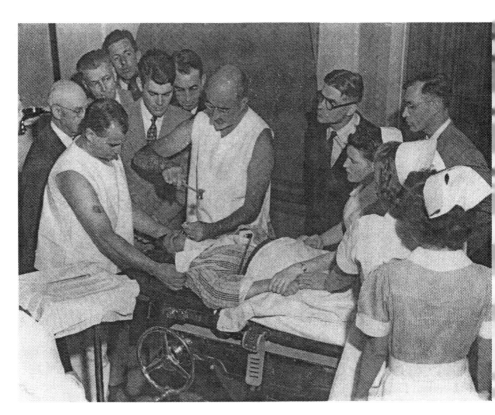

Dr. Walter Freeman, the greatest American advocate of lobotomy as a cure for mental illness, prepares to demonstrate an ice pick lobotomy. Conventional brain surgery required drilling holes in the skull; here the brain was entered by way of the eye socket. Part of the appeal of psychoanalysis was that alternatives like this were so brutal. UPI / Corbis-Bettmann

Seymour Kety was the first scientific director of the National Institute of Mental Health. Kety was the most prominent of those striving to find a biochemical explanation of schizophrenia and the archenemy of those who believed the disease was caused by bad parenting. Christopher S. Johnson. Reprinted with permission from McLean Hospital, Belmont, MA.

Leo Kanner, the Johns Hopkins psychiatrist. In 1943 Kanner wrote a groundbreaking paper that proclaimed the existence of a new psychiatric disorder. He named it "autism," for "self," because the strangest feature of the eleven children Kanner described was that they seemed utterly without interest in other people.
Blakeslee Group

Bruno Bettelheim, the University of Chicago psychologist. Bettelheim was a much acclaimed authority on autism. He accused parents of causing their child's autism. "All my life," he declared, "I have been working with children whose lives have been destroyed because their mothers hated them."
University of Chicago Library

Temple Grandin. The best-known person with autism, Grandin is a professor in the animal sciences department at Colorado State University. She can sense intuitively what cattle are feeling, she says, but she has enormous difficulty fathoming the moods and motives of her fellow humans.
© Rosalie Winard

Harry Harlow. A renowned psychologist at the University of Wisconsin, Harlow studied such questions as why infants are devoted to their mothers. He took infant monkeys from their mothers and turned them over to puppetlike surrogates. They vastly preferred soft, cuddly surrogates to bare, wire ones (right). The behavior of autistic children looked to Harlow like that of these timid monkeys, and he concluded that autism was caused by mothers who were little more than wire surrogates. Both photos Harlow Primate Laboratory, University of Wisconsin

Nikolaas Tinbergen and a pair of courting gulls. Tinbergen won the Nobel Prize in 1973 for a lifetime's study of these birds and other animals. On the basis of this "highly relevant" research, he announced that he had unlocked the mystery of autism. The problem was bad parenting, which made children as skittish as gulls. The remedy was "a solid dose of 'supermothering,'" especially hugging. Both photos Lary Shaffer

Bernard Rimland and his son Mark. When Mark was born, in 1956, his incessant screaming and odd mannerisms exhausted and bewildered his parents. On learning that Mark was autistic, Bernard Rimland set out to read everything ever written about this new and barely understood condition. He eventually wrote his own book attacking conventional psychiatric wisdom and defending parents of autists. © Carol Constantine

Howard Hughes, the billionaire industrialist and recluse. A victim of obsessive-compulsive disorder, Hughes ended his days trapped in a hotel room and encumbered by endless rituals. These photos show him in 1947, when he was one of the most recognizable men in the world, and (apparently) in 1972 (UPI published the second photo but could not confirm that Hughes was the subject).
UPI / Corbis-Bettmann

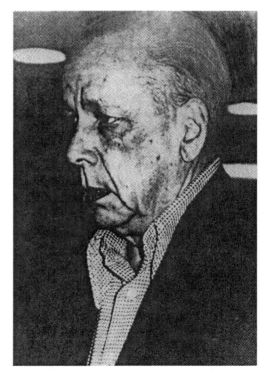

message. "Throughout this book," he declared, "I state my belief that the precipitating factor in infantile autism is the parent's wish that his child should not exist."

It is important to note that from the mid-1940s to at least the mid-1960s, the antiparent message was proclaimed everywhere. Bettelheim was a loud voice, but only one voice, in a large chorus. Psychiatrists filled learned journals with debates on the nature of parental misdeeds — were the mothers of autistic children too remote, say, or were they too engulfing? — but the underlying premise, that the parents were at fault, was conventional wisdom.

There were two sets of reasons for this orgy of parent-bashing, one simple and the other more arcane. The simple reasons had nothing to do with the intricacies of psychiatric or psychoanalytic theory. On the contrary, they arose from a feature of autism that struck even the most casual observer: the children *looked* bright and alert — in short, normal. "These were beautiful children," says Anne Donnellan, a University of Wisconsin psychologist and the editor of *Classic Readings in Autism*, "so right away there was a problem. Because people will believe almost anything about someone who looks strange. But if someone looks 'normal,' then they insist on an explanation. In the postwar period, that meant someone to blame, and the blame usually fell on Mom."

Plainly *something* had happened to these lovely children. Moreover, it had happened when they were very young, for autism is typically diagnosed by age two. And so parents were the obvious suspects, even more than in the case of schizophrenia, which appears only at age fifteen or twenty. Who else but the parents had been with the child from birth? Who else had been caught at the scene of the crime?

Any jury might have been suspicious. As it happened, this particular jury was composed almost exclusively of psychiatrists, whose training and inclination was to look for psychological explanations rather than physiological ones. There was little doubt what they would find.

That jury-packing was not the result of some dark conspiracy. "Remember," Donnellan says, "that at the time there was almost no notion that psychology and neurology were linked. From the turn of the century until very recent times, disorders belonged either to 'bodiless psychology' or 'soulless neurology,' in Oliver Sacks's phrase." And even if there had been a medical specialty that offered insight into autism, it would have been pushed aside. In its early days, autism belonged to psychiatry for a simple reason. Autism was psychiatry's for the same reason that North America was once the Indians', because they had gotten there first.

So parents had little chance. Their children's good looks sent a message that autism was an emotional disturbance rather than an organic problem. Although there were prominent dissenters who argued that autism was organic, such as Lauretta Bender at Bellevue Hospital in New York, they were badly outnumbered. Most psychiatrists knew perfectly well where to look for the roots of a child's emotional problems.

As if all that were not enough, nature itself seemed to have dropped another heavy hint that there was an intact child somewhere inside the autistic one. From Kanner on, every observer of autism has remarked that many autistic people show startling, although often startlingly narrow, intellectual skills. One autistic boy who has been studied at Yale, to choose an example almost at random, can rattle off each day's winning number in the state lottery for the past several *years.* He scores only 60 on IQ tests, but it is hard not to imagine that where there is smoke like this, there may be fire, too.

These signs of intelligent life arrive unpredictably and unfathomably, like news bulletins interrupting long stretches of static. Ruth Sullivan, the woman whose son was a model for Dustin Hoffman in *Rain Man,* recalls riding in the station wagon when Joseph was about four. His speech consisted of rudimentary two-word sentences — "Want juice," say, or "Go car" — but more often he sat silent. On this day, he threw off the blanket he had wrapped around his head, took his thumb from his mouth, and declared (apparently to no one), "Dangerous intersection, twenty-one letters." Then he retreated back into silence.

As such tales go, Ruth Sullivan's is almost run-of-the-mill. About 60 percent of autistic people have so-called splinter skills, talents in particular areas that far surpass their general abilities. These skills tend to pop up repeatedly in a handful of areas — music, art, calculation, calendars, spatial orientation. As one small example of the depth of these special skills, and also of their narrowness, consider the case of an autistic girl named Jessy Park. At age three, when she could barely speak or understand anyone else's words, she could assemble jigsaw puzzles without hesitation, and she performed just as quickly whether the puzzle was facedown or right side up.

Stranger still are autistic savants, whose skills in certain areas vastly outstrip those of ordinary people. These savants — perhaps 10 percent of the autistic population — present a bizarre intellectual skyline, in which an occasional gleaming skyscraper stands amid blocks of ruined and bombed-out shells. An autistic person might be able to compute the square root of 58,081 in his head, for example, and not know how many days are in a week.

One famous pair of autistic identical twins could instantly name the day of the week of any date over an *eighty-thousand-year* span. January 17, 1941? They knew it at once. April 29, in the year 18,214? No problem. The twins, skinny figures with squeaky voices and thick glasses, sometimes entertained themselves by taking turns rattling off enormous prime numbers, some of them twenty digits long! (Primes are numbers that cannot be broken into a product of smaller numbers. Seven and eleven and fifty-nine, for example, are prime; six and fifteen are not.)

This would be a startling feat for anyone, no matter how mathematically sophisticated. No one, least of all the twins themselves, could explain how they performed their magic. They could not count as high as thirty, and the simplest abstraction — how much change would you get if you paid a dollar for something that cost a quarter? — left them baffled. Multiplication, which is absolutely crucial to understanding what prime numbers *are*, seemed out of reach. Asked to multiply seven times four, for example, one of the twins replied, "Two."

"What does that mean, seven times four?" a psychiatrist persisted.

"It means two."

The psychiatrist David Viscott described a musical autistic savant named Harriet, who was the sixth of seven children and the daughter of a music teacher. At seven months, she could hum on pitch the arias her mother's voice students had been practicing. But music seemed almost her only human connection. When she was a year old, she spent hours at a time rocking silently back and forth in her crib and banging her head. Never speaking, never crying, never smiling, her only "communication" was to howl in pain if a student missed a note. At age seven, when she was just beginning to learn to speak, it became clear that Harriet's memory was prodigious. As a test, her father read her the first three pages of the telephone book; for years afterward she could recall any of the phone numbers.

Harriet had perfect pitch. She could immediately identify any tone, musical or otherwise, including a spoken word. She could instantly name the notes in any chord played on the piano. She could name the notes struck at random with a fist slammed down on the keyboard, and the notes struck simultaneously by two fists. She could play any composition in any key and change key on the fly, without losing a beat.

Nor were Harriet's skills pure mimicry. As a test, Viscott asked her to play "Happy Birthday" in the style of Mozart, then Beethoven, Schubert, Debussy, Prokofiev, and Verdi. That was easy, and it was just as easy to play the right hand in the style of one composer and the left hand in the style of another.

At the same time, though, Harriet was unable to grasp the most basic nonmusical abstraction. Asked how a nickel was like a dime, for example, she could not reply that both were round, or both were made of metal, let alone that both were forms of money. Her reply, no matter how much Viscott coaxed and hinted, was simply, "A nickel is a nickel and a dime is a dime. They are not alike at all."

Parents, who saw these mingled talents and disabilities close-up, found them eerie and bewildering. Psychiatrists were equally fascinated but not nearly as puzzled. The savant stories, they explained, were straightforward demonstrations of three related lessons.

First, these so-called splinter skills were more than demonstrations of intellectual talent. They were cries from a trapped child to the world outside, like the weak calls for help of a person caught inside a collapsed building. Here was proof positive that inside the wounded, autistic child was a bright, normal one.

Second, these stories of autistic prowess provided still more proof that these were children who had been victimized by their parents. The problem was a pushy mother in quest of a "perfect" child. "She puts excessive pressure on the growing baby to achieve feats of development which are considerably beyond his age level and interests," observed J. Louise Despert, a leading psychiatrist and an authority on autism. These "overintellectual" and "emotionally detached" mothers, Despert explained in 1951, sought "gratification from intellectual sources rather than from contact with people." Small wonder that they pushed their children to such sterile pursuits as the "acquisition of knowledge of musical records, license plate numbers, astronomical data, large and inappropriate vocabulary, word spelling, etc."

The psychiatrist Leon Eisenberg, who studied autism with Kanner and would later become chairman of Harvard's psychiatry department, seconded Despert. In a paper in 1957 on the fathers of autistic children — Eisenberg found them as unappealing a lot as their wives, "obsessive, detached, and humorless" — he noted that they, too, had pushed their children beyond their abilities. "Such interest as they have in the children is in their capacity as performing automata," Eisenberg wrote. "Hence, the frequent occurrence among autistic children of prodigious feats of recitation by rote memory."

Psychiatrists drew yet a third moral from studying autistic savants. The reason that autistic children had such mismatched skills, prodigious in some areas and hopeless in others, was that their parents had never given them an opportunity to develop normally. Instead, as the prominent psychoanalyst Beata Rank explained, the child had come to have a "scattered and fragmented personality," normal in some aspects but frozen in infancy in others. "The tenuous relationship with an emotionally disturbed mother we recognize as the chief source of this condition," Rank observed.

This was the standard psychiatric thinking on the origin of savantism, but it should be noted that it was not the only view. On the one hand, there were even more dubious theories that focused on toilet training and the like. "It has been suggested," one writer observed, "that giving prolonged attention to the task of memorizing (or 'taking in') large numbers of facts may represent a person's unconscious desire to undo or compensate for the loss of narcissistic play, as a result of the enforced removal of feces in childhood."

On the other hand, there were more down-to-earth theories based on observation rather than speculation. Some were even sympathetic to parents. The psychoanalyst Albert Cain, for example, noted in 1969 that although he had seen children whose parents paraded their talents in the way that Despert and Eisenberg had decried, he had "also seen such children where the ability was *not* hammered in, where it was, in fact, *unhammerable;* where parents took no visible pride or notice of it, and even one instance where the parents were totally unaware of the special ability."

The typical pattern, Cain observed, was that parents trying to cope with an autistic child found themselves exhausted, bewildered, and over-whelmed. Then, to their astonishment, their child revealed a narrow but extraordinary talent, a tiny garden blooming in a wasteland. Parents wel-comed the discovery that their child had a special talent not because they had ambitions of creating a prodigy but because they craved some oasis in their chaotic lives. The discovery of a safety zone where their child's behavior was innocuous, even praiseworthy, provided "a relatively safe, neutral haven" where both sides could avoid "sinking into emotional quicksand."

But to this day, no one has come up with even the rudiments of a satisfactory explanation of the savant's skills. The "experts," biological and psychological alike, have done little more than produce great clouds of ink, squidlike, to camouflage their ignorance. For the time being, the cryptic pronouncement of George, one of the calendar twins, will have to serve as a tantalizing last word. "It's in my head," he says simply, "and I can do it."

So the parents of autistic children found themselves ripe for attack. Their children *looked* normal, and many of them displayed prodigious, if narrow, skills. And there was one last, painfully simple reason that parents found a finger of blame pointing at them. Often their children had seemed fine, even precocious, until they reached eight months or a year. The experi-ence of a woman named Catherine Maurice was typical. Her first twinges of concern about her daughter began when Anne-Marie was about ten months old. In a powerful memoir called *Let Me Hear Your Voice,* Maurice described the scene two months later, when it had become undeniable that matters were growing rapidly worse:

> She no longer even looked up at anyone coming into or leaving the apartment. Seated on the floor, she would stare at a piece of dust, then slowly bring it up in front of her eyes and gaze at it, enthralled. She pulled little pieces of string off the rugs or the furniture, or a hair out of her doll's head. These she would twirl between her fingers, endlessly fascinated. At other times she seemed mesmerized by a combination of sight and sound, tapping two objects rhythmically in front of her face.
>
> Her activities were becoming stranger, more bizarre. I watched her, feeling very close to panic, as she repetitively sorted through puzzle pieces, then held them up two by two, always at right angles, and stared at them. Oh please baby. Please don't do that. Why are you doing that?
>
> We had given her a teddy bear for Christmas, hoping that she might

cuddle it and hold it the way a normal child would. Instead, she developed a strange ritual where she would push the bear through the bottom rungs of a certain chair, over and over again.

Her mannerisms increased as well. She had intermittently walked on her toes ever since she began to walk, but now she toe-walked almost exclusively. One day she added a new item to her repertoire: while seated on the floor and gazing dreamily into space, she extended her neck, held the position, and ground her teeth together. I was finding it hard not to cry out in terror at the sight of these strange behaviors. The sense of help-lessness was overwhelming. Sometimes I would actually catch myself whimpering as I witnessed each new sign of her alienation.

One morning, without any preamble of frustration or anger, she raised both of her hands and calmly struck herself in the face: once, twice, three times before I rushed at her, trembling, and jerked her hands down.

For parents, their child's remorseless slipping away, a kind of slow-motion sinking beneath the waves, was terrifying. For psychiatrists, it was simply additional proof that autism was an emotional disorder. The child had been normal, after all — even the parents said so — and then something had gone wrong. What other explanation could there be?

The psychiatrists assembled great stacks of evidence. Nearly all of it was anecdotal, and some of the anecdotes did indeed seem to cry out for psychological interpretation. One observer after another noted, for example, that autistic children pushed aside dolls and toy animals and played instead with blocks or cars. It was hard to know just what this preference meant, but it certainly seemed to show a rejection of human society in favor of a world "peopled" by inanimate objects.

Psychological explanations of other autistic traits were less compelling. Often, for example, people with autism are fascinated by such things as numbers and timetables and weather reports. In *The Empty Fortress*, Bettel-heim explained the weather obsession of a girl at the Orthogenic School. The key was that the word "weather" contained the message "we/eat/her." "Convinced that her mother (and later all of us) intended to devour her," Bettelheim wrote, "she felt it imperative to pay minutest attention to this 'we/eat/her.' "

At another point, Bettelheim interpreted a story that Kanner had told. One of Kanner's original patients was a boy named Paul who would invari-ably exclaim "Peten eater" each time his mother took out a saucepan. The behavior had begun one day when Paul was two, his mother recalled, when she had happened to drop a saucepan while reciting the "Peter, Peter, pumpkin eater" nursery rhyme to her son.

Kanner told the story to show that the seemingly random phrases that dot autistic speech may in fact have a private meaning. Bettelheim thought that Kanner had missed the real point. "Peter was changed to Peten in the typical way that autistic children tend to hide and reveal at the same time. In changing the name, Paul indicates that he was not quite referring to the Peter of the nursery rhyme, and may even have referred to himself, since Peter starts with the same letter as Paul, and since the names Peter and Paul are so often cited together that he may have thought them a unit."

This was a game that anyone could play. In France, for example, one psychiatrist informed the parents of an autistic girl that her very name betrayed their hostility toward her. The couple had named their daughter Sylvie, the psychiatrist noted, which sounded like "s'il vit," meaning "if he lives." Worse still, the pronoun did not fit — "il" is "he," not "she" — as if to hammer home the parental rejection.

But parent-blaming moved far beyond wordplay. In a well-received book called *Pathways to Madness*, published in 1965, for example, an anthropologist and Bettelheim protégé named Jules Henry reported on five families he had observed in their homes. All five families had mentally disturbed children. Trained as a neutral observer, Henry (or an assistant) spent about a week observing each family in what he referred to as its "native habitat." Although parents of autistic children did feed and clothe their children, Henry wrote, they neglected their deeper needs. They were not "available" to their children, not attuned to them. "Every culture has to strive to make adults available long enough to keep children sane," Henry declared, "and the existence of infantile autism in our culture proves that the struggle has not been completely won. In contemporary society, though a parent may drive a child mad through isolation, he cannot be 'held' for 'cruelty' as long as the child appears fat, round, and clean, because a cruelty of isolation, without starvation, without welts, without blood, is merely an invisible cruelty that is only of the mind."

Again, the dispute was not over whether parents were indeed driving their children mad — that went without saying — but over how that had come to pass. Few authorities believed that parents were intentionally malicious. On the contrary, as a well-regarded psychoanalyst named Margaret Ribble observed, "The fact that parents can be sick emotionally without being aware of it and can have their pathological symptoms brought to light in the setting of parenthood with such tragic effects on the child is shocking and challenging."

The problem, Ribble explained, was that mothers come in two varieties. The "positive" mother loves her baby "without hesitation, without feeling of duty, . . . and without a feeling of sacrifice." She communicates to her child "that he is intensely wanted as a part of the family group."

But then there was the "negative" mother. "The negative mother does not truly want her child," Ribble went on. "She has little capacity to devote herself to him and this fact comes to light very clearly in the way she handles the infant. Her mothering is a duty and often produces a negative response in the baby, who is made uneasy by her ministrations. No matter how many books she reads on child care or how diligently she attempts to do all the prescribed things for the infant, she somehow manages to do them inappropriately and without warmth. She is practically unteachable."

The lesson, Ribble concluded, was clear. "It seems to me that the mother of the child who develops autistic behavior is an extreme case of this negative woman, and unfortunately the infant is the first to sense her unconscious hostility."

Earnest and duty-bound, but mechanical, clumsy, and unconsciously hostile — this was the portrait of motherhood that three decades of therapists labored to flesh out. But if the broad contours of the picture emerged early on, the details were always evolving.

The influential psychoanalyst Beata Rank, for example, added a twist to the neglectful-mother theory. (She was the beautiful and elegant ex-wife of Otto Rank, once one of Freud's most devoted disciples, and was herself one of Freud's great favorites.) Rank agreed with others that the main source of the autistic child's problems was "the tenuous relationship with an emotionally disturbed mother." Mothers of autistic children, she said, were inadequate women in whom "the sunshine which is radiated by the spontaneous, tenderly devoted mother is missing." That much was standard fare. But Rank went on to depict that emotional disturbance in her own way. Her views, it is important to emphasize, were the mainstream conclusions of a major thinker.

The mothers of autistic children *appeared* well adjusted, Rank conceded, and many of them were highly intellectual and accomplished. But Rank's predecessors had missed the point. These mothers were not merely cold and mechanical, like robots or zombies, but something worse.

They were parasites so lacking in vitality that, vampirelike, they were driven to stealing it from someone else. "The need to be a mother, the hope and expectation that through this experience she may become a real person capable of true emotions," Rank wrote, "is so desperate that of itself it may create anxiety, ambivalence, fear of failure." The mother's "hope," Rank explained, was "that through identification with the child, her own flesh and blood, she may experience vicariously the joys of real living, of genuine feeling."

For a woman woefully short on motherly feelings, this "need to be a mother" was risky business. The solution was a good baby, in the sense of a nondemanding one. Rank was not taken in. "The passive child is less of a threat," she wrote, "because he does not make exaggerated demands on the mother, who feels constantly in danger of revealing that emotionally she has little or nothing to offer, that she is a fraud."

Jules Henry, the anthropologist, had seen the strategy in action. One of the families he observed had an autistic son who lived in an unreachable world of his own. Henry explained that the parents had brought their fate on themselves. They had wanted a quiet child, and their son had sensed the meaning behind that wish. Like King Midas, they had wished without thinking, and they had gotten what they had asked for. "The child has 'obeyed' his parents' wishes," Henry noted somberly. "He has grown indifferent to society. The wish that the child be quiet has become the magic jest — the child is quiet forever."

A second school of therapists, equally vehement, reached a similar conclusion by an opposite route. They turned their guns not on maternal hostility but on its opposite, a kind of doting overinvolvement. The psychiatrists Maurice Green and David Schecter, for example, found that the mothers of autistic children raced "to give the baby the bottle before he cries for it, to get the toy to him before he reaches for it, to say the words before he says them, thus encouraging, if not forcing, the child to be increasingly helpless and supplicant."

The mothers' motivation was simple, if hardly admirable. They were "all very lonely, frightened women" — there were a total of three women in Green and Schecter's sample — "who found overt comfort in the clinging, infantile behavior of their children." They did not want their children to grow up, and they did their best to prevent it.

Here, Green and Schecter pointed out, was the explanation of the muteness that is so common in autism. Mothers of autistic children were so quick to anticipate their every wish that the children never *bothered* to speak: "There was little need or opportunity for them to develop 'public' or conventional symbols."

In one article after another, psychiatrists spelled out the hazards of such overinvolvement. To do too much for a child was as dangerous as to do too little. "By excessive anticipation of his needs," one typical case history explained, "the parents denied [their son] the right to demand. As a result of this anxious oversolicitousness, the normal cycle of frustration-gratification-rest was seriously disturbed." Small wonder that little Billy soon showed all the signs of autism. By age seven, he had been institutionalized.

Psychiatrists had trapped the parents of autistic children in a no-win predicament. Either they were hostile and had driven their children mad by neglecting them, or they had smothered them with love and transformed them into permanent infants. Or both.

For there was yet a third psychological explanation of autism, this one combining both the other views. There was "hostility" and "suffocation," and now there was what one could call a "pothole" theory. Parents who were *consistently* neglectful or suffocating, the argument ran, were at least predictable. Perhaps children could learn to cope with them. The real danger came when parents were cold one day and warm the next, rejecting now and smothering later. The child would eventually buckle under the strain, like a road subjected to repeated cycles of freeze and thaw. In confusion and desperation, he would eventually retreat into silent seclusion.

The common feature of all such theories was the belief that, behind their glass wall, autistic children were normal and intact. The corollary was that the child's strange behavior was willful, and the therapist's task was to learn why he had chosen not to speak or decided to avoid eye contact. Autistic children, Bruno Bettelheim declared, were "those who, on weighing the question 'to be or not to be,' elect not to be."

There was, for example, a symbolic message in an autistic child's incessant rocking and spinning. "The child longs for mutuality," Bettelheim explained. "He wants to be part of a circle consisting of him and his parents, preferably with him as the center around which their lives revolve. This the autistic child states in his back-and-forth rocking and his circling."

Another crucial hint, the therapists felt sure, lay hidden in the autistic child's strange use of pronouns. Until about the age of six, Kanner had pointed out in his first paper, autistic children almost never refer to themselves as "I." Instead, they call themselves "you." When five-year-old Donald, Kanner's first autistic patient, stumbled but stayed on his feet, he said of himself, *"You* did not fall down."

Kanner described this peculiar behavior but did not interpret it. His successors were less cautious. This, they maintained, was a clue skywritten across the heavens. Could there be plainer evidence of a battered ego than a child's refusal to call himself "I"? (*Newsweek* headlined a 1967 story on autism, "World Without 'I.' ") Bettelheim did not even bother to spell out the argument. "Clearly the nonuse of personal pronouns, or what Kanner terms pronominal reversal, has nothing to do with innate disabilities," he wrote, "but with how the child experiences the world and himself within it."

To parents of autistic children, it was not so clear. The misuse of "you" and "I," they contended, reflected a weak intellect rather than a weak sense of self. "Elly knew who she was," declared Clara Park, the mother of an autistic daughter and the author of a superb memoir called *The Siege.* "She was 'you.' The usage was exact, denotative, certain. The whole family understood it. It simply reversed the usual meaning."

Park's explanation, in contrast with the psychoanalysts', was utterly mundane and down-to-earth. "Elly thinks her name is 'you' because everyone calls her that. No one ever calls her 'I.' People call themselves 'I,' and as a further refinement Elly began to call them 'I' herself."

CHAPTER TWELVE

The Scientists

In saying this we are not blaming these unfortunate parents.

— NIKOLAAS TINBERGEN, Nobel Prize acceptance speech

THE EXPERTS ON AUTISM paid little heed to explanations like Clara Park's. The mothers of autistic children, after all, were seen not as authorities but as perpetrators. Turning to such a mother for insight was not quite on a par with asking an abusive parent for tips on child discipline, but it was not far different.

In any event, there was no need to turn to parents for advice, for some of the biggest names in science had pronounced on autism. The scientific trail began in wartime Europe and made its way through England and across the Atlantic to the American Midwest.

In 1948, in the aftermath of World War II, Europe had yet to struggle to its feet. Children suffered especially. "Thousands of children, ragged and barefoot, still live in wartime bunkers, bombed-out houses and dank cellars below the bombed buildings," the *New York Times* reported. "Hundreds of thousands are orphans who live in makeshift institutions. . . . Uncounted thousands wait in special centers for artificial limbs which have never come to replace arms, hands, and legs." The *Times* illustrated its story with a photograph of an eleven-year-old boy named Italo Renzetti, "with double amputation and totally blind, reading Braille with his tongue."

Beggars and child prostitutes dotted the streets of the biggest cities and the most isolated villages. Starvation and tuberculosis hovered everywhere. Nor were all the problems physical. Recognizing this grim fact, the World Health Organization set out to study the mental health of these child victims of the war. The project was headed by a maverick British psychoanalyst named John Bowlby, who would publish an account of his work in 1951.

For years afterward, long after Europe had returned to prosperity, Bowlby's findings would reverberate throughout the world of psychology. In the narrow confines of autism, in particular, they echoed almost deafeningly, for Bowlby seemed to have provided the scientific underpinnings for the view that autism was caused by parental neglect.

Bowlby was after big game. He knew — everyone knew — that a close, loving relationship with one's mother was a key to a child's mental health. The point of his World Health Organization book was to document what happened when circumstances fell short of this ideal. What were the consequences, Bowlby wanted to know, of "maternal deprivation"?

It was a timely topic, and not only because of postwar chaos. Mother-infant bonds had been the subject of tremendous intellectual interest since 1945, when the psychoanalyst René Spitz had published a groundbreaking (and heartbreaking) study comparing two groups of infants who had been raised in institutions. The first lived in an orphanage that tended to their physical needs but took no notice of their emotional well-being. The second lived in a nursery annexed to a prison for delinquent girls; the mothers, who were serving time, were essentially in charge of their babies. The second group, the doted-on babies, fared far better.

To live without nurturing, Spitz found, was hardly to live at all. Children left to themselves soon grew weak and depressed, barely able to summon the strength to walk or talk. By age two, one in three had died.

The importance of parent-child bonds had once been a commonplace. As long ago as 1890, foster homes had been invented precisely because children raised in institutions fared so poorly. But by Spitz's day, the trend had gone the other way. Hospitalized children, for example, were allowed only the briefest of visits from their parents, out of fear that they would grow spoiled.

The authority of science was sometimes invoked to "prove" that the commonsense notion that children needed loving parents was empty sentiment. In 1936, for example, a University of Virginia researcher named Wayne Dennis reported an astonishing experiment to the American Psychological Association. For thirteen months, Dennis explained, he and his wife had raised a pair of adopted twins in their home.

No one but Dennis and his wife came near the twins, who were kept in separate cribs separated by an opaque screen. The infants had no toys, no pictures, no dealings with other human beings. "We did not smile at the subjects nor did we speak to them, romp with them, or tickle them except as these actions occasionally were incorporated into routine experiments," Dennis reported.

Beginning at seven months, Dennis eased the routine ever so slightly. "On day 192, we began to speak to the subjects and occasionally to romp and play with them . . . ," he noted. "Rattles, the only toys which were presented to them, were introduced on day 341."

The results, Dennis reported, were a clear blow against fuzzy-minded notions of child-rearing. "A large number of acts on the part of the adult which have been held by some people to be of importance may be dispensed with," he declared. "Fondling is not necessary," he went on, sounding like Mr. Gradgrind in Dickens's *Hard Times*, for "the infant within the first year will 'grow up' of his own accord."

Spitz and his followers had put an end to such complacency. As a result, even before he set out, Bowlby had a good notion of where he was likely to end up. In any event, Bowlby's earlier work had already convinced him of the crucial role of mothers. His first acclaimed work, published in 1944, had been a study called *Forty-Four Juvenile Thieves.* The title seemed to promise a tale of derring-do, but reality was more prosaic. Bowlby compared two groups of emotionally disturbed children, one group who had been caught stealing and one who had not. What set the two groups on different roads, Bowlby reported, was that seventeen of the forty-four thieves had endured long separations from their mothers when they were small; only two of the forty-four controls had experienced similar separations.

Bowlby's postwar book, published to much acclaim in 1951 as *Maternal Care and Mental Health*, now served as a full-length fleshing out of that earlier hint. Bowlby painstakingly reviewed some fifteen years' worth of studies of children and parents. They came from around the world and reflected a variety of approaches, but virtually all pointed in the same direction. In Bowlby's summary, "Mother-love in infancy and childhood is as important for mental health as are vitamins and proteins for physical health."

Bowlby's conclusion sounds bland to the point of banality. Who would stand up to denounce motherhood? In practice, Bowlby made clear, his prescription was a radical one.

In a chapter with the no-nonsense title "The Purpose of the Family," Bowlby spelled out the challenge to parents. "Much emphasis has already been laid on the necessity of continuity for the growth of a child's personality," he noted. The point was not merely that a child needed care, but that he needed *continuous* care. Bowlby made sure that there could be no misunderstanding him, and he acknowledged that not every mother would be up to the challenge. "The provision of constant attention day and night, seven days a week and 365 in the year, is possible only for a woman who derives profound satisfaction from seeing her child grow from babyhood, through the many phases of childhood, to become an independent man or woman, and knows that it is her care which has made this possible."

For parents, the stakes could hardly have been higher. In a discussion of "family failure," for example, Bowlby provided a list of factors that could deprive a child of proper parental support. The list began with such catastrophes as "social calamity — war, famine" and "death of a parent" and moved through "imprisonment of a parent" to such items as "separation or divorce" and "full-time employment of mother." Lest anyone miss his point, Bowlby repeated it: "Any family suffering from one or more of these conditions must be regarded as a potential source of deprived children."

For the psychiatrists trailing in Bowlby's wake, the application of all this to autism was obvious. Hadn't they said all along that there was something cold and distant about the mothers of autistic children? And now here was proof, in study after study, with tables and statistics and percentages and control groups and the imprimatur of the World Health Organization, that the children of inadequate mothers were emotional disasters.

This scholarly apparatus, and his own reputation, gave Bowlby's findings great weight. But his argument found favor for another reason as well. Bowlby had done more than compile facts and figures, like a squirrel gathering nuts. His data on the crucial importance of mother-child bonds fit neatly within a new theoretical framework that Bowlby and his followers had recently happened on.

The new field was called ethology. Bowlby was "addicted," he would say later, to the work of Konrad Lorenz and Nikolaas Tinbergen and its other pioneers. (We will meet Tinbergen again later.) These students of animal behavior had spent years in the field describing and analyzing animal interactions. Lorenz in particular had become famous for his discovery of animal "imprinting": newborn ducks and geese automatically follow the first moving object they happen to see. Almost always, in nature, that object was their mother. But, as Lorenz demonstrated, ducklings or goslings would just as happily parade along behind a golden retriever or a goateed Austrian biologist.

The relevance to humans, Bowlby believed, was that they, too, were primed by nature to respond to certain cues from the environment. The right cues at the right time would promote normal development. The wrong cues, or the right cues delivered too early or too late or not at all, could lead to disaster.

Decades later, psychoanalysts still joined with Bowlby in hailing this breakthrough. Ethologists were researchers in muddy boots who spent their days tramping through barnyards and skulking in marshes — could anyone have had less in common with the fastidious Sigmund Freud, office-bound in Vienna? — and yet these field scientists had provided key support for Freud's most fundamental observation. Here, at last, was insight into *why* childhood experiences exerted lifelong pulls.

"Konrad Lorenz noticed that if you walk in front of a little chick at a certain time in the chick's life he'll follow you, and if you do it at other times he won't," one New York analyst explained in 1980, summing up what had become conventional psychiatric wisdom. "There's a particular time when he gets 'set.' And we have found out in psychoanalysis that in human development, too, there is a time that is uniquely formative. . . . The Oedipal period — roughly three and a half to six years — is like Lorenz standing in front of the chick, is the most formative, significant, molding experience of human life, is the source of all subsequent adult behaviors."

Bowlby himself did not make an explicit connection to autism, but his successors did. Here were infants whose cold-fish mothers had never provided the proper nurturing, the cooing and hugging and lullaby-singing, that humans require. The result, inevitably, was stunted, timid, withdrawn children. Therapists had seen it, and now science had explained it.

In the meantime, additional scientific support for Bowlby's views had come along from an unexpected quarter. The mothers of autistic children would not know it for several years, but the unlikeliest of psychologists had launched an attack on them from the unlikeliest of directions.

Harry Harlow was a psychologist at the University of Wisconsin who had begun his career as a "rat runner" and had later moved on to experiments with monkeys. His academic life began inauspiciously — he was so poor a lecturer that his students booed him off the stage — but over the course of fifty years at Wisconsin, he became a major figure in psychology.

A showman and a scholar and, eventually, a confident, wisecracking lecturer, Harlow brought the sunniest of temperaments to the grimmest of subjects. His great interests were in such areas as depression and mother-infant bonding and the effects of isolation, and his papers make unsettling reading. With transparent pride in his inventiveness and uncalled-for good humor, he described the most gruesome experiments. In order to study fear, for example, Harlow designed a "terror trap." It was, he noted, a "diabolical" setup that permitted him to lower a monkey's cage into a chamber where it was confronted, no matter where it turned, by an "assault of arm-flapping, light-flashing, buzzing, or shrieking monsters."

Much of his work dealt with depression, which he studied in characteristically direct fashion. "Depressed human beings report that they are in the depths of despair or sunk in a well of loneliness and hopelessness," Harlow noted in a paper in 1969. "Therefore we built an instrument that would meet these criteria and euphemistically called it the pit." And, indeed, the accompanying photograph showed a stainless steel well, its sides too slick to be climbed, with a monkey cowering at the bottom. The caption read, "Typical posture of animal during pit incarceration."

In the same paper, Harlow went on to discuss another invention that he called "the tunnel of terror." This was essentially the "terror trap" all over again, with the refinement that Harlow had attached the mechanical "monster" to a long pole, the better to direct it at the cowering monkey. He went on to explain how the pit and the tunnel of terror could be used in tandem "to shorten, intensify, and possibly stereotype the depressive syndrome."

Autism seemed a long way off. But, at least as he would tell the story later, Harlow had a grand strategy in mind all along. The goal was understanding insanity in humans. Tormenting monkeys was merely a means to that end.

The aim of Harlow's much-celebrated work, he explained, was to drive monkeys mad and thereby gain insight into mental illness in humans. "We have inadvertently produced schizophrenia-like behavior in individual monkeys," Harlow reported in 1973, "and we are initiating research designed to produce such states under deliberate defined and definitive conditions. In other words, we are seeking to exhaust the monkeys' psychopathic capabilities, so that we know where simian insanity ends and human hopelessness begins and how and where they overlap."

Harlow's scientific career had begun much more conventionally, with studies of memory and learning. The switch to simian insanity came about by happenstance, when Harlow noticed severe problems with the monkeys in his breeding colony. Because of the threat of tuberculosis, monkeys destined for breeding were raised one to a cage, able to see other monkeys but not touch them. These soon-to-be breeders grew strong and healthy. When they reached sexual maturity, a male was put into the cage of a female. But then . . . nothing. "The two monkeys sat staring out from the cage as if still all alone," recalled Clara Mears Harlow, Harry Harlow's wife and colleague. "Neither showed any interest in the other nor in anything else."

Harlow had, he realized, inadvertently created "a brooding, not a breeding" colony. From that glum observation, though, it was only a small step to think of studying the impact of isolation on social animals. He set to work with a will.

By 1958, Harlow's reputation was at its zenith, and he set out to tell the world of his discoveries. He began with his presidential address to the American Psychological Association. His title was "The Nature of Love." The topic itself was startling: to speak on "love," a term that did not even appear in psychology texts, was as unexpected as to speak about UFOs at a physics convention.

But Harlow did not recite a sonnet or speculate on the nature of romance. Instead, he reported on an experiment he had designed to learn why infant monkeys were devoted to their mothers. Harlow took newborn monkeys away from their mothers and raised them with two surrogates instead. One was simply a block of wood wrapped in rubber and covered in cloth and topped with a puppetlike head; the other was a wire-mesh cylinder with a puppet head. Both "mothers" were warmed by a nearby lightbulb, and both were rigged so they could provide milk.

The result, considered shocking in its day, was that infants hugely preferred the soft, cuddly surrogate to the wire-mesh mother even if it was the wire mother that provided milk. Infants spent hours each day clinging to this soft surrogate, they played happily when it was nearby, and they ran to it for protection when confronted with Harlow's fright-producing "monsters."

For both the reigning schools in psychology, Freudians and behaviorists, this was a surprise. Both groups had arrived at essentially the same explanation of the mother-infant bond — this was, Harlow liked to say, the solitary issue on which they had ever agreed—each school arguing that a child "bonded" with his mother because he identified her as his source of milk. The moral was clear, at least for a thinker as bold as Harlow. Above all else, he insisted, children crave security and "contact comfort." A child's first need is for love, not food.

Harlow presented this insight as an indisputable laboratory finding, but it was not quite that. Harlow had simply taken an observation about monkeys and assumed that it applied to human beings as well. More cautious psychologists would spend years worrying about whether such generalizations were valid. While they peered nervously across the chasm that separated monkeys in a psychology laboratory from human beings living their ordinary lives, Harlow blithely jumped the gap.

Most of those who heard him speak leapt with him. "A charming lady once heard me describe these experiments," Harlow recalled, "and, when I subsequently talked to her, her face brightened with sudden insight: 'Now I know what's wrong with me,' she said, 'I'm just a wire mother.' "

For Harlow, this was not a cautionary tale about jumping to conclusions. This mother's self-accusation, he emphasized, was exactly on target. For years, he pursued the analogy between monkeys and humans, between wire-mesh surrogates and inadequate human mothers. In 1971, writing in the *Journal of Autism and Childhood Schizophrenia*, he summarized his insights. Some families, he observed, are "characterized by coldness, ambivalence, double binding messages and lack of physical contact."

The result, Harlow went on, could be "the development of infantile autism, other forms of childhood psychosis, or severe behavioral disorders." He cited the "striking" similarities between the behavior of monkeys reared in isolation and autistic children. "Both exhibit marked social withdrawal. In a play-setting with peers both may retreat to a corner of the room to avoid social contact. The autistic child may be preoccupied with his inanimate surroundings and be intolerant of changes in these surroundings. The isolate monkeys also can relate only to their physical environment, if at all, and try to shut out outside stimulation."

Both monkeys and children seemed bent on shutting out the outside world. Both injured themselves intentionally on occasion, often by biting. Then Harlow dropped in a caveat. "The interpretation of such behavioral similarities is a matter of conjecture and should be done cautiously at this time."

The warning in that last sentence was disingenuous. If studies of monkeys were *not* relevant to autism, why publish a paper on monkeys in the *Journal of Autism and Childhood Schizophrenia?*

In any event, readers focused their attention on Harlow's grand claims, not on his throat-clearing. Psychiatrists were not eager to experiment with monkeys themselves, but they happily embraced Harlow's findings. What news could have been more welcome? A highly regarded scientist from an unrelated discipline had ventured into the psychiatrists' territory and announced to an admiring world that they had been right all along.

For psychiatrists eager to have a scientific seal of approval, there was more good news ahead. On December 12, 1973, a Dutch scientist named Nikolaas Tinbergen bowed his head so that Sweden's King Carl XVI Gustaf could drape the Nobel Prize medal around his neck. The medal was for medicine, and Tinbergen was a surprising choice. He and his cowinners, Konrad Lorenz and Karl von Frisch, were not doctors or medical researchers but, in Tinbergen's words, "mere animal watchers." Tinbergen himself had devoted years of his life to studying the behavior of two varieties of seagull.

Now, as Tinbergen launched into his Nobel Prize acceptance speech, the surprises continued. His topic, it became clear almost immediately, had nothing directly to do with birds or behavior or indeed with animals at all. Instead, Tinbergen proposed to demonstrate how "watching and wondering" might also "contribute to the relief of human suffering." He had learned, Tinbergen announced at this august forum, the secret of autism.

His words — backed with all the authority of his Nobel Prize — would eventually come to serve as one of the sturdiest supports for the notion that autism was caused by bad parenting. "To a trained observer," Tinbergen told his audience in Stockholm, it was "very obvious" why autistic children behaved as they did. Their problems "can often be traced back to something in the early environment — on occasion a frightening accident, but most often something in the behavior of the parents, in particular the mothers.

"Let me hasten to add," Tinbergen continued, "that in saying this we are not blaming these unfortunate parents. Very often they seem to have been either simply inexperienced . . . ; or overapprehensive; or overefficient and intrusive; or, perhaps most often, they are people who are themselves under stress. For this and many other reasons, the parents of autists deserve as much compassion, and may be as much in need of help, as the autists themselves."

Tinbergen's diagnosis of the problem led straight to a remedy. Mothers simply needed to learn "maternal, protective behavior." Autism could be reversed, Tinbergen insisted, if mothers were "willing to cooperate." "Many autists can attain a full recovery," he declared, "if only we act on the assumption that they have been traumatized rather than genetically or organically damaged."

Tinbergen was a sophisticated man from a sophisticated family (his older brother was also a Nobel laureate, in economics), and he was renowned for his painstaking field work. Nonetheless, his approach to autism was strikingly amateurish. He had dealt with autism before his Nobel Prize talk and he would return to it repeatedly in the years to come, but his writings always fell far short of what one would have expected from a celebrated and tough-minded scientist.

Tinbergen's pronouncements on autism relied heavily on anecdotes, often involving his family. Once, for example, he had brought his two-and-a-half-year-old daughter to the doctor, where "she suddenly showed . . . total withdrawal, alternating with extreme restlessness" and other signs of anxiety. Another child, "again a close relative," was so timid that "in slightly unfamiliar situations he often withdraws from social contact." These two cases demonstrated, Tinbergen had written in 1972, that "normal children can easily be made 'temporarily autistic.' " This buttressed his claim that a *relentlessly* bad environment could make for full-fledged autism.

This was hardly a Nobel-caliber experiment — it was more akin to the idle speculation of nannies at the park, comparing their charges — and Tinbergen had gone on to propose evidence of a different sort. It was scarcely more impressive. He and his wife, Tinbergen said, had long paid close attention to how children behaved when they encountered strangers in "three semi-controlled situations in particular." One was in the supermarket, while the child rode in a shopping cart; the second, on a bus; the third at home, when visitors arrived.

In all three situations, the Tinbergens had noticed, the child's attitude toward strangers was a mixture of curiosity and wariness. This informal observation brought Tinbergen to the heart of his argument: the child's behavior seemed strikingly like that of "a group of species to which we have devoted a lifetime of research: the Herring Gull and relatives, and the Black-headed Gull."

To Tinbergen's frustration, "this highly relevant work [had] either been ignored or insufficiently understood." He set out to remedy that problem. In breeding season, Tinbergen explained, a female gull would slowly venture near a male, but the male, aggressive by nature, might threaten to drive her off. The female was caught in a "motivational conflict," uncertain whether to approach or to run away.

And here, Tinbergen reassured his presumably puzzled readers, was the essence of autism. Like a female gull, the autistic child is caught betwixt and between, not knowing whether to embrace the world or flee it. In contrast, a normal child learns to negotiate the delicate dance that every new encounter represents: she advances a wary step if a stranger smiles; or gathers herself by turning away momentarily if he is too frightening; or retreats behind the safety of a mother's dress; and so on.

For an autistic child, matters are more charged. Because she has never learned to read other people's signals, or because her parents failed to send the right ones, the autistic child's world is composed of permanent strangers. There is neither safe haven nor retreat, and life is paralyzingly frightening. Tinbergen italicized his conclusion: *"The core of the problem would seem to be found in desperate, frustrated attempts at socialization combined with constant and intense fear."*

In 1983, in a book with the audacious title *"Autistic" Children: New*

Hope for a Cure, Tinbergen and his wife Elisabeth put all the pieces together. Using detailed descriptions of gull behavior as a model, they began by recapping their picture of autism. Then they moved on to the cure. This was as homespun as their diagnosis and interpretation had been. Autistic children, it turned out, could be hugged back to health. "It would seem to make eminently good sense to give a child who has missed out on adequate mothering or has otherwise been 'hurt' a solid dose of 'supermothering,' however belatedly," the Tinbergens wrote, "and to do this by treating him the way one would have done when he *began* to 'derail'; i.e., by behaving towards him as if he were a very young child, or treating him the way any mother would deal with even older normal children when they need support or consolation after moments of distress, or when ill or sickening for an illness, etc."

What could be simpler? Children who had been driven to autism by their inadequate or neglectful parents could still be reclaimed, and the medicine was no more exotic than a mother's hug.

CHAPTER THIRTEEN

The Parents

*The parents believed what the professionals told them,
and the professionals believed Bettelheim. No one
questioned his authority.*

— CATHERINE MAURICE

FOR PARENTS, the mood was not as cheery as Tinbergen had implied. The great pooh-bahs of psychiatry had accused them of rejecting their children. Then a string of scientists, each more eminent than the ones before, had endorsed the same message. In the meantime, the story had been taken up and passed along by an army of therapists and social workers and psychologists. After three decades, it had seeped its way into every nook and cranny of American life.

Parents staggered under the blows like outmatched boxers. The reaction of Jacques May, a father of autistic twins, was typical. "I was made to feel that the doctor knew everything and that I knew nothing, that the problem was really no problem at all," May lamented at the dawn of the parent-blaming era, "since there was an accepted, unchallenged explanation for our children's condition."

May, a physician himself, seemed especially wounded to realize that his fellow healers had written him off:

> As the conversation developed, I had more and more the feeling that my wife and I were finding aloofness instead of understanding, coldness instead of warmth, distrust instead of sympathy. Then it became quite clear; to our amazement it dawned upon us that, in the doctor's eyes, we were being held responsible for the children's situation. This was the accepted view, we found, the official doctrine, the only explanation offered and recognized, the sole basis for treatment. Further, we soon realized that instead of being anxious and desperate people seeking understanding and help, as I had thought we were, we had become culprits hiding something, people with some dark secret whose words were not a simple expression of

the facts but a shield to cover our guilt, a way of concealing the truth from ourselves and misleading others.

May lashed back at his accusers, but most parents sat back and absorbed the blows. Why? Because they believed (mistakenly) that if their child's problem was organic, then it was hopeless. If it was an "emotional" problem, on the other hand—even if it was the parents' fault—then it might be fixable. Biology meant a life sentence without the possibility of parole; psychology meant hope.

There were other reasons, too, that the psychiatrists' attacks found their mark. Frightened, baffled parents were deferential to authority, especially medical authority. In addition, their confidence in their own judgments was eroded by guilt. Finally, their usual skepticism was suspended—in the face of their child's extraordinary behavior, parents were prepared to believe a therapist's extraordinary explanations.

It was guilt above all that made parents vulnerable. "I was carrying around this terrible secret," recalls Annabel Stehli, the Brooklyn Heights woman who had gathered her nerve to read *The Empty Fortress*. "I didn't want to talk to anyone about Bettelheim. My husband said that he thought it was baloney, but I didn't talk to my friends about it. I was very alone. I really felt as if I had a scarlet letter on, only the 'A' was for 'Abuse.'

"I felt that I'd hurt Georgie in some subtle way that I couldn't grasp," Stehli adds sadly, "and if I could just figure it out, then maybe she'd be okay. There was a part of me that *wanted* to believe Bettelheim, because that would mean that if I got better, Georgie would get better."

On occasion, Stehli says, she could convince herself she was not to blame for her daughter's autism. But her faith in herself was shaky. "I said that on a good day, and that's what I felt in my heart of hearts, but when everybody was accusing me, it was like a witch hunt. Those witches in the 1600s often confessed to being witches when they weren't—there's something sinister in the human character that does this. People love a scapegoat."

So much so that sometimes they nominate themselves for the role. "I had been disdainful of 'bovine' women who were content with their lot and just wanted to raise babies," Stehli recalls. "I wanted life beyond motherhood. I was a real *Feminine Mystique* type, and I thought I was being punished for those attitudes."

Jacques May was a surgeon and not much inclined to psychological explanation, but Stehli was an easy mark. A college dropout who had been raised in a household where psychiatrists were regarded as only a step below deities—"my mother was teaching me about Freud, Jung, and Adler when my friends were learning about Matthew, Mark, Luke, and John"—she was terrorized even by a hostile social worker. "She was sniffing for pathology in me like one of those guys on Miami Beach with a metal detector," Stehli recalls uncomfortably.

"*I* had flunked out of Vassar, and *she* had a master's degree," Stehli goes on. "I was very hierarchically inclined, and I felt that she knew something I didn't know. She'd studied it, she was the pro, she was the expert, and I was *dying* to get out of this morass. I would follow *anybody* who offered me any way to get at the truth."

Stehli's motives could hardly have been simpler. "If I changed, Georgie would get better. And I wanted my daughter to get well."

Parents with far more self-confidence than Stehli found themselves just as panicky. Catherine Maurice is the mother of *two* autistic children. "You can have all kinds of credentials, all kinds of degrees," she says — Maurice has a Ph.D. in French literature — "you can think of yourself as a real smart cookie, but when something starts stealing your kid away, reason is the first thing to go. It hits you at a gut level, and you grasp at anything, cling to anything, suspend disbelief."

To have children with a terrifying illness, or disability, or whatever mysterious thing autism was, would have been heartache enough. To have *caused* it besides made it almost too much to bear. "I was a mother losing my children," Maurice says incredulously, "and I found myself blamed for it.

"I thought of myself as an intelligent woman and a loving mother, but both of those things were just *battered.* Intellectually, I saw through the accusations, but emotionally it really didn't matter. I was willing to take on the blame and the responsibility for having caused it, if that meant I could cure it. And that happens over and over again with parents."

Leo Kanner was too old and too ill to deliver a speech, he had said, but here he was at the podium. His audience at the Sheraton Park Hotel in Washington, D.C., on this July night in 1969 — later this same weekend the world would watch Neil Armstrong step onto the moon — was a group of four hundred American outcasts. They were parents of autistic children, gathered in force for the first time, and they might almost have been untouchables in India.

Now Leo Kanner stood before them. He had been the first to recognize autism, and even in retirement he was still the reigning figure in the field. It was a coup for a barely organized band of nonprofessionals to have lured such a distinguished visitor. But the audience was wary, too, for everyone in the room knew that it was Kanner who had labeled them "refrigerator" parents.

He was seventy-four years old, a small man with thick glasses, bent and fragile, with a weak voice. He began his talk by recounting the story of his first encounters with autism. A few more sentences and he was done with history. Then came the climax of the short talk. "Herewith I especially acquit you people as parents," Kanner declared, speaking for the first time in formal and forceful tones. "I have been misquoted many times. From the very first publication until the last I spoke of this condition in no uncertain terms as 'innate.' But because I described some of the characteristics of some of the parents as persons, I was misquoted often as having said that 'it is all the parents' fault.' Those of you parents who have come to see me with your children know that this isn't what I have said."

The parents were on their feet, clapping and cheering. They knew full well that Kanner had been the first to brand them, one member of that audience recalls today, "but because he *was* Leo Kanner, and autism belonged to him, that sentence of acquittal made all the difference to parents, and to those psychologists and psychiatrists who were swimming against the tide."

In any case, the truth was not nearly as simple as Kanner had claimed. Kanner had indeed spoken of autism as innate even in his first paper on the subject. And he had in fact concluded that landmark paper with an emphatic declaration, in italics so that no one could miss it, that he was discussing *"inborn autistic disturbances."*

He meant it. In a staff conference at Johns Hopkins in April 1943, shortly after this first paper, Kanner's fellow psychiatrists had taken him angrily to task for having called autism "innate." Back and forth they argued, Kanner alone making the case for autism as inborn, his colleagues joined together in pinning the blame on parents. The point that Kanner kept missing, the psychiatrist Hilde Bruch insisted, was "the emotional significance of the mother's intellectual overfeeding" of her child.

Kanner would have none of it. He knew plenty of intellectually overbearing parents with perfectly healthy children. Were the parents of autistic children so different? It was one thing to claim that parents were at fault, Kanner challenged his colleagues, and quite another to show it. "Why are these children developing differently?" he demanded. "Can we explain that entirely on the basis of the kind of parents and the activities and attitudes, on their faces when they come to the crib? I don't know what can explain these things."

But by 1949, as we have seen, Kanner had reversed course. At that point, he began to argue not merely that parents were strange, as he had been saying all along, but that their strangeness had *caused* their child's illness. More important, Kanner began delivering the new message to a huge, nonprofessional audience. In 1960, to cite the most notable example, *Time* ran an adoring profile of Kanner. A photograph showed him smiling benignly above a caption that read "In defense of mothers." The text was less soothing. "There is one type of child to whom even Dr. Kanner cannot get close," *Time* wrote. "All too often this child is the offspring of highly organized professional parents, cold and rational — the type that Dr. Kanner describes as 'just happening to defrost enough to produce a child.' "

Few parents read the *American Journal of Orthopsychiatry* or the other journals Kanner published in. Few of them could miss a giant finger of accusation pointed at them in *Time* magazine, especially when relatives and neighbors hurried to bring it by. To this day, virtually every parent who had an autistic child in 1960 recalls that issue of *Time* with a shudder.

Time's use of the "in defense of mothers" phrase was significant. Kanner had written a book by that title years before, in 1941, two years before his first paper on autism. It was indeed a defense of mothers, and through all the years to come Kanner continued to see himself as a mother's staunchest ally. The book was subtitled "How to Bring Up Children in Spite of the More Zealous Psychologists," and it was a wise, sensible, and reassuring reminder to mothers that on questions of child-raising, *they* were the real experts. "Let us, contemporary mothers, together regain that common sense which is yours," Kanner had declared, "which has been yours before you allowed yourselves to be intimidated by would-be omniscient totalitarians of one denomination or another."

There was no need to censor children's reading or radio-listening, Kanner wrote, nor to worry about every bite of food they swallowed. If a child stayed up a few minutes past bedtime or didn't finish her milk, there was no harm done. Children were sturdy, not fragile.

He made a gleeful detour to mock the "weird words and phrases which are apt to confuse and scare [parents] no end: Oedipus complex, inferiority complex, maternal rejection, sibling rivalry, conditioned reflex, schizoid personality, repression, regression, aggression, blah-blah, blah-blah, and more blah-blah." It would be hard to imagine a more generous and welcome defense, especially coming in what Kanner correctly labeled an "atmosphere full of isms and doctrines and 'schools.' "

Curiously, though, in the same year as *In Defense of Mothers*, Kanner had published a paper on a similar topic. The two works overlapped considerably, but the new paper was a very different piece of work. Its most strident passages might have qualified it for the title *An Attack on Mothers*. The essay, in a medical journal called *Mental Hygiene*, bore the ominous title "Cultural Implications of Children's Behavior Problems." Kanner had presented it as a talk to the American Neurological Association the year before. Like a politician who changes his message when he changes his audience, Kanner had told the neurologists a story quite different from the one he would tell the mothers.

For the neurologists, he had focused on the dangers a bad mother poses. The family home was no longer the cozy refuge of *In Defense of Mothers*, where curtains rustled gently in the breeze and the smell of fresh-baked bread wafted from the oven. Instead, it was "a field of battle." Parents, especially mothers, ruled "dictatorially" over their children. "The mother continues to think, will, and act for the child. Compliance is taken for granted. Noncompliance is lamented as ominous rebellion, which must be crushed with all the means at the mother's disposal." In this civil war, no tactic was forbidden. "The parents fight with scolding, beating, and other punitive measures. The child retaliates with ever more refusals and temper outbursts. Rules of fairness are suspended; both parties hit below the belt."

This early confusion on Kanner's part — were mothers paragons of warmth and common sense or were they domestic dragons? — presaged a deeper confusion to come. When it came to autism, Kanner never did sort out his thinking on the role of the family. Were parents the culprit or was biology?

For a quarter century, Kanner tried on one answer and then the other, as he zigged and zagged across the nature-nurture boundary line. In one paper, he damned coldhearted and "mechanical" parents. In the next, he let parents off the hook and highlighted the child's "constitutional inadequacies." Sometimes he offered *both* explanations in a single paper.

Kanner's 1949 paper set out the defective-parent case in full. "I have dwelt at some length on the personalities, attitudes, and behavior of the parents," he concluded, "because they seem to throw considerable light on the dynamics of the children's psychopathologic condition." Through the fifties, Kanner continued to harp on the same theme. In the sixties, he was still at it. In 1965, for example, he observed, "The coincidence of infantile autism and the parents' mechanized form of living was startling. This was confirmed by most observers. These were realities which were impossible to ignore."

It is hard to know how to reconcile this record with Kanner's own summary of it. On the one hand, he was utterly sincere when he told parents at the 1969 autism conference that he had never blamed them and that he had been misquoted. On the other hand, he was indisputably mistaken. With the exception of a few articles in *Time* and other magazines, his pronouncements on autism were from his own hand. Kanner's denial of his own words was especially unworthy; it calls to mind the basketball player Charles Barkley, who explained away controversial statements in his autobiography by claiming that he had been misquoted.

Some authorities on autism flatly deny Kanner's version of events. "I had several long conversations with him when I published my book," says Marian DeMyer, a psychiatrist now retired from the Indiana University School of Medicine and the author of a highly regarded book called *Parents and Children in Autism*. "He wanted to talk to me, and I made a journey down to Baltimore and spent a Sunday talking with him. He *really* wanted to deny that he had ever implicated the parents in any way. But he had," she says quietly. "He started a trend. He really did, and it was a very tenacious trend."

Mary Coleman, a neurologist now retired after many years at Georgetown University, tells a similar story. "I investigated all the claims for the first chapter of my book," she says, referring to a medical text called *The Biology of the Autistic Syndromes*. "He was an out-and-out liar."

That is too simple. Kanner was certainly mistaken about the historical record, but it seems clear that he was not out to deceive anyone (with the possible exception of himself). The great majority of articles cited above, for example, can be found proudly gathered in a volume of Kanner's most significant papers. There was no cover-up. Kanner was no Nixon.

Harvard's Leon Eisenberg, who trained under Kanner at Johns Hopkins, believes that Kanner was simply swept up in the fervor of that era. "At a time when most everybody who was academic and thoughtful was looking for environmental causes of disorders," Eisenberg says, "Kanner wrote this paper that suggested that autism began so early in life that it must be inborn." Psychiatrists leapt to the attack.

Kanner fought back, but he was not the kind of rebel willing to stand against the world. "I think that despite himself," Eisenberg continues, "and *not* with a sense of conscious deceit to curry favor, he began to be influenced by the character of the times. He came to stress the 'schiz-y' mothers and how maybe the mother had never given much to the child, and so on and so on."

Then, having given in, Kanner did what most of us do. He recast the past in a way that put the best light on it. Kanner delighted in teasing Freudians, but it seems that Freud had his number here. Each of us constructs a personal, rose-tinted version of his own biography, Freud had written in 1909, a process "analogous in every way to the process by which a nation constructs legends about its early history." Generations of schoolchildren believed that George Washington could not tell a lie; Leo Kanner believed he had never maligned parents.

The audience at the Sheraton Park Hotel burst into cheers and cries of jubilation when Leo Kanner "acquitted" them. But that announcement was not the highlight of Kanner's speech. That had come a few moments earlier.

In the fight against autism, Kanner had said, "many people are trying their best, but there are many people who, while trying their best, are exchanging misinformation and misinterpretation. I need not mention to you *the book,* an 'empty' book I call it." The reference was to Bruno Bettelheim and *The Empty Fortress.* No one in the audience missed it.

For although Leo Kanner had vastly more credibility than Bettelheim in the medical community, it was Bettelheim who had the public's ear. A small man with a large, bald head and a thick German accent, Bettelheim was an unlikely celebrity. Even a close friend like the psychiatrist Alvin Rosenfeld described his notoriously short-tempered colleague as "abrasive" and "aggressive" and "difficult, indeed thorny." Kanner was an altogether gentler character. Even his harshest critics tempered their judgments. Mary Coleman, the neurologist who called Kanner a "liar," for example, added in the next breath that "he was a very decent man, a brilliant man, and a very perceptive man . . . he was not an unsympathetic, noncompassionate man. He was probably a very nice man."

Bruno Bettelheim was many things, but he was not "nice." "He was a sadistic son of a bitch," recalls Harvard's Leon Eisenberg. "He once came to Baltimore and gave a talk in one of the state hospitals. I don't remember what the talk was about, but I do remember some young psychologist in the audience got up to ask a question, and as young men and young women will do sometimes, instead of asking a question, he gave a long disquisition that everybody else was bored with and nobody gave a shit about.

"So the audience began to titter a bit, because this was going on too long, and he sat down, and Bettelheim said"—here Eisenberg drops his standard gruff manner in favor of a polite but authoritative voice—" 'Young man, please stand up.' And the kid stands up, and Bettelheim says, 'Do you understand *why* the audience began to laugh at you?'

"And then he stripped the skin off this kid, so that by the end of it, everybody who disliked the kid in the first place was cringing inside and felt terribly sorry for him. And apparently, that's what happened to parents or anybody else who riled him up."

Eisenberg is famously plainspoken, but he is hardly unique in his judgment. Kenneth Colby, for example, is a retired UCLA psychiatrist and a psychoanalyst. "Bettelheim," he says flatly, "was just a real son of a bitch, one of the worst people that psychoanalysis ever produced."

Bettelheim had zealous admirers, too. Many of his students at the University of Chicago declared him the greatest teacher they had ever encountered. A good number of the counselors who worked for him at the Orthogenic School praised him with almost cultlike fervor. Dazzled audiences who heard him speak at fund-raisers raced one another to tear open their checkbooks.

He was charismatic, brilliant, and provocative, able to take the most familiar subject and convince an audience that they had never until that moment really thought about it. To take one of countless examples, consider this brief passage from Bettelheim's review of a Helen Keller biography:

> By pretending to have a full life, by pretending that through touch she knew what a piece of sculpture, what flowers, what trees were like, that through the words of others she knew what the sky or clouds looked like, by pretending that she could hear music by feeling the vibrations of musical instruments, she fooled neither her teacher nor herself. But we loved her for making it possible for us to fool ourselves. . . . And we fool ourselves about it out of our anxiety that we might lose the ability to hear or see. Helen's pretenses reassured us that this would not be so horrible.

That gleeful bursting of bubbles was a favorite move. "You *really* believed in the Easter Bunny?" he seemed always to be asking. (When it came to children, however, he vehemently opposed hurrying to expose Santa and other favorites.) But Bettelheim had more than one move in his repertoire. He could play the sage *or* the iconoclast, strike a calming note as well as a provoking one. In an article in the *Atlantic Monthly*, for example, he reassured parents who worried about their children's toy guns. "As playing with blocks does not indicate that a child will grow up to be an architect or builder, and playing with cars and trucks does not foretell the future auto mechanic or truck driver," he noted calmly and wisely, "so playing with toy guns tells nothing about what a child will do and be later in life."

The Helen Keller passage and the gun one share nothing but a voice, but that voice was as distinctive as a fingerprint. The note of utter self-assuredness was key. Others might be taken in, it seemed to say, but not Bruno Bettelheim. Especially not when it came to autism. Let Leo Kanner waver and wonder where he stood, a Hamlet of the hospital. Bettelheim knew what *he* believed.

He made sure that no one else could have any doubts either. Autism had always been seen as a terrifying, lifelong curse. No one dared talk of recovery. But Bettelheim claimed astonishing success rates. "Altogether we have worked with forty-six autistic children," he wrote in *The Empty Fortress*, "all of whom showed marked improvement."

For various reasons, the group of forty-six was winnowed down to forty. Of those forty autistic children, seventeen had had a "good outcome" and another fifteen had shown "fair improvement." Only eight of these supposedly incurable cases had "poor results."

Mere figures could not portray just what had been accomplished. "The seventeen children whose improvement we classified as 'good' can for all practical purposes be considered 'cured.' " They were in school or at work with nothing to prevent them from "functioning well on their own in society." The "fair improvement" group had done strikingly well, too. "The fifteen classified as 'fair' results are no longer autistic, though eight of them should now be classified as borderline or schizoid, since they have only made a fair social adjustment." Thirty-two out of forty, then, were cured or no longer autistic.

In a 1967 *Newsweek* interview pegged to the publication of *The Empty Fortress*, Bettelheim elaborated a bit. "One of my former boys is a professor at Stanford," he declared proudly. "Another is finishing a Ph.D. at Harvard, another is making his first million on Wall Street."

In 1973, he would repeat his claims in a television interview. The Orthogenic School, Bettelheim said, "cured eighty-five percent" of the autistic children it admitted before age seven or eight.

For parents, it was Bettelheim's accusations that made him the enemy. For his fellow professionals, it was this talk of miracle cures and the inevitable false hopes they inspired. "He told a tremendous lie," says Colby, the UCLA psychiatrist. "He used to tell these stories, and it was an absolute lie."

There is a marginally less damning explanation. Perhaps the cures were real, but the autism was not. "Bettelheim reported an *enormous* cure rate, or improvement rate, unlike what *anybody else* has achieved," Leon Eisenberg bellows incredulously, "and I have to believe he must have had a large number of children who weren't autistic in the collection he described in that book."

It was a problem that Leo Kanner had anticipated years before. No sooner had Kanner written his original paper on autism than psychiatrists across the United States took up the diagnosis. Intended as a description of one of the rarest of conditions, "autism" became a catchall label that could be hung around the neck of virtually any emotionally disturbed child. The new diagnosis had become a fad. "Almost overnight," Kanner lamented in 1965, "the country seemed to be populated by a multitude of autistic children."

Many of these troubled but nonautistic children ended up at the Orthogenic School. Exactly how many was never clear; of the forty-five students at the school at any one time, Bettelheim wrote in *The Empty Fortress,* no more than six to eight were "truly autistic." But there was no way to check the numbers or the diagnoses. The Orthogenic School, Bettelheim liked to boast, was his private fiefdom. *"He* decided who was autistic," recalls Benson Ginsburg, at that time a University of Chicago biologist and an acquaintance of Bettelheim's who had tried and failed to interest him in a study comparing various forms of psychotherapy. *"He* decided on the diagnosis, and *he* decided when they were cured. Some of the other people there used to say, 'You let *me* decide who's got what and when they're cured, and *I* can have an eighty percent cure rate, too.'"

It was not a charade that could be kept up indefinitely, since no one else had remotely similar success. Even Bettelheim eventually gave up the game. In his last book, *The Art of the Obvious,* he conceded that "nobody knows how to treat these children." (It was late to make amends. The book was published in 1993, after Bettelheim's death.) But Bettelheim had realized that he did not know how to cure autism decades before, around 1964 — *The Empty Fortress,* with its bold talk of cure, was published three years later, in 1967. This startling finding is one of the few points of agreement in two recent Bettelheim biographies, a critical one by Richard Pollak and an admiring one by Nina Sutton.

In Sutton's summary — bear in mind that this is the favorable account — "the Ford Foundation grant [to treat autistic children] had expired in 1963, and Bettelheim had still not written the book he was announcing back in 1960, when he had asked for an extension of the deadline. He was caught. Having arrogantly promised so much, what definitive answers could he now provide to the puzzle of autism; what happy ending could he find to a heartbreaking story, whose victims failed to respond to his best efforts to understand and heal them?"

Bettelheim kept his doubts to himself, proclaimed cures instead, and basked in the glory of having rescued children the rest of the world had given up on. That was shabby, but Bettelheim maintained later that he had had no choice. He had set out with genuinely high hopes, he explained, and though they had fizzled, he still had a school to fund and a reputation to maintain. "Success in helping autistic children would, more than anything else," he wrote later, "establish the merit of the school's philosophy and of its methods."

On the evening of March 12, 1990, Bruno Bettelheim washed down some barbiturates with a bit of liquor and then tied a plastic bag over his head. Old and sick and lonely, stuck in a retirement home that he saw as little better than a condemned man's cell, he had been discussing suicide for some time. The *New York Times* marked his death with a page-one headline — BRUNO BETTELHEIM DIES AT 86; PSYCHOANALYST OF VAST IMPACT — and a long, admiring story.

Within weeks, the legacy of a lifetime began to crumble. First came reports from some former students at the Orthogenic School. The school was not a haven for the emotionally wounded, they maintained, but a minigulag presided over by Bettelheim. They told of beatings and episode after episode of physical and verbal abuse.

The stories came as a shock. Bettelheim had preached against violence for decades. He had given the school thirty years of his life, in exhausting days that often stretched out well past midnight. He had handpicked counselors for their empathy and their patience rather than their experience or their academic credentials. A *Time* magazine profile in 1968 had dubbed him "Chicago's 'Dr. Yes' " for his generous ways with his students. Every Christmas, for example, found Bettelheim shopping for the best Santa Claus suit in Chicago for a counselor to wear, and happily presiding over nights of elaborate preparations — the sewing of toys and stuffed animals and the baking of cookies and the hanging of stockings.

The whole idea behind the school was to take the lessons Bettelheim had learned from the concentration camps and invert them by substituting kindness for cruelty. "He turned it upside down when he started his school for disturbed children," explained Rudolf Ekstein, a psychoanalyst and one of Bettelheim's closest friends. "It was a protected, caring environment, the mirror opposite of the camps."

Physical discipline was the great taboo. "Punishment teaches a child that those who have power can force others to do their will," Bettelheim had written. "And when the child is old enough and able, he will try to use such force himself." He invoked Shakespeare: "They that have power to hurt and will do none . . . They rightly do inherit heaven's graces."

Still, there had been clues over the years that philosophy was one thing and practice another. In 1983, for example, an ex-student named Tom Lyons wrote a thinly disguised novel about the Orthogenic School (and dedicated it, "with gratitude and affection," to Bettelheim). In one representative scene, Lyons described an encounter between "Dr. V" (Bettelheim was known as Dr. B) and a boy named Ronny, who had hit a classmate during a game of dodgeball:

> "Since ven do ve hit people in zhe eye?" The question that broke the silence was soft and menacing.
>
> "I didn't *mean* to," Ronny's voice was a subdued, protesting whine. Tony winced as Dr. V's left hand caught Ronny on one side of the face, then returned with a swift backhand across the other. SMACK! SMACK! SMACK! SMACK! SMACK! Dr. V's left hand moved quickly, methodically back and forth across Ronny's face. Then: SMACK! SMACK! SMACK! SMACK! with both hands on the back of the head as Ronny ducked forward. Dr. V grabbed a small tuft of his hair and shook. And with both hands he caught Ronny by the shirt and hauled him halfway out of his chair.
>
> "Vhy did you hit her in zhe eye?"
>
> Tony realized that he felt helplessly, humbly subdued before Dr. V's thundering anger.
>
> "It was an accident," Ronny's voice was distinctly tearful.
>
> Dr. V stepped back; he watched Ronny while the latter sniffled once or twice. Suddenly he extended his hands, palms up, in grandiose gesticulation. "I didn't mean to! It vas an accident!" he shrilled mockingly. This made him appear less frightening. In his more normal, but still menacing voice, he asked, "Does zat make it feel any better?" Ronny shook his head. "All right, zhen, remember zat ven you have accidents, I vill have zem also. Is zat clear?"

Such hints went largely unheeded while Bettelheim was alive. But soon after his death, one former student and counselor after another came forward to confirm the rumors. Today, Bettelheim's supporters as well as his critics concede that the beatings took place.

The dispute has moved on from a debate over facts to one of motives. The simplest interpretation, as spelled out by Bettelheim's biographer Richard Pollak, was that Bettelheim was a monumental hypocrite. A more forgiving view is that Bettelheim was a good man who, understandably and perhaps inevitably, sometimes lost patience with his hugely difficult charges.

Bettelheim's admirers are more forgiving still. They maintain that Bettelheim's seeming violence was actually a ploy. Their position, which takes open-mindedness to the verge of empty-headedness, was that Bettelheim intentionally took on the role of human lightning rod in order to divert the aggression that festered inside his disturbed students. As his biographer Nina Sutton explains, "He had discovered at Buchenwald that nothing is more effective in defeating self-destructive anxieties than a high-profile, visible enemy, someone one can hate without reservation."

•   •

Parents of autistic children were quick to take up that invitation. Bettelheim had made perfectly clear what he thought of them, parents across the nation believed, and they returned the favor. In fact, though, Bettelheim had occasionally hedged his bets. In *Truants from Life*, for example, he had devoted a long section to arguing *against* parent-blaming. "We, too, have sometimes been guilty of looking to parental difficulties for an easy explanation of a child's disturbance," he conceded in that 1955 book, his second on the Orthogenic School. But it was not even clear, he went on, that it was the parent and not the child who was the original source of trouble. Perhaps, Bettelheim suggested, a mother who had originally been "merely anxious or insecure" became indifferent or rejecting as a defense "against the unbearable pain and anxiety inflicted by the indifference or strange responses of the infant."

Even in *The Empty Fortress*, he tiptoed around the chicken-and-egg question of whether autism was a matter of cold mothers who neglected their children or of unreachable children who ignored their mothers. "It is not the maternal attitude that produces autism," Bettelheim wrote, "but the child's spontaneous reaction to it." The problem, in other words, was not as simple as a mother turning her back on her child. The actual scenario was that a child felt persecuted by his mother, whether rightly or wrongly, and drew away from her. If she withdrew in turn, the child would draw away still further, and the two would be launched on a downward spiral that ended in autism.

Bettelheim never repudiated that measured, complex position — indeed, he could always point to it if accused of parent-blaming — but he downplayed it in favor of the clearer, more dramatic theory that autistic children were akin to terrorized prisoners in a concentration camp. In his actions, too, he made it plain that he did not welcome parents as allies.

Bettelheim's University of Chicago colleague Benson Ginsburg recalled an encounter between Bettelheim and the mother of an autistic child. The woman had asked Ginsburg to phone Bettelheim on her behalf. "I called Bruno and asked if there was any room for this child, or at least if he could talk to her," Ginsburg said. "He said no. The mother was on the line at the time. Her words were, 'But Dr. Bettelheim, you're my only hope. If you won't take my child, what can I do?' He said, 'Lady, haven't you done enough already?' "

This was a credo, not a fit of pique. Years later, in 1981, a publisher asked Bettelheim to write a preface for a book on the maternal instinct. He declined. "All my life," he replied, "I have been working with children whose lives have been destroyed because their mothers hated them."

Leo Kanner was never as harsh as that, but he and Bettelheim agreed on one crucial question. Both men believed that autistic children could improve only if they were away from their parents. Even before his "refrigerator parents" papers, Kanner had declared himself as favoring a "change of environment," which "means a change of people," as necessary for "weaning the schizophrenic child away from the temptation of schizophrenic withdrawal."

Bettelheim had quoted that remark approvingly in *Truants from Life.* (Like Kanner, he sometimes used the term "childhood schizophrenia" rather than "infantile autism." The usage reflected a then-current notion that autism was the earliest stage of schizophrenia.) "Our own experience," Bettelheim had gone on, "suggests that the treatment of schizophrenic children proceeds best within a total therapeutic environment and through the cooperative effort of several people."

And so parents who were genuinely devoted to their child's welfare would not keep her at home. Bringing her for daily psychotherapy sessions might be better than nothing—at least the child would have *some* contact with genuinely well-intentioned adults—but it was far from adequate. "As soon as we began our work at the Orthogenic School," Bettelheim wrote, "we concluded that to treat the schizophrenic child, he must be provided with truly need-satisfying persons not just for one hour a day, but as much as possible all the time, every day of the year."

Beginning in the mid-fifties, Bettelheim demanded that new students at the Orthogenic School not see their parents for at least nine months. Students had once been allowed to go home on vacations, but Bettelheim changed that policy because he believed they returned in worse shape than they had been in when they left. To insure that parents could not harm their children even at long distance, counselors at the school read letters from home before passing them on to the children.

Bettelheim had explained the need for such precautions in a 1956 essay called "Schizophrenia as a Reaction to Extreme Circumstances." "We must protect the child from any hostility coming from the external world," he wrote, "particularly from his parents." A decade later, in *The Empty Fortress,* he threw the full weight of his authority behind the notion that parents had to give up their child if they hoped to save her. "Trying to rehabilitate autistic children while they continue to live at home, or by treating mother and child simultaneously, is a questionable procedure. It has been our experience that this works only when the disturbance is relatively mild and the child still very young."

Therapists dubbed the complete and permanent removal of child from parents a "parentectomy."

CHAPTER FOURTEEN

Parent-Blaming Put to the Test

*From this observation a testable hypothesis can be
formulated.*

— MARIAN DEMYER

T HE DECLARATION OF WAR was only a single paragraph long, and easy
to overlook. On March 12, 1967, in a letter to the *New York Times*, a
psychologist named Bernard Rimland lambasted Bruno Bettelheim. The
Times had just run an article by Bettelheim and a glowing review of *The
Empty Fortress*. "Parents of mentally ill children have anguish enough already," Rimland responded. "To heap guilt, based on disproven, circumstan-
tial evidence, on these parents, is an act of irresponsible cruelty."

Academics of various stripes had occasionally criticized Bettelheim, but
those rebukes had been confined to dusty journals and couched in opaque
language. (Rimland had contributed to this critical literature himself.) This
public cry of outrage was something new.

On paper, Rimland was hardly a match for Bettelheim. He was not an
academic or a therapist but a research psychologist at a U.S. Navy lab in
San Diego. Little more than an amateur in the field of child psychology —
he had made a point, in his student days, of avoiding all such "irrelevant"
courses — Rimland had only one credential that Bettelheim lacked: he had
a son with autism.

Bernard and Gloria Rimland's son Mark was born in 1956. For the
excited young couple, the birth of their first child capped what seemed to
them "the perfect setup." Bernie had landed the job he wanted in San
Diego, his hometown; they had found a two-bedroom house they could
afford. "We'd painted one of the bedrooms yellow, because we didn't care if
we had a boy or a girl," Bernard Rimland recalls. "We got the crib and we
had everything all prepared. Everything was *perfect*. The pregnancy was
perfect, the delivery was perfect. The only problem was, the baby was born
screaming" — even today, as Rimland remembers this four-decades-old saga,

his exuberance melts away at this point in the story—"and he continued to scream for hours and weeks."

It took a little while for the message of that screaming to sink in. "Mark was screaming in the hospital when I first came to see him," Bernie Rimland recalls. "Remember the old days where the father stood outside the glass window and looked at the kid? I was the third father in line that day. The first kid was brought out, a little limp rag doll, eyes glazed and half-closed, and the father admired this wonderful little kid. And the second kid the same way. And then the nurse brought out Baby Rimland, and he was looking around wide-eyed, just as though he could talk. I was very proud of that. I thought, 'Gee, what a precocious-looking little guy.' And I went down to see Gloria. She said, 'Oh, he's got your lungs'—I used to be a very good underwater swimmer. She said, 'All the kids cry, but my golly, you can hear Mark all the way down the hallway; he's got the best lungs of all.'

"Little did we know," Rimland laughs. He is a big, shambling bear of a man, nearly seventy now. With his burly frame and his tangled gray beard, he looks like a retired Jewish lumberjack. But he is no chuckling *zayde* with a fund of cracker-barrel wisdom. Rimland is a sharp-tongued, angry man spilling over with righteous indignation. "So it was obvious right in the hospital that something was wrong," he observes sardonically, "before our pernicious personalities had had a chance to exert themselves on the kid."

Life at home proved nearly impossible. Mark banged his head on the walls so hard that he went around with a perpetual black-and-blue knot on his forehead. He could not tolerate even the slightest break in routine—it was Gloria Rimland who found herself forced to buy identical dresses for herself and her mother and mother-in-law.

Any change could trigger disaster. "I would wash my hair and set it, and he would cry until it was dry again, like it was before," Gloria recalls. "We opened the back door to let the beautiful summer breeze come in," she continues, "and then came winter and we couldn't shut the door, because he would just scream and scream and scream. And so we went through the winter with an open door."

Mark spent his days staring into space, banging his head, tearing his crib apart with his wild rocking. He seemed oblivious to his parents and to everyone else. And always, hour after hour, there was the sound of "violent, uncontrolled, furious screaming."

Gloria remembers timing Mark's crying, to see just how long it went on. "When he got to be about a year old," she recalls, "he only cried twelve hours by the clock in a twenty-four-hour period, and we thought we were really living—that was so wonderful, only twelve hours!" Neighbors would call the police to complain about the noise. "The police got to know us," Gloria laughs. "They said they were just glad he was ours, not theirs."

Exhaustion dominates all other memories of those years. "If it was a good day, I got my teeth brushed," Gloria recalls. *"Heaven* was washing my hair and taking a shower." For five years, she was almost unable to leave the house. When a neighbor volunteered to stay with Mark one day, Gloria scarcely knew how to deal with her unaccustomed freedom. Finally, she went to a department store and wandered up and down in a happy daze. "When I came back home," Gloria says, "my neighbor was sitting on the floor, crying, and that was the last time she offered to help out with Mark."

Gloria Rimland is not one to complain, and she has a knack for story-telling that helps transmute the miseries of those early years into comedy. But she knows there is really no explaining to anyone else what life with Mark was like. "People would say to me," and here she mimics a sweetly inane questioner: " 'Oh, what do *you* do?' " She bursts into raucous laughter.

Mark was the oldest of Bernard and Gloria Rimland's three children and the only one with any sort of troubles. "Our daughter was born in 1958, two years after Mark," Bernard says. "What a difference! She was cuddly, she looked at us, she was interested in us, she was the exact opposite of Mark. It was just obvious that from the moment of birth they were totally different kids."

The Rimlands' pediatrician, who had been in practice for thirty-five years, was at a total loss with Mark. "He had never seen a kid, or heard of a kid, like this," Bernard says. "Mark seemed precocious in some ways. He started talking early, repeating words when he was eight months old, like 'bear' and 'done' and 'all gone' and 'spoon' and things like that. And then all of a sudden whole sentences — 'Come on, let's play ball.' "

"What about 'Mommy' or 'Daddy'?" I asked.

"Never," Bernard says briskly. And then, primly, "Heavens, no."

After that early start, Mark began talking less and less, except to echo someone else's words or to recite a few pet phrases. "It's all dark outside, honey," for example, meant "window," apparently because Gloria had used that phrase one evening while holding Mark in front of a window. He stopped talking altogether for a time, and then he whispered for a year. No one knows why.

There seemed to be no reaching him. "He stopped using his hands," Gloria recalls. "He would just grab somebody else's hand and use that." By way of illustration, she grabs her right wrist with her left hand and moves it around, like a crane operator directing his shovel through the air.

It took the Rimlands two years to put a name to Mark's endless scream-ing and his withdrawal from the world. The turning point came when something in her son's parrotlike recitations of radio commercials tweaked a memory of Gloria's. Husband and wife raced to the garage and tore open a box of old college textbooks. There, in a section headed "infantile autism," they found a "perfect point-by-point description" of their son.

That was in 1958. Rimland, by his own account "obsessed," devoted himself to reading every account of autism that had ever been written. Fifteen years after the syndrome had been discovered, this was still barely possible. San Diego had no medical school in those days, but the Navy occasionally sent Rimland to conferences in other cities. Between sessions and at the end of each day's work, Rimland would race to the nearest university library. In New Orleans, for example, he skipped the French Quarter and headed off to Tulane, where he talked a guard at the library into letting him into the locked building after hours. Photocopies were still uncommon, so Rimland took meticulous notes on four-by-six cards. He recruited friends and acquaintances to translate articles he copied from medical journals in French, German, Dutch, Czech, and Portuguese.

In 1959, Rimland contacted Kanner. The eminent researcher encouraged the young unknown's solo assault on the received psychiatric wisdom, much of it his own. Did this represent yet another instance of Kanner's ambivalence? Was it a display of open-mindedness? Of moral courage?

Rimland himself has never resolved the issue. But in 1964, he was ready to present his case. (It took a push from Gloria, who pointed out to her husband that, whether he realized it or not, his self-education project had grown into a book.) He laid out the evidence in a small volume called simply *Infantile Autism*. Leo Kanner wrote an encouraging preface.

In methodical and plodding fashion, Rimland moved through the medical literature. By chapter three, he had taken care of the preliminaries. Now came the main event.

First, Rimland took up the evidence that parents were to blame. Yes, he agreed, the psychiatric case sounded plausible. The question was, was the case proved?

Other once-mysterious conditions, after all, had eventually turned out to have organic causes. Psychiatrists might have leapt to a conclusion when they assumed that a mute autistic child, say, had *refused* to speak. Perhaps, for biological reasons, the child was unable to speak. Think of stroke victims who could no longer talk, Rimland suggested. Were they silent out of hostility?

Why, he asked, did psychiatrists take the symptoms of autism as clues to the *origin* of the condition? If someone with schizophrenia reported that Martians were beaming messages into his head, that was taken as a sign that something was wrong. No one ran off to look for Martians. When an autistic child drew away from his parents, on the other hand, that withdrawal was taken not as a symptom but as evidence that the parents had done something wrong.*

Then Rimland shifted ground. If psychology was not the key to autism, what was a better explanation?

Biology. Autism, Rimland argued, was a biological bolt from the blue, a not-yet-understood disease that struck one child in a thousand. Parents were no more to blame than they were for Down's syndrome or cerebral palsy.

Here was the payoff for Rimland's years in the library stacks. Little of the evidence he had compiled was original, but no one had ever assembled all the scattered bits of information into one place. Gathered together and put in order, they made a compelling picture.

"Number one," Rimland wrote. "Some clearly autistic children are born of parents who do not fit the autistic parent personality pattern." "Number two" was the flip side. "Parents who do fit the description of the supposedly pathogenic parent almost invariably have normal, non-autistic children."

And so on. Calmly, quietly, relentlessly, Rimland proceeded through his case. "Number three. With very few exceptions, the siblings of autistic children are normal. Number four. Autistic children are behaviorally unusual 'from the moment of birth.' "

Rimland made nine observations in all, backing each one with reference after reference. None was as conclusive as a report of a particular brain defect or chromosome abnormality — to this day autism remains poorly understood — but they were certainly more than debaters' points. Rimland noted, for example, that autism afflicted three or four times as many boys as girls. For believers in biology, like Rimland, that was not especially puzzling; a host of conditions, from color blindness to heart disease, strike males more often than females or strike males at younger ages. But for those who looked to explain autism psychologically, this sex discrepancy should have set off warning bells. In our culture, after all, baby boys are at least as welcome as girls. How does that fit with the theory that autism was caused by parental neglect? Rimland posed such questions, but he never raised his voice. He ended his chapter with a plea "to let conviction be subordinated to evidence."

At the time his father's book was published, Mark Rimland was seven years old and still in diapers. Mark never appears in the book, nor did Bernard Rimland ever drop a hint of his special interest in his subject.

---

* Richard Hunter and Ida Macalpine, the distinguished historians of psychiatry, made a similar observation in *George III and the Mad-Business*. They criticized modern-day psychoanalysts who have written on the case for reading meaning into the king's ravings, which are now generally attributed to an organic disease called porphyria. "Who would seek the cause of pneumonia in the delirious utterances of a sick child and judge its personality by them?" Hunter and Macalpine ask. "Yet this is precisely what has been done in George III's case."

Mark is forty now. He still lives with his parents. (When Mark was five, the Rimlands were advised that he was "hopeless" and should be institutionalized.) About five feet ten, with neatly combed brown hair, he is a handsome man with an appealing smile. From certain angles, he looks remarkably like his father did as a young man. He reads at about an eighth-grade level and goes off every day to a school for disabled adults, by himself, on a city bus.

It takes a moment or two before it becomes clear that there is something odd about him. The eyes are the first clue. Mark does not avoid eye contact, but he tends to look a foot or two to the side of the person he is with. There is nothing there to see — or nothing that an ordinary person would think to look at — and this intent gazing at emptiness makes Mark seem blind. He is easy to talk with, though, and he likes to talk.

He speaks swiftly and enthusiastically, and loudly enough that heads turn. His tone is not robotic but the rhythm is choppy, and he repeats himself. "A man once took me to play golf. His first name was Bob, his last name was Wilson. Once he hit a golf ball and a squirrel picked up the golf ball and ran away with it. He picked up the golf ball. Picked up the golf ball."

His father reminds him "dozens of times every day" to lower his voice, but the lesson does not sink in. Mark absorbs the rebukes with no signs of embarrassment or irritation. In a world preoccupied with image, he seems eerily unself-conscious.

It can be unsettling. Mark has learned "proper" behavior, but it is plain that his skills are memorized rather than heartfelt. He shakes hands, for example, but there seems nothing in it for him (although no discomfort either), no hint of connection with another person. He extends his hand as he has been taught, and it lies there limp, like an empty glove clipped to the end of a child's jacket sleeve.

It is hard not to wonder if there is a "there" there. Certainly, Mark seems cheery enough ("Wasn't I a cute little boy?" he likes to ask his mother. "You were just perfect," Gloria replies). The screaming ended decades ago, and Mark is a good companion today.

But it may be a mistake to try to probe too deeply. After we had spent a fair bit of time together, I felt stymied. Mark had told me about his school, his teachers, his pets, but we had never quite engaged in conversation. It was clear that Mark *knew* about a lot, I complained to his father, but I could not tell what he *cared* about.

Rimland responded with a bemused shrug. "Mark's just not tied in to that aspect of things."

Perhaps cruelly, I pursued the topic. "What would happen if you were hit by a bus today? Would Mark be sad if you didn't come home after work?"

Rimland thought a moment. "Would he *notice?* Yes, he'd notice. Would he be sad? I don't know."

Mark is not cold — on the contrary, he seems sweet, guileless, good-humored — but he is not empathetic. People do not seem to rouse much interest. Birthdays, on the other hand, have been an endless source of fascination since Mark was little. He likes to buttonhole strangers and ask them their birthday. Then he stands stock still, head tilted slightly, eyes focused on the middle distance, smiling. In ten seconds or so, he will announce, "That was a Monday."

He knows the birthdays of everyone he has met. He cannot explain how he knows what day of the week November 10, 1952, was, but he seems never to make a mistake and never to forget. If I happen to bump into Mark a decade from now, his father told me, he will recall my birthday. At a family dinner one night, someone mentioned the date. Exactly twenty-three years ago today, Mark chimed in, the next-door neighbors moved in. The routine events that other families scribble on the kitchen calendar — the dentist appointments, the pet checkups, the upcoming visits of one person or another — are all carried in Mark's head.

Mark has another talent as well, which he discovered only at age twenty-one. He has a genuine gift for art. He draws and paints, and anyone would be glad to claim the results as his own. The subjects are everyday ones — a sleeping cat, a grove of birches, a woman in profile — drawn in a realistic but sophisticated way. This is not "folk art" but the real thing, and there is no need to know Mark's story to admire his style.

Mark likes painting, and he seems pleased that visitors admire his work, but he has little to say about it. Like his calendar skills, Mark's art is both gift and mystery. He seems unable or unwilling to ponder the source of his talent; his curiosity does not seem to turn inward. "Do you remember when you got interested in art?" I asked.

"September 15, 1977. It was Thursday."

Infantile Autism won the award that its publisher gave each year to "a distinguished manuscript in psychology," but few readers paid attention. Rimland had been especially eager for a response from Bettelheim. While he was working on the book, Rimland had written to Bettelheim, asking for data on his autistic students. Bettelheim had turned him down. Rimland's project was "ill-conceived," Bettelheim wrote, and in any event he was working on his own book. Rimland wrote back. He would give Bettelheim five pages at the end of *his* book to make a rebuttal argument if Bettelheim would do the same for Rimland.

Bettelheim rejected the suggestion, and Rimland seethed at this latest insult. "When I was working on the book," Rimland recalls today, "we'd finally get the kids to bed by about ten o'clock or so, and it would be quiet. I'd work at the dining room table until two or three every morning, and then go off to work for the Navy a few hours later. And while I was sitting there late at night, tired and bleary-eyed, I'd shake my fist and say, 'You son of a bitch, Bruno Bettelheim, I'm going to show you.' And I'd keep working."

Infantile Autism appeared three years before *The Empty Fortress*. Bettelheim had not spent those years pondering Rimland's arguments. He dismissed his would-be rival in a few sharp paragraphs. "Rimland, a psychologist, seems uninterested in the psyche of autistic children," Bettelheim wrote, "since he did not study them as persons but inquired only into the neurological structure of their brains."

This belief that psychological explanations ran deep, whereas biology skated along the surface, was one that psychotherapists of the day all embraced. Bettelheim never abandoned it. Biological "explanations" of autism were glib and beside the point, he implied, akin to attempts to explain suicidal depression as caused by a tendency to skip breakfast.

But Bettelheim went further. The biological approach, he insisted, was not only an intellectual mistake but a moral one. It represented a panicky and misguided attempt to draw a boundary between us, the sane, and them, the sick.

"In the last decades," he argued in his last book, published posthumously in 1993, "we seem to have gone back to those old views of mental patients as basically different from the rest of the human race, to distance ourselves from them. Only now, instead of demonic possession, we have made the basis of the difference a behavioral or molecular oddity. They are different because something in their symptomatology or in the biochemistry that underlies their behavior makes them alien to so-called normal beings. This rejects and attacks Freud's view that all human beings array themselves on a continuum without any hard dividing lines. What differences exist between people are only differences of degree."

This was Bettelheim at his best and worst, in the same breath infuriatingly self-righteous and stubborn and yet somehow also morally imposing and humane. He knew, though, that he had lost the battle. Long before his death in 1990, it had become clear that the neurological approach he so disliked had won the day.

The parent-blaming view that Bettelheim had championed began losing ground in the mid-seventies, roughly a decade after the publication of Rimland's *Infantile Autism*. In hindsight, that book seems almost to outline a research program that would have allowed psychologists to move from anecdote to experiment. At the time, though, Rimland's voice was too isolated, and too little known, to shift the debate.

The idea that autism was caused by bad parents was too imposing to demolish at a single blow. It took assault after assault, like a series of floods finally undercutting a towering sycamore on a riverbank, to bring it down. Many of those assaults came in the form of clinical reports. Independently and one after another, researchers began reporting unmistakable signs of brain abnormalities in many autistic patients. Epilepsy, for instance, was indisputably a brain disorder, and doctors found, to their surprise, that one autistic person in three became epileptic. Retardation was common as well, and everyone agreed that, except in cases of the grimmest abuse, retardation was an organic problem rather than a man-made one.

Marian DeMyer, an Indiana University psychiatrist, unearthed much of the crucial data. In hindsight, DeMyer's great breakthrough seems embarrassingly straightforward. Rather than take for granted that the parents of autistic children were strange souls, for example, she tested that claim over the course of a dozen years. In a series of painstaking comparisons complete with rigorously chosen control groups (this by itself set DeMyer's work above nearly everyone else's), she compared the personalities of three groups of parents. Parents in the first group had an autistic child; parents in the second group had only normal children; those in the third group had a brain-damaged child.

DeMyer administered standard personality tests to all three groups. The result, it turned out, was that the three groups of parents were indistinguishable. In addition, DeMyer compared the parents of autistic children with parents who were outpatients in a psychiatric clinic and who had normal children. The parents of the autistic children, DeMyer found, had significantly *fewer* problems than the outpatient parents.

So the healthier parents had the sicker children. It was a finding that was hard to reconcile with the widespread belief that autistic children were so badly off because they had had the bad fortune to be born to emotionally disabled parents.

In DeMyer's view, the great mystery that Kanner and all his descendants had been out to solve was scarcely a mystery at all. Why did parents seem so aloof and wary? Because they knew that the psychiatrists who were interviewing them had already decided on their guilt. "Most of them were just bewildered," she says. "They'd heard that there was something wrong with them, and they were frozen with fear when they first came to be interviewed. They could *seem* to be very distant, not very interactive, not very emotional, but once you'd had two or three interviews with them and gotten to know them, that broke down."

In the same straightforward fashion in which she had looked at parents, DeMyer set out to study the intelligence of autistic children. This had been considered impossible, on the grounds that the children could not be made to cooperate. DeMyer's notion was that the problem was not testing per se but finding suitable tests. She began with tests normally used for infants and slowly worked her way along until the tests grew too difficult. "If you give them items that they're capable of doing, they will do them," DeMyer says with characteristic matter-of-factness. "This is no different from a normal child. If you take a four-year-old and give him items that we know two-, three-, and four-year-old children can do, he will be happily engaged in doing the test. If you then start giving him items that only five- and six-year-olds can do, he may start to try on a few of them but then he'll very rapidly lose interest, and he'll run away from the test."

The result of such testing, she reported in the mid-1970s, was that somewhere around 80 percent of autistic children are retarded. At the time that finding was controversial, because it undermined the notion that there was a bright child trapped within the autistic shell. Today it is widely accepted. "Kanner thought that autistic kids had underlying intelligence," says Leon Eisenberg, the Harvard psychiatrist who began his career working with Kanner at Johns Hopkins. "Well," he says, with a philosophical shrug, "they're retarded."

Neither DeMyer's findings nor any of the others were decisive in themselves. It was just barely conceivable that callous parents could somehow predispose their children to epilepsy, though no one could quite think how. Perhaps parental coldness could raise the risk of retardation. Perhaps the host of other symptoms — the hand-flapping, the spinning, the lack of eye contact, the selective hearing — all somehow reflected parental misdeeds.

But as one study followed another, and as more autistic people were followed for longer periods of time, it began to seem increasingly unlikely. Bettelheim and Niko Tinbergen and their intellectual allies continued to make the case that autism was psychological, but now they had to share the floor. Perhaps a simpler explanation really was called for. Perhaps autism really was a physical disorder.

At last, with psychological theories under attack by clinicians, Rimland's arguments of a decade before finally got a hard look. What *about* the healthy siblings? What about the loving parents? The two-sided squeeze on psychology, from the clinic and the library, proved decisive. Yesterday's heresy had become today's common sense.

With forgivable pride, Rimland let down the cloak of neutrality. (Even in *Infantile Autism,* his call-to-arms against the psychotherapists who had condemned him and his fellow parents, he had given the crucial chapter the bland title "The Problem of Biological versus Psychological Causation.") Now he no longer needed to appear above the battle. "In 1979," he boasted recently, "a national magazine article on autism said that ninety percent of the people in the field credited *Infantile Autism* with 'blowing the "refrigerator mother" theory to hell.' "

That is an exaggeration. What Rimland did was to light a fuse that smoldered and smoked for a decade before it ignited. Still, it *had* caught fire in the end, and the case against refrigerator parents *had* been blown to hell. And that, Rimland notes with grim satisfaction, is "a good place for it."

Epilogue:
Current Theories of Autism

HAVING SPENT so much time discussing what autism is not, let us briefly consider what it might be. Recall "splinter skills," first of all. These are the isolated but sometimes extraordinary talents that are so frequent in autism. As poorly understood as these skills are, they may nonetheless be a crucial clue.

The key, suggests the psychologist Uta Frith, is that "the 'islets' of abilities are not so much tranquil oases as volcanoes, blatant signs of underlying disturbance." Take the astonishing memory feats that are so common in autism. Telephone directories, railroad timetables, strings of made-up words — none seems to present any challenge. Kanner himself marveled at the "truly phenomenal memory that enables the child to recall and reproduce complex 'nonsense' patterns, no matter how unorganized they are, in exactly the same form as originally construed."

But, as Frith notes, Kanner fell into a trap here. He presumed that if a child could memorize nonsense, then his memory for *useful* information would surely be all the more remarkable. Matters turn out not to be so simple.

Recite a random string of words, for instance, and a normal child and an autistic one will both recall the last few words. Asked to repeat "what-see-where-leaf-is-ship-we," for example, both will say something like "is-ship-we." But repeat the experiment with a string of words that is not completely random — "where-is-the-ship-that-see-was-leaf" — and something curious happens.

This time, the normal child will recall the words that made sense together — "where is the ship" — and forget the rest. But the autistic child will do exactly as she did before! She will still repeat only the last words, as if she did not detect the pattern or found it no help.

Somewhere in this tale a clue lies buried. We know, from calendar calculations and prime-number tricks and such everyday challenges as jigsaw puzzles, that autistic children can sometimes detect even the most subtle of patterns. Yet this "where is the ship" puzzle seems to convey the contrary moral.

Here the autistic person's approach to the world seems to be exactly the opposite of the ordinary person's. *They* cannot see a pattern even when it is right before their eyes, and *we* cannot help seeing patterns even when we know they do not exist. Autism, at least in this one tiny instance, seems to be defined by an inability to find the unity that ties together seemingly random events. It is a condition of permanent inability to see the forest for the trees.

In recent years, a number of scientists have built on such hints to pioneer a new approach to autism. The new view, associated primarily with Frith and other London-based psychologists, has won wide though far from universal support. More a rough draft than a proper theory, it is not so much an attempt to explain autism as to pin down just what it is that is missing. The new theory, named for its most surprising feature, goes by the name of "mindblindness."

The idea is that autistic people seem blind to other people's minds, unable to put themselves in anyone else's shoes. In Frith's formulation, the problem is that the autistic child "makes no distinction between what is in his own mind and what is in anybody else's mind."

The picture emerges most clearly in a series of simple but startling experiments. In one, Frith and her colleagues acted out a kind of puppet show while an autistic child looked on. A doll named Sally took a marble and put it in a basket. Then Sally left the room. While Sally was gone, a doll named Anne took the marble out of Sally's basket and put it into her own. When Sally came back into the room, the psychologists asked, where would she look for her marble?

Normal children gave the right answer at once. Sally would look for her marble in her basket, where she had put it before she left. Children with Down's syndrome also answered correctly. But nearly all autistic children got the answer wrong. Sally would look for the marble in Anne's basket, they said, presumably because that was where *they* would look.

The results are hard to fathom. The problem was not one of memory — further questions made clear that the autistic children had certainly not forgotten where the marble had been. Nor was it a question of deductive power. By conventional measures such as the ability to solve logical puzzles, the autistic children were intellectually far more able than the Down's syndrome children.

Time and again, related experiments have turned up similar results. In one of the simplest, one actor looked inside an open box. Later, a second actor placed her hand on the box while keeping her head turned away. Which actor would know what was in the box?

Three-quarters of mentally handicapped children answered that question correctly. But only one autistic child in three knew the answer. It was as if they were doubly handicapped — not only did they not know *what* other people knew, but they did not know *how* they knew it.

The problem, Uta Frith believes, is not with understanding in general but with understanding what is in other people's minds in particular. Autistic children can understand "mechanical" events: they know that if a balloon hits a thorn bush, it will pop. They can understand rote behavior: they know that if a person brings a candy bar to a cashier and gives him money, she will receive change in return. But they have enormous difficulty understanding events that require imagining what someone else is thinking: they cannot understand that someone will be hurt if he is called big and fat even if he is big and fat, or that someone who is crying will resent it if people laugh at her.

The result is that the world becomes a bewildering place, governed by rules that everyone else seems to know automatically. The autistic person is caught in the position of an American tourist in England drafted into a cricket match. "The same autistic child who can understand very well why a customer pays the shopkeeper, or why a person jumps out of the way of a falling rock," Frith writes, "may not understand why a polite guest declines a further offer of food when he is still hungry; why an employee who wishes to be promoted gives flowers to the boss's secretary; why a schoolgirl complains of a stomachache whenever she has not done her homework, or why a toddler exaggerates his hurt by crying when his brother pushed him."

More important, the notion of mindblindness suggests a less charged interpretation of what looks likes emotional aloofness in people with autism. Perhaps the seeming indifference to others is in fact an inability to decipher other people's emotions or to express one's own feelings. In that case, to talk of an autistic person's "coldness," say, would be to overinterpret symptoms in much the same way that psychiatrists did.

In any event, the inability to read other people makes for a risky kind of unworldliness. Donna Williams, an autistic woman who is nonetheless a college graduate and the author of several acclaimed volumes of autobiography, described an encounter with an aggressive cab driver in Sri Lanka. " 'You married? Do you have a boyfriend? Do you like Sri Lanka? Do you like men? Have you ever had a boyfriend? Are you afraid of AIDS? Would you like to get married? Would you like to get married to me?' The taxi driver went on and on as I answered each question honestly. It wasn't until he got to the last question and he explained his intentions that I understood what was happening. I thought that it was a sort of factual quiz, a culture study on his behalf, or that maybe he was into sociology or something."

Every student of autism is familiar with such displays of naïveté. People tend to use such terms as "open" and "innocent," but the behavior seems to have more to do with cognition than with morality. Psychologists have found, for example, that autistic children have terrible trouble with a simple puzzle involving deception. If he is asked to hide a penny in one hand, an autistic child will know to close a fist around it. But he will give the game away with other clues. He may show the experimenter that his other hand is empty, or he may "hide" the penny without turning away from the guesser. Normal and mentally handicapped children have no such problems.

Autistic people seem to see other people as unpredictable, self-propelled machines. ("Everything over which I did not have complete control . . . always took me by surprise," Donna Williams wrote, "often either shocking or confusing me. It often felt like the effect one gets in a 3-D movie where you duck and weave as everything seems to be coming at you.") It is easy to imagine that life in such a world would be exhausting and overwhelming. Is this a clue to the avoidance of people and the preference instead for such reliably consistent bits of the world as street directories and square-root tables?

As Frith suggests, other people's emotions are especially hard to decipher. "I was always trying to please people, and to do everything right," a high-functioning autistic man named Paul McDonnell recalled in an autobiographical essay. "I tried so hard that it had the opposite effect on everyone, including my parents. When people got upset with me, I felt like a failure. Even today I feel the same way. I feel it isn't fair that people get angry with me when I never *try* to do anything bad. I just *can't* understand human emotions, no matter how hard I try.

"For many years I would ask people, 'Are you mad at me?' " McDonnell went on. "Usually I asked my parents that question several times a day. My dad would occasionally get upset with me for asking that question over and over. I would feel very anxious about certain tones of voice. I would think that a surprised tone, or an emphatic tone, would mean anger."

A book of advice for parents of autistic children makes a related point. Losing your temper, the author cautions, will be no help in disciplining a child who has no idea what a parent's loud voice and red face mean: "A young autistic child who does not understand the implications of the signs of rage may feel that an angry parent is an interesting and exciting event, and he will therefore be encouraged rather than deterred."

Even Temple Grandin, who is savvy enough in the ways of the world to have earned a Ph.D. and a university professorship, talks about her difficulties in trying to "decode" other people's emotions. "I can tell if a human being is angry, or if he's smiling," she says, but she notes that "my emotions are simpler than those of other people. I don't know what complex emotion in a human relationship is. I only understand simple emotions, such as fear, anger, happiness, and sadness. I cry during sad movies, and sometimes I cry when I see something that really moves me. But complex emotional relationships are beyond my comprehension. I don't understand how a person can love someone one minute and then want to kill him in a jealous rage the next. I don't understand being happy and sad at the same time."

Grandin has learned to mimic ordinary behavior more or less success-fully — she can look people in the eye and keep her voice down to a normal conversational level, for instance — but she relies on logic and analysis where the rest of us get by on intuition and experience. It is as if a baseball player had to calculate, by applying the laws of physics, where to hold his glove to catch a fly ball. It might work, if he could calculate quickly enough, but his performance would always have a mechanical, herky-jerky quality.

"I can act social," Grandin says, "but it is like being in a play." Donna Williams writes that she, too, has had to learn acting skills. In her memoir *Somebody Somewhere*, she described an encounter with an autistic man named Malcolm, who had "the most extensive store of copied gestures, accents, facial expressions, and standard verbal anecdotes I had ever seen outside myself."

Still, something was off. Williams tried to explain to Malcolm what he was doing wrong. "Poses are meant to say something," I said, "they're meant to go together with what you are saying or feeling."

Malcolm tried another of his "characterizations" and asked what it meant. Williams did not know. "I am not very good at reading poses," she said. "I just know that other people use them to go with what they are saying or feeling and that you are supposed to use ones that come from your feelings and not just ones you have copied."

For the great majority of autistics, who are not nearly as able as Temple Grandin and Donna Williams, the challenge is far more than learning social routines. The deeper problem is that without the ability to empathize, to read other minds, the autistic person is at a handicap that no anthropologist would ever face. *Anything* is possible. One autistic girl, for example, was at the doctor's office. "Please give me your hand," the nurse told the bright ten-year-old, because she needed to take a blood sample. The girl panicked. It turned out that she had thought the nurse wanted her to cut off her hand and pass it over!

Such astonishing literal-mindedness is virtually a defining trait of au-tism. It shades into yet another characteristic feature of the disorder, often described as simply a preference for the concrete over the abstract. An autistic child is far quicker to learn words like "house" or "dog," for example, than "love" or "hate." But Clara Park noted in her memoir *The Siege* that something more subtle was going on.

Park's autistic daughter Elly could instantly learn words that stood on their own, independent of context. "Giraffe," "box," "heptagon," were all easy. It made no difference that some were abstract, some concrete. But words that depended on a relation between two things — "sister," "friend" — were vastly harder. For nearly everyone else, learning is far easier when it has some personal connection; for Elly, human connection was an irrelevance or an actual hindrance. She learned the world "man" — meaning "short-haired, trousers-wearing creature" — a full year before she learned the name of any particular man, "rectangle" and "heptagon" long before "happy" and "sad."

Clara Park, Elly's mother, is a professor of English, not a psychologist. But she is an acute observer who has become an undisputed authority on autism. Her descriptions of Elly (in time, she came to use her real name, Jessy) were not written in support of any theory, but simply to convey a picture of an utterly "other" way of living in the world.

The mindblindness work, she says today, fits with what she has seen firsthand over the past thirty-eight years. "Jessy doesn't know what's in anybody's mind," Clara Park says. "If we're cooking together and she knows the recipe, she *will* give me the garlic that I need, already cut up, and I'll congratulate her — 'You read my mind!' But she didn't, really. She can read a recipe, but she can't read body language, or faces. She can say *she's* happy or sad, but she would *never, never* pick up if I were sad or happy."

Clara Park has little patience with the notion that an autistic child may feel an emotional connection with the rest of the world that she cannot express. "Maybe, maybe, maybe," she says. "We'd all like to believe that." But she's no more convinced than Bernard Rimland that her child will grieve significantly when she dies. "She'll miss me," Park says. "She's used to me. She'll even be sad. But all kinds of trivial things — things we'd call trivial — would distress her more." To expect otherwise, she says, would be "pure sentimentality."

I tiptoe around that remark. What is the etiquette for discussing whether a beloved child returns a parent's love? And how could she not, for surely even a *pet* will show that it feels love? "A pet will and an autistic person won't," Park bursts out, her calm manner tested by this failure to grasp the essential point. "If autistic people were as empathetic as pets, we wouldn't have a problem."

PART FIVE

Obsessive-Compulsive Disorder

Certainly this is a crazy illness.
— *SIGMUND FREUD*

CHAPTER FIFTEEN

Enslaved by Demons

FAILED SUICIDE ATTEMPT
SUCCEEDS AS "SURGERY"

Bullet Ripped Through Brain,
Freed Youth from Obsessive-Compulsive Behavior.

Beset with psychiatric problems, the Canadian teen-ager
pointed the barrel of a .22 rifle at the roof of his mouth
and pulled the trigger.
The shot failed to kill him but, by a bizarre
happenstance, served as inadvertent brain surgery,
according to the psychiatrist who was treating him.
The bullet that tore into his brain released the
18-year-old from the grip of his most disturbing psychiatric
problem. Until the day he attempted suicide, he had a
fierce compulsion that led him to wash his hands more
than 50 times a day and take frequent, sometimes
hours-long showers.

—Washington Post, *February 26, 1988*

HOWARD HUGHES, one of the richest men in the world, prepared to eat lunch. For Hughes, obsessed with a fear of germs, food was a special problem. He had devised a series of decontamination rites, but they were so elaborate that no one person could manage them. Hughes managed with the help of his aides. He had prepared, for example, a meticulous memo on how to open a can of food to keep it germ-free:

> The man in charge turns the valve in the bathtub on, using his bare hands to do so. He also adjusts the water temperature so that it is not too hot nor too cold. He then takes one of the brushes, and, using one of two special bars of soap, creates a good lather and then scrubs the can from a point two inches below the top of the can. He should first soak and remove the label, and then brush the cylindrical part of the can over and over until all particles of dust, pieces of paper label, and, in general, all sources of

contamination have been removed. Holding the can at all times, he then processes the bottom of the can in the same manner, being very sure that the bristles of the brush have thoroughly cleaned all the small indentations on the perimeter of the bottom of the can. He then rinses the soap from the cylindrical sides and bottom of the can.

Clothes demanded equal care. Aides were forbidden to bring Hughes's clothes to him bare-handed, lest they transfer germs. Instead, Hughes instructed them to "obtain a brand new knife, never used, to open a new box of Kleenex, using the knife to open the slot. After the box is open you are to take the little tag and the first piece of Kleenex and destroy them; then using two fingers of the left hand and two fingers of the right hand take each piece of Kleenex out of the box and place it on an opened newspaper and repeat this until approximately fifty sheets are neatly stacked." That made a protective shield for one hand, and Hughes went on to provide page after page of similarly detailed instructions.

By the end of his life, to guard himself from contamination, Hughes had virtually withdrawn from the world. He lived in isolation, half-starved, behind tight-shut windows painted black to keep out germs emitted by the sun, watching the same movie time after time after time. The simplest act — picking up a spoon, throwing away a tissue — required elaborate and enormously time-consuming precautions. Hughes died imprisoned in his hotel room, a billionaire unable to walk out the door or even to eat a sandwich from room service.

Obsessive-compulsive disorder Hughes's affliction is called, and the commonplace words tempt us to think that we know what this bizarre illness is like. We tease a "compulsive" friend who keeps her CDs in alphabetical order or scrupulously knocks on wood for luck, and we all know people "obsessed" with food or sports or gardening. But these everyday examples smack of harmless eccentricity — they call to mind A. A. Milne and cozy verses about bears "who wait at the corners all ready to eat / The sillies who tread on the lines of the street" — and they miss the point badly.

For obsessive-compulsive disorder is in fact deeply *un*familiar. People whose lives had seemed utterly ordinary suddenly find themselves tormented by unwelcome thoughts and compelled to carry out meaningless rituals. Patients describe themselves as in thrall to a capricious demon, as if they are stuck in a malevolent version of "Simon Says." "Simon says, tap your right foot three times." "Simon says, now tap your left foot." "Simon says, right foot again." "Simon says . . ."

They wash their hands for hours each day, in a frenzied fear of contamination, until the flesh is raw and bleeding. They replay, helplessly and endlessly, a single horrifying scene in their minds — their child trapped in a fire, say. They check ten times, thirty times, fifty times, that the doors are locked and the stove is off.

Once the spell is broken, people can talk about their obsessions and compulsions with total clarity and can get on with completely normal lives. The paradox is that they themselves recognize that their rituals are pointless and "crazy," superstitions to the nth degree, and yet they remain powerless to resist. Victims of obsessive-compulsive disorder are perfectly sane people who find themselves marooned on islands of madness.

The most commonplace act can suddenly become mired in ritual. One woman explained to her therapist how she turned on her television, a process that took about half an hour:

> Before I start to turn it on, I have to wash and dry my hands. Then I go and touch the corner curtain, followed by touching the side of the TV two times. Then I have to go back and wash my hands. When I am finished with that, I will look behind the lamp two times, go back and wash my hands, come back, move the lamp to the left and look behind it, move the lamp two times to the right and look behind it, go back, wash my hands, and then look in back of the TV on the left four times, washing my hands in between each one. Then I look in back of the TV on the right eight times, wash my hands, and put the TV on channel six. Then I turn the knob from channel six to seven, four times, and from channel six to channel eight, four times. Then finally I turn it on.

As in Howard Hughes's case, these rituals can consume lives. One seven-year-old girl felt compelled to color in the round part of every *o* and *p* and *a* and *q* and *e* and *d* and *g* and *b* she encountered, and to count to fifty after every word she read or wrote. A woman with an obsessive fear of germs saw cockroaches in the supermarket one day and for the next *fourteen years* washed her groceries before putting them away. In time, she began washing everything else she brought into the house as well — "books, paint cans, mail, newspapers, toys, tools, pictures, everything."

Even psychiatrists who have heard all the stories shake their heads in disbelief. "I've learned never to tell a patient with compulsions that 'everybody does that,' or 'I know just how you feel,'" one therapist observes. *"They* don't and *you* don't." Consider, for example, a woman named Stacie Lewis, who traveled across Europe after college. If she violated any of her self-imposed rules about proper behavior — by showing impatience with a stranger, for example — Lewis felt compelled to return to the Spanish fishing village where she had begun her trip. Over the course of two years of travel, Lewis sometimes got as far as Germany or Scandinavia but she returned to her starting point in Spain over two hundred times.

Why do they do it? Obsessive-compulsives try valiantly to explain, but in the end they cannot quite convey to us what they are feeling. Simultaneously like everyone else and terribly cut off from them, they are like prisoners who can hear the ordinary sounds of street life wafted on the breeze. "What drives me and other obsessives to do this," one patient wrote, in an earnest attempt at explanation, "is the pain — the ceaseless anxiety that if we don't do it some unimaginably horrible event will occur."

The guru of obsessive-compulsive disorder is Judith Rapoport, chief of the child psychiatry branch at the National Institute of Mental Health. Rapoport is a tall, thin woman with short gray hair and the rat-tat-tat speech patterns of her native New York. She is an unusual scientist, happy to talk about the brain in conventional fashion, in terms of neurotransmitters and PET scans and so on, but more than willing to roam far afield as well. She peppers her conversation with references to Levi-Strauss and anthropology and religion, and she hops from discussions of serotonin levels over to *The Golden Bough* and back again.

That is partly because obsessive-compulsive disorder is a hard disease to confine — it forces one to confront such topics as free will and superstition and primitive ritual. And it is partly because Rapoport herself is hard to pigeonhole. She was trained as a psychoanalyst and her specialty, she notes, is "the illness most cited to illustrate the fundamental principles of psychoanalysis." And yet she has never worked as an analyst, and she brushes off most of psychoanalysis as unscientific and silly.

A few figures at the top *were* titans, she agrees, especially in the early days, but then there was a drastic drop in quality. "From 1950 on," she says, "the bulk of those who went into the field had IQs forty points lower" than their predecessors.

That impatient, irreverent tone is characteristic, and it comes with a characteristically conspiratorial, aren't-we-being-naughty grin. "One of the reasons why smart people left psychoanalysis," Rapoport goes on enthusiastically, "is because you were *brain dead* by the end of the first day. You just couldn't *stand* hearing the same thing people had been saying for forty years. You can go to church if you want that."

Rapoport herself, her manner makes plain, is not one to listen politely to someone else's sermon. But though she long ago abandoned psychoanalysis in favor of biological psychiatry, she hardly turned her back on psychology. "There's *no question*," she says in her emphatic way, "that if you know someone's family and their relationship with their family, you *really* know something important about them. One is simply, *totally* convinced."

Rapoport's account of obsessive-compulsive disorder, *The Boy Who Couldn't Stop Washing*, is the best book on the subject. The illness had fascinated her for decades. She had written about it in her undergraduate days, in an honors thesis at Swarthmore. Later, when she was a resident in psychiatry at Harvard in 1961, the first patient she ever treated was obsessive-compulsive. Sal was a family man, a churchgoer and a hard worker, a proud resident of Boston's North End. Out of the blue, on one perfectly ordinary day, he felt a compulsion to pick up a piece of trash he happened to see in the street. And another, and another. He *had* to do it, he said, although he could not say why.

He began to gather trash in bags and bring it home. The bags soon filled the house, blocking the halls and hiding the furniture. Still Sal gathered, now hunting down even the tiniest scraps of paper. Trash-gathering took more and more time. Before long, it took *all* his time. When he was no longer able to get to work, he entered the hospital.

The strangest feature of the story, Rapoport thought, was the specificity, the narrowness, of Sal's craziness. We think of madness as far-ranging — its victims are bludgeoned, not skewered. But Sal's memory was intact, his emotions were unchanged, his reason and judgment were unimpaired. With one devastating exception, he was the same person he had always been.

There is the strangeness that sets obsessive-compulsive disorder apart. The hallmark of this disease is normality pierced by a shaft of madness. That confined strangeness, that sliver of madness, hooked Rapoport three decades ago, and it holds her today.

Because the symptoms are so restricted, people can sometimes hide their obsessions from the world. This is not necessarily a plus; many times what it provides, Rapoport notes, is an opportunity "to suffer secretly." At work, for example, a lawyer compulsively checking and rechecking a document for typos may simply strike a casual observer as conscientious. (The professional basketball player Mahmoud Abdul-Rauf has Tourette's syndrome, which can include symptoms also seen in obsessive-compulsive disorder. Abdul-Rauf is dogged by rituals that range from tying his shoes over and over until they are perfectly symmetrical to opening the refrigerator door time and again. One of these compulsions — shooting basket after basket, to the point of exhaustion, until he swishes ten in a row — has made him a rich man.)

Even spouses might not know that their mates, once out of sight, are devoting hours a day to obsessive rituals. Freud made the same observation as long ago as 1907. "Sufferers from this illness are . . . able to treat their affliction as a private matter and keep it concealed for many years," he noted. "They are quite well able to fulfill their social duties during a part of the day, once they have devoted a number of hours to their secret doings."

Rapoport and her colleagues in psychiatry have worked hard to penetrate that secrecy. They have come up with at least the outline of a natural history of obsessive-compulsive disorder. It turns out to be far more common than anyone had suspected, afflicting millions of people in the United States alone. Depending on who is doing the counting, the incidence is between 1 and 3 percent of the population. That is at least as common as schizophrenia, perhaps on a par with asthma or diabetes. "You know someone with this disease," Rapoport says flatly.

The stories of these millions of people, though, fall into a tiny number of categories. Like TV sitcoms, patients' case histories tend to repeat the same half-dozen themes again and again. They wash, they check, they count, so predictably that psychiatrists talk casually about "washers," "checkers," and so on. The patients themselves, in contrast, usually are astonished to learn that there are countless strangers who carry out secret rituals identical to their own. For they have each invented their rituals. No one showed them what to do, after all, and often they had no idea that there was anyone who *could* have shown them.

It is an uncanny picture — people with obsessive-compulsive disorder literally form a secret society, each member hidden in his solitary cell unbeknownst to the others, each one convinced he is suffering uniquely and responding uniquely, and yet each one acting in parallel. It is as if an enormous studio of dancers, each one isolated in a separate room, should suddenly begin to move in perfect and complex synchrony.

The disease usually comes on insidiously, but it can begin abruptly, as in Sal's case. Rapoport has treated "kids who just woke up one morning with awful, sterile rituals and phrases stuck in their heads." Obsessive-compulsive disorder can strike at any age, though somewhere around eighteen or twenty is most common, and it occurs equally often in men and women.

The most common symptom, by far, is endless washing. Eighty-five percent of her patients, Rapoport says, go through a phase of scrubbing their hands for hours because of a deathly fear of contamination. It is tempting to put the blame on an American fixation with spic-and-span kitchens and germ-free bathrooms, but that seems incorrect. For the disease strikes around the world and across vastly different cultures, and it appears remarkably the same. Obsessive-compulsive disorder takes immediately recognizable forms in England and India and Sweden and the Sudan and the United States and Nigeria. Among Australian aborigines and Balinese priests and Israeli Jews, case histories of the disease are almost interchangeable.

What differences there are have more to do with local geography and customs than with the disorder itself. "In rural Nigeria, where it's a day's walk to water, you still see contamination rituals, but they take the form of women beating the bedding to pieces for lice," Rapoport says. "If they had any water, they would be running to a washing machine instead." In Jerusalem, she goes on, a psychiatrist who is himself an Orthodox Jew described a series of Orthodox Jewish patients he treated for obsessive-compulsive disorder. "This was an amazingly isolated group," Rapoport says. "It was a better cross-cultural study than going to some Berber tribe where they all listen to the radio and go to a bar and watch television. They're proscribed from doing that in the ultra-Orthodox community. And they showed all the classic symptoms, contamination and counting and the rest."

Similar stories echo down through the centuries. In the early 1600s, for example, one English physician described a patient whose fear of dirt ("dust") was so extreme that she felt "tortured until that she be forced to wash her clothes, be them never so good and new. Will not suffer her husband, child, nor any of the household to have any new clothes until they wash them for fear the dust of them will fall upon her. Dareth not to go to the church for treading on the ground, fearing any dust should fall on them." The details have changed through the years — once plague was the great fear, then syphilis, later cancer, and now AIDS — but the theme has remained the same.

Though obsessive-compulsive symptoms fit within a few broad categories like washing and counting, the details are always changing. One two-year-old boy spent hours each day lining up crayons and sorting out Tinkertoys. As he grew older, he began organizing his books alphabetically and arranging the shoes in his closet. At age twenty-two, his primary compulsion was walking through the exact center of doorways. It might take fifty passes through a doorway before he felt satisfied that he had done it right.

Rapoport once tried to compile a family tree of symptoms — do people begin as "washers," say, and later become "counters"? — but any patterns soon disappeared under a giant tangle of zigzagging arrows and switchbacks and cloverleafs. The mother of a teenage boy with severe obsessive-compulsive disorder showed me a list of his symptoms that she had compiled. It ran half a page. "Unable to shower without compulsively washing one foot," it read, and "fear of someone behind him" and "repeating sentence or words while trying to override intrusive thoughts" and "checking doors" and a dozen more.

In psychiatric jargon, "compulsions" are acts, like hand-washing. "Obsessions" are thoughts, akin to vignettes from waking nightmares. They are shameful, and they can be terrifying. Robert, a graduate student in chemistry and an obsessive-compulsive since he was seventeen, confessed that "thoughts would pop into my head of putting my daughter — I love my daughter very much — of putting her into the autoclave when I was working and watching her scream and suffer, and I couldn't get that thought out of my head."

Odder still, obsessive thoughts often take the form of doubts. (The French call obsessive-compulsive disorder *folie de doute*, the doubting disease.) Perhaps the strangest feature of this strange disease is that its victims literally do not believe their senses. Their fears recall the skeptical views of the philosopher David Hume, who asked how we can be sure that the universe does not change utterly every time we turn our backs. For most of us, this is merely an academic riddle, amusing or annoying according to our tastes, but certainly not urgent. For obsessive-compulsive people, though, Hume's query is literally of compelling interest — they cannot stop checking to see if the stove is off, the doors are locked, the windows are shut, no matter that they have checked ten or one hundred or one thousand times already.

Each check is complete, down to the smallest detail, and each is identical. None ever brings peace of mind. Each check momentarily quells panic, but then it returns almost at once, sometimes even stronger than before. "You say, 'Is the stove off? Is the stove off?'" one obsessive woman explained, "and then you get to the point of saying, 'Well, what's *off?* When I turn the knob to the off position, how do I know that's really the off position?'" Many patients say that if not for fear of losing their job or their family, they would literally continue checking all day long.

"I check *everything*," says Robert, the chemistry graduate student. "We have four cats, and when my wife washes the clothes, I say, 'Don't turn it on yet. Did you make sure there's no cats in there?' I push all the clothes aside to make sure there aren't any cats in the washing machine. When I open the refrigerator door, I open it, close it, open it, close it, two or three times, to make sure there's no cats in the refrigerator. I check the dishwasher two or three times to make sure there's no cats in *there,* and they would never climb in there. Even though I open it up and look in and see no cats" — his voice is rising in incredulity now — "I still think there might be a cat in there. Same with the oven."

Sometimes the doubts turn inward. A thirty-two-year-old college librarian was obsessed with the fear that he was a mass murderer who sneaked out of his house in the middle of the night in a memoryless trance, went on a killing spree, and then crawled back into bed. For the two years before he finally sought admission to a hospital, he had tied himself to bed with a rope each night to make sure he could not go out and kill. Even so, he was unable to rid himself of his obsession.

CHAPTER SIXTEEN

Freud Speaks

In obsessive actions everything has its meaning and can be interpreted.

— *SIGMUND FREUD*

LISTEN TO PEOPLE tell stories of the obsessions and compulsions that entrap them, and again and again they insist that this is something that fell out of the sky and hit them. "This is not *me*," they proclaim. "It is something that *happened* to me."

But it is hard to listen to these case histories and not conclude that they are symbolic tales. Even Emil Kraepelin, Freud's great rival and a devout believer that mental diseases had organic roots, made an exception for obsessiveness. Schizophrenia was certainly a brain disease, Kraepelin maintained, but obsessiveness was not. Look at how insightful these patients were, at how normally they behaved most of the time, at how clearly they saw that their rituals were meaningless.

The case histories do seem to carry disguised messages. Nor do the disguises seem especially cunning. Consider, for example, a case described in a recent psychiatric text. "A young married woman," the authors write blandly, "began to avoid the number four." Convinced that she had to avoid fours in order to fend off some looming but unidentified danger, she would never write a four. Nor would she ever eat four potato chips or four grapes or four of anything else, nor read the fourth page of any book or magazine. The rules grew ever stricter. She also began to avoid numbers beginning in four, or ending in four, or multiples of four, or one bigger or smaller than a multiple of four, and on and on, confining herself within an ever-shrinking prison cell.

Now listen to the explanation of how this had all started. "Her husband's birthday was on the fourth day of a month and . . . if she did not avoid the number, she would cause some great harm to him." Aha! Who among us could resist raising a knowing eyebrow?

Who, for that matter, could hear of people perpetually washing their hands and not think of Lady Macbeth?

Not Sigmund Freud. In an 1895 paper called "Obsessions and Phobias," he provided several examples of patients whose symptoms had a symbolic meaning. "A woman kept washing her hands constantly and touched door-handles only with her elbow," Freud wrote, by way of summarizing one such case. *"Reinstatement:* It was the case of Lady Macbeth. The washing was symbolic, designed to replace by physical purity the moral purity which she regretted having lost. She tormented herself with remorse for conjugal infidelity, the memory of which she had resolved to banish from her mind."

Obsessive-compulsive disorder was one of Freud's favorite subjects, one he returned to again and again throughout his long career and the neurosis he discussed more than any other. It was the illness he knew best, he declared, and "unquestionably the most interesting and repaying subject of analytic research." He would return to it again and again — obsessively, one is tempted to say — proposing a sequence of ever-deeper, ever-more-complex explanations.

His clinical descriptions are clear and compact. "Obsessional neurosis is shown in the patient's being occupied with thoughts in which he is in fact not interested, in his being aware of impulses in himself which appear very strange to him, and in his being led to actions the performance of which give him no enjoyment, but which it is impossible for him to omit," he told a lecture audience in 1916.

"Certainly this is a crazy illness," he went on, among other reasons because the patient's insight into his predicament did him no good. "Do not suppose, however, that you will help the patient in the least by calling on him to take a new line, to cease to occupy himself with such foolish thoughts and to do something sensible instead of his childish pranks. He would like to do so himself, for he is completely clear in his head, shares your opinion of his obsessional symptoms and even puts it forward to you spontaneously. Only he cannot help himself."

For Freud, the subject also had a personal tug. He himself, he wrote in a letter to Jung, was a representative of "the 'obsessional' type, each specimen of which vegetates in a sealed-off world of his own."

Even more than usual, Freud's views on what he called "obsessional neurosis" merit a close look. When it came to schizophrenia and autism, Freud's followers spoke loudly, and Freud spoke softly or not at all. When it came to obsessions and compulsions, on the other hand, Freud's descendants did little more for fifty years than echo their master's voice.

His first insight into obsessiveness, Freud wrote, had come from one of his early patients, a government official "troubled by innumerable scruples." When this patient paid Freud's consultation fees, the florin notes were invariably clean and smooth. Freud made a passing remark about the new bills, and the patient explained that they were by no means new. He had the money ironed at his home, he went on, as a matter of conscience. It was not right to risk harming innocent people by handing them dirty, bacteria-carrying florins. Freud let it pass, and on another occasion asked the man about his sex life:

> "Oh, that's quite all right," he answered airily [Freud wrote]. "I'm not at all badly off in that respect. I play the part of a dear old uncle in a number of respectable families, and now and then I make use of my position to invite some young girl to go out with me for a day's excursion in the country. Then I arrange that we shall miss the train home and be obliged to spend the night out of town. I always engage two rooms — I do things most handsomely; but when the girl has gone to bed I go in to her and masturbate her with my fingers."
>
> "But aren't you afraid of doing her some harm, fiddling about in her genitals with your dirty hand?"
>
> At this he flared up: "Harm? Why, what harm should it do her? It hasn't done a single one of them any harm yet, and they've all of them enjoyed it. Some of them are married now, and it hasn't done them any harm at all."

Here was the clue, and Freud pounced. At some level, he wrote, the man knew that his behavior was wrong. Nonetheless, he was not about to reform, and so his unconscious had come up with a neat compromise. "The self-reproachful affect had become *displaced*," Freud explained. "The aim of this displacement was obvious enough: if his self-reproaches had been allowed to remain where they belonged he would have had to abandon a form of sexual gratification to which he was probably impelled by some powerful infantile determinants. The displacement therefore ensured his deriving a considerable advantage from his illness."

That same clear idea would recur in all Freud's writings on obsessiveness. The key was always that "the sufferer from compulsions and prohibitions behaves as if he were dominated by a sense of guilt, of which, however, he knows nothing."

It sounded odd, Freud acknowledged, to say that someone could feel guilty but not know it. Yet he was certain he was correct. Throughout his career, Freud's view of obsessiveness changed in major ways. But he always held fast to this core belief in what might be called unconscious guilt. Through the years, he tried out his prize insight in one context after another, like a jeweler who cannot quite find the setting that does justice to a particularly handsome stone.

From the start, Freud was convinced not only that guilt lay at the heart of obsessiveness but that the guilt had to do with sex. "We can always find in the previous history of the patient," he wrote in 1895, *"at the beginning of the obsession*, the original idea that has been replaced. The replaced ideas all have common attributes; they correspond to really [i.e., real rather than imaginary] distressing experiences in the subject's sexual life which he is striving to forget." (Italics in original.)

He cited, for example, "a girl [who] reproached herself for things which she knew were absurd: for having stolen, for having made counterfeit money, for being involved in a conspiracy, etc., according to what she happened to have been reading during the day." Freud had no trouble explaining the true reason for those false confessions: "She reproached herself with the masturbation she had been practicing in secret without being able to renounce it." The remedy, he noted in passing, was as self-evident as the diagnosis: "She was cured by careful surveillance which prevented her from masturbating."

Other cases struck him as equally transparent. They were so simple to interpret that, contrary to his usual practice, Freud skipped the details and simply tossed a variety of similar-sounding case histories into a single grab bag of a sentence. "Several women complained of an obsessional impulse to throw themselves out of the window, to stab their children with knives, scissors, etc.," he wrote. His explanation made clear that details would have been superfluous: "These were women who, not being at all satisfied in marriage, had to struggle against the desires and voluptuous ideas that constantly troubled them at the sight of other men."

This seemed awfully simple, even pat. Did it really go without saying that stabbing a baby was a more acceptable fantasy than lusting after a stranger? And, indeed, Freud quickly went on to show that the unconscious had more than one trick up its sleeve. Just as obsessions and compulsions allowed a person to replace an unacceptable idea with a less disturbing one, he argued, so they made it possible to replace a forbidden wish with an innocuous *act*.

Consider, for example, "a woman [who] found herself obliged to count the boards in the floor, the steps in the staircase, etc. — acts which she performed in a ridiculous state of anxiety." Why count? Freud asked, as decades later Rapoport would ask, why pick up trash?

For Freud, the explanation was at hand: "She had begun the counting in order to distract her mind from obsessional ideas (of temptation). She had succeeded in doing so, but the impulse to count had replaced the original obsession." Rituals were shaky defenses against "constantly threatening" impulses "lurking in the unconscious." The obsessive could never relax his guard; his "ceremonials" were not routine precautions, like a driver's fastening his seat belt, but desperate attempts to stave off disaster.

And the pressure was always growing. "The process of repression which leads to obsessional neurosis must be considered as one which is only partly successful and which increasingly threatens to fail," Freud went on. "Fresh psychical efforts are continually required to counterbalance the forward pressure of the instinct." Freud wrote as if he had in mind the horror movie scene where the monster pounds the bedroom door, which shakes and quivers under the assault, while the young couple inside whimper in terror and try frantically to shove chairs and dressers under the knob.

As time passed, and Freud considered his patients' cases in more detail, his explanations would grow ever more arcane. No clue was too small. "In obsessive actions," Freud declared, "everything has its meaning and can be interpreted." In 1909, for example, he devoted nearly one hundred pages to his most famous obsessive patient, a prominent young lawyer in Vienna named Ernst Lanzer. He has gone down in history as the Rat Man (Freud coined the name), because he was plagued by obsessive thoughts of a particularly gruesome torture someone had once described to him. A criminal was tied up, a metal pot with rats trapped inside was fastened to his buttocks, and the rats bored their way into the victim's rectum. The image horrified him, the Rat Man told Freud, but he could not rid himself of it. Worse still, he was consumed by the thought that this punishment was being applied to his fiancée and to his father (even though he knew perfectly well that his father had died years before!).

Freud's resolution of the case is too complex to summarize briefly — we will come back to the Rat Man later — but even the smallest features of the story reveal how ornate Freud's interpretations had become. At one point, for example, Freud discussed a magical word, a sort of one-word prayer, that the Rat Man had invented to ward off danger. It was essentially an acronym, with an "amen" tacked on at the end. The word was "glejisamen." The Rat Man explained that the first two letters came from the word *glückliche*, meaning "happy," the letter *j* stood for *jetzt und immer,* meaning "now and forever," and so on.

Freud was in no doubt about the real meaning of this mysterious word. "I could not help noticing," he wrote, "that the word was in fact an anagram of the name of his lady." (This was a bit of a reach. Freud was referring to the Rat Man's fiancée, whose name was Gisela.) But Freud was only warming up.

"Her name contained an 's,' and this he had put last, that is, immediately before the 'amen' at the end. We may say, therefore, that by this process he had brought his 'samen' [in English, 'semen'] into contact with the woman he loved; in imagination, that is to say, he had masturbated with her. He himself, however, had never noticed this very obvious connection."

In comparison with other examples of Freud's code-breaking, such explanations would indeed come to seem endearingly straightforward. Consider the case of another of Freud's patients, a woman in her late twenties bedeviled by obsessions and compulsions. Among them was this: many times a day she ran out of her bedroom into the next room, stood beside a table there, rang a bell for the housemaid and sent her off on some errand, and then ran back to her own room.

She could not explain why she did it, but soon she and Freud figured it out. "More than ten years before, she had married a man very much older than herself," Freud wrote, "and on the wedding night he was impotent. Many times during the night he had come running from his room into hers to try once more, but every time without success. Next morning he had said angrily: 'I should feel ashamed in front of the housemaid when she makes the bed,' took up a bottle of red ink that happened to be in the room and poured its contents over the sheet, but not on the exact place where a stain would have been appropriate."

This was certainly a beginning. Not only did his patient's running back and forth make some kind of sense, but so did her calling the housemaid. In addition, Freud's patient soon added another key insight: her table was covered with a tablecloth that *did* have a stain, and the maid had surely seen it. Freud was certain that he was on the right track, but he conceded that he was still confused.

Then the light dawned. "It was clear, in the first place, that the patient was identifying herself with the husband," Freud explained. "She was playing his part by imitating his running from one room into the other. Further, to carry on the analogy, we must agree that the bed and the sheet were replaced by the table and the tablecloth. This might seem arbitrary, but surely we have not studied dream-symbolism to no purpose. In dreams too we often find a table which has to be interpreted as a bed."

So far, so good. Now, what was behind the young woman's obsessive ritual?

Its kernel was obviously the summoning of the housemaid, before whose eyes the patient displayed the stain, in contrast to her husband's remark that he would feel ashamed in front of the maid. Thus he, whose part she was playing, did not feel ashamed in front of the maid; accordingly the stain was in the right place. We see, therefore, that she was not simply repeating the scene; she was continuing and at the same time correcting it; she was putting it right. But by this she was also correcting the other thing, which had been so distressing that night and had made the expedient with the red ink necessary—his impotence. So the obsessional action was saying: "No, it's not true. He had no need to feel ashamed in front of the housemaid; he was not impotent." It represented this wish, in the manner of a dream, as fulfilled in a present-day action; it served the purpose of making her husband superior to his past mishap.

Freud was proud of this bit of detective work—he published two versions of the story a decade apart—and he proclaimed that his interpretation "led directly to the inmost core of an illness."

Not all readers were won over. In 1924, Virginia Woolf wrote a letter to a friend about the publishing firm she and Leonard Woolf had founded. "We are publishing all Dr. Freud," she wrote impatiently, "and I glance at the proof and read how Mr. A.B. threw a bottle of red ink on to the sheets of his marriage bed to excuse his impotence to the housemaid, but threw it in the wrong place, which unhinged his wife's mind — and to this day she pours claret on the dinner table. We could all go on like that for hours; and yet these Germans think it proves something — besides their own gull-like imbecility."

Virginia Woolf should have kept reading. In the same essay that recounted Mr. A.B.'s misadventures, Freud went on to weave a story that made the first one seem as mundane as a road map. The essay's title was "The Sense of Symptoms." By way of demonstrating how to unearth the meanings concealed in symptoms, Freud told a long and involved story about a woman who could fall asleep only after elaborate preparations. It was a story that revealed Freud at the height of his rebus-solving powers.

The patient was nineteen years old. She was bright and well educated, an only child who lived at home. Once lively and high-spirited, she had grown depressed and irritable over the past few years. Along with these general symptoms was a specific one: she found herself unable to fall asleep until she had gone through a complicated "ceremony." First, in order to insure absolute quiet during the night, she took all the clocks from her room, even banishing her tiny wristwatch. She put all the flowerpots safely on the writing table, so they would not fall over in the night. Then the pillows on the bed had to be precisely arranged, the quilt shaken and reshaken and laid down just so, her own head placed atop the pillow in a particular way, and so on.

The young woman acknowledged that her preparations made no sense — her watch was too quiet to hear, for example, nor was there any chance that a flowerpot would topple on its own — but she had no choice in the matter. Every step had to be carried out and then checked and double-checked, all in an atmosphere of terrible anxiety. Each night, the routine took an hour or two.

This case, Freud noted, did not resolve itself as easily as the previous one had. "I was obliged to give the girl hints and propose interpretations," Freud wrote, "which were always rejected with a decided 'no' or accepted with contemptuous doubt." In time, though, Freud's patient overcame her doubts and accepted his interpretations.

It cannot have been easy. "Our patient gradually came to learn that it was as symbols of the female genitals that clocks were banished from her equipment for the night," Freud explained. "Clocks and watches," he reminded his readers, "have arrived at a genital role owing to their relation to periodic processes and equal intervals of time."

The meaning of the young woman's fear that the ticking of a clock might disturb her sleep was similarly clear. "The ticking of a clock may be compared with the knocking or throbbing in the clitoris during sexual excitement." Similarly, "flowerpots and vases, like all vessels, are also female symbols. Taking precautions against their falling and being broken at night was thus not without its good sense."

What about the rule that the pillow must not touch the headboard? "The pillow, she said, had always been a woman to her and the upright wooden back a man. Thus she wanted — by magic, we must interpolate — to keep the man and woman apart — that is, to separate her parents from each other, not to allow them to have sexual intercourse."

At this point, the interpretation built to a pitch that makes the reader fear for Freud's equilibrium. Explaining why his patient first fluffed her quilt and then smoothed it down, he tells us that "if a pillow was a woman, then the shaking of the eiderdown till all the feathers were at the bottom and caused a swelling there had a sense as well. It meant making a woman pregnant; but she never failed to smooth away the pregnancy again, for she had for years been afraid that her parents' intercourse would result in another child and so present her with a competitor."

There was more to come. "On the other hand, if the big pillow was a woman, the mother, then the small top-pillow could only stand for the daughter. Why did this pillow have to be placed diamond-wise and her head precisely along its centre line? It was easy to recall to her that this diamond shape is the inscription scribbled on every wall to represent the open female genitals. If so, she herself was playing the man and replacing the male organ by her head."

Freud seemed to fear he had gone too far. "Wild thoughts, you will say, to be running through an unmarried girl's head. I admit that is so." But after all, he protested — perhaps he protested too much — *he* had not put these ideas in his patient's head. "But you must not forget that I did not make these things but only interpreted them."

The theory behind such interpretations had evolved over the years. In its first incarnation, Freud had seen obsessiveness as caused by sexual experiences in childhood. Not fantasies, it should be noted, but *experiences.* And not just any experiences.

Obsessiveness was special, as Freud explained "in a simple formula" in an essay in 1896. "Obsessional ideas are invariably transformed self-reproaches which have re-emerged from repression and which always relate to some sexual act that was performed with pleasure in childhood." (Freud's zeal in pursuit of a sexual interpretation was formidable. "The connection between obsessional neurosis and sexuality is not always all that obvious," he once confided to his friend Fliess, and "someone who had not searched for it as single-mindedly as I did would have overlooked it.")

The "pleasure" theory was soon discarded. When Freud publicly abandoned the "seduction hypothesis" in 1906 — when he announced that his patients were not recalling true incidents of sexual abuse from their childhood but were instead relaying sexual fantasies — he moved to a new view of obsessiveness as well.

In the case history of the Rat Man, published in 1909, Freud spelled out his new thinking. It is a long, tangled essay, and the Rat Man's story is so complex that whole paragraphs are almost impenetrable — "it would not surprise me to hear that at this point the reader had ceased to be able to follow," Freud confesses early on* — but there are dazzling passages as well.

In these sections, we see Freud at his best. His Lady Macbeth interpretations, arguing that hand-washing symbolizes guilt, were too simple to be surprising. The sexual theories, about the secret significance of stained tablecloths and spilled ink, were too far-fetched to be compelling. But at several points in the Rat Man's story, Freud wins us over. While we are still contemplating the facts of the case in bafflement, like dim Watson, Freud has come on like Holmes and presented us with an explanation that leaves us muttering "Of course!" and "How did I miss it?"

He begins by telling us about the relationship between the patient and his late father. The two had been close, best friends even, though the father had disapproved of the son's fiancée. The young couple, we soon learn, had conflicts of their own. They had a long history together; the Rat Man had proposed ten years before, and been turned down. Even he conceded that their relationship was far more complex than a mere love affair.

Now Freud leapt in. The relationship of the Rat Man and his father, and also of the Rat Man and his fiancée, shared one crucial feature. Both were compounds of love and hate. The difference was that the young man was at least dimly aware of his hostile feelings for his fiancée; his resentment of his father was unconscious.

The key to the Rat Man's character, Freud wrote, was not simply that he felt both love and hate, but that he felt them both *permanently*. "Poets tell us that in the more tempestuous stages of love the two opposed feelings may subsist side by side for a while as though in rivalry with each other," Freud noted. "But the *chronic* co-existence of love and hatred, both directed towards the same person and both of the highest degree of intensity, cannot fail to astonish us."

Here was the explanation of small but perplexing mysteries. The Rat Man had once seen a stone in the roadway, for instance, and had felt compelled to move it because his fiancée would later be traveling along the same road and might hit it. But a few minutes later, he had realized that the whole performance was silly. This time, he felt an equally irresistible compulsion to go back and return the stone to its original position in the middle of the road. Once Freud has opened our eyes, we can hardly imagine a clearer symbolic display of love and hate in uneasy coexistence.

More important, the same explanation untangled a whole class of symptoms. Here, too, was the explanation of the perpetual doubts that

---

* In a letter to a colleague, Jung praised the paper but noted that it was *"very hard to understand.* I will soon have to read it for the third time. Am I especially stupid? Or is it the style? I cautiously opt for the latter."

plagued the Rat Man, as they plague so many obsessives to this day. "The doubt is in reality a doubt of his own love—which ought to be the most certain thing in his whole mind; and it becomes diffused over everything else, and is especially apt to become displaced on to what is most insignificant and small. A man who doubts his own love may, or rather *must*, doubt every lesser thing." (Italics in original.)

The deciphering of the Rat Man's torture fantasy was less satisfactory. The reason for the Rat Man's obsessive visions, Freud explained, was his unconscious guilt for harboring fantasies of having anal intercourse with his father and his fiancée. The pressure of those repellent fantasies burbling away in his unconscious gave rise to marginally more presentable, conscious obsessions.

This translation hinged on a lengthy series of dubious connections—as a boy, the Rat Man had once been punished for biting, rats are sharp-toothed, therefore rats symbolized the patient; rats carry disease, a penis can transmit disease, therefore the rats symbolized a penis; and so on—and any general insights sank beneath wave after wave of details unique to the Rat Man's story.

But a general theory of obsessiveness would not be long in coming. By 1913, only four years after his Rat Man essay, Freud would hit on the explanation he would stick with forever after. The answer, as always, lay in childhood. The obsessive-compulsive adult had, years before, been the victim of harsh toilet-training. The infant's fear of losing control of his bowels had become the adult's all-pervasive fear of losing control of anything.

Control, order, routine—these were the watchwords, the guiding themes, of the adult obsessive's life. There was one more crucial theme. This was the urge to impose one's will on others. "Compulsive orderliness is at the same time an expression of the patient's desire for domination," Freud's disciple Karl Abraham explained. "He exerts power over things. He forces them into a rigid and pedantic system."

Think of the homemaker with a compulsion for cleaning, Abraham went on, or the unbending bureaucrat who goes strictly by the book. They imposed their rules on themselves and on everyone else as well. "In extreme cases of an obsessional character, as it is met with in housewife's neurosis and in neurotic exaggerations of the bureaucratic mind," Abraham noted, "this craving for domination becomes quite unmistakable. Or again, we need only think of the sadistic elements that go to make up the well-known anal character-trait of obstinacy to realize how anal and sadistic instinctual forces act together."

This explanation of obsessiveness would dominate psychiatry for the next half century. Every paper on the subject took "anal-sadism" as its central theme. (It is surprising that the Rat Man story, which had anal obsessions as its major theme, had not provided Freud with the crucial clues.)

Freud had nearly hit on the answer a few years earlier, in a paper called "Character and Anal Erotism," published the year *before* the Rat Man essay. Time and again, Freud had noted then, he saw patients who were "noteworthy for a regular combination of the three following characteristics. They are especially *orderly, parsimonious, and obstinate*." (Italics in original.)

This was a favorite theme of Freud's, one he had been mulling over for years. What connected the elements of this mysterious triad? The crucial clue was that these people "as infants . . . seem to have belonged to the class who refuse to empty their bowels when they are put on the pot because they derive a subsidiary pleasure from defecating; for they tell us that even in somewhat later years they enjoyed holding back their stool, and they remember — though more readily about their brothers and sisters than about themselves — doing all sorts of unseemly things with the feces that had been passed."

The child, Freud had written in this early paper, was father to the man. The adult's exaggerated insistence on neatness and order was a defense against the infant's unseemly interest in filth and feces. The adult's obstinacy originated in the infant's wish that he himself, and not his parents, be in control of his performance on the toilet. The adult's miserliness . . . well, that was a bit trickier.

To hold on to money with a penny-pinching "tightness," Freud argued, was the counterpart of retaining one's feces. After all, he noted, in "the ancient civilizations, in myths, fairy tales and superstitions, in unconscious thinking, in dreams and in neuroses," money and feces were equated. The most valuable of substances was identified with the most worthless. Did not the Babylonians call gold "the feces of Hell"? Do we not today speak of "filthy lucre"?

For Freud and his followers, such potty talk would prove irresistible. The discovery of "anal character traits" explained, for example, the impulse to create art. The artist, Karl Abraham noted in an influential paper, was one whose delight in playing with his feces had become "sublimated into pleasure in painting, modelling, and similar activities." The same theory also explained the impulse to *admire* art. "The pleasure in looking at one's own mental creations, letters, manuscripts, etc., or completed works of all kinds," Abraham wrote, had as its prototype "looking at one's own feces, which is an ever-new source of pleasure to many people." And the theory explained the impulse to *collect* art, or stamps, or odds-and-ends that might someday come in handy. "Pleasure in having a mass of material stored up," Abraham observed, "entirely corresponds to pleasure in the retention of feces."

Soon the theory was an essential item in every psychiatrist's tool kit. "An attack of diarrhea at the beginning of the analysis heralded the important subject of money," the analyst Ruth Mack Brunswick noted succinctly in an essay in 1928, knowing there was no need to explain or justify the connection.

There were almost no limits to the bounty provided by this new theory. It explained both generosity and miserliness, tidiness and slovenliness, docility and rebelliousness, and countless other traits besides. Generosity, for example, was a telltale sign of infantile behavior; the adult's gifts harkened back to his infancy, when he believed that his feces, which he had made himself, were a great prize. Even a seemingly unrelated trait like procrastination was revealed in its true guise. Procrastination simply reenacted the infant's attempts to defy his parents by retaining his feces until the last possible moment.

Why is the toilet-training era so crucial? Because, said Freud, "it is here for the first time . . . that [children] encounter the external world as an inhibiting power, hostile to their desire for pleasure, and have a glimpse of later conflicts both external and internal. An infant must not produce his excreta at whatever moment he chooses, but when other people decide that he shall. . . . This is where he is first obliged to exchange pleasure for social respectability." And so the toilet is indeed a seat of tremendous power and responsibility, the always earnest Karl Abraham observed, and deserves its designation as "the throne."

With his 1907 insight into the "anal" character, Freud had virtually solved the mystery of obsessiveness. All that was left was a single, tiny step, although it took Freud until 1913 to see it—people who suffered from obsessions and compulsions were simply those at the extreme end of the spectrum of "anality." They were not merely neat but consumed by a frantic need to impose order on the world. Drafted against their will, they fought an endless and panicky battle against the forces of chaos and confusion.

Character explained everything. "Obsessive neurosis" was no longer a bizarre kind of modern-day possession but merely a well-mapped quirk of personality. What had long seemed bewildering soon became mundane.

In a passage that reflected psychiatry's comfort with this now-tamed neurosis, for example, the eminent Leo Kanner summarized current thinking in 1948. "Obsessive and compulsive phenomena," Kanner declared matter-of-factly, "are most frequently encountered in persons who are overconscientious, shy, pedantic, punctilious, painstakingly addicted to minutest order and symmetry, not satisfied until everything is 'just so.' "

For decades, this Just So story reigned unchallenged as a universal insight into human nature. This is, perhaps, a bit of a surprise, for anthropologists had found that attitudes toward toilet-training varied enormously around the world. In some cultures, for example, infants were toilet-trained as early as six months. As the anti-Freudian psychiatrist E. Fuller Torrey points out, this would have led one to predict "an exceptional number of bookkeepers, cleaning ladies, and stamp collectors, and . . . villages which rival Swiss villages in immaculateness."

Psychiatrists carried on undaunted. In 1965, for example, Anna Freud delivered a lecture on the newest psychoanalytic thinking on "obsessive neurosis." The talk, intended as a summary of the field rather than a personal view, might have been lifted from her father's groundbreaking paper of fifty years before. The key observation was "the fact that in clinical work we always uncover anal-sadistic material."

But eventually, for reasons beyond the scope of this book, Freud's "developmental theory" of oral, anal, phallic, and genital stages disappeared. We do continue to use the word "anal" to denote a certain persnickety character. But the word is a ghost of a buried theory, much as words like "good-humored" and "phlegmatic" are ghosts that have long outlived the theories that gave rise to them.

When the theory of "developmental stages" sank, it created a whirlpool, like the vortex around a capsized ship. The main casualty was the theory itself. But its intellectual offspring became casualties as well. In particular, Freud's anal theory of obsessiveness was also, and unceremoniously, dragged beneath the waves. "We have, of course," the psychiatrist Aaron Esman wrote in a 1989 essay on obsessions and compulsions, "long ago given up the id-psychological connection associated with toilet-training traumas." The casually dismissive tone, making clear that no argument was called for, was as significant as the message.

Still, it is easy to believe that Freud was on to *something* when he talked of obsessiveness, even if it is hard to tag along on some of his more exuberant flights of fancy. When he resisted the impulse to peek through the bedroom or bathroom keyhole, he could be compelling.

His explanation of obsessive doubts as symbolizing love-hate ambivalence, as discussed earlier, was one example. There were many others. One of his grand themes, for example, was that obsessiveness was a kind of religious devotion gone mad. Always scornful of religion, Freud had here a subject that gave full scope to his malice, and his genius.

He began an essay called "Obsessive Actions and Religious Practices" by summarizing "the resemblances . . . between neurotic ceremonials and the sacred acts of religious ritual." Both called for the utmost concentration and conscientiousness; both caused tremendous guilt if neglected. But Freud conceded that the differences were great, too. Some were "so great that they make the comparison a sacrilege."

For Freud, that was an irresistible temptation. He listed some of these differences: the obsessive carried out his neurotic rituals in secrecy and isolation, while the religious worshiper prayed in company. More important, the neurotic's rituals seemed "foolish and senseless," while every element of the believer's ceremonies was "full of significance" and "symbolic meaning."

Then Freud sprang the trap. "It is precisely this sharpest difference between neurotic and religious ceremonial which disappears when, with the help of the psychoanalytic technique of investigation, one penetrates to the true meaning of obsessive actions."

He went on to probe those "true meanings" in characteristic, sex-soaked fashion and then returned to his religious theme. First came another tie between the neurotic obsessive and the religious believer — both risked focusing so intently on rituals as performance that they lost sight of their true significance. And there was still another, deeper tie.

Both the obsessive and the believer renounced "instincts that are constitutionally present." Not the same instincts, to be sure. The religious believer tried to submit his own will to God's will. He fought down his impulse toward vengeance, for example, and turned the other cheek instead. The obsessive renounced, or repressed, unacceptable *sexual* impulses.

In the end, Freud argued, the obsessive and the believer were acting out the same play on different stages. One performance was private, one public, but that was the only difference. That one performer was mad, or the next thing to it, while the other was engaged in the solemn observance of his faith was beside the point. It was best, Freud declared magisterially, to think of "[obsessive] neurosis as an individual religiosity and religion as a universal obsessional neurosis."

Such virtuoso displays were a specialty of Freud's — he happily ventured off into literature and anthropology whenever he could slip his therapeutic leash — but Freud did not rely on literary artistry to win over his peers. The proof of *this* pudding, he noted repeatedly, was easy to find: he cured obsessive patients.

The Rat Man's case, for example, was "moderately severe," Freud wrote, and "the treatment, which lasted for about a year, led to the complete restoration of the patient's personality, and to the removal of his inhibitions." Seven years later, he repeated and broadened the same claim. Psychoanalysis had begun by *explaining* hysteria and obsessiveness, Freud declared, and it had quickly moved on to *curing* those illnesses. "Obsessional neurosis and hysteria are the forms of neurotic illness upon the study of which psychoanalysis was first built," he proclaimed in 1916, "and in the treatment of which, too, our therapy celebrates its triumphs." Nor was this boast a momentary lapse. "We have found from psychoanalysis," he emphasized elsewhere in the same lecture, "that it is possible to get permanently rid of these strange obsessional symptoms. . . . I myself have succeeded repeatedly in this."

Freud was so matter-of-fact about curing obsessive patients that he tossed off references to cures in passing. They were cited not as the climax of clinical tales but almost grudgingly, as interruptions that slowed the narrative flow. Consider this example from 1900, from Freud's most ambitious work, *The Interpretation of Dreams:*

> I had an opportunity of obtaining a deep insight into the unconscious mind of a young man whose life was made almost impossible by an obsessional neurosis. He was unable to go out into the street because he was tortured by the fear that he would kill everyone he met. He spent his days in preparing his alibi in case he might be charged with one of the murders committed in the town. It is unnecessary to add that he was a man of equally high morals and education. The analysis (which, incidentally, led to his recovery) showed that the basis of this distressing obsession was an impulse to murder his somewhat over-severe father.

By 1926, Freud's talk of cures had grown bolder and more sweeping. The psychoanalytic treatment of obsessiveness and other neuroses was "a kind of magic," he wrote, that *"would* be magic if it worked rather quicker. An essential attribute of a magician is speed — one might say suddenness — of success. But analytic treatments take months and even years; magic that is so slow loses its miraculous character."

Appropriately, Freud is practicing sleight of hand here. By admitting so openly that psychoanalysis is slow to cure, he draws our attention away from the real question — never mind speed, does it cure at all? While we are left pondering whether a slow miracle is a true miracle, Freud has snatched our wallet and darted off.

It is hard to know what to make of Freud's therapeutic "triumphs." Neither he nor anyone else ever wrote up most of these cases. The great majority came unaccompanied by names or dates or even the sketchiest details. The most basic questions — how many triumphs were there? how many failures? how were success and failure judged? — went undiscussed.

Even in the tiny number of cases where Freud did provide details, matters remain murky. The Rat Man seems not to have been cured. (He was killed in World War I, only a few years after his treatment with Freud.) Freud's claims of a cure, according to the psychoanalyst and Freud partisan Patrick Mahony, were a "therapeutic exaggeration." Mahony, who devoted an entire book to the case, notes that the Rat Man had previously been treated by Vienna's most renowned psychiatrist, Julius Wagner-Jauregg. (It was Wagner-Jauregg who would win the Nobel Prize for treating general paralysis of the insane by inducing malarial fevers.) Eager to succeed where his better-known rival had failed, Mahony wrote, "Freud was bent on making the case a psychoanalytic showpiece."

At the time, in 1909, Freud was hardly the titan he would become. The head of a fledgling movement, he had climbed only a few rungs on the ladder of fame. Freud "desperately wanted the appearance of a complete case," Mahony wrote, "to impress his recently won international followers and to promote the cause of the psychoanalytic movement."

And so he proclaimed success in public, while at the same time acknowledging in private correspondence that the case was still far from closed. Mahony is sympathetic. Freud was a bit reckless, he implies, but, after all, he had made an astonishing discovery. Would we rebuke Columbus for having discovered America without the proper number of lifeboats?

The story of the Wolf Man, perhaps Freud's most famous patient, was strikingly similar. Sergei Pankejeff (known as the Wolf Man because of the dream that became the centerpiece of his analysis) was a slender Russian aristocrat with large pale eyes and a wispy mustache. In his early twenties when he saw Freud, he had grown up on an immense estate, in a home that looked like a palace. In 1910, he arrived in Vienna, traveling with a personal physician and a valet, and seeking help for a variety of woes including a host of obsessive fears. The most prominent psychiatrists in Europe, including Freud's archrival Emil Kraepelin, had been no use. Now it was Freud's turn.

His new patient, Freud noted, was "entirely incapacitated and completely dependent upon other people." Freud worked with the Wolf Man from 1910 to 1914. At first, he was as unsuccessful as his rivals, and then he hit on a bold strategy. Freud told the Wolf Man that he would end treatment on a particular day in the near future, regardless of how matters stood. It worked. "In a disproportionately short time," Freud announced in his presentation of the Wolf Man's case, "the analysis produced all the material which made it possible to clear up his inhibitions and remove his symptoms." It made a compelling tale, and indeed the story of the Wolf Man is generally considered "the most elaborate and no doubt the most important of all Freud's case histories."

If only Freud's talk of cure were true. For, inconveniently for mythmakers, the Wolf Man lived to a ripe and troubled old age. Far from cured, he flitted from one psychoanalyst to another for over half a century (including another go-round with Freud five years after the first), still troubled by a variety of neurotic woes. Two of these analysts, notably Freud's protégée Ruth Mack Brunswick in 1928 and Muriel Gardiner in 1971, wrote their own Wolf Man case histories.

Despite the odds, these were remarkably rosy. "Thanks to his analysis," Anna Freud observed in 1971, "the Wolf-Man was able to survive shock after shock and stress after stress — with suffering, it is true, but with more strength and resilience than one might expect. The Wolf-Man himself is convinced that without psychoanalysis he would have been condemned to lifelong misery."

Even with it, he was hardly consumed by joy. In an essay on the Wolf Man in old age, Muriel Gardiner reported that the chief features of "his more disturbed periods" were "obsessional doubting, brooding, questioning,

. . . being completely engrossed in his own problems and unable to relate to others, unable to read or to paint. On the other hand," she added brightly, "he has seldom if ever since his analysis with Freud been completely unable to function."

Other therapists made similar evaluations. "The analyst whom the Wolf-Man saw once every few months after 1956 and the second analyst whom he has been seeing at more regular intervals in recent years," Gardiner noted, "both diagnosed his disorder as obsessional-compulsive personality."

The Wolf Man's own assessment, in a series of detailed interviews shortly before his death, was even bleaker. He emphatically denied that he had been cured, by Freud or any of his successors. "That was the theory," he told the journalist Karin Obholzer, "that Freud had cured me 100 percent. . . . And that's why Gardiner recommended that I write memoirs. To show the world how Freud had cured a seriously ill person. . . . It's all false."

The Wolf Man, then eighty-six years old, summarized his view of the whole story for Obholzer. "In reality, the whole thing looks like a catastrophe. I am in the same state as when I first came to Freud, and Freud is no more."

Now, a first-person account is not necessarily reliable, especially when it comes from so troubled a figure as the Wolf Man surely was. But even the most devout Freudians concede the Wolf Man's claim that he was hardly cured. They retreat instead to the unassailable position that, troubled as he was, without psychoanalysis he would have been worse off still.

Well, perhaps. And perhaps the death of a devout jogger at forty-five is an argument in favor of exercise, since he might have died even sooner if not for his running. But whether it is fair to blame psychoanalysis for not making the Wolf Man healthy, wealthy, and wise, it *is* fair to say that Freud claimed to deliver more than he had.

It is no rebuke to Freud to say that he did not cure his obsessive patients — even today, they are notoriously difficult to treat. But Freud's behavior here was dishonest, in fact doubly so. He claimed, first of all, to have cured patients though he knew those claims were false or exaggerated. Second, he advanced those same fictional cures as proof that his theory of obsessional neurosis was valid.

Freud's followers were equally prompt to proclaim their own successes. If anything, they were bolder than their mentor. Where Freud had talked about "the truly complicated phenomenon of obsessional neurosis," for example, his descendants tended to see what one of them called a "comparatively simple" illness.

It was not that they claimed to understand some point that Freud had missed. The difference was not a matter of new ideas but of a new tone — familiarity had bred complacency. Freud's exotic explanations reemerged muffled in generalities, stripped of their particularity and much of their quirkiness. The tangle and complexity of Freud's almost mythological tales gave way to the bare-bones outlines of a Cliffs Notes summary. Consider this characteristic discussion from 1934, by the British psychotherapist Muriel Hall:

> A child who is by nature timid, lacking in confidence, sensitive to criticism, and who is over-conscientious in that he sets an unduly high standard of morals for himself and for others, comes in touch, for the first time, either at school or in the streets, with a more robust make of child to whom the facts of coitus, pregnancy and childbirth, among other information, are common knowledge. He sees, hears discussed, and becomes aware of the existence of such matters for the first time, but in such a way that his sensitive nature revolts and refuses to accept them. The instinctive curiosity born of his own half-awakened sexual impulses does not allow him to forget the incidents and facts. Thus, his mind is involved in a difficult conflict. On the one hand stand his moral standards, often taking dramatic form in an imaginative child who carries in his mind vivid mental pictures of religious punishments, disease and death. On the other hand, he is urged forward by his tardily developing instinctive trends. The latter are not sufficiently forcible to declare themselves so openly as in his more robust fellows; they therefore only express themselves behind a screen of behavior to which no exception can ever be taken. Thus an endless succession of ceremonial acts based on scruples of apparently hygienic or religious significance become substitutes for the thoughts and acts which are abhorrent to the timid mind.

Cures were easy, too. "The average length of time required for recovery," Hall noted, "will be six months."

CHAPTER SEVENTEEN

The Biological Evidence

These children were catching *obsessive-compulsive disorder.*

—JOHN RATEY

B Y THE TIME Judith Rapoport came along, in the early 1960s, psychoanalysts had pulled off a neat trick. No one talked much about curing obsessive-compulsive disorder anymore, for the simple reason that no one could point to any cures. Indeed, some of the most prominent analysts warned explicitly that psychoanalysis could *not* cure obsessive patients. To the present day, despite the claims of cure from Freud and his successors, there are virtually no such authenticated claims. In a recent survey of obsessive-compulsive disorder, Michael Jenike, a Harvard psychiatrist sympathetic to analysis, notes flatly that "there is not a single case report in the modern psychiatric literature" of a cure attributed to psychoanalysis.

Somehow, though, Freud's view of obsessiveness prevailed through the 1950s and '60s, even without the benefit of the cures that Freud had cited as proof that his ideas were correct. It was as if the partygoers in a penthouse apartment continued to carry on as cheerily as ever even though all the supporting girders beneath them had melted away.

At Harvard in the sixties, Rapoport learned to treat obsessive-compulsive patients as Freud had treated the Rat Man. Careful, patient listening would eventually reveal the guilty wish, or the unacceptable longing, behind the patient's washing and checking and so on.

Rapoport changed her mind in 1972 on a visit to Sweden, where she heard a curious story. Swedish psychiatrists testing the effects of antidepressants on suicidal patients had noticed an unexpected side effect. For the tiny group of suicidally depressed people who also happened to be obsessive-compulsive, the medication intended to ease their depression somehow ended their obsessions as well.

Those surprising experiments were clear hints at a biological view of obsessive-compulsive disorder. Before long, similar trickles of evidence would join to form a torrent. Today, Freud's favorite subject, Exhibit A in his hall of symbolic diseases, has been snatched away from psychology and grabbed up by biology.

Rapoport is an emblem of that change, for the lapsed psychoanalyst has become a leader among those who argue that obsessive-compulsive disorder is a straightforward, nonsymbolic, brain-based disorder. (The claim is not that psychology is completely irrelevant. It may help to explain the "choice" of a person's obsessions — why one NIMH patient lived in terror of green pens and another of spearmint gum — but it will not explain why someone is obsessive in the first place.)

Evidence that biology is key comes from two different but converging lines of evidence. First, though psychoanalysis and other "psychodynamic" therapies have failed to produce cures, nonpsychological approaches have succeeded. About two-thirds of all obsessive-compulsive patients seem to respond to antidepressants. Behavior therapy, too, seems to help about 60 or 70 percent of patients. The behavioral approach could hardly be more straightforward and less analytic. It bypasses all talk of what symptoms mean, or where they come from, or what purposes they serve, and focuses exclusively on learning to combat them. Like a physical therapist helping a stroke victim learn to walk again, the behavioral therapist concentrates all her attention on the obsessive patient's problems in the here-and-now.

The patient learns to whittle away at her rituals ever so gradually — a woman afraid of germs, say, might begin by touching a "contaminated" object and then trying to refrain from washing her hands for a few minutes afterward. Once she can manage that degree of anxiety, she can take on a bigger challenge and then one bigger still. In time, if all goes well, she can pry herself entirely free of the rituals that once had her by the throat.

The effectiveness of drugs and of behavior therapy both run contrary to psychoanalytic doctrine, which holds that there is no point in treating symptoms. If the heart of the problem is unbearable anxiety, then dealing with symptoms rather than the underlying anxiety should be useless. Tamp down one symptom and another will emerge. Push down the pillow over here and it will puff up over there. But, in fact, it does not.

More broadly, psychoanalysis has failed theoretically as well as practically. The central assumption of the entire Freudian theory — that victims of obsessive-compulsive disorder are distinctively fussy, neat, stubborn, punctual; in short, "anal" — has crumbled. Patients turn out to be all over the lot. Only one in five fits the stereotype, according to Rapoport.

(It is worth noting that psychotherapy may help people who are obsessive and compulsive in the ordinary sense of those words. People who are tense and perfectionistic and rigid may indeed learn to find more joy in life with the help of a good therapist. But unlike victims of obsessive-compulsive disorder, who are desperate for relief, they rarely see themselves as needing help. "Compulsive personalities don't usually come for treatment for their habits," Rapoport notes. "Their complaints are about everyone else.")

Freudians made the mistake of viewing obsessive-compulsive patients as "anal" because they looked at a patient's rituals and assumed that they were seeing his overall character. A closer look would have revealed that a victim of obsessive-compulsive disorder who seems, at a glance, to fit the Freudian pigeonhole may in fact not fit it at all. A consuming anxiety in one domain need not carry over into others. Rapoport has treated boys so obsessed with cleanliness that they washed their hands for hours a day but who nonetheless left their rooms as filthy as any other teenagers do. Another psychiatrist describes a thirty-five-year-old woman who was so afraid of germs that she could open doors only after she had covered the knob with a paper towel. But this woman who was afraid to touch a doorknob was also a sky diver who was happy to jump out of airplanes.

A second and more powerful stream of evidence bolsters the conclusion that obsessiveness is a brain disorder. Some of this evidence is as brutal as a bullet in the brain, as in the newspaper story cited as the epigraph to chapter 15, and some is as subtle as a PET scan.

The case of the would-be suicide stands alone only in its strangeness. (Perhaps one *could* argue that the psychological trauma of nearly dying somehow dislodged the young man's obsessions, as a scare drives away hiccups, but it would be a challenge that would require the ingenuity of Freud himself.) Brain surgeons, after all, have also rid patients of obsessions and compulsions, though operations are out of favor because they can cause personality changes. Rapoport's first obsessive patient, for example, the Boston man who felt compelled to pick up trash, had been lobotomized years before Rapoport ever met him. He woke up from surgery "cured" of the obsessions that had ruled his life for twenty years, but permanently unfit for life outside the hospital.

And just as obsessions can sometimes be extinguished by bullets and scalpels, they can sometimes arise, full-blown and apparently out of nowhere, as a result of blows to the head or epileptic seizures or strokes. That evidence is not disputed. Moreover, it is beyond dispute that several neurological diseases, among them Tourette's syndrome and Sydenham's chorea (St. Vitus' dance), can include obsessions and compulsions among their symptoms.* That link was suspected centuries ago. In the 1700s, for

---

* A determined psychiatrist of the symptom-decoding school can explain away even this evidence. Why, asks Peter Breggin, do brain damage, disease, and accidents sometimes cause obsessions and compulsions? "Faced with increased helplessness in dealing with the world, the brain-injured person attempts to control inner anxiety and the outer environment alike with repetitive rituals." The patient's odd behavior is not a direct result of his brain damage but "more likely it is a psychological defense aimed at increasing the individual's sense of security in the face of reduced mental function."

Rapoport pushes "radical biological theories," Breggin contends, in an attempt "to appeal

example, Samuel Johnson was nearly as well known for his tics and grimaces as for his writing and conversation. "He often had, seemingly, convulsive starts and odd gesticulations," his future stepdaughter once noted, "which tended to excite at once surprise and ridicule." Johnson's appearance was strange enough that he was turned down for a teaching job, in his twenties, on the grounds that he "had the character of being a very haughty, ill-natured gentleman, and that he has such a way of distorting his face (which though he can't help) the gentlemen think it may affect some young lads."

Johnson's symptoms, which had troubled him from childhood on, sound to modern ears much like Tourette's syndrome. But what startled his contemporaries more than his tics were his compulsions. Frances Reynolds, the sister of the painter Joshua Reynolds, described Johnson's "extraordinary gestures or antics with his hands and feet, particularly when passing over the threshold of a Door, or rather before he would venture to pass through *any* doorway. On entering Sir Joshua's house with poor Mrs. Williams, a blind lady who lived with him, he would quit her hand, or else whirl her about on the steps as he whirled and twisted about to perform his gesticulations; and as soon as he had finish'd, he would give a sudden spring and make such an extensive stride over the threshold, as if he were trying for a wager how far he could stride." Moments later, on coming to another doorway, he would go through the entire bewildering ritual again.

Boswell cited "another peculiarity," which no one dared ask the formidable Johnson to explain. "It appeared to me some superstitious habit," Boswell wrote in his *Life of Samuel Johnson,* "which he had contracted early, and from which he had never called upon his reason to disentangle him. This was his anxious care to go out or in at a door or passage, by a certain number of steps from a certain point, or at least so that either his right or his left foot (I am not certain which) should constantly make the first actual movement when he came close to the door or passage."

Once through the door, Johnson's troubles had only begun. He never stepped in the cracks between paving stones, for example, and he insisted on touching every post on the roadside as he walked by. If he missed one, he turned back to retrace his steps and right the wrong before rejoining his puzzled companions.

In Johnson's case, the Tourette's diagnosis is only educated guesswork. But present-day cases point the same moral even more starkly — known brain diseases can cause obsessive behavior. As usual, the transition from historical cases to present-day ones is accompanied by a change from anecdote to statistic. We lose color and gain rigor.

Today, Tourette's disease has been extensively studied. Rapoport reports

---

to those who cannot bear to face their own self-destructive mental processes. Her views also will appeal to some parents who don't wish to believe that they have had anything to do with their offspring's problems."

that about *one-third* of all Tourette's patients suffer from obsessions and compulsions. (Gilles de la Tourette, the French neurologist who described the disease that would later be named for him, had noted the connection in his first, landmark paper, in 1885.)

Susan Swedo, a child psychiatrist and a colleague of Rapoport's at the National Institute of Mental Health, has gone after the brain in a different way. Swedo discovered that some of her patients had suddenly become obsessive-compulsive as the result of a commonplace sore throat. An ordinary strep infection had somehow triggered their immune system to attack their own brain cells.

It would be hard to imagine more compelling evidence that a disease was biological. An ordinary ten-year-old could go to bed sick one day and wake up the next morning obsessed with a belief that he had to climb the stairs while skipping every other step or feeling compelled to wash his hands for hours. "The news that a completely symptom-free, altogether normal little boy . . . could develop a flagrant case of the disorder *overnight* was profoundly shocking," the Harvard psychiatrist John Ratey has written. "Acute onset cases like these wrenched obsessive-compulsive disorder radically out of a psychodynamic, interpretive framework — even the updated, biologically aware versions. Essentially, these children were *catching* obsessive-compulsive disorder . . . the way a person catches cold."

Josh Brown caught his "cold" sometime in the winter of 1992. Josh was thirteen then, an eighth-grader and a friendly, good-looking boy. The previous June his family had moved from St. Louis to the suburbs of Washington, D.C., and settled into a big, handsome house in a cozy, tree-lined neighborhood. By February, it was clear that something was amiss. Small and thin but a good athlete, Josh had become fanatical about exercise.

For hours at a time, long after his muscles had given out, he would force himself to do push-ups and sit-ups. "He'd be screaming in agony," his mother recalls, "but he couldn't stop exercising. One time a neighbor came over and asked if someone had fallen down the stairs, because she heard someone screaming in pain."

It was May 1992, near the end of eighth grade, before anyone came up with an explanation. Josh was diagnosed as having obsessive-compulsive disorder. Neither he nor his parents had ever heard the phrase.

Josh's compulsions grew worse through the summer. Exercise was only part of the problem. On the first day of his freshman year in high school, Josh sat in Spanish class, eyes squeezed closed, picking his pencil up from his desk and then placing it back down, picking it up and placing it down, picking it up and placing it down, over and over again. For fifteen minutes, his classmates and teacher tried, unsuccessfully, to divert him. "People were touching me and asking if I was okay," Josh recalls, embarrassed at the memory, "and one person thought I was having a seizure." He pauses. "It was a big mess." Then, in his next class, Josh was unable to sit down. He would settle on his chair for a moment and then stand up, sit down and stand up, sit down and stand up.

Spurred by the Browns' panic, one of Josh's doctors arranged for him to be seen at the National Institute of Mental Health. There, Susan Swedo and her colleagues confirmed the obsessive-compulsive diagnosis. Beyond that, they found that, though he had none of the usual symptoms, Josh had a raging strep infection. When Josh gets strep throat, these doctors found, his immune system churns out antibodies that target certain brain cells as well as the strep itself. These cells are in the basal ganglia, the region of the brain at the core of obsessions and compulsions. An MRI scan of Josh's brain confirmed that ominous finding: structures within the basal ganglia were swollen and damaged.

Josh had been on medication for obsessive-compulsive disorder, more or less ineffectually, since shortly after he was diagnosed in May 1992. A few months after that, at the start of his freshman year, with the illness ruining his life, the NIMH doctors tried a new and drastic tack. "That was when it all peaked," Josh's mother Tina recalls. "He couldn't get into bed at night without doing two hours of gymnastics; he couldn't talk without repeating his words over and over and over; he couldn't eat a bowl of cereal because he had to put his spoon in just the right way. We just thought he was" — she searches for a word — "going."

Obsessive-compulsive disorder's toll is not limited to those who have the illness. Tina Brown had to give up her job to help care for Josh and to accompany him to an unending series of doctor's visits. In the bad stretches, it was a welcome break if Josh didn't wake up once or twice in the night to exercise compulsively, screaming in agony for an hour or two. No outing, no matter how minor, was ever routine. On a Fourth of July trip to the beach, for example, Josh was playing in the waves, but suddenly the game changed character and he began swimming compulsively, straight out to sea. Josh's brother and his father, not much of a swimmer, had to race after him and drag him back to shore against his will. Josh fights so hard and screams so loud on such occasions that his father has to carry a doctor's letter in his wallet, explaining that Josh is his son and that he is not abducting or abusing him.

The NIMH doctors opted for a harrowing, but straightforward, plan. They would clean Josh's blood, straining out the destructive antibodies. Six times in the next two weeks, for about two and a half hours each time, doctors put a needle connected to a tube into Josh's forearm, drew his blood out and "cleaned" it in a centrifuge, and then returned it to his body through a needle in the other arm. Josh lay in bed at the center of a network of blood-filled tubes reading Stephen King novels.

"They did brain scans, and there was a decrease in the swelling after just two treatments," Tina Brown says. "It was amazing to see — Josh started smiling again, the muscles in his face relaxed, it was unbelievable."

After six blood-cleanings, Josh's obsessions and compulsions were far weaker, though not entirely gone. Then came three weeks of intensive behavior therapy. "At that point," Tina says, "he was completely in control again. There were no symptoms, nothing. We felt that we had come through the tornado and somehow we'd been among the lucky ones. It had been enormously scary, but we'd been lucky and we'd gotten through it."

Josh was among the first patients to have been treated for obsessions triggered by a strep infection. (It is not yet clear how often strep and obsessiveness are linked.) Blood-cleaning is a formidable and last-ditch procedure, but NIMH physicians have shown that it works: when they treat these strep patients by cleaning their blood of strep antibodies, the obsessive symptoms disappear and the swollen brain structures shrink back to normal size. And if the strep recurs, the obsessions recur; and if the blood is cleaned again, the obsessions vanish again.

The pursuit of the strep connection has led to still more support for the idea that obsessiveness is biological. Swedo has identified a particular marker — a protein found on the surface of certain cells — that seems to be a red flag that predicts who will fall ill with obsessive-compulsive disorder. Only 2 percent of the general population carry the marker, but 98 percent of obsessive-compulsive patients carry it.

But even if this "marker" story holds up, and it is essential to note that at this early stage it could still fizzle out, it would not clinch the case that obsessiveness is biological. For psychiatry is a field where individual findings can rarely be decisive. Alternative, though perhaps convoluted, explanations are always possible. One could imagine, for example, that strict toilet training created such stress in an infant that it altered his immune response and therefore his "marker" profile.

And so controversies are resolved slowly, by a preponderance of the evidence rather than by a single Eureka!-style revelation. Each bit of evidence is an arrow that points one way or another. It is only when arrow after arrow seems to point in the same direction that minds begin to change.

In the study of obsessive-compulsive disorder, the drug findings were a hard-to-ignore arrow. Though older than the strep findings, these were a surprise in their own right. Just as it would have been hard to invent an illness that had symptoms as specific as coloring in the letter *e* or checking the dishwasher for cats, it would have been hard to guess that a drug could relieve such narrow symptoms. Most drugs, Rapoport points out, work best for pervasive mood disorders such as anxiety or depression. An anti-cat-checking drug seemed a ludicrous notion. And yet there are such things.

Several antidepressants — including Anafranil and Prozac — can sharply cut down on obsessions and compulsions, even ones that have endured for years, and can do so in a matter of weeks. No one knows why. They know only that all the successful antidepressants share a chemical property: they all affect the brain's metabolism of a chemical messenger called serotonin. Antidepressants that happen not to affect serotonin don't affect obsessions and compulsions either.

The antidepressant story has a curious footnote. Rapoport was on a radio talk show promoting *The Boy Who Couldn't Stop Washing* and talking about children who washed their hands until they bled. A day or two later, a woman contacted Rapoport. She had a black Labrador dog, she said, and it licked its paw so persistently, so compulsively, that it had given itself an ugly, serious, open wound. The veterinarian had said the injury was life-threatening. The reason the dog was licking itself to death, the vet had suggested, was that an older, companion dog had died and the Lab was bored.

He had recommended a puppy as a playmate. The woman had bought one, and her Lab was ecstatic to have company, but the canine psychiatry was off-base. The dog was still licking its paw. The owner was desperate. Would Rapoport give the dog an antidepressant?

The next day Rapoport had another call — new dog, same problem. (And a new vet, with a new psychological explanation. It, too, sounded plausible. This dog licked itself bloody, the vet said, because it was lonely. The owner, who had been thinking of working at home anyway, set up a home office. The dog was thrilled, but it kept licking.) With the help of her own veterinarian, Rapoport set out to round up more dogs who couldn't stop licking. Soon, in typical Washington fashion, it became a status symbol to have a dog who received house calls from a National Institute of Mental Health psychiatrist.

Rapoport set up a study with seventy-eight dogs and all the proper safeguards and statistical controls. The results turned out to be just like those in humans — the same antidepressants that helped humans with obsessive-compulsive disorder helped the dogs; antidepressants that had no effect on compulsive humans had no effect on compulsive dogs; and placebos helped neither humans nor dogs.

This, Rapoport notes gleefully, made a nice bit of evidence in favor of the biological model. It is hard to imagine that the real problem underlying Fido's symptoms is a crushing sense of shame about his animal-like sexual urges.

Treating obsessive-compulsive disorder is one thing, and explaining it is another. Rapoport can only guess at the origin of this bewildering disease, and few of her colleagues will go even that far. The crucial clue, she believes, is that of the infinity of possible obsessions and compulsions, nature in fact seems to have come up with only a few.

She makes an argument analogous to one that evolutionary psychologists have made in the case of phobias. Why, they ask, should modern, urbanized humans be so afraid of snakes and spiders? Why do all phobias center on the same few dangers, ones which in fact we seldom encounter, and not on realistic hazards like guns and cars?

Their answer is that phobias are legacies of our hundreds of thousands of years as hunter-gatherers. For countless generations, our ancestors faced mortal danger from venomous snakes and slippery cliffs. Those with an abiding fear of snakes and heights and similar dangers were more likely to live to have descendants than those without such qualms. The result is that *we* quake at bygone threats. Today's phobias represent yesterday's dangers.

In monkeys at least, such fears seem to be lying in wait in the brain, so to speak. Wild monkeys are afraid of snakes; laboratory-raised monkeys who have never seen snakes are not. But a lab-raised monkey who sees another monkey panic at the sight of a snake will itself panic from then on. (The monkey cannot be made afraid of a harmless object like a flower, on the other hand, no matter how often it is shown [doctored] films of other monkeys terrified of flowers.)

To Rapoport, the obsessions and compulsions that she hears about daily — washing, checking, fretting about doorways — sound uncannily like the preoccupations that fill an animal's day. Animals groom by the hour, they perpetually check and recheck their territory, and they focus special attention on thresholds and boundaries. The behavior is fixed, rigid, repeated identically time after time.

If Rapoport is right, obsessions and compulsions are ancient "programs" in the brain, which start up accidentally as a result of some kind of internal short circuit and then cycle and recycle in endless loops. Obsessive hand-washing, for example, might be a kind of "grooming behavior run amok." Once upon a time, the senseless ritual did make sense, just as a dog's turning in circles before it lies down once made sense. It is only when the ritual persists out of context — as in a dog that sleeps on an Oriental carpet but still turns in circles as if to flatten the grass on the African savannah — that we look on in bewilderment.

Jeffrey Schwartz, a UCLA psychiatrist who studies PET scans of obsessive-compulsive patients, has taken such theories a step further. His patients tell him, he writes in *Brain Lock*, that their problem is that they cannot stop worrying that the stove is on or that their hands are dirty. But the real anguish, Schwartz contends, is not that they worry about what is not worth worrying about. The true dilemma is that "no matter what they do in response to what's worrying them, the urge to check or to wash will not go away." Schwartz described one woman who suffered agonies of doubt about whether she had turned off the coffeemaker before she left the house. She would be panic-stricken hundreds or even thousands of times a day, and "she could have that all-consuming worry even while holding the unplugged cord from Mr. Coffee in her hand!"

Schwartz believes the reason is that a gatekeeping filter that should function automatically and subconsciously has somehow gone wrong:

> In all likelihood, what happens in [obsessive-compulsive disorder] is that evolutionarily old circuits of the cortex, like those for washing and checking, break through the gate, probably because of a problem in the caudate nucleus. . . . The thought comes in the gate, the gate gets stuck open, and the thought keeps coming in over and over again. People then persevere in washing their hands or checking the stove, even though it makes no sense to do so. These actions may bring them momentary relief, but then —boom—because the gate is stuck open, the urge to wash or check breaks through again and again.

All that said, it is still hard to resist thinking that a disease that seems to shout from the rooftops that it is psychological really *is* psychological. These evolutionary theories, after all, are as much "Just So" stories as any of Freud's. The antidepressant story, though certainly a major advance, is still in its early stages. Drugs free only a few people from all their symptoms. For a typical patient, the improvement is somewhere between 30 and 70 percent. And even in the best of cases, patients will likely need their medicines for a lifetime.

Moreover, drugs are no help at all to one patient in three. *Something* differentiates the lucky from the unlucky, but none of the obvious guesses —mild cases versus severe ones, for instance, or new ones versus old, or children versus adults—has proved correct. And even in those cases where drugs do work, there is no more than a rudimentary understanding of why they are effective.

The serotonin connection, for example, is still mysterious. Any antidepressant that affects serotonin affects another ten or more brain chemicals as well. Furthermore, no one has yet found any differences in the serotonin levels of healthy and obsessive people. Finally, all the antidepressants that are effective in treating obsessiveness change the brain's serotonin levels almost at once. Why, then, does it take two weeks for symptoms to start to disappear?

Behavior therapy has even less intellectual appeal. It seems to work, and that is no small matter, but it is hardly a theory to win devotees. It is begrimed with ugly jargon—psychologists talking about their patients' anxiety use such terms of art as "subjective units of discomfort"—and it is mechanical and plodding.

So "deeper" explanations continue to beckon. Even some patients interpret their symptoms symbolically. A woman named Sarah, for example, told me that her obsessions and compulsions began when she was eleven, when she learned that her mother had breast cancer. She could not fall asleep until she had made sure that the dresser drawers in her bedroom were shut completely; her shoes had to be lined up just right; her toys had to be arranged with their noses facing up, so they could breathe, "even though I *knew* they were stuffed animals and didn't breathe anyway, so it didn't matter." Looking back two decades (she is now free of symptoms), Sarah recalls that "it felt to me as if the world was thin and fragile and the veneer of order had to be maintained at all costs. I had this horrible, vague fear of looming chaos. It was trying to suck me in, and my response was to try to make everything perfect, including me, to keep the world safe."

Some therapists, too, continue to see obsessive-compulsive disorder as fraught with meaning. By taking Freud's theories as metaphorical rather than literal, they have recast his insights into a new and appealing form. A recent book by the psychologist George Weinberg, for example, is a fine example of what might be called Freud Lite, or perhaps Reform Freudianism.

Weinberg declares in his opening sentences that "every compulsion is an act of terror. It is an attempt to regulate something concrete and controllable because the person cannot identify and control some real psychological problem."

That message echoes Freud, but Weinberg briskly rubs his hands clean of any lingering Freudian dust. "Today we dismiss as an early guess Freud's connection of compulsions with the toilet-training period," he writes. "Few believe that all compulsions are the continual replaying in different guises of an anal urge for control."

But there was a baby in that bathwater. "However," Weinberg continues, "it is true that compulsive people are seeking symbolic control and are trying to stem unconscious fears, just as Freud said. . . . But what drives the compulsive is a fear more general than any connected with the bathroom. The compulsive adult may have evolved his unconscious fear in any context. All that matters is that he has the fear and is attempting to minister to it. The control sought by the compulsive is that of a person terrified of what he or she sees as chaos and imminent danger all around him. Such a person feels that he has no hope but to regulate everything that can be regulated."

It is an alluring theory, but it does not win Rapoport over. She remains deeply skeptical of all such personality-based theories. Studies at NIMH and elsewhere of people with obsessions and compulsions, she says, turn up run-of-the-mill biographies, with no telltale personality patterns and no more than the usual quota of miseries. Once the illness is in place, Rapoport concedes, fear and stress do make its symptoms worse, but she contends that mental woes are not the *source* of the problem. Rapoport says she can only recall "one case out of thousands" — a victim of a gang rape who became obsessed with showering — where she believes that a specific trauma precipitated the disease.

Attempts at psychological explanations, she says, are understandable but mistaken efforts to make sense of what would otherwise seem utterly random. It is a view that echoes an observation of Elaine Pagels, the historian of religion, who has written on humankind's curious willingness to believe in such doctrines as eternal damnation and original sin. How can we believe, Pagels asks, that the world is set up in such a way that many among us, perhaps even we ourselves, will burn in everlasting flames?

We believe it, she says, because we are desperate to view the world as making sense, even terrifying and violent sense. A game played by cruel rules is better than one with no rules at all. "People," writes Pagels, "often would rather feel guilty than helpless."

Rapoport acknowledges the seductiveness of psychological explanations, and not only when it comes to obsessiveness. They do seem to cut to the heart of the matter, after all, while biology skitters across the surface. "Psychology *seems* deeper," she says emphatically. "It's always impressive when someone authoritative looks you in the eye and says, '*You think* the reason you're so angry is that you couldn't get a ticket to the play' "— here she leans forward in her chair, eyes wide, eyebrows raised — " 'but *I know* that's just a smokescreen, and you're really telling me how mad you are at your mother for not giving you things that you wanted.'

"That's *very* impressive," Rapoport repeats. "It rocks everyone on their heels." Then she pauses a moment and scowls impatiently. When she resumes speaking, her voice is louder and her words are quicker.

"But if someone keeps on saying that to you over and over and it turns out to be mostly wrong, then after a while it's not so impressive anymore. And so in this area, psychology no longer seems deep to me."

PART SIX

Conclusion

Sometimes it is very difficult to keep firmly in mind the fact that the parents, too, have reasons for what they do — have reasons, locked in the depths of their personalities, for their inability to love, to understand, to give of themselves to their children.

— VIRGINIA AXLINE

CHAPTER EIGHTEEN

Placing the Blame

*It's the easiest thing in the world to come up with a
hypothesis. Any fool can do it. The question is whether
there's any evidence to substantiate it.*

— DONALD KLEIN

BEFORE HIS DEPRESSION HIT, before he had been locked in a mental
hospital, before he had bloodied his feet by pacing hour upon hour and mile
upon mile up and down the hospital hallways, Raphael Osheroff seemed to
have everything in the world a person could want. Osheroff was a forty-one-
year-old doctor, a kidney specialist with a $300,000-a-year practice. He was
married, the father of three children, and lived in a handsome house in
Alexandria, Virginia, outside Washington.

But on January 2, 1979, Osheroff needed help. He had been depressed
for two years and lately he had grown suicidal. He asked his medical partner
to drive him to Chestnut Lodge, the prestigious private mental hospital just
north of Washington where Frieda Fromm-Reichmann had once presided.
There psychiatrists diagnosed Osheroff as suffering from depression and a
"narcissistic personality disorder." They recommended talk therapy to "re-
structure" his personality and vetoed the use of antidepressant drugs.

Over the course of the next seven months, Osheroff grew steadily more
pitiable. Unwashed, unshaven, unable to sleep, he spent his days pacing the
corridors and pleading for help. His weight fell by forty pounds. Finally, in
despair that their son seemed to be deteriorating despite his four-times-a-
week psychotherapy sessions, Osheroff's parents had him transferred to
another private hospital, Silver Hill, in Connecticut. The Silver Hill psychiatrist who admitted Osheroff would later describe him as "the most pathetic
person I've ever seen" and prescribed antidepressants at once. The turn-
around was almost immediate. In three weeks Osheroff stopped pacing; in
nine weeks he was discharged, fully functioning, to resume his medical
career.

In 1982, Osheroff filed a lawsuit against Chestnut Lodge. The hospital was guilty of malpractice, he charged, for treating his depression with talk alone rather than with a combination of antidepressants and talk. An expert witness testifying on Osheroff's behalf, Gerald Klerman, a psychiatrist then at Harvard Medical School, called Chestnut Lodge's treatment "criminal" and "cruel and negligent." The use of antidepressant medications was standard practice, Klerman observed, and Osheroff's depression was so plain that a first-year resident could have diagnosed it. The state of Maryland agreed. In 1984, the Health Claims Arbitration Board awarded Osheroff $250,000.

This was a devastating symbolic blow, a door slammed shut on the psychological era. The medical community had followed the case closely — they saw it as "psychiatry on trial" — and no one missed the message. Chestnut Lodge had long represented the state of the art in psychotherapy; now this haven of healing had been proclaimed a danger to its patients. For decades, "talk therapy" had dominated psychiatry and held its rivals in open contempt, but its day was gone. From all sides — from those studying schizophrenia, autism, obsessive-compulsive disorder, and now depression — came the message that in the future psychotherapy would play a considerably diminished role. The more serious the illness, the less likely that anyone would treat it by talk alone.

The saga of psychoanalysis in the twentieth century is a tale of rise and fall. When it came to treating madness, the fall was sharpest of all. The story of therapists in collision with madness was a tale that abounded in grief needlessly inflicted. Still, it was a tragedy and not a scandal. With the possible exceptions of Bruno Bettelheim and of John Rosen, the psychiatrist who brutalized his hapless schizophrenic patients, it was a tale almost without villains. Indeed, the central irony of the whole story is that the therapists had only the best intentions. Earnest but misguided, like American communists in the forties and fifties who sincerely wanted a better world but refused to acknowledge Stalin's crimes, psychoanalysts in the golden age were led astray by their own laudable ambitions.

Their story is a true tragedy because, with hindsight, it is clear that the psychotherapeutic approach was doomed from the start. Schizophrenia and its grim brethren turned out to be brain diseases that could no more have been cured by talking than could lung cancer. The medical establishment now declares unequivocally that the psychiatrists who tried to treat severe mental illness with "talk therapy" alone would have done as much good if they had donated their couches to the Salvation Army.

But they did try, and for that they deserve commendation. Unlike most of their psychiatric colleagues, they never turned their backs on these desperately ill patients. Their fault was not in trying to help distressed and despised outcasts. The fault was that, having labored valiantly but in vain, they condemned their patients and their families for having brought on their own troubles.

For the psychoanalysts we have been discussing had a tragic flaw, like all tragic heroes. It was hubris, as we have discussed, and for the analysts it took the shape of certainty that they alone possessed the truth. Few beliefs could have been as dangerous. The risk was of wandering miles off course, at full speed, since the impossibility of being in error meant that there was no need to slow down to listen to outside opinions.

The tendency to ignore dissenting voices is a sad fact of human nature and hardly unique to psychoanalysis. But from its earliest days, when Freud banished "heretics," psychoanalysis *did* face a heightened risk of isolation because it took pains to insure that critical voices would not be heard. "Here's the bind they were in," says Leon Eisenberg, the Harvard psychiatrist. "In order to become a researcher in the field, you had to be psychoanalyzed, and if the analysis was done by someone who *knew* that his theory was right, one of the things that he *had* to do was treat your skepticism about it as a symptom." Eisenberg laughs in wonderment, as if contemplating an especially cunning mousetrap. "So there was no way out — you got psychoanalyzed out of your interest in doing significant research. It was a Catch-22."

And so the effectiveness of "talk therapy" was assumed and proclaimed rather than tested and questioned. In the short run, this made for harmony. The odds that someone would cry out, "The emperor has no clothes!" were a lot less when the emperor and his coterie had ruled ahead of time that only those on record as admiring the emperor's wardrobe could attend his parade. But in the end, a system without outside feedback is doomed. As crashes go, the final crash of the analysts who had taken on madness was not especially spectacular. What marked it as special was that this time the pilots themselves were the ones who had disabled the warning lights in the cockpit and shut off communication with air traffic control on the ground.

Hubris aside, how did things go so wrong? One key is that the psychoanalysts were the victims of a kind of cosmic practical joke. In the cases of schizophrenia and autism and obsessive-compulsive disorder in particular, nature itself seemed to have conspired to lead them astray. To those trained to seek out hidden meanings, the "word salad" of a schizophrenic, the silent withdrawal of an autist, the endless hand-washing of an obsessive, were irresistible temptations. These were diseases crying out to be interpreted. Analysts rushed to take the bait, never for a moment suspecting it was poisoned.

But even the wary might have been led astray, for mental illness *looks* fundamentally different from ordinary illness. The distinction is that the symptoms of mental illness involve behavior. It is far harder to know what to make of a person who claims that the CIA is sending him secret messages than to deal with a temperature of 103 degrees or a face covered with red spots.

From the simple observation that mental illness is marked by odd behavior flows a host of troubles, as if from a poisoned cornucopia. For nothing seems clearer than that we are responsible for our behavior; from there, it seems only a small step to the conclusion that a disease character-ized by strange behavior must be a disease under our control. And so we appeal to willpower in the devout belief that we can think our way to mental health. We advise the victim of depression to look on the bright side; we tell the person in the midst of a sky-high manic episode to take a deep breath and calm down. When it comes to mental illness, we are all Christian Scientists.

Psychoanalysts fell into the same trap. Was it ludicrous for them to have thought that talk could cure? No, for the symptoms of schizophrenia, say, are strange behaviors, and we know that talk can change behavior. It is why we continually tell our children to mind their manners and clean their rooms. If the symptoms of schizophrenia had been as straightforward as those of appendicitis, no one would have spent years trying to talk patients into health.

Many problems *are* helped by psychotherapy, after all. No one believed that more deeply than the psychoanalysts, who had all been through analyses of their own. Their mistake was in generalizing from their own relatively mild problems to those of the desperately ill. Aspirin may cure a headache; it is not a treatment for a brain tumor.

In fact, psychotherapy may play a useful role even for a patient with a brain tumor. The key is to recognize the limits of that role — psychotherapy will not *cure* a patient's cancer or schizophrenia; it may help him *cope* with the anger and fear and isolation that accompany his disease.

The psychoanalysts we have been considering never acknowledged that distinction. Instead, they reasoned that all emotional problems were essentially alike and that what worked for one would work for all. In similar fashion, they took a well-founded observation — some parents are guilty of horrendous abuse and inflict lifelong emotional scars on their children — and assumed that what was true in some cases was true in all cases.

The problem was not with psychological explanations in principle. The problem was that the psychological approach was badly flawed in practice. Psychological explanations of behavior were too easy to devise and too hard to test.* As the psychoanalysts' joke had it, "The person who arrives at a

---

* In literary circles especially, such glib explanations are still fashionable. The acclaimed English novelist Julian Barnes recently noted, for example, that "the British empire was the product of sexual repression. The conquerors set off on their voyages for sexual motives."

party early is anxious; the one who arrives on time is compulsive; and the one who arrives late is hostile." It was a joke with considerable bite. Recall, for example, the psychiatrists who "explained" schizophrenia as caused by mothers who shunned their children; mothers who gave every appearance of doting on their schizophrenic children, according to these authorities, were in truth overcompensating for their true feelings of hostility.

The deeper problem with psychological explanations was that they so quickly transformed themselves into patient-blaming and family-bashing. Without ever considering schizophrenia, autism, or obsessive-compulsive disorder, we could drown in examples. Take Nancy Gibbons, a sixty-four-year-old Florida woman who recently brought an old complaint to a new doctor, Joseph Wassersug. A pastry chef for a catering service, Gibbons had been troubled for years by a chronic cough, "like a tickle in my throat." Lately it had grown especially bothersome. With considerable embarrassment, Gibbons told Wassersug a story from more than sixty years before. When Gibbons was still a baby, her mother had come to pick her up from her crib one day and seen her playing with a coin. Somehow, before her mother could snatch the coin away, it disappeared. Off they raced to the doctor. He looked down the little girl's throat, didn't see anything, and sent her home. On a return visit, he repeated that there was nothing to see.

Over the years, Nancy Gibbons had told the story to various doctors, but they had dismissed her complaints. Her real problem, they noted, was neither a cough nor a coin but hysteria. One pointed out that "it's your womb that's stuck in your throat, not a coin."

Wassersug took a direct approach. Positioning Gibbons in front of an X-ray machine, he took a photograph that revealed a quarter nestled in her throat, where it had lain for the previous six decades.

Bonnie Burke's predicament was far graver. In 1978, her psychiatrist had diagnosed her as suffering from a "hysterical neurosis." Burke was a twenty-seven-year-old California woman whose strength seemed to be leaking away by the minute. Once active, she had gotten to the point where she could no longer walk; she could not lift her arm to brush her teeth; she could barely summon the strength to dress herself. Following the advice of her psychiatrist, Roderick Ponath, she combed through her past in search of the repressed anger at the root of her problems.

In 1990, twelve years into her work with Ponath, Burke happened to be at the eye doctor's for a checkup. He saw that she was too weak even to keep her eyelids from drooping and asked if she had ever been tested for myasthenia gravis, a disease in which the muscles waste away. The eye doctor referred Burke to a specialist, who promptly tested her. The test procedure, an injection of a substance called Tensilon, had been developed in 1952, nearly four decades before. If a person has myasthenia gravis, even if she is too weak to sit upright or talk, a Tensilon injection will restore her full strength *within moments.*

Burke did indeed have myasthenia gravis. She is now on medication (a longer-lasting variant of Tensilon) and is living a normal life. "It turned out to be as easy as a pill," she later recalled. "It was like a miracle." Her psychiatrist, Ponath, who had once served as medical director of the well-regarded Brea Hospital Neuropsychiatric Center, had never sent her to another psychiatrist for a second opinion or to a neurologist for an exam. The reason Burke had grown steadily weaker through their years together, Ponath told her, was that she had too little confidence in his therapy and was not trying hard enough. In 1995, a Santa Ana jury awarded Burke $97,500 in a malpractice lawsuit against Ponath.

The story of "David," a patient with another muscular disease, this one called dystonia musculorum deformans, is if anything even grimmer. A cruel disease of the central nervous system, dystonia advances slowly and unevenly, beginning subtly but eventually twisting its victims into grotesque pretzel shapes, arms and legs frozen in strange grimaces, backs bowed, necks contorted, and in the end unable to move but for uncontrollable spasms. David's disease had first appeared at age seven, when the toes of his right foot began curling uncontrollably. By age seventeen, still undiagnosed but nearly overwhelmed by his symptoms, he was admitted to a psychiatric hospital. When he was discharged, in 1950, his psychiatrist wrote up his case:

> When this seventeen-year-old single, white male was admitted, he had a severe motor disturbance in walking, giving him a grotesque, uncoordinated gait so that his arms and legs and trunk seemed to have no control. They would flail about, his trunk would move backwards and forwards so that his buttocks would be protruding or his pelvic area protruding in front, and this would alternate back and forth. His head was always bent forward so that he was looking down toward the ground. . . .
>
> The patient was seen in psychotherapeutic interviews three times a week; the interviews being a half hour in duration. In all, he had 146 therapy sessions while at the hospital. . . . He gained insight into the exhibitionistic quality of his symptoms. . . .
>
> He learned in good time a good deal about the meaning of his symptoms, how his sticking his stomach out was, on the one hand, imitating his mother's pregnancy with his younger sister, whereas, on the other hand, it was putting his penis forward and asserting himself as a man. Inevitably, whenever he sticks his stomach out, he withdraws it rapidly and sticks his buttocks out. He could see in time how this was, in part, related to his fear that harm would be done to his penis when it is stuck out, and sticking out his anus prominently was an invitation for sexual attack from the rear. This would protect his penis. . . . he never fully accepted his sexual wish toward his mother. . . .

Despite his one-hundred-plus psychotherapy sessions, David's condition had not improved during his hospital stay, his psychiatrist noted, but that was to be expected. "It seems he wasn't at all ready to give up his symptoms as yet because they were giving him much too much gratification to be relinquished."

For decades, and across a wide variety of medical ailments, patient-blaming accounts like these were so common that they passed almost unnoticed, like rain on the roof. When it came to schizophrenia and autism, though, the blaming became so virulent and sustained that it could no longer be overlooked. Suddenly, the steady rain had become a howling thunderstorm.

Why? What was it about these conditions in particular that inspired such abuse? The short answer is that schizophrenia and autism struck the young, which immediately directed suspicious eyes to the children's parents. Like unwary tourists caught in a gang fight, these unfortunate parents happened to be in the wrong place at the wrong time. For mothers especially, to live in America in the 1940s, '50s, and '60s was to stand convicted.

Convicted of what? Virtually everything. Of causing such childhood ailments as colic and eczema. "The mother's personality acts as the disease-provoking agent, as a psychological toxin." Of causing a swarm of emotional ills by setting impossible standards. "A child needs love, acceptance, and understanding. He is devastated when confronted with rejection, doubts, and never-ending testing." Of harboring feelings of murderous hostility. "Most mothers do not murder or totally reject their children, but death pervades the relationship between mother and child. The child never ceases to be a threat to her and she never ceases to be a threat to it."

Name a hazard, in short, and mothers were to blame. Edward Strecker, a highly regarded professor of psychiatry at the University of Pennsylvania and a past president of the American Psychiatric Association, summed up the mood in a 1946 book called *Their Mothers' Sons*. "We have gone a long way toward cutting down the yearly toll due to cancer, tuberculosis, and venereal diseases by a threefold program — talking about them freely, presenting the cold hard facts for all to see, and continuous unrelenting public education," Strecker wrote. "The same program could be applied to the threat of moms."

Women had never fared well at the hands of Freudians. Freud's own views on women are too well known to need another airing, and in any event it should be clear without extensive argument that a theory that says that females see themselves as maimed males is not without bias. But the mother-bashing in the postwar decades went beyond anything in Freud. In so hostile a climate, it was almost inevitable that when it came time to make sense of problems as overwhelming as schizophrenia and autism, it would be mothers who took an especially hard hit.

Every generation finds it tempting to sneer at the mistakes of its predecessors. In looking at a bygone era, there is always the risk of cozy condescension, of playing the role of indulgent parents watching a toddler's clumsy attempts to run and jump. In fields like science and medicine where there is a clear-cut sense of progress, the danger is especially acute. Should psychoanalysts in the 1950s and '60s have known better? *Could* they have?

No one would blame a mapmaker in 1400 for having portrayed the earth as flat, after all. And though the history of medicine is overall a tale of progress, it is nonetheless a history besmeared with countless stains. For two hundred years, for example, surgeons "helped" wounds heal by pouring boiling oil into them. The practice ended only when Ambroise Paré, a French army surgeon, ran out of oil on the battlefield and was forced to resort to gentle cleaning instead. Similarly, bloodletting (with unsterilized razors) had a centuries-long run as the preferred remedy "for everything and against anything from plague to dandruff." There are countless other examples. Why single out psychoanalysts for *their* mistakes?

It is a good question, and it has a good answer. Richard Hunter, a psychiatrist himself and an eminent historian of psychiatry, put it succinctly. "No other specialty blames illness — and therapeutic failure — on patients," he declared in a 1972 lecture. Blaming was the key; other physicians had subjected patients to reckless and ill-conceived therapies, but they chalked up their failures to their own shortcomings or (more likely) to having been called on too late. When their treatments failed, they blamed fate, not their patients. The behavior of the analysts was shabbier. It was not simply that they kicked patients when they were down. Even worse, they first knocked patients (or their parents) to the ground, by blaming them for having caused their own illness, and *then* they kicked them.

This was not simply ugly, though it was certainly that. Patients in severe trouble, and schizophrenics and autists in particular, needed all the support they could get. By accusing parents of causing their children's illness — or, in the case of autism, by advising parents to stay away from their children in order to avoid harming them further — psychiatrists deprived these nearly friendless patients of their natural allies. In an essay with the forthright title "Mistreatment of Patients' Families by Psychiatrists," the Harvard psychiatrist William Appleton spelled out the consequences. "Badly treated families retaliate in ways that are detrimental to the patient," Appleton wrote. "They become less willing to tolerate the problems he causes, are less agreeable to changing their behavior toward him, do not give much information when interviewed, and pay few visits to the hospital."

The patient, the family, and even the psychiatrists lost out. "By abusing the family," Appleton continued, "the psychiatric profession also deprives itself of extremely important information. It is the relatives who can quickly give information that the psychotic patient is unable or unwilling to divulge. But the family will not reveal facts and certainly not admit the faults if they are made to feel more guilty and defensive than they already do."

Is such criticism fair, or is it second-guessing? Could psychiatrists in the heyday of psychoanalysis have known better? Yes. The claim that odd families caused a disease as crushing as schizophrenia, for example, should have raised red flags; in any case, it was a charge so certain to cause lifelong pain that anyone making it should have provided reams of supporting evidence. "People who read books like *I Never Promised You a Rose Garden* don't know what untreated schizophrenia looks like," the Columbia psychiatrist Donald Klein observes. "They have this picture of fey creatures with airy fantasies. When I worked at Creedmoor in 1953, we had no drugs — all we had was [electroconvulsive therapy] and nursing care and a ward full of, literally, raving lunatics. To say that *that* was because of subtle differences in their upbringing made no sense. They were just too crazy."

More generally, anyone proposing psychological explanations of mental illness should have asked some fundamental questions. Was the toilet-training of obsessive-compulsives in fact stricter than that of other people? If schizophrenia was caused by stress — whether from overbearing mothers or inept fathers or contradictory messages or some other source — one would expect the incidence of the disease to vary from culture to culture and era to era. Did it? Was there more schizophrenia in times of war or famine or revolution? Did the disease take different forms in sprawling, smoke-belching industrial cities and in tiny, remote agrarian villages?

Why, if stress was the culprit, was schizophrenia three to seven times more common in preadolescent boys than in preadolescent girls? Did boys really suffer so much more stress, or suffer so much more from it? If so, what was different about the era between adolescence and age thirty, when schizophrenia hit males and females in *equal* numbers? And what changed yet again to explain why, among the elderly, schizophrenia struck *fewer* males than females?

One might have asked similar questions about autism. The opportunities to challenge conventional wisdom were there. Unlike mapmakers before the Age of Discovery, psychiatrists in the 1950s had the crucial puzzle pieces lying before them. Nor was a conceptual breakthrough required. Isaac Newton might have *asked* himself Einstein's famous question about what it would be like to ride on a beam of light, but he would not have arrived at Einstein's answer because he presumed that time was absolute, not relative. But anyone could have asked, and answered, the question "Were the parents of schizophrenics different from other parents?" Anyone could have posed such a question in 1950. Almost no one did.

The problem was that the psychoanalysts assumed that their work was done when it was barely beginning. It was possible that parents drove their children mad. It sounds unlikely, but it sounds unlikely that a cowlike animal found in Africa has a seven-foot-long neck. You can't know until you look. But the analysts did *not* look. Having come up with a theory that purported to explain mental illness, they put their feet up on their desk and knocked off for the day. "It's the easiest thing in the world to come up with a hypothesis," Donald Klein snaps. "Any fool can do it. The question is whether there's any evidence to substantiate it."

If for the sake of argument we grant that the analysts should have known better, we come immediately to another question: why didn't they? Beyond hubris, beyond ideological zealotry, beyond the shutting out of outside voices, two factors played key roles. The first had to do with medicine, the second with science.

Ironically, it was the psychoanalysts' optimism about what therapy could accomplish that made for trouble. The analysts' approach was fundamentally different from the conventional medical one. Ordinary medicine comes with no guarantees. If we are sick, it may be that there is no saving us, even if we put ourselves in the hands of the greatest experts and they are armed with the latest weapons. Psychoanalysis, on the other hand, explicitly placed itself outside the world of medical science. Its domain was "soulcraft," so to speak, and souls could always be mended. "The underlying assumption of psychoanalysis is that progress toward a 'healthy' personality is possible, given hard work, good faith, enough time, and enough money," the psychiatrists Miriam Siegler, Humphry Osmond, and Harriet Mann observed. "In medicine, there is no such contract; an illness may become suddenly worse, for no known reason, in spite of everyone's hard work and good faith."

The distinction between the two approaches was fundamental. The key was that the psychoanalytic approach left no room for chance or for unexplained setbacks. "In the psychoanalytic model, these sudden reversals must be explained 'dynamically,' i.e., they are somebody's fault," Siegler, Osmond, and Mann went on. "Either the family does not really wish the patient to get well, or the patient is 'afraid' to get well, or the analyst has not solved the countertransference problem. The fact that failure must be explained, either implicitly or explicitly, as someone's fault places a great additional burden on the schizophrenic and his family."

The second factor driving the analysts astray was their lack of respect for science. Ignorant of science and disdainful of it, they failed to follow up on leads they should have checked out. In a 1951 paper on autism, for example, the eminent psychoanalyst J. Louise Despert brushed aside the question of why, if the mothers of autistic children were so dangerous, the great majority of their children were healthy. "It must be remembered," Despert wrote, "that a mother, *biogenetically identical for all her children*, may nevertheless psychogenetically differ widely from one child to the other." (Italics added.) The explanation, in other words, was that a mother's children might turn out differently because she treated them differently. But Despert casually dismissed the possibility that the children might differ biologically, and she dismissed that possibility because of a fundamental misunderstanding of genetics. A faculty member at Cornell University Medical College, Despert was a major figure in psychiatry and an authority on children's mental health. It is telltale that she apparently did not know that a mother passes on different genes to different children.

The problem was not merely ignorance. Just as important, Despert and her peers felt no inclination to take other views seriously. This smugness and intellectual complacency struck Peter Medawar, a Nobel laureate in medicine, as the besetting sin of psychoanalysis. Scientists, he argued, saw themselves as engaged in a difficult, disorienting, high-risk enterprise, making their way through a maze that might or might not eventually lead to an exit door. Psychoanalysts, to Medawar's astonishment, seemed free of all such doubts. "Where shall we find the evidence of hesitancy or bewilderment, the avowals of sheer ignorance, the sense of groping and incompleteness that is commonplace in an international congress of, say, physiologists or biochemists?" Medawar asked. "A lava flow of *ad hoc* explanations pours over and around all difficulties, leaving only a few smoothly rounded prominences to mark where they might have lain."

The reliance on anecdotes was the most important example of this nonrigorous approach. Psychoanalysts seldom bothered with controls and steered away from statistics, partly out of distaste, partly in recognition of genuine difficulties, and partly out of a humane impulse to focus on patients rather than on abstractions. Instead, they placed enormous weight on anecdotes and case histories. On the basis of six or ten or twenty cases, they laid down sweeping generalizations about diseases that affected thousands or millions.

David Levy, an influential child psychiatrist and a past president of the American Psychiatric Association, put the case clearly. In yet another indictment of mothers, a popular 1943 book called *Maternal Overprotection*, Levy observed that "it seems evident that in the study of human relationships as intimate as those of family life, intensive study of a handful of cases, selected because the relationships depicted are unusually clear, yields more knowledge than a statistical study of several thousand unselected cases." That said, and on the basis of twenty case histories, Levy went on to discuss the ways in which a generation of American mothers had failed their children.

The problem was not simply that analysts drew sweeping generalizations from tiny samples, like lazy journalists who chatted with their taxi driver on the way in from the airport and then pronounced confidently on "what Frenchmen are thinking." The deeper problem had to do with standards of evidence. In science, wrongheaded theories cannot endure because they must be tested and verified by scientists *who do not necessarily accept the theory beforehand.* In psychoanalysis, this safeguard was missing. Almost from the start, psychoanalysts split apart into warring factions espousing contradictory doctrines. Where Freud's explanations of behavior centered on sex, for example, Adler emphasized the inferiority complex. The rival camps did not communicate. Instead, each went its own way, treating patients in line with its own views, growing ever more confident as one "verification" after another of the truth of its beliefs rolled in. The problem, never addressed, was that the various "truths" were in conflict.*

When it came to proving the merits of particular treatments, though, it is important to acknowledge that standards were low not only in psychoanalysis but in medicine generally. Until the mid-1940s, most new medical treatments were introduced informally: a senior physician who had tried a new treatment on a series of patients and obtained encouraging results would report his observations. The more reliable, more cumbersome modern-day approach, which relies instead on so-called randomized double-blind controlled trials, is remarkably recent. (The "double blinding" is an acknowledgment of the power of positive thinking; in order to insure that no one's expectations somehow muddle an experiment's results, neither patients nor physicians are allowed to know which pills are real and which are placebos.) The first such trial in the history of medicine did not take place until 1948, in Britain, when the Medical Research Council tested the effect of streptomycin on tuberculosis.†

For psychoanalysts, who believed devoutly that each patient was unique unto himself and whose therapy relied on hard-to-quantify talk rather than on mass-produced and identical drugs, such elaborate ventures had almost no appeal. In any event, the analysts believed as an article of faith that only talk therapy produced deep, lasting cures. Other approaches offered only the dubious advantages of theft over honest toil. "The physician must go to the root of the trouble, and his triumph is not complete until the root has been hacked out completely," Flanders Dunbar had written in one of her

---

* The psychoanalyst Judd Marmor, one time president of the American Academy of Psychoanalysis, acknowledged that each analytic school unearthed exactly the evidence it had announced ahead of time it would find. But Marmor's explanation was not that psychoanalysts interpreted their patients' stories to fit their own doctrines; instead, patients unknowingly shaped their stories in response to cues from their therapists. "Depending upon the point of view of the analyst," Marmor wrote, "the patients of each school seem to bring up precisely the kinds of phenomenological data which confirm the theories and interpretations of the analysts! Thus each theory tends to be self-validating. Freudians elicit material about the Oedipus complex and castration anxiety, Jungians about archetypes, Rankians about separation anxiety, Adlerians about masculine strivings and feelings of inferiority, Horneyites about idealized images, Sullivanians about disturbed interpersonal relationships, etc. What the analyst shows interest in, the kinds of questions he asks, the kind of data he chooses to react to or ignore, and the interpretations he makes, all exert a subtle but significant suggestive impact upon the patient to bring forth certain kinds of data in preference to others."

† This was a full *two centuries* after the first medical study to have used controls of any sort. That was James Lind's classic demonstration, in 1747, that citrus fruit served to combat scurvy. A twenty-eight-year-old surgeon in the Royal Navy, Lind took a dozen sailors sick with scurvy and put all of them in the same quarters, with the same food. In addition, the men were given various purported remedies — two were given a quart of cider each day, for example, another two a pint of seawater, two more a paste of garlic, horseradish, and a few other ingredients, and two others two oranges and a lemon every day. The sailors who gulped down the oranges and lemons were back on their feet in days.

psychosomatic medicine texts. "Every gardener knows that it is much easier to mow weeds than to uproot them. But every gardener knows which is the sensible course in the long run."

Philip May showed in 1968 when he compared various treatments for schizophrenia that it *was* possible to evaluate psychotherapy objectively. But there was no question that it was difficult; the analysts' resistance was more than special pleading. Even Seymour Kety, perhaps the leading debunker of the psychoanalytic approach to schizophrenia, acknowledged that it was natural for medicine to be less rigorous than other scientific fields. Unlike science, Kety pointed out, medicine had as its core purpose the relief of suffering. "The neutron did not come begging to be discovered," Kety wrote, "but the patient suffering from disease or trouble or incapacitated by conflict cannot wait. The physician to whom he turns for help can hardly say, 'Come back in three centuries or so when we may really understand these things.'"

But the analysts' casual talk of cures was nonetheless deeply harmful. In the short term, it raised false hopes. In the longer term, it diverted energy and attention away from genuinely promising research and instead beckoned psychiatrists down a dead end. The problem, it bears emphasizing, is not that psychotherapists failed to cure their severely ill patients but that they *claimed* to have cured them, without evidence. If they had simply done their best, they would deserve honor for having done all that a person could do. To hold a sick person's hand is a good deed; to go on to proclaim hand-holding as a cure is something else entirely.

Today the biological picture of mental illness has triumphed completely. For now. We are as sure that "everything is biological" as our predecessors of a generation ago were that "it's all in the mind." More than 20 million people around the world take Prozac; in the United States alone, sales of this wonder drug have passed the $2-billion-a-year mark. Every morning's headlines contain announcements that scientists have found a gene for manic-depression or a drug that conquers phobias. The "discovery" may be retracted the next day, but the underlying premise stays unquestioned — mental diseases have their roots in biology, and the more serious the disease, the deeper the roots. A recent *Newsweek* cover spelled out today's conventional wisdom: "Shy? Forgetful? Anxious? Fearful? Obsessed?" it asked, and went on to announce a story on "How Science Will Let You Change Your Personality with a Pill."

As if to hammer home the point that psychoanalysis has had its day, the National Institute of Mental Health has officially dubbed the 1990s the "Decade of the Brain." But scientists in the Victorian age might have used the same label to describe the 1890s or perhaps an earlier decade. "So far as the phenomena of deranged mind reach, the battle has been won and the victory is complete," the eminent English psychiatrist Henry Maudsley declared in 1873. "No one whose opinion is of any value pretends now that they are anything more than the deranged functions of the supreme nervous centers of the body."

Then came the Freudian era, according to one's perspective either a welcome interlude of lucidity or a decades-long reign of error. Could the pendulum swing back again?

It would be a mistake to conclude that biology's rise represents the enshrinement of some fixed and final truth. Even today, when it rules unchallenged, it is conspicuously incomplete. Today's antischizophrenia drugs relieve symptoms, for example, but the disease itself remains in place. Nor does anyone even claim to understand in more than the most rudimentary way how the drugs work. Knowing how to treat a disease is one thing, understanding its cause something else. "Although aspirin is well known for its relief of headache," one authority on schizophrenia reminds us, "headache is not caused by a shortage of aspirin in the body."

But we are unlikely to see a return from biology to psychology. The reason is that the pendulum is the wrong model for science. Old scientific theories, unlike old soldiers, *do* die. Political debates may return to eternal themes, like the merits or drawbacks of a strong central government, but science has no reverence for its own history. On the contrary, each generation bulldozes the graves of its ancestors. No one today argues the case for a flat earth or the spontaneous generation of life from heaps of old rags.

Science operates not in a pendulum's back-and-forth but in cycles of a different sort. The process begins with a group of scientific explorers venturing into new territory. Only rarely are they conquistadores. Typically, in fact, in their caution, their years of preparation, their reliance on exotic equipment, they seem more akin to polar explorers. After checking carefully for hidden dangers, they warily stake their territory, if all seems well.

Perhaps their pioneering venture will thrive. Rudimentary shops and rutted streets may grow up where once stood only tents; a makeshift outpost may someday grow into a real village. Eventually, newcomers may arrive and build on the work of their predecessors. But the good times cannot last forever. The first hints of trouble may be misunderstood at first, possibly even taken as signs of still better times to come. The perpetual fog may finally lift, the wind at last lose some of its bite. Sooner or later, though, the trouble signs will be unmistakable. Ultimately, the ground itself will begin to crack apart. Then it will finally become clear that what had seemed solid earth was really nothing but a giant ice floe on a frozen bay.

There will be casualties, but the most agile of the pioneers will jump into a boat or onto a new chunk of ice in time to save themselves. On shore again, they will catch their breath and relax. They may find that in many ways their new surroundings resemble the old ones. In time, as the weather grows colder and the ground grows firmer and each day comes to resemble its predecessors, they will begin to feel at home. They will come to believe, despite some vague historical memories to the contrary, that this time is different. This time, they will tell themselves, they really *are* on solid ground.

In post–World War II America, psychology's reign seemed as secure as biology's does today. The shift from yesterday's psychological explanations to today's biological ones was in part a matter of scientific discoveries. But not entirely. Shifts from one view of mental illness to another have never been simply a matter of which side could muster the stronger arguments. The clash between psychology and biology is part of a familiar story, though this time played out in unfamiliar costumes.

Americans have always wavered between two poles, proclaiming in one breath the virtues of hard work and self-sacrifice and in the next the delights of instant gratification. We solemnly declare that there is no such thing as a free lunch, and we line up for "Instant Millionaire" lottery tickets. We buy a NordicTrack in the morning and a "How to Eat Everything You Want and Still Lose Weight" diet book in the afternoon.

We cannot seem to resolve this clash of attitudes — we are Puritans in party hats — and it reappears in one guise after another. The psychology-versus-biology debate, in particular, is really about hard work versus instant gratification. The dispute turns on whether lengthy, painful, introspective bouts of psychotherapy provide a true cure while drugs offer only a skin-deep "quick fix." In the fifties, psychiatrists asked whether Thorazine, which can ease schizophrenia's symptoms, was a breakthrough or simply a mask. Today we debate whether Prozac is truly a cure for depression or whether a real cure must be "earned."

Such questions leave us uneasy because we believe in *both* hard work and instant cures. But they are unsettling for another reason, too. Just as we are ambivalent about how to treat mental illness, so are we of two minds about what causes it. The problem is that we hold two fundamentally different views of human nature.

According to the psychological view, everyday language has it right — a disturbed person really is twisted, like a telescope pulled from a furnace. He sees the world askew, through distorting lenses. The biological view presents a different picture — it is not that the disturbed person himself is fundamentally flawed but simply that, by bad fortune, something *happened* to him. Disease is a mugger who picks his victims at random.

Neither view captures the whole truth and neither can be dismissed altogether. As a culture, we flip back and forth between the two, like readers confronting the textbook drawings that show either a wine goblet or two faces in profile. At intervals, the entire society seems to shift its point of view at once, and one view leaps into temporary prominence.

We are now witnessing a new round of attempts to see the goblet and the faces simultaneously. Researchers are trying to meld psychology and biology together, by showing, for example, that our happiness (or sadness) affects our immune system and thereby determines how well we are able to fight off colds, or AIDS, or heart disease. The goal is an old one — it is essentially an attempt to try psychosomatic medicine again, this time getting it right — and in a sense its most surprising feature is that anyone ever thought that psychology and biology could be separated in the first place. When we climb the stairs to the high board at a swimming pool, knees trembling, and then look down to the water *miles* beneath us, what are our dry mouth and sweaty hands and pounding heart but the physical signs of a mental state? And when we savor the melting, bittersweet smoothness of a bite of chocolate soufflé, what is our momentary glow of contentment but a mental state induced by a few grams of matter on a spoon?

In medicine as in everyday life, such examples are commonplace. Even Descartes, the person who did more than any other to separate mind from body, took for granted that physical ailments could have mental causes. Sorrow, he wrote to Princess Elisabeth of Bohemia in 1645, was the most likely cause of her lingering fever. Similarly, a renowned eighteenth-century physician noted that aristocrats who spent their days at court were liable to a physical ailment called *mal de cour.* The cause was loss of the king's favor, and the symptoms included pallor and lack of appetite. At the Russian court, one ambassador observed, *"Il n'y a que deux maladies, les hémorroïdes et le mal de cour."* ("There are only two illnesses, hemorrhoids and court sickness.")

For a modern example of the ties between mind and body, take the use of placebos in drug trials. Placebos don't earn much respect. They are dismissed as "dummy" pills whose only role is negative — if a placebo helps patients as much as a genuine pill does, the assumption is that the pill is worthless and the trial is a bust. But the same findings could be taken as evidence of the mind's influence over the body — a placebo, a sugar pill that works solely by the power of suggestion, can be a match for a pharmaceutical giant's latest million-dollar creation.

And just as mind and body (or psychology and biology) are inextricably intertwined, so are nature and nurture, and heredity and environment. We think of height as a hereditary trait, for example, and so it is, but a person's "tallness" genes can express themselves fully only if the environment provides her with adequate nutrition. Thus we have the familiar phenomenon of first-generation Americans growing taller than their immigrant parents.

Even genetic diseases can be less than straightforwardly genetic. Favism, for example, is a hereditary blood disorder that is relatively common in Mediterranean countries. Its name reflects its defining feature — in susceptible individuals, certain compounds in fava beans can be lethal. The genetics have been worked out in detail — the problem stems from a single gene, which specifies the production of a particular enzyme. But favism appears only in those individuals who have the bad gene *and* who eat fava beans — avoid the beans, and thereby "manipulate" the environment — and an indisputably genetic disease can be completely forestalled and its "victims" can lead normal lives.

The point is that any theory that attempts to draw sharp lines between psychology and biology (or mind and body, or nurture and nature, or environment and heredity) is doomed. This is especially plain when it comes to unraveling the workings of the mind. "I've made up my mind," we say, or "I've changed my mind again," and we think we are simply using figures of speech. But we are speaking literally — we *are* making up our minds, constantly, and we have been since birth. The way that the neurons in a person's brain communicate with one another changes when she learns to speak Italian, or talks with a friend (or a therapist), or sees a horror movie, or survives a mugging. No one brain is fixed and unchanging, and no two brains are identical. Even identical twins have nonidentical brains. Their experiences are not identical, for one thing, and even if they were, the countless connections in the developing brain are not specified in detail. An infant's brain follows general rules as it grows, but there is considerable room for improvisation; the brain's development is more akin to a jazz soloist's impromptu creations than to a player piano's rote unrolling of an ordained melody.

And so it may well be that medicine in the future will make more room for psychology, in the sense of acknowledging the biological impact of experience and emotions. But it is *not* likely that in the future disease-decoding à la Freud will once again become the standard way of thinking of mental illness. The reasons are simple enough. New books and films appear every day, so psychoanalytically minded critics will never run short of raw material to decipher. Nor is there any objective way to evaluate the interpretations they come up with. Matters are crucially different when it comes to mental illness. First, there are only a handful of severe mental illnesses to speculate about, and (presuming that schizophrenia *is* new) it has been nearly two centuries since the last one came along. Second and more important, psychological interpretations of disease have to pass the test of the marketplace. It is not enough to claim to have deciphered a disease; one must go beyond asserting that, for example, paranoia is caused by unacknowledged homosexual impulses and put the claim to the test. Beyond that, one would need to show that the symptom-decoding approach helps patients at least as much as other therapies do. Those are formidable challenges.

Generations of clever analysts have tried to find meaning concealed in the symptoms of madness. They did find solutions — the butler did it! — but the butler turned out to have an alibi. They may yet revive the game in the future, but they will need either new diseases or new solutions, and neither prospect is likely.

• •

But that is speculation. Let us conclude by turning from guesswork about the future to evaluation of the past. In the end, what can one say about the psychoanalysts who ventured to take on madness?

Future generations will look back on psychoanalysis, Peter Medawar wrote, as "the most stupendous intellectual confidence trick of the twentieth century." Brilliant scientist and caustic writer though he was, Medawar was surely wrong here. Con men know exactly what they are up to. The sidewalk sharp taking money from the rubes would be in trouble if he himself believed that the Red Queen was still where he had so ostentatiously placed it. The truth was more interesting and more complicated than in Medawar's depiction. Unlike con men, the psychoanalysts fervently believed their own patter and ended up bewitched by their own spells.

They compounded that intellectual error with a moral one. There is a tendency in the human heart, or brain, to find meaning where there is only happenstance. Worse, there is a tendency to assign blame where there is only bad fortune. The psychoanalysts gave in to this perennial temptation. In doing so, they caused long-lasting, needless harm to those already bowed low by fate. Unable to acknowledge the wisdom of Robert Frost's definition of a tragedy — "something terrible happens and nobody is to blame" — they blamed the victims of illness for the misfortune that had befallen them.

Notes

Throughout these notes, "SE" is used for *The Standard Edition of the Complete Psychological Works of Sigmund Freud*, 24 volumes, translated by James Strachey.

"Freud-Fliess" is used for *The Complete Letters of Sigmund Freud to Wilhelm Fliess, 1887–1904*, translated and edited by Jeffrey M. Masson.

Many titles have been shortened. They are cited in full in the bibliography.

PROLOGUE: *IN SEARCH OF EL DORADO*

11 *I am actually not:* Freud-Fliess, p. 398.

12 *"Psychoanalysis," Freud observed:* Ernst L. Freud, ed., *The Letters of Sigmund Freud*, p. 278.

12 *"The past is pus":* Lauren Slater, *Welcome to My Country*, p. 117. Slater is paraphrasing Freud, "Studies on Hysteria," SE, vol. 2, p. 305.

13 *From the Enlightenment:* This "organic" view never went unchallenged. In the Romantic era, in particular, theories that emphasized psychological factors in mental illness enjoyed a considerable vogue. These psychological theories lost favor again beginning in roughly 1840. See Henri F. Ellenberger, *History of the Unconscious*, pp. 210–215, 284.

13 *"A lunatic is a sick man":* Voltaire's observation, from his *Philosophical Dictionary*, is cited in Roy Porter, ed., *The Faber Book of Madness*, p. 17. Porter is a renowned historian of medicine in general and of madness in particular; this excellent collection is organized thematically and is perhaps the broadest of several such anthologies.

14 *Freud's disciples explained:* See, for example, Smith Ely Jelliffe, "The Parkinsonian Body Posture: Some Considerations on Unconscious Hostility." Jelliffe explains in this 1940 essay that he "sees in the specific Parkinsonian posture an involuntary attitude of defense, comparable to the stealthy approach of the boxer or wrestler to his opponent" (p. 468). He notes, in addition, that the characteristic Parkinsonian tremor "is the same as that which we observe in anxiety and rage" (p. 474) and remarks that "the tremor of the Parkinsonian syndrome corresponds to a repressed sadism" (p. 475).

14 *The "rigidity" of an arm or leg:* Sándor Ferenczi, "Psycho-Analytical Observations on Tic," p. 5.

14 *"If the motor accomplishments":* The quotation is from Isador Coriat, a two-time president of the American Psychoanalytic Association, in "The Psychoanalytic Conception of Stuttering." Coriat is quoted in Benson Bobrick, *Knotted Tongues,* p. 123.

14 *"The critical factor":* Terence Monmaney, "Annals of Medicine: Marshall's Hunch," *New Yorker,* Sept. 20, 1993, p. 64.

14 *Most often, as it turns out:* The discovery was made by Barry Marshall, then an unknown Australian physician. He first published his heretical theory in 1984. See Barry Marshall and J. Robin Warren, "Unidentified Bacilli in the Stomach of Patients with Gastritis and Peptic Ulceration." In 1989, the guilty bacterium was dubbed *Helicobacter pylori,* and by the early 1990s, Marshall's shocking doctrine had won general acceptance. For excellent accounts of Marshall's assault on entrenched belief, see Monmaney's *New Yorker* article and Martin J. Blaser, "The Bacteria Behind Ulcers."

15 *The last blow:* René Dubos and Jean Dubos, *The White Plague: Tuberculosis, Man, and Society,* p. 11.

16 *It seems certain:* Ernest Gellner devotes chap. 5 of *The Psychoanalytic Movement* to this topic. The book is elegantly slim and uniformly excellent.

PART ONE: *FREUD*

17 *A layman will no doubt find:* Sigmund Freud, "Psychical (or Mental) Treatment," SE, vol. 7, p. 283.

CHAPTER ONE: *THE GOSPEL ACCORDING TO FREUD*

19 *[Freud] is extraordinary:* Norman Malcolm, *Ludwig Wittgenstein: A Memoir,* p. 100. Italics in original.

19 *We possess the truth:* Vincent Brome, *Freud and His Disciples,* p. 132. The passage was in a letter from Freud to Ferenczi written on May 13, 1913.

19 *spreading the toothpaste:* Paul Roazen, *Freud and His Followers,* pp. 56–57.

19 *a therapist by trade:* Freud confided to his friend Wilhelm Fliess that "I became a therapist against my will." See Freud-Fliess, p. 180.

19 *"We do analysis for two reasons":* Franz Alexander, *Psychoanalytic Pioneers,* p. 255.

19 *"not the main":* Smiley Blanton, *Diary of My Analysis with Sigmund Freud,* p. 116.

20 *"I'm glad you ask":* Abram Kardiner, *My Analysis with Freud,* p. 68.

20 *"In the depths of my heart":* Ernst Freud, ed., *Letters of Sigmund Freud,* p. 390.

20 *"I have found little that is 'good' ":* Heinrich Meng and Ernst L. Freud, eds., *Psychoanalysis and Faith: The Letters of Sigmund Freud and Oskar Pfister,* p. 61.

20 *"I cannot put up with":* Sigmund Freud, "On Beginning the Treatment," SE, vol. 12, p. 134.

20 *"The doctor should be opaque":* Sigmund Freud, "Recommendations to Physicians Practicing Psycho-Analysis," SE, vol. 12, p. 118.

20 *"emotional coldness":* Ibid., p. 115.

20 *"a situation in which":* Sigmund Freud, "On the History of the Psycho-Analytic Movement," SE, vol. 14, p. 49.

21 *"When I would protest":* Todd Dufresne, "An Interview with Joseph Wortis," p. 593.

21 *"Do you suppose":* Freud-Fliess, p. 417.

21 *"the interpretation of dreams":* Sigmund Freud, "Five Lectures on Psychoanalysis," SE, vol. 11, p. 33.

21 *"It contains," he wrote:* Freud made the remark in 1931, in the preface to the third English edition of *The Interpretation of Dreams.* It is cited in Peter Gay's *Freud: A Life for Our Time,* p. 4.

21 *Dreams seem strange:* John Farrell notes, in *Freud's Paranoid Quest,* that just this sort of press censorship was in fact the rule in Freud's Vienna. See p. 145.

21 *"Do not let us forget":* Sigmund Freud, "My Contact with Josef Popper-Lynkeus," SE, vol. 22, p. 222.

21 *"wolves in sheep's clothing":* Sigmund Freud, "The Interpretation of Dreams," SE, vol. 4, p. 183.

22 *"the irritating and clumsy process":* Sigmund Freud, "The Psychopathology of Everyday Life," SE, vol. 6, p. 176.

22 *"pressing out the content":* Sigmund Freud, "The Unconscious," SE, vol. 14, pp. 199–200.

22 *"writing, which entails":* Both this example and the next are from Sigmund Freud, "Inhibitions, Symptoms, and Anxiety," SE, vol. 20, p. 90.

22 *Even intellectual curiosity:* Sigmund Freud, "Leonardo da Vinci and a Memory of his Childhood," SE, vol. 11, p. 78.

22 *"When a member of my family":* Sigmund Freud, "The Psychopathology of Everyday Life," SE, vol. 6, p. 180.

22 *"I believe in external (real) chance":* Ibid., p. 257.

22 *"We cannot fail to admire":* Ibid., pp. 179–180.

22 *"To the observer of human nature":* Ibid., p. 199. In a different context, Freud made an X-ray comparison of his own. Psychoanalysis was so powerful a tool, he wrote, that it could prove risky to the analyst himself, in "disagreeable analogy with the effect of X-rays on people who handle them without taking special precautions." See "Analysis Terminable and Interminable," SE, vol. 23, p. 249.

23 *"I asked her what":* Sigmund Freud, "Fragment of an Analysis of a Case of Hysteria," SE, vol. 7, p. 39. In later references, this essay is cited as "Dora."

23 *"Later on it no doubt":* Ibid., p. 39.

23 *"Dora's symptomatic acts":* Ibid., pp. 79–80.

24 *"In many cases, as in Dora's":* Ibid., p. 80.

24 *Herr K. had "suddenly clasped":* Ibid., p. 28.

24 *"The behavior of this child":* Ibid.

24 *"Hysterical headaches rest":* Freud-Fliess, p. 340.

24 *"the repression of the intention":* Freud-Fliess, pp. 217–218.

24 *"I observed one of his attacks":* Hilda C. Abraham and Ernst L. Freud, *The Letters of Sigmund Freud and Karl Abraham,* p. 15.

24 *"obvious hostile significance":* Karl Abraham, "Contribution to a Discussion on Tic," in his *Selected Papers,* p. 324.

25 *"Just in the same way":* Karl Abraham, "Ejaculatio Praecox," in his *Selected Papers,* pp. 292–293.

25 *"It was discovered that":* Quoted in Daniel Rogers, *Motor Disorder in Psychiatry: Towards a Neurological Psychiatry,* p. 12.

25 *"Illness has a purpose":* Georg Groddeck, *The Book of the It,* p. 101.

25 *"wild analyst"*: Ronald Clark, *Freud*, p. 403.

25 *"the dark, inaccessible part"*: Sigmund Freud, "New Introductory Lectures," SE, vol. 22, p. 73.

25 *"Groddeck is quite certainly"*: Ibid., pp. 434–435.

25 *"He alone will die"*: Groddeck, *Book of the It*, p. 101.

25 *"it is possible that death"*: Christopher Silvester, ed., *Norton Book of Interviews*, p. 266.

25 fn *It should also be noted*: Freud's comment appears in Ernst L. Freud, ed., *The Letters of Sigmund Freud*, p. 318.

26 *"I believe that"*: Ernest Jones, *Freud*, vol. 2, pp. 416–417.

26 *"For a Jew-boy"*: Ernest Jones, *Freud*, vol. 3, p. 208.

26 *"son and heir"*: Ernest Jones, *Freud*, vol. 2, p. 33.

26 *"So we are at last rid"*: Clark, *Freud*, p. 336.

26 *"adversaries, diluters"*: Ibid., p. 334.

26 *"In the execution of this duty"*: Ibid., p. 333.

26 fn *The use of the word "heresy"*: Freud's reference to "the two heretics" is from Roazen, *Freud and His Followers*, p. 244.

27 *"Overtly and without apology"*: Trilling's remark is from the introduction to his one-volume abridgement of Ernest Jones's three-volume biography of Freud. See Lionel Trilling and Steven Marcus, eds., *The Life and Work of Sigmund Freud*, p. viii.

27 *"I know that I have a destiny"*: Sigmund Freud, "Contributions to a Discussion on Masturbation," SE, vol. 12, p. 250.

27 *"human megalomania"*: Sigmund Freud, "Introductory Lectures," SE, vol. 16, pp. 284–285.

27 *Joseph, Moses*: Farrell, *Freud's Paranoid Quest*, p. 51.

27 *"had the support of a long series"*: Ernest Jones, *Freud*, vol. 3, p. 131.

27 *"invariably and indisputably"*: Sigmund Freud, "The Interpretation of Dreams," SE, vol. 5, p. 561.

28 *"Was not this the sharpest"*: Sigmund Freud, "The Interpretation of Dreams," SE, vol. 4, p. 151.

28 *(To his dismay)*: Gay, *Freud*, pp. 456–457.

28 *"I'm sick of this"*: Percival Bailey, "The Academic Lecture: The Great Psychiatric Revolution," p. 395.

29 *"Reporting on it now"*: Freud-Fliess, p. 131.

29 *"The pig finds truffles"*: Clark, *Freud*, p. 309.

29 *"distribution of menu-cards"*: Sigmund Freud, " 'Wild' Psychoanalysis," SE, vol. 11, p. 225.

29 *"Superstition is in large part"*: Sigmund Freud, "The Psychopathology of Everyday Life," SE, vol. 6, p. 260.

29 *"We have long observed"*: This is the opening sentence of Freud's essay "Formulations on the Two Principles of Mental Functioning," SE, vol. 12, p. 218.

29 *"Yet every single hysteric"*: Sigmund Freud, "Five Lectures on Psycho-analysis," SE, vol. 11, pp. 16–17.

29 *Let us suppose*: Ibid., pp. 25–27.

30 *"He that has eyes to see"*: Sigmund Freud, "Dora," SE, vol. 7, pp. 77–78.

31 *"purely descriptive"*: Sigmund Freud, "Introductory Lectures," SE, vol. 15, p. 20.

31 *"first understanding"*: Sigmund Freud, "Introductory Lectures," SE, vol. 16, p. 251.

31 *Neurotic patients of all sorts*: Sigmund Freud, "The Question of Lay Analysis," SE, vol. 20, pp. 186–187.

31 *"Such practitioners casually recommend"*: Ernest Jones, *Papers on Psycho-Analysis*, p. 342.

32 *Dreams had been considered meaningful:* Henri F. Ellenberger, *The Discovery of the Unconscious*, p. 506.

32 *"it hardly seems necessary"*: Josef Breuer, "Studies on Hysteria," SE, vol. 2, p. 222.

32 *"guesses and intuitions"*: Ellenberger, *Discovery*, p. 277.

32 *" 'I did this,' says my Memory"*: Freud quotes Nietzsche (more precisely, he quotes a patient quoting Nietzsche) in his "Notes upon a Case of Obsessional Neurosis," the case history of the Rat Man, SE, vol. 10, p. 184.

32 *"coincides with my concept"*: Sigmund Freud, "On the History of the Psycho-Analytic Movement," SE, vol. 14, p. 15.

32 *"The current legend"*: Ellenberger, *Discovery*, p. 548.

33 *Freud did not create:* Allen Esterson explores these claims in *Seductive Mirage*, pp. 219–224. Esterson's examination of Freud's arguments is a model of scholarship.

33 *he brought the prestige:* Ernest Gellner makes this point about the prestige and vocabulary of medicine in *The Psychoanalytic Movement.* See pp. 26, 110–112.

33 *"I have the distinct feeling"*: Freud-Fliess, p. 74.

CHAPTER TWO: *THE POWER OF CONVICTION*

34 *In such a case:* Sigmund Freud, "Dora," SE, vol. 7, pp. 58–59.

34 *"Whatever case and whatever symptom"*: Sigmund Freud, "The Etiology of Hysteria," SE, vol. 3, p. 199.

34 *"universal validity"*: Ibid.

34 *"At the bottom of every case"*: Ibid., p. 203.

34 *"I can only repeat"*: Sigmund Freud, Postscript to "Dora," SE, vol. 7, p. 115.

35 *"If the* vita sexualis": Sigmund Freud, "My Views on the Part Played by Sexuality in the Etiology of the Neuroses," SE, vol. 7, p. 274.

35 *"Every new arrival"*: This remark is part of a long footnote that Freud added in 1920 to his "Three Essays on the Theory of Sexuality," SE, vol. 7, p. 226n.

35 *"It became ever clearer"*: Sigmund Freud, "A Short Account of Psycho-Analysis," SE, vol. 19, p. 198.

35 *"the central experience"*: Sigmund Freud, "An Outline of Psycho-Analysis," SE, vol. 23, p. 191.

35 *"no human individual"*: Ibid., p. 185.

35 *"unsavory and incredible"*: The passage is from Freud's essay "Dostoevsky and Parricide." The sentence that immediately follows the one quoted in the text reads: "This key, then, we must apply to our author's so-called epilepsy." See SE, vol. 21, p. 184.

35 *"the delusion of persecution"*: Sigmund Freud, "A Case of Paranoia Running Counter to the Psycho-Analytic Theory of the Disease," SE, vol. 14, p. 266.

35 *"With boys the wish"*: Sigmund Freud, " 'A Child Is Being Beaten,' " SE, vol. 17, p. 188.

35 *"The motive for being ill"*: The remark is from a footnote that Freud added in 1923 to "Dora," SE, vol. 7, p. 43n.

35 *"Is this the explanation"*: Sigmund Freud, "Introductory Lectures," SE, vol. 15, p. 44.

35 *"It was the same"*: Sigmund Freud, "Totem and Taboo," SE, vol. 13, pp. 127–128.

35 *"The insight has dawned"*: Freud-Fliess, p. 287.

36 *"Mankind," he declared*: Freud-Fliess, p. 25n.

36 *"smoothly opened"*: Freud-Fliess, p. 427.

36 *"Freud is a man"*: Quoted in Paul Cranefield, "Josef Breuer's Evaluation of His Contribution to Psychoanalysis," p. 320.

36 *Breuer's caution is especially noteworthy*: Robert Coles, for example, wrote that Freud's "patients were people apart, people looked down upon, people who annoyed and even enraged their doctors, let alone everyone else in Vienna's middle-class world. . . . In contrast Freud wanted to understand and heal. He treated those 'neurotics' with a revolutionary kind of respect. He listened to them. He watched them. He held off judging them, or labeling them, unlike his colleagues, who seemed to feel that if only we can classify people into categories, we have done our job as scientists." See *The Mind's Fate*, p. 226.

36 *"to furnish a psychology"*: Sigmund Freud, "Project for a Scientific Psychology," SE, vol. 1, p. 295.

36 *"I no longer understand"*: Freud-Fliess, p. 152.

36 *"The* Project, *or rather"*: This is from James Strachey's introduction to Freud's "Project for a Scientific Psychology," SE, vol. 1, p. 290.

36 fn *Freud's great rival*: Carl Jung, *Modern Man in Search of a Soul*, p. 229.

37 *"You should not for a moment"*: Sigmund Freud, "Introductory Lectures," SE, vol. 16, p. 244.

37 *"In the sexual processes"*: William McGuire, ed., *The Freud/Jung Letters*, pp. 140–141.

37 *"Mechanical agitation"*: Sigmund Freud, "Beyond the Pleasure Principle," SE, vol. 18, p. 33.

37 *The child fell ill*: Sigmund Freud, "The Psychopathology of Everyday Life," SE, vol. 6, p. 146n.

38 *"The 'No' uttered by a patient"*: Sigmund Freud, "Dora," SE, vol. 7, pp. 58–59.

38 *"So that's your technique"*: Sigmund Freud, "Introductory Lectures," SE, vol. 15, p. 50.

38 *"Heads I win, tails you lose"*: In his essay "Constructions in Analysis," Freud attempts to rebut the charge that he relies on what he calls (on p. 257) "the famous principle of 'Heads I win, tails you lose.' " See SE, vol. 23, pp. 257–269.

38 fn *Freud acknowledged*: Ibid.

39 *"there are, however"*: Sigmund Freud, "Introductory Lectures," SE, vol. 16, p. 438.

39 *"remain on the whole"*: Ibid., pp. 438–439.

39 *Freud's only direct experience*: Anthony Storr, *Freud*, p. 59.

39 *All the patients were rich*: Ronald Clark, *Freud: The Man and the Cause*, p. 65.

39 *"I do not care for these"*: Max Schur, *The Id and the Regulatory Principles of Mental Functioning*, p. 21.

39 *"Even we cannot withhold"*: Sigmund Freud, "New Introductory Lectures on Psycho-Analysis," SE, vol. 22, p. 59.

39 *"They reject the doctor"*: Sigmund Freud, "Introductory Lectures," SE, vol. 16, p. 447.

39 *"are inaccessible to our efforts"*: Ibid., p. 447.

39 *"unfamiliarity with schizophrenia"*: Paul Roazen, *Freud and His Followers*, p. 142.

40 *"We know that the mechanisms"*: Ernest Jones, *Freud*, vol. 3, p. 449.

40 *"Do not suppose"*: Sigmund Freud, "Introductory Lectures on Psychoanalysis," SE, vol. 16, p. 432.

40 *"the grain of sand"*: Sigmund Freud, "Dora," SE, vol. 7, p. 83.

40 *"Are [neuroses] the inevitable result"*: Sigmund Freud, "Introductory Lectures on Psychoanalysis," SE, vol. 16, pp. 346–347. Freud often made such remarks. In "Analysis Terminable and Interminable," for example, he observed, "The etiology of every neurotic disturbance is, after all, a mixed one. . . . As a rule there is a combination of both factors, the constitutional and the accidental." See SE, vol. 23, p. 220.

41 *The more striking*: Sigmund Freud, "Introductory Lectures," SE, vol. 15, p. 154.

    41 *water-taps, watering-cans*: Ibid., p. 155.

41 *"pits, cavities, and hollows"*: Ibid., p. 156.

41 *We "began to turn"*: Sigmund Freud, "The Interpretation of Dreams," SE, vol. 5, p. 355n.

42 *(though not to conventional scholars)*: David Stannard devotes a chapter to Freud's essay on Leonardo in *Shrinking History*, his dissection of psychohistory. See esp. pp. 4–7.

42 *"There is no doubt"*: Sigmund Freud, "Leonardo da Vinci and a Memory of His Childhood," SE, vol. 11, p. 121.

42 *In 1909, to take a clinical example*: Freud's essay, "Analysis of a Phobia in a Five-Year-Old Boy," is usually referred to as the case of "Little Hans." It can be found in SE, vol. 10, pp. 3–149. The case is discussed in a fine debunking essay called "Psychoanalytic 'Evidence': A Critique Based on Freud's Case of Little Hans," by Joseph Wolpe and Stanley Rachman.

42 *"were both among my closest"*: Freud explains his interactions with Hans and his parents in the opening paragraphs of his essay. See SE, vol. 10, pp. 5–6.

42 *Here was the Oedipal drama*: "Hans really was a little Oedipus who wanted to have his father 'out of the way,' to get rid of him, so that he might be alone with his beautiful mother and sleep with her." Ibid., p. 111.

42 *"The horse must be his father"*: Ibid., p. 123.

42 *"by what horses wear"*: Ibid., p. 41.

42 *"directly transposed"*: Ibid., p. 123.

42 *"The content of his phobia"*: Ibid., pp. 139–140.

42 *seconded Hans's account*: Ibid., pp. 49–50.

42 *the fearsome black object*: Ibid., pp. 42, 49, 53, and esp. 69, where Hans was finally able to show his father a horse with the fearsome object, even though his father had denied that there were such things. "Once he called out, almost with joy: 'Here comes a horse with something black on its mouth!' And I was at last able to establish the fact that it was a horse with a leather muzzle."

42 *For Freud and his followers*: In *The Memory Wars*, Crews comments on Freud's "always preferring the arcane explanation to the obvious one" (p. 37).

43 *"I knew very well"*: Sigmund Freud, "On the History of the Psycho-analytic Movement," SE, vol. 14, p. 48.

43 *"The whale and the polar bear"*: Sigmund Freud, "From the History of an Infantile Neurosis." This is the celebrated case of the Wolf Man. SE, vol. 17, p. 48.

43 *"How then could I expect"*: Sigmund Freud, "The Question of Lay Analysis," SE, vol. 20, p. 199. Freud made a similar remark in "An Outline of Psychoanalysis," SE, vol. 23, p. 144: "The teachings of psycho-analysis are based on an incalculable number of observations and experiences, and only someone who has repeated those observations on himself and on others is in a position to arrive at a judgment of his own upon it."

43 *"One cannot properly deny":* Sigmund Freud, "Further Remarks on the Neuro-Psychoses of Defense," SE, vol. 3, p. 220.

44 *"It may seem tempting":* Sigmund Freud, "From the History of an Infantile Neurosis," SE, vol. 17, p. 14n.

44 *"if the enlightenments":* Wolpe and Rachman, "Little Hans," p. 145.

44 *"refuse to give up the punishment":* Sigmund Freud, "The Ego and the Id," SE, vol. 19, pp. 49–50.

45 *Eckstein was a young woman:* Her photograph appears in Freud-Fliess, facing p. 112.

45 *No surviving records:* Jeffrey M. Masson, *The Assault on Truth,* p. 57.

45 *"very charming and old-fashioned":* Edward Shorter, *From Paralysis to Fatigue,* p. 67, quoting Alix Strachey.

45 *the closest friend:* Frank Sulloway, *Freud, Biologist of the Mind,* p. 135.

45 *"almost reverential":* Freud-Fliess, p. 2.

45 *"Your praise is nectar and ambrosia":* Freud-Fliess, p. 87.

45 *"How much I owe you":* Freud-Fliess, p. 2.

45 *Troubles in certain "genital spots":* Sulloway, *Freud,* pp. 138–141; see also Masson, *Assault,* pp. 72–78.

45 *(Fleiss laid out this aspect):* Masson, *Assault,* p. 78.

45 *Treatment was, to begin with:* Ibid., pp. 74–77.

45 *Emma Eckstein appears:* Ibid., pp. 60, 78.

45 *many skeptics thought so:* See, for example, Freud-Fliess, p. 310n.

45 *but Fliess was:* Sulloway, *Freud,* pp. 147–152; Shorter, *From Paralysis to Fatigue,* pp. 64–68.

45 *In any event, Fliess operated:* Masson, *Assault,* p. 67.

45 *"Eckstein's condition is still":* Freud-Fliess, p. 113.

46 *"There still was moderate bleeding":* Ibid., pp. 116–117.

46 *"Poor Eckstein is doing less well":* Ibid., pp. 120–121.

46 *"I know what you want":* Ibid., p. 122.

46 *"Dearest Wilhelm, Gloomy times":* Ibid., pp. 123–124.

47 *"Emma E. is finally doing":* Ibid., p. 130.

47 *"a completely surprising explanation":* Ibid., p. 181.

47 *"Her episodes of bleeding":* Ibid., p. 183.

47 *"When she saw how affected":* Ibid., p. 186.

47 *permanent disfigurement:* Masson, *Assault,* p. 70.

47 *"For me you remain":* Freud-Fliess, p. 125.

47 *(Freud* had *put himself):* Sulloway, *Freud,* pp. 143, 145; Jones, *Freud,* vol. 1, p. 309; Shorter, *From Paralysis to Fatigue,* p. 67.

47 *"[Emma's] story is becoming":* Ibid., p. 191.

47 *"As for the biographers":* Clark, *Freud,* p. 63.

48 *He got away with it:* One of the closest examinations of this central point is in Jean Schimek, "Fact and Fantasy in the Seduction Theory: A Historical Review." Among the key references are Freud's "Constructions in Analysis": "[The analyst's] work of construction, or, if it is preferred, of reconstruction, resembles to a great extent an archeologist's excavation of some dwelling-place that has been destroyed and buried or of some ancient edifice" (SE, vol. 23, p. 259); also, "The Analysis of a Phobia in a Five-Year-Old Boy": "This is how, basing my conclusions upon the findings of the analysis, I am obliged to reconstruct the unconscious complexes and wishes, the repression and reawakening of which produced little Hans's phobia" (SE, vol. 10, p. 135); also, "Analysis Terminable and Interminable": "The therapeutic effect depends on making conscious what is repressed, in the widest sense of the word, in the id. We

prepare the way for this making conscious by interpretations and constructions" (SE, vol. 23, p. 238); also, "From the History of an Infantile Neurosis": "So far as my experience hitherto goes, these scenes from infancy are not reproduced during the treatment as recollections, they are the products of construction." Such scenes "are as a rule not reproduced as recollections, but have to be divined — constructed — gradually and laboriously from an aggregate of indications" (SE, vol. 17, pp. 50–51).

48 *In part, this blurring:* But only in part. See Esterson, "Jeffrey Masson and Freud's Seduction Theory: A New Fable Based on Old Myths," pp. 13–15.

48 *He was not, he insisted:* See, for example, "Constructions in Analysis": "I can assert without boasting that such an abuse of 'suggestion' has never occurred in my practice" (SE, vol. 23, p. 262). Allen Esterson examines this question with characteristic insight and thoroughness in *Seductive Mirage*, pp. 236–239.

48 *"it is true that":* Sigmund Freud, "A Phobia in a Five-Year-Old Boy," SE, vol. 10, p. 104.

48 *"we may then boldly":* Sigmund Freud, "Sexual Etiology of the Neuroses," SE, vol. 3, p. 269.

48 *(Often these "memories"):* Esterson cites several examples in "Jeffrey Masson and Freud's Seduction Theory," pp. 5–9. In his essay "On Beginning the Treatment," for example, Freud wrote: "Telling and describing [the patient's] repressed trauma to him did not even result in any recollection of it coming into his mind" (SE, vol. 12, p. 141).

48 *"The technique of psychoanalysis":* Sigmund Freud, "Hysterical Phantasies and Their Relation to Bisexuality," SE, vol. 9, p. 162.

49 *"self-deprogramming":* Frederick Crews, *Skeptical Engagements*, p. xi. For an example of Crews's work before his deprogramming, see his *Sins of the Fathers*, a study of Nathaniel Hawthorne.

49 fn *By far the most important:* The Crews quote is from *Memory Wars*, p. 57.

50 *If you set about measuring:* Martin Gardner, *Fads and Fallacies*, pp. 176–177. Cioffi quotes Gardner in "Freud and the Idea of a Pseudo-Science," in Robert Borger and Frank Cioffi, eds., *Explanation in the Behavioral Sciences*, p. 491.

50 *"I would often give":* Joseph Wortis, "Fragments of a Freudian Analysis," pp. 844–845. Wortis's remark is cited in Frank Cioffi, "Wittgenstein's Freud," pp. 204–205, in Peter Winch, ed., *Studies in the Philosophy of Wittgenstein.*

51 *"The popular picture of psychoanalysis":* Janet Malcolm, *In the Freud Archives*, pp. 8–9.

PART TWO: *THE HEYDAY OF PSYCHOANALYSIS*

53 *There has been nothing:* Ernest Gellner, *The Psychoanalytic Movement*, p. 11.

CHAPTER THREE: *THE HIGH GROUND*

55 *In America today:* Philip Rieff, *Freud: The Mind of the Moralist*, p. xi.

55 *"I remember seeing":* Author interview, Dec. 15, 1995.

56 *even at their peak:* Edward Shorter, *A History of Psychiatry*, p. 307.

56 *"The possibilities have to be":* John R. Seeley, "The Americanization of the Unconscious," p. 72.

56 Scientific American *carried:* See Erich Fromm, "The Oedipus Myth," *Scientific American*, Jan. 1949; and "Books," *Scientific American*, September 1959.

56 *The* Atlantic Monthly *devoted:* See "Psychiatry in American Life," *Atlantic Monthly,* July 1961; quote, p. 62.

56 Life *produced:* The series ran between Jan. 7 and Feb. 4, 1957.

56 Look *ran a first-person article: Look,* Oct. 2, 1956, pp. 48–49. This reference is cited in E. Fuller Torrey's *Freudian Fraud* (now out of print), the best account of Freud's influence on American culture. Many of the references cited in this section are based on my interviews with Torrey and on passages in *Freudian Fraud.*

56 *"The theoretical underpinning":* Torrey, *Freudian Fraud,* p. 135.

57 *"A boy loves his mother":* Nathan G. Hale, Jr., *The Rise and Crisis of Psychoanalysis in the United States,* p. 286.

57 *"From 1945 to 1955":* Bertram S. Brown, "The Life of Psychiatry," p. 492.

57 *Of the 89:* This sentence and the next one are from Hale, *Rise and Crisis,* p. 253.

57 *"By the mid-1960s":* This quote and the figures in the previous sentence are from Shorter, *A History of Psychiatry,* p. 174.

57 *three memorial meetings: Time* devoted its April 23, 1956, cover story to Freud and discussed the upcoming birthday plans on p. 70.

57 *"No other system":* Alfred Kazin, "The Freudian Revolution Analyzed," p. 22.

57 *"undoubtedly . . . the most insightful":* M. F. Ashley Montagu, "Man — And Human Nature," p. 403.

57 *"the nearest to a miracle": Life,* Feb. 4, 1957.

57 *"Immeasurably great":* Ernest Jones, *Freud,* vol. 1, p. xiii.

58 *"reached out to touch":* Brendan Gill, "Dreamer and Healer," p. 153.

58 *"European psychoanalysis found itself":* Laura Fermi, *Illustrious Immigrants,* p. 142.

58 *The Vienna Psychoanalytic Society:* The 1937 date and the figures in the following sentence are from Fermi, pp. 142, 147, 151.

58 *Of those psychoanalysts who escaped:* Fermi, *Illustrious Immigrants,* p. 147.

58 *By the end of World War II:* Reuben Fine, *A History of Psychoanalysis,* p. 90.

58 *"Our readers will be thrilled":* Ben Hecht, *Gaily, Gaily,* p. 65.

58 fn *The Viennese seemed as intrigued:* Freud-Fliess, p. 57.

59 *"Freudian psychology had flooded":* Nathan Hale, *Freud and the Americans,* p. 434, quoting Morton Prince.

59 *shell shock accounted:* Hale, *Rise and Crisis,* p. 189.

59 *Overall, 60 percent:* Gerald Grob, "Origins of DSM-I: A Study in Appearance and Reality," p. 427.

59 *"It looks ridiculously simple":* Hale, *Rise and Crisis,* p. 196.

60 *"It helped* them": Author interview, May 22, 1996.

61 *"Psychiatrists before Freud":* Author interview, Dec. 15, 1995.

61 *"Freud, even more than Lincoln":* These are the opening words of Kaufmann's "Freud and the Tragic Virtues," p. 469.

61 fn *Freud himself switched sides:* The quote is from Mitchell and Black, *Freud and Beyond,* p. 208.

62 *At Boas's suggestion:* Derek Freeman, *Margaret Mead and the Heretic,* p. 75.

62 *"Adolescence represented no period":* Margaret Mead, *Coming of Age in Samoa,* p. 157.

62 *The gentle Samoans:* The quotations in the rest of this paragraph are from different articles Mead wrote on Samoa. They are cited (pp. 90–91, 94) and referenced in Freeman, *Margaret Mead and the Heretic,* in the chapter entitled "Mead's Depiction of the Samoans."

63 *"Familiarity with sex":* Mead, *Coming of Age,* p. 151.

63 *("because he had been psychoanalyzed"):* Catherine Bateson, *With a Daughter's Eye,* p. 31.

CHAPTER FOUR: *HOPE AND GLORY*

64 *The nature of men:* Karl Menninger, "Hope," p. 490.

64 *"In those days":* Author interview, Dec. 15, 1995.

65 *"The reason why twenty-five people":* Author interview, Dec. 14, 1995.

65 *"I wanted to be":* Author interview, Dec. 4, 1995.

67 *"the happy man would not get":* Susan Sontag, *Illness as Metaphor,* p. 54.

67 fn *It was an upholsterer:* Robert Sapolsky, "On the Role of Upholstery in Cardiovascular Physiology."

68 *Freud himself had predicted:* Franz Alexander and Sheldon Selesnick, *The History of Psychiatry,* p. xv.

68 *putting "psychoanalysis on the map":* Nathan Hale, *Rise and Crisis,* p. 132.

68 *"in the main":* Edward Shorter, *A History of Psychiatry,* pp. 151–152.

68 *"an engaging and energetic":* Hale, *Rise and Crisis,* p. 180.

68 *"They asked for it":* Flanders Dunbar, *Mind and Body,* p. 26.

68 *"Men, women and children":* Ibid., p. 34.

68 *"seeking compensation":* Ibid., p. 33.

68 *"The sufferers lose":* Ibid., p. 34.

69 *(This also marked the end):* Hale, *Rise and Crisis,* p. 181.

69 *"Only about ten to twenty percent":* Dunbar, *Mind and Body,* pp. 97–98.

69 *allergy victims:* Ibid., p. 181.

69 *Those with skin diseases:* Ibid., p. 191.

69 *Diabetics, for example:* Ibid., p. 199.

69 *The key was "smother love":* Ibid., p. 174.

69 *"Smother love has enveloped":* Ibid., p. 190.

69 *In 1948, for example:* "How's Your Psychosoma?" *Time,* July 12, 1948.

70 *"We are now ready":* Franz Alexander, *Psychosomatic Medicine,* pp. 139–140.

70 *"girls who do not get along":* "Rejection Dyspepsia," *Time,* Jan. 26, 1953.

70 *the historian Nathan Hale:* Hale, *Rise and Crisis,* p. 182.

71 *In 1951, Kety was named:* Kety has described these events in an autobiographical essay, "The Metamorphosis of a Psychobiologist." The story about his psychoanalysis is from my interview, Oct. 19, 1995.

71 *a remarkable mini-essay:* Seymour Kety, "A Biologist Examines the Mind and Behavior." See esp. pp. 1867–1869.

72 *"I blush to admit":* Jerome Kagan, *Unstable Ideas,* p. 89.

72 *In Holland in the 1600s:* The classic account is in Charles Mackay's *Extraordinary Popular Delusions and the Madness of Crowds.*

72 *"What I'm trying to tell you":* Author interview, Dec. 14, 1995.

72 *"we were taught or led":* Coles was speaking at a 1970 symposium on R. D. Laing. See Robert Boyers and Robert Orrill, eds., *R. D. Laing and Anti-Psychiatry,* p. 221.

73 *"Kennedy had just been elected":* Author interview, Dec. 14, 1995.

73 *"America is a mistake":* Nathan Hale, *Freud and the Americans,* p. 433.

73 *("As I stepped onto"):* Sigmund Freud, "An Autobiographical Study," SE, vol. 20, p. 52.

73 *The wretched American food:* Ernest Jones, *Freud,* vol. 2, pp. 59–60.

73 *an "obsession":* The biographer is Ronald Clark, in *Freud: The Man and the Cause,* p. 279. Peter Gay also discusses Freud's anti-Americanism at length in his Freud biography. See Gay, pp. 562–570.

74 *"hysterical misery"*: Sigmund Freud, "Studies on Hysteria," SE, vol. 2, p. 305.
74 *"The difference between"*: Sigmund Freud, "Analysis Terminable and Interminable," SE, vol. 23, p. 228.
74 *"Men are not gentle"*: Sigmund Freud, "Civilization and Its Discontents," SE, vol. 21, p. 111.
74 *"a savage beast"*: Ibid., pp. 111–112.
74 *"the mental constitution"*: Sigmund Freud, "Introductory Lectures," SE, vol. 15, p. 146.
74 *"born afresh with every"*: Sigmund Freud, "The Future of an Illusion," SE, vol. 21, p. 10.
74 *"Life, as we find it"*: Sigmund Freud, "Civilization and Its Discontents," SE, vol. 21, p. 75.
75 *"The intention that man"*: Ibid., p. 76.
75 *"Freud astonished us"*: Gay, *Freud*, pp. 394–395.
75 *"Ye shall know the truth"*: Karl Menninger, "Hope," p. 490.
76 *"more Freudian than Freud"*: See, for example, "Karl Menninger, 96, Dies; Leader in U.S. Psychiatry," *New York Times*, July 19, 1990.
76 *"a man whose intrepidity"*: Karl Menninger, "Death of a Prophet," p. 23.
76 *Freud was a "genius"*: Karl Menninger, "Sigmund Freud," pp. 373–374. All the quotations in this sentence and the next are from this article, except the statement that Freud had "discovered psychology," which is from "Death of a Prophet."
76 *"The old point of view"*: Karl Menninger, *The Vital Balance*, p. 2.
76 *"We know there is a possibility"*: Ibid.
76 *"At the risk of tiring the reader"*: Ibid., p. 251.
76 *"Words are the essential tool"*: Sigmund Freud, "Psychical (or Mental) Treatment," SE, vol. 7, p. 283.
77 *"Our concern now"*: Menninger, *Vital Balance*, p. 2.
77 *"We tend today to think"*: Ibid.
77 *"The assumption was"*: Author interview, Dec. 4, 1995.
77 *"For Menninger"*: Donald Klein and Paul Wender, *Mind, Mood, and Medicine*, p. 331.
77 *"It is now accepted"*: Menninger, *Vital Balance*, p. 33.
77 *"Every normal person"*: Sigmund Freud, "Analysis Terminable and Interminable," SE, vol. 23, p. 235.
77 *"The idea of continuity"*: Author interview, Dec. 4, 1995.
78 *"It would be superficial"*: Abram Kardiner, "Freud: The Man I Knew, the Scientist, and His Influence," in *Freud and the Twentieth Century*, ed. Benjamin Nelson, p. 56.
78 *Its special strengths derive*: John Gunderson and Loren Mosher, eds., *Issues and Controversies in the Psychotherapy of Schizophrenia*, pp. 209–210.
78 *Psychoanalysis was "the most powerful"*: Leo Stone, "The Widening Scope of Indications for Psychoanalysis," p. 593.
79 *"he offers a challenge"*: Beata Rank, "Adaptation of the Psychoanalytic Technique for the Treatment of Young Children with Atypical Development," pp. 132–133.

PART THREE: *SCHIZOPHRENIA*

81 *Healing schizophrenia establishes:* Arthur Burton, "The Adoration of the Patient and Its Disillusionment," p. 200.

CHAPTER FIVE: *THE MOTHER OF THE*
"SCHIZOPHRENOGENIC MOTHER"

83 *We think of a schizophrenic:* Frieda Fromm-Reichmann, "Transference Problems in Schizophrenics," in *Psychoanalysis and Psychotherapy: Collected Papers of Frieda Fromm-Reichmann,* p. 117.

83 *She did not see any phantoms:* Frieda Fromm-Reichmann, *Principles of Intensive Psychotherapy,* pp. 179–180.

84 *lauded her as a "hero":* Robert Coles, *The Mind's Fate,* p. 138.

84 *"you'll find out that":* Joanne Greenberg, *I Never Promised You a Rose Garden,* p. 188.

84 *"technical rules":* Dexter Bullard, ed., *Selected Papers of Frieda Fromm-Reichmann,* p. 126.

84 *"the basic attitude":* Ibid., p. 126.

85 *"aloof, detached, and uncommunicative":* Ibid., p. 6.

85 "It is certainly not": Ibid., p. 125.

85 *"You dirty little stinking":* Frieda Fromm-Reichmann, "Transference Problems in Schizophrenics," pp. 117, 122, in Bullard, *Selected Papers.*

85 *"it is true that she threatened":* Fromm-Reichmann, *Principles of Intensive Psychotherapy,* p. 26.

85 *"well-brought-up":* Leslie H. Farber, "Schizophrenia and the Mad Psychotherapist," in Robert Boyers and Robert Orrill, eds., *R. D. Laing and Anti-Psychiatry,* pp. 98–99.

85 *Fromm-Reichmann would "sit":* The colleague was Theodore Lidz, quoted in "Schizophrenia, R. D. Laing, and the Contemporary Treatment of Psychosis: An Interview with Dr. Theodore Lidz," in Boyers and Orrill, eds., *R. D. Laing and Anti-Psychiatry,* pp. 163–164.

86 *"Schizophrenia is the cancer":* Donald Klein, "Psychosocial Treatment of Schizophrenia, or Psychosocial Help for People with Schizophrenia?" p. 128.

86 *"awesome holocaust":* Harold Searles, "Transference Psychosis in the Psychotherapy of Chronic Schizophrenia," in Harold Searles, *Collected Papers on Schizophrenia and Related Subjects,* p. 654.

86 *There was a message here:* Carol North, *Welcome, Silence,* p. 93.

86 *"juxtaposition of lunacy and sanity":* Donald Klein and Paul Wender, *Mind, Mood, and Medicine,* p. 117.

87 *"My son is crazy":* Author interview, Jan. 26, 1996.

87 *firsthand accounts of insanity:* See, for example, Robert Sommer and Humphry Osmond, "A Bibliography of Mental Patients' Autobiographies, 1960–1982"; and Anne Hudson Jones, "Literature and Medicine: Narratives of Mental Illness."

87 *"Environmental stimuli":* North, *Welcome, Silence,* p. 41.

87 *"I spent hours marveling":* Ibid., p. 54.

87 *"The walk of a stranger":* Norma MacDonald, "Living with Schizophrenia," p. 218.

88 *"chattering away nonsensically":* North, *Welcome, Silence,* p. 42.

88 *"I could find no rest":* Autobiography of a Schizophrenic Girl: The True Story of "Renée," pp. 58–59.

88 *"my skin turning gray":* North, *Welcome, Silence,* p. 139.

88 *"molten blobs of thoughts":* Ibid., p. 177.

88 *fate of the world:* Dilip V. Jeste et al., "Did Schizophrenia Exist Before the Eighteenth Century?" p. 498.

88 *"so that a good stew":* E. Fuller Torrey, *Surviving Schizophrenia* (1988 ed.), p. 207.

89 *King Charles VI:* Vivian Green, *The Madness of Kings,* p. 13.
89 *"In the interval":* quoted in Gottesman, *Schizophrenia Genesis,* p. 6. The best introductions to schizophrenia are Gottesman's *Schizophrenia Genesis* and E. Fuller Torrey's *Surviving Schizophrenia.* Gottesman, a geneticist and clinical psychologist, focuses more on science and history, Torrey, a psychiatrist, more on day-to-day coping.
89 *"We had a wonderful":* Sylvia Hoff, "Frieda Fromm-Reichmann: The Early Years," p. 119.
89 fn *A favorite topic for historical:* Irving Gottesman, *Schizophrenia Genesis,* p. 5.
90 *"withdrawn, detached":* Frieda Fromm-Reichmann, "Remarks on the Philosophy of Mental Disorder," in Bullard, *Selected Papers,* p. 19.
90 *"The schizophrenic has, above all":* Fromm-Reichmann, "Transference Problems in Schizophrenics," in Bullard, *Selected Papers,* p. 126.
90 *"Sooner or later":* Edith Weigert, "In Memoriam: Frieda Fromm-Reichmann," p. 94.
91 *"Anyone who has ever worked":* Joann Rodgers, "Roots of Madness," p. 85. Some psychiatrists have also disputed Carol North's schizophrenia diagnosis.
91 *one-third of all patients recovered:* E. Fuller Torrey, *Surviving Schizophrenia* (3rd ed., 1995), pp. 130–131.
91 *in 1903 he published:* See Ida Macalpine and Richard Hunter, eds. and translators, *Memoirs of My Nervous Illness,* by Daniel Paul Schreber. Freud's essay is "The Case of Schreber," SE, vol. 12, pp. 3–82. Years after Freud wrote, psychiatrists took the Schreber story in an unexpected direction. Schreber's father was a physician and a renowned social reformer with eccentric, not to say sadistic, views on educating children. As the American psychoanalyst William Niederland was the first to show, many bizarre passages in Schreber's memoir seem like distorted echoes of his father's advice on child-rearing. For contrary views of the implications of Niederland's discovery, see W. G. Niederland, "The 'Miracled-up' World of Schreber's Childhood," and subsequent essays; and Morton Schatzman, "Paranoia or Persecution: The Case of Schreber."
91 *"even now the miracles":* Hunter and Macalpine (Daniel Schreber), *Memoirs of My Nervous Illness,* p. 131.
91 *The aim of the book:* Hunter and Macalpine, "Translators' Introduction," *Memoirs of My Nervous Illness,* pp. 4–5.
92 *Freud read Schreber's book:* Jung called Freud's attention to Schreber's memoirs. See Phyllis Grosskurth, *The Secret Ring,* p. 42.
92 *This was Freud's first report:* Hunter and Macalpine, "Translators' Introduction," *Memoirs of My Nervous Illness,* p. 10.
92 *Unable to acknowledge:* Freud makes this argument in "The Case of Schreber," SE, vol. 12, pp. 62–63.
92 *He was an odd character:* The best biography of Sullivan is Helen Swick Perry, *Psychiatrist of America: The Life of Harry Stack Sullivan.*
92 *"as tender as a pat of butter":* Don Jackson, "The Transactional Viewpoint," p. 543.
92 *"a lonely person":* Clara Thompson, "Harry Stack Sullivan, the Man," p. 436.
92 *"The individual is simply not":* Stephen Mitchell and Margaret Black, *Freud and Beyond,* pp. 62–63.
92 *some biographers suspect:* A. H. Chapman, *Harry Stack Sullivan,* p. 26.
92 *he put his theories into practice:* Sullivan's main papers on schizophrenia are collected in Harry Stack Sullivan, *Schizophrenia as a Human Process.* His prose is distressingly murky. Chapman, Perry, and Patrick Mullahy provide clearer accounts. For the particular points cited in the text, see Chapman, pp.

45–47; Perry, pp. 193–200; and Mullahy, "Harry Stack Sullivan's Theory of Schizophrenia," esp. p. 520.

92 *Sullivan chose the patients:* Chapman, *Sullivan,* p. 47; and Mullahy, "Harry Stack Sullivan's Theory of Schizophrenia," p. 520.

92 *This down-to-earth:* Nathan Hale, *Rise and Crisis,* p. 173.

93 *The results were extraordinary:* Chapman, *Sullivan,* p. 47; Mullahy, "Sullivan's Theory," p. 521.

93 *"Intimacy," he declared:* Perry, *Sullivan,* p. 195.

93 *"Like the animal in the woods":* John Rosen, *Direct Analysis,* p. 19.

93 *"In working with these patients":* Harold Searles, "Schizophrenic Communication," in Searles, *Collected Papers,* p. 395.

94 *"a profound influence":* Virginia K. Dunst, "Memoirs — Professional and Personal: A Decade with Frieda Fromm-Reichmann," pp. 111–112.

94 *Well before Frieda:* The studies mentioned in this paragraph are cited (approvingly) in Suzanne Reichard and Carl Tillman, "Patterns of Parent-Child Relationships in Schizophrenia," pp. 247–257.

94 *"The schizophrenic is painfully distrustful":* Frieda Fromm-Reichmann, "Notes on the Development of Treatment of Schizophrenics by Psychoanalytic Psychotherapy," p. 265. This page number refers to the original appearance of Fromm-Reichmann's paper on schizophrenogenic mothers, in *Psychiatry;* the article is reprinted in a collection of Fromm-Reichmann's papers, *Psychoanalysis and Psychotherapy,* where it is perhaps easier to find.

95 *"All the mothers were tense":* Trude Tietze, "A Study of Mothers of Schizophrenic Patients," p. 56.

95 *but "all of the mothers":* Ibid., p. 57.

95 *"openly tried to dominate":* Ibid.

95 *"appeared docile and submissive":* Ibid.

95 *"they seemed quite unaware":* Ibid.

95 *"These mothers 'cooperated' ":* Ibid.

95 *They tended to become solicitous:* Ibid.

96 *"They did not seem to be aware":* Ibid.

96 *"It was impossible to obtain":* Ibid., p. 62.

96 *"The majority of mothers":* Ibid., p. 58.

96 *"The children were uniformly described":* Ibid., p. 62.

96 *"The acute onset of the psychosis":* Ibid., p. 63.

96 *their mothers' "rejection":* Ibid., p. 65.

96 *These "sick" women:* Ibid., p. 64.

96 *"It is this intuition":* Ibid., p. 61.

97 *"It is the subtly dominating mother":* Ibid., p. 65.

97 *"All schizophrenic patients":* Ibid.

97 *"the most thorough-going research":* Reichard and Tillman, "Patterns of Parent-Child Relationships," p. 248.

97 *"perhaps [the] best known":* Don D. Jackson et al., "A Study of the Parents of Schizophrenic and Neurotic Children," p. 387.

97 *"definitely unwanted siblings":* Tietze, "A Study of Mothers," p. 60.

97 *"In order to arrive":* Ibid., pp. 63–64.

97 *"To obtain such a control group":* Ibid., p. 64.

98 *"revealed no significant":* All quotations in this paragraph are from Tietze, p. 64.

98 *"There is a common belief":* Curtis Prout and Mary Alice White, "A Controlled Study of Personality Relationships in Mothers of Schizophrenic Male Patients," p. 251.

99 *"guileful and potentially deceitful":* Jackson et al., "A Study of the Parents," p. 394.

99 *The vogue lasted for decades:* See John Neill, "Whatever Became of the Schizophrenogenic Mother?" The quotes in this paragraph are from p. 502.

99 *"the immediate response":* Tietze, "A Study of Mothers," p. 55.

99 *"Those mothers whose children":* Ibid., pp. 55–56.

99 *"warmly human error":* Jackson et al., "A Study of the Parents," p. 388.

CHAPTER SIX: DR. YIN AND DR. YANG

101 *"I felt as though":* Harold Searles, *Collected Papers,* p. 258.

101 *"I'm a psychiatrist":* John Rosen, *Direct Analysis,* p. 132.

101 *"probably the most widely read":* Robert Knight, preface to Searles, *Collected Papers,* p. 15.

102 *"ruthlessly honest":* Ibid., p. 17.

102 *"obnoxious condescension":* Harold Searles, "Schizophrenic Communication," in Searles, *Collected Papers,* p. 393.

102 *"anxiety, confusion":* Harold Searles, "The Schizophrenic Individual's Experience of His World," p. 119.

102 *"He has no reliable way":* Ibid.

102 *"violently hateful":* All the quotations in this paragraph are from Harold Searles, "Positive Feelings in the Relationship Between the Schizophrenic and His Mother," in Searles, *Collected Papers,* pp. 244–245.

103 *Treatment could last:* Knight, preface to Searles, *Collected Papers,* p. 16.

103 *months of silence:* Searles, "Schizophrenic Communication," in Searles, *Collected Papers,* p. 410.

103 *"At the end of each":* Ibid., p. 405.

103 *One paranoid woman:* Harold Searles, "Transference Psychosis in the Psychotherapy of Chronic Schizophrenia," in Searles, *Collected Papers,* pp. 660–661.

103 *"once declared to me":* Ibid., p. 671.

103 *"overwhelming and deeply discouraging":* Ibid., p. 655.

103 *an "advertisement":* Ibid., p. 686.

103 *"confirmation of his own lack":* Harold Searles, "Anxiety Concerning Change, as Seen in the Psychotherapy of Schizophrenic Patients—With Particular Reference to the Sense of Personal Identity," in Searles, *Collected Papers,* p. 462.

103 *"cold annoyance":* Searles, "Schizophrenic Communication," in Searles, *Collected Papers,* p. 392.

103 *"at a moment when I had withdrawn":* Searles, "Positive Feelings," in Searles, *Collected Papers,* p. 246.

104 *"in mutually vindictive comments":* Searles, "Schizophrenic Communication," in Searles, *Collected Papers,* p. 412.

104 *Of his eighteen schizophrenic patients:* Knight, preface to Searles, *Collected Papers,* p. 16.

104 *"a physically attractive":* Harold Searles, "The Effort to Drive the Other Person Crazy—An Element in the Etiology and Psychotherapy of Schizophrenia," in Searles, *Collected Papers,* p. 258.

104 *"Ambiguous and unpredictably shifting":* Searles, "The Schizophrenic Individual's Experience of His World," pp. 119–120.

104 *"What is traumatic":* Searles, "Positive Feelings," in Searles, *Collected Papers,* p. 229.

105 *"unconscious defenses":* Searles, "The Schizophrenic Individual's Experience of His World," p. 125.

105 *"his streaming tear glands"*: This example and the one cited in the next sentence are from Harold Searles, "The Sources of the Anxiety in Paranoid Schizophrenia," in Searles, *Collected Papers*, p. 475.
105 *"unaware of her murderous rage"*: Ibid.
105 *"felt a literal"*: This example and the one in the next sentence are from Searles, "The Sources of the Anxiety in Paranoid Schizophrenia," in Searles, *Collected Papers*, p. 472.
105 *"a world which is"*: Ibid.
106 *"One patient's drooping shoulders"*: Searles, "Schizophrenic Communication," in Searles, *Collected Papers*, p. 402.
106 *"freakish demeanor"*: Ibid.
106 *"It feels as though"*: Ibid., p. 398.
106 *"a defiant, contemptuous"*: Ibid., p. 414.
106 *"felt that my accidental dropping"*: Ibid., p. 388.
106 *"The therapists — including myself"*: Harold Searles, "Schizophrenia and the Inevitability of Death," in Searles, *Collected Papers*, p. 489.
106 *"There is a great deal of literature"*: Searles, "Positive Feelings," in Searles, *Collected Papers*, p. 217.
107 *"intense, mutual hostility"*: Ibid., p. 221.
107 *"as a being unworthy"*: Ibid., p. 224.
107 *"Mrs. Matthews"*: Searles, "The Sources of the Anxiety in Paranoid Schizophrenia," in Searles, *Collected Papers*, p. 477.
107 *"He wasn't anything"*: Ibid., p. 478.
107 *"snow man in a glass"*: Ibid., p. 479.
107 *"the mother's failing"*: Searles, "Positive Feelings," in Searles, *Collected Papers*, p. 233.
108 *"You're speaking about one"*: "Dr. Rosen: Praise, Fear in the Cocktail Set," *Miami Herald*, Sept. 18, 1977.
108 *"direct analysis"*: John Rosen, *Direct Analysis*, p. 45.
108 *"He was always spoken of"*: Raymond Corsini, ed., *Handbook of Innovative Psychotherapies*, p. 241.
108 *"an inspired young doctor"*: This is from the copy in a full-page advertisement for *Savage Sleep* in the *New York Times Book Review*, Oct. 27, 1968.
108 *Man of the Year:* Jeffrey M. Masson, *Against Therapy*, p. 126.
108 'I can castrate you': Rosen, *Direct Analysis*, p. 151.
108 *"The patient gets the feeling"*: Ibid., p. 151.
108 *"forcefulness, closeness"*: Ibid., p. 2.
108 *"confronting the patient with reality"*: Ibid., p. 149.
109 *He had treated:* Ibid., p. 46.
109 *He took on schizophrenic patients:* Ibid., table 1, pp. 50–57.
109 *"It looks very easy"*: Ibid., p. 84.
109 *"A schizophrenic is always one"*: Ibid., p. 97.
109 *"begged and pleaded"*: Ibid., p. 102.
109 *"the deeper explanation"*: Ibid., p. 103.
110 *"built on a shallow, uneven"*: Ibid., pp. 100–101.
110 *"governing principle"*: Ibid., pp. 8–9.
110 *"the ever-giving, ever-protecting"*: Ibid., pp. 139–140.
110 *"tended her, fed her"*: Ibid., p. 45.
111 *"gain the sense"*: Ibid., p. 13.
111 *"to let the sufferer know"*: Ibid., p. 12.
111 *"the psychosis begins"*: Ibid., p. 13.
111 *"self-evidently" the key:* Ibid., p. 3.

111 *"Let the dreamer walk about"*: Silvano Arieti quotes Jung's remark in his *Interpretation of Schizophrenia*, p. 29.

111 *"What is the psychosis"*: Rosen, *Direct Analysis*, p. 4.

111 *"every symptom, each remark"*: Ibid., p. 44.

111 *"There always is meaning"*: Ibid., p. 13.

111 *"Anything from a stomach rumble"*: Ibid., p. 13.

111 *"One must, therefore, take"*: Ibid., p. 42.

112 *"I grabbed the pillow"*: Ibid., pp. 149–150.

112 *"to that tiny portion"*: Ibid., p. 150.

112 *"Over the next five weeks"*: Ibid., pp. 146–148.

112 *"So far as the patient"*: Ibid., p. 139.

113 *the first verbatim psychiatric transcripts:* Author interview with Jay Haley, April 10, 1996.

115 *"four weeks to the day"*: This dialogue appears in Rosen, *Direct Analysis*, pp. 131–136.

115 *the psychiatrist William Horwitz:* William Horwitz et al., "A Study of Cases of Schizophrenia Treated by Direct Analysis."

115 *A second study:* Robert Bookhammer et al., "A Five-Year Clinical Follow-up Study of Schizophrenics Treated by Rosen's 'Direct Analysis' Compared with Controls."

115 *"almost uncanny insight"*: O. Spurgeon English, "Clinical Observations on Direct Analysis," p. 160.

116 *"blunt force injuries"*: "Doctor Settles Suit in Patient's Death for $100,000," *Miami Herald*, Sept. 3, 1981.

116 *Rosen gave up his license:* Jeffrey Masson devotes a chapter of *Against Therapy* to Rosen and details a number of horror stories, some involving sexual abuse as well as beatings. Rael Jean Isaac and Virginia Armat also discuss Rosen in *Madness in the Streets*.

CHAPTER SEVEN: *FROM BAD MOTHERS TO BAD FAMILIES*

117 *We now know:* Theodore Lidz, "A Developmental Theory," in John Shershow, ed., *Schizophrenia: Theory and Practice*, p. 71.

117 *"like a bombshell"*: Luc Ciompi, *The Psyche and Schizophrenia*, p. 127.

117 *"more limbs and height"*: Mary Catherine Bateson, *With a Daughter's Eye*, p. 20.

118 *"His car had termites"*: Author interview with Jay Haley, April 10, 1996.

118 *"the most physically unattractive"*: Jane Howard, *Margaret Mead: A Life*, p. 154.

118 *"a prince of the muddleheaded"*: See Bateson's obituary in *American Anthropologist*, p. 382.

118 *"As the war engulfed us"*: Margaret Mead, *Blackberry Winter: My Earlier Years*, p. 238.

118 *"Gregory's students"*: Bateson, *With a Daughter's Eye*, p. 109.

118 *"forty hours a week"*: In 1990, John Weakland and Jay Haley videotaped themselves reminiscing about their collaboration with Bateson. The comments in this paragraph are from that tape, which Haley was kind enough to allow me to watch.

119 *"There was money"*: Author interview with Jay Haley, April 10, 1996.

119 *from Mary Poppins:* The Mary Poppins excerpt appears in Milton Berger, ed., *Beyond the Double Bind*, p. 220n.

120 *"would not know what kind"*: Ibid., p. 13.

120 *"If he chooses this alternative"*: Ibid.
120 *"A little boy complained"*: Ciompi, *The Psyche and Schizophrenia*, p. 127.
121 *"The person caught"*: Ibid., p. 153.
121 *"hostile"* and *"anxious"*: Berger, *Beyond the Double Bind*, pp. 14–17.
121 *"bread-and-butterfly"*: Ibid., p. 212.
122 *"The theoretical possibility"*: Berger, *Beyond the Double Bind*, p. 14.
122 *"Bateson put in the grant"*: This is from the 1990 Haley-Weakland film on Bateson.
122 *"not been statistically tested"*: Berger, *Beyond the Double Bind*, p. 14.
122 *"the family situation[s]"*: Bateson's discussion of the schizophrenic's predicament is from Berger, *Beyond the Double Bind*, pp. 14–16.
123 *"a family-borne disease"*: Don D. Jackson, "A Note on the Importance of Trauma in the Genesis of Schizophrenia," p. 184.
123 *"He was glad to see her"*: Berger, *Beyond the Double Bind*, p. 18.
124 *"a research group undertook"*: Theodore Lidz, "Schizophrenia and the Family," in Lidz, Stephen Fleck, and Alice Cornelison, eds., *Schizophrenia and the Family*, p. 81.
124 *"We now know"*: Lidz, "A Developmental Theory," p. 71.
124 *"constantly critical"*: Theodore Lidz, "The Fathers," in Lidz, Fleck, and Cornelison, *Schizophrenia and the Family*, p. 107.
124 *"Mr. Grau was paranoically bitter"*: Theodore Lidz, "The Transmission of Irrationality," in Lidz, Fleck, and Cornelison, *Schizophrenia and the Family*, p. 178.
124 *"an unusually vague"*: Theodore Lidz, "The Mothers of Schizophrenic Patients," in Lidz, Fleck, and Cornelison, *Schizophrenia and the Family*, p. 315.
125 *"needed and used"*: Ibid., p. 314.
125 *"typical 'schizophrenogenic' mothers"*: Lidz, "The Transmission of Irrationality," p. 176.
125 *"aloof, hostile"*: Lidz, "The Mothers of Schizophrenic Patients," p. 323.
125 *"The fathers were as pathological"*: Lidz, *Schizophrenia and the Family*, pp. 82–83.
125 *"Few of the fathers"*: Lidz, "The Fathers," p. 103.
125 *"disease or an illness"*: See "An Interview with Dr. Theodore Lidz," in Robert Boyers and Robert Orrill, eds., *R. D. Laing and Anti-Psychiatry*, pp. 151–152.
125 *"that has inserted itself"*: Lidz, "Schizophrenia and the Family," p. 76.
125 *A person could be schizophrenic*: Boyers and Orrill, *R. D. Laing and Anti-Psychiatry*, p. 152.
125 *"When the path into the future"*: Lidz, "Schizophrenia and the Family," p. 80.
125 *He liked to point out*: Theodore Lidz, "A Psychosocial Orientation to Schizophrenic Disorders," p. 214.
125 *"I came to understand"*: Author interview, Nov. 14, 1995.
126 *Lidz had been a serious*: Lidz, "A Psychosocial Orientation to Schizophrenic Disorders," p. 214.
126 *"After spending an hour"*: Ibid.
126 *"Talking to the parents"*: Author interview, Nov. 14, 1995.
126 *"Psychiatrists have not been able"*: Lidz, "The Fathers," p. 102.
126 *"spoke incessantly"*: Lidz, "The Transmission of Irrationality," p. 185.
126 *"in one of her most insightful"*: Lidz, "The Fathers," p. 116.
126 *"freely poured out"*: Lidz, "The Transmission of Irrationality," pp. 180, 182.
126 *"We have had medical students"*: Boyers and Orrill, *R. D. Laing and Anti-Psychiatry*, p. 174.
127 *"That stuck with me"*: Author interview, Nov. 14, 1995.

127 *"We wanted to know":* Ibid.
127 *"In each aspect":* Lidz, "Schizophrenia and the Family," p. 27.
127 *"each of the families":* Ibid.
127 *"We began to consider":* Theodore Lidz, "Family Studies and a Theory of Schizophrenia," in Lidz, Fleck, and Cornelison, *Schizophrenia and the Family,* p. 363.
128 *"training in irrationality":* Lidz, "Schizophrenia and the Family," p. 83.
128 *This "brainwashing":* Lidz, "Family Studies and a Theory of Schizophrenia," p. 374.
128 *"the child's achievement":* Ibid., p. 371.
128 *"We now realize":* Lidz, "A Developmental Theory," p. 73.
128 *"I'd like to see":* Author interview, Nov. 14, 1995.
128 *Families were not simply bad:* The theory of "schism" and "skew" laid out in the first four paragraphs of this section is from Lidz, "A Developmental Theory," pp. 74–77.
129 *"My tendency has been":* Boyers and Orrill, *R. D. Laing and Anti-Psychiatry,* pp. 159–160.
129 *"We don't do it":* Author interview, Nov. 14, 1995.
129 *had been "very great":* Boyers and Orrill, *R. D. Laing and Anti-Psychiatry,* p. 182.
129 *"nevertheless, Freud kept":* Theodore Lidz, "The Relevance of Family Studies and Psychoanalytic Theory," in Lidz, Fleck, and Cornelison, *Schizophrenia and the Family,* p. 355.
129 fn *After comparing psychoanalysis:* Sigmund Freud, "Introductory Lectures," SE, vol. 16, p. 459.
130 *"There was no sense":* Author interview, Nov. 14, 1995.
130 *"intensive studies of a few":* Author interview, Nov. 14, 1995.
130 *"we went back far enough":* Ibid.
130 *"They're not":* Ibid.
130 *"and it made for trouble":* Ibid.
130 *"Whatever the shortcomings":* Theodore Lidz and Stephen Fleck, "Schizophrenia, Human Integration, and the Role of the Family," in Don Jackson, ed., *The Etiology of Schizophrenia,* p. 332.
131 *"Although it is the mother":* Silvano Arieti, *Interpretation of Schizophrenia,* pp. 52–53.
131 *"The child wants to be approved":* Ibid., p. 45.
131 *"Each child has to be disapproved":* Ibid., p. 46.
132 *"Madness need not be all":* R. D. Laing, *The Politics of Experience,* p. 133.
132 *In a world of doomsday:* See, for example, *The Divided Self:* "A little girl of seventeen in a mental hospital told me she was terrified because the Atom Bomb was inside her. That is a delusion. The statesmen of the world who boast and threaten that they have Doomsday weapons are far more dangerous, and far more estranged from 'reality' than many of the people on whom the label 'psychotic' is affixed" (preface to the Pelican ed., p. 12).
132 *Bumper stickers proclaimed:* Bob Mullan, *Mad to Be Normal: Conversations with R. D. Laing,* p. 8.
132 *"no less respect":* Laing, *The Politics of Experience,* p. 129.
132 *"see that what we call":* Ibid., p. 129.
132 *"never opened the door":* Mullan, *Mad to Be Normal,* p. 320.
133 *"civilized courtesy":* Ibid., p. 321.
133 *"I said, 'I mean you haven't' ":* Ibid., p. 322.
133 *"Freud was a hero":* R. D. Laing, *The Divided Self,* p. 25.

133 *Laing said that he:* Daniel Burston, *The Wing of Madness,* p. 224.
133 *"in her psychosis":* Laing, *The Divided Self,* p. 192.
133 *In a book published:* R. D. Laing, *Conversations with Adam and Natasha,* p. 116.
134 *"persons diagnosed as schizophrenic":* See, for example, Laing, *The Politics of Experience,* p. 102.
134 *"A good deal":* Laing, *The Divided Self,* p. 164.
134 *"To regard the gambits":* Laing, *The Politics of Experience,* p. 102.
134 *"To the best of my knowledge":* Ibid., p. 114.
134 "Without exception *the experience":* Ibid., pp. 114–115.
134 fn *The notion that "madness":* Nathaniel Lee is quoted in Roy Porter, *Mind-Forg'd Manacles,* p. 2.
135 *"One might do better":* Laing, *The Divided Self,* p. 190.
135 *"We are driving":* Laing, *The Politics of Experience,* p. 104.
135 *His own mother:* This account of Laing's mother is from Burston, *The Wing of Madness,* pp. 10–12. The last sentence of the paragraph, about Laing's biggest regret, is from Burston, p. 142.
136 *a lecture to the Oxford:* Burston, *The Wing of Madness,* p. 137.
136 *a woman named Nancy:* Author interview, Jan. 17, 1996.

CHAPTER EIGHT: *ICE PICKS AND ELECTROSHOCKS*

138 *Surgeons now think:* "Explorers of the Brain," *New York Times,* Oct. 30, 1949, p. E8.
139 *"He may bleed":* Karl Menninger, *The Vital Balance,* p. 305.
139 *"Researchers have examined":* Silvano Arieti, *Interpretation of Schizophrenia,* p. 8.
139 *"In contrast to":* Theodore Lidz, *The Origin and Treatment of Schizophrenic Disorders,* pp. 6–7.
139 *"in every country":* Nancy Andreasen, *The Broken Brain,* p. 16.
139 *"If I had died":* Edward Shorter, *From Paralysis to Fatigue,* p. 243.
140 *"impenetrable darkness":* Irving Gottesman, *Schizophrenia Genesis,* p. 82.
140 *"It is difficult to exaggerate":* Nathan Hale, *Freud and the Americans,* p. 50.
141 *one Frankfurt professor:* Edward Shorter, *History of Psychiatry,* pp. 54–55.
141 *For decades, doctors had speculated:* This account is from Martin Seligman, *What You Can Change and What You Can't,* pp. 31–32.
142 *"There was a series":* Author interview, Oct. 19, 1995.
142 fn *In 1917, the Viennese:* Shorter, *History of Psychiatry,* pp. 193–194.
142 fn *Kraepelin could hardly contain:* Gottesman, *Schizophrenia Genesis,* p. 15.
143 *"as in frustration one kicks":* *New York Review of Books,* April 24, 1986.
143 *"a chair in which agitated":* Andreasen, *The Broken Brain,* p. 190.
144 Great and Desperate Cures: My account closely follows Valenstein's superb history. For another perspective and an excellent bibliography, see Victor Swayze, "Frontal Leukotomy and Related Psychosurgical Procedures in the Era Before Antipsychotics (1935–1954): A Historical Overview." For discussions of the current use of neurosurgery in mental illness, see Poynton, and Malhi et al.
144 *"This method":* William Sargant, *Battle for the Mind,* p. 64.
144 *"With faint hope":* The quoted phrase is from Meduna's unpublished autobiography and is cited in Max Fink, "Meduna and the Origins of Convulsive Therapy," p. 1035.
145 *(Bini had experimented):* Franz Alexander and Sheldon Selesnick, *The History of Psychiatry,* p. 282.

145 *frontal-lobe surgery:* Elliot Valenstein, *Great and Desperate Cures,* pp. 77–79; see also Swayze, "Frontal Leukotomy," pp. 505–515.
146 *"Some three hundred people":* "Psychosurgery," *Time,* Nov. 30, 1942, p. 48.
147 *"What's going through your mind":* Ibid.
147 *Of their 136 cases:* Ibid., p. 49.
147 *Freeman and Watts neglected:* Robyn Dawes makes this point in *House of Cards,* p. 48.
147 *"The freedom from painful":* "Psychosurgery," p. 48.
147 *"I have also been trying":* Valenstein, *Great and Desperate Cures,* p. 203.
148 *"he saw Freeman leaning over":* Ibid., p. 204.
148 *"anxiety neuroses":* "Mass Lobotomies," *Time,* Sept. 15, 1952, p. 86.
148 *"Strapped to an operating table":* Ibid.
148 *"It is safer to operate":* Ibid.
148 *the ice-pick variety:* Valenstein, *Great and Desperate Cures,* p. 229.
149 *"hypochondriacs no longer":* "Explorers of the Brain," *New York Times,* Oct. 30, 1949, p. E8.
149 *"a crude business":* Frank T. Vertosick, Jr., "Lobotomy's Back," *Discover,* Oct. 1997, p. 68.
149 *"His soul appears to be":* Swayze, "Frontal Leukotomy," p. 507.
149 *"schizophrenics are the usual":* "Grey Matter," *Time,* May 28, 1951, p. 81.
149 fn *Today, in a tiny number:* For a journalistic account of the current role of neurosurgery in treating mental illness, see "Brain Surgery Is Back in a Limited Way to Treat Mental Ills," *The Wall Street Journal,* Dec. 1, 1994, p. 1. See also Poynton, and Malhi et al.

CHAPTER NINE: *THE TIDE TURNS*

150 *To have forgotten:* Maria Ron and Ian Harvey, "The Brain in Schizophrenia," p. 725.
151 *"Most of them had spent":* This account is based on my interview with Klein, Dec. 4, 1995, and on his account in *Mind, Mood, and Medicine.*
151 fn *The discovery of many:* See John Cade, "The Story of Lithium," in Frank Ayd and Barry Blackwell, eds., *Discoveries in Biological Psychiatry.* This excellent collection consists of essays by the discoverers themselves.
152 *"Rip van Winkle":* Donald Klein and Paul Wender, *Mind, Mood, and Medicine,* p. 148.
152 *"a medical miracle":* Author interview, Dec. 4, 1995.
152 *"The big change":* Author interview, Dec. 14, 1995.
152 *Some medication has the same:* Quoted in Martin Gross, *The Psychological Society,* p. 106.
153 *"You could see it":* Author interview, Dec. 14, 1995.
153 *The first cousin:* These figures are from Irving Gottesman, *Schizophrenia Genesis,* p. 96. Gottesman provides the layman the most detailed, and simultaneously the clearest, account of the genetics of schizophrenia.
154 *Consider twins:* The figures in this paragraph are from ibid.
155 *"I just met with a swarm":* This account is based on my interview with Heston on Dec. 21, 1995, and on Leonard Heston and Duane Denney, "Interactions Between Early Life Experience and Biological Factors in Schizophrenia."
158 *"hardly help but wonder":* This account is from Rosenthal's *Genain Quadruplets.* The quote is from p. 7.
158 *"I'd noticed an interesting":* Author interview, Oct. 19, 1995.
159 *Testing that prediction:* This account of Kety's work is based on my interview

with Kety on Oct. 19, 1995, and on his published findings. The major papers are listed in the Bibliography. The first and most important was "The Types and Prevalence of Mental Illness in the Biological and Adoptive Families of Adopted Schizophrenics." A more accessible overview is in Kety's essay "Heredity and Environment." Gottesman's discussion of Kety, in *Schizophrenia Genesis*, is characteristically clear.

160 *If you looked not only:* Gottesman, *Schizophrenia Genesis*, p. 143.
160 *"Thank you, Ted Lidz":* Author interview, Oct. 27, 1995.
161 *(They did tend to tell):* Klein and Wender, *Mind, Mood, and Medicine*, p. 175.
161 *"undoubtedly the single treatment":* Philip May, *Treatment of Schizophrenia*, p. 262.
161 *"expensive and ineffective":* Ibid., p. 262.
161 *"startling" and "traumatic":* Ibid., p. 26.
161 *"the effect of psychotherapy":* Ibid., p. 232.
162 *"overly aggressive treatments":* Robert Drake and Lloyd Sederer, "The Adverse Effects of Intensive Treatment of Chronic Schizophrenia," p. 314. E. Fuller Torrey discusses May, and Drake and Sederer, in *Surviving Schizophrenia* (pp. 167–169) and also provides more current references.
162 *"Only a person":* Karl Menninger, *The Vital Balance*, p. 294.
162 *Think of a bullying boss:* Irving Gottesman, personal communication.
162 *"For perhaps 5 percent":* Torrey, *Surviving Schizophrenia*, p. 192.
162 *The most feared:* Ibid., pp. 202–204.
163 *"We were told":* Author interview, Dec. 14, 1995.
163 *consider Hobson's experience:* This account is based on my interview with Hobson on Dec. 14, 1995, and on Hobson's account in *The Chemistry of Conscious States.*
164 *Rüdin had served:* R. C. Lewontin, Steven Rose, and Leon Kamin, *Not in Our Genes*, p. 207; Gottesman, *Schizophrenia Genesis*, p. 207.
164 *"the predominant medical presence":* Robert Jay Lifton, *The Nazi Doctors*, p. 27.
164 *"decisive . . . path-breaking step":* Ibid., p. 28.
164 *A key part of the study:* Philip May, *Treatment of Schizophrenia*, p. 60.
164 *Stars or journeymen:* See, for instance, L. Grinspoon, J. R. Ewalt, and R. I. Shader, *Schizophrenia: Pharmacotherapy and Psychotherapy.*
165 *"a need to deny":* Annemargret Osterkamp and David Sands, "Early Feeding and Birth Difficulties in Childhood Schizophrenia: A Brief Study," p. 365.
165 *"subtle malignancy":* Don D. Jackson, "A Note on the Importance of Trauma in the Genesis of Schizophrenia," p. 183.
166 *"has plagued therapists":* Lyman Wynne, "Knotted Relationships, Communication Deviances, and Metabinding," in Berger, *Beyond the Double Bind*, p. 180.
166 *"A new scientific truth":* Thomas Kuhn, *The Structure of Scientific Revolutions*, p. 151.

PART FOUR: *AUTISM*

167 *The precipitating factor:* Bruno Bettelheim, *The Empty Fortress*, p. 125.

CHAPTER TEN: *A Mystery Proclaimed*

169 *There have come:* Leo Kanner, "Autistic Disturbances of Affective Contact,"
p. 217.

169 *For Bruno Bettelheim:* This account of Bettelheim's early life is based on his
autobiographical writings, especially *Surviving* and *The Informed Heart,* and
on two recent biographies, one by Richard Pollak and the other by Nina Sutton.
Pollak's *The Creation of Dr. B,* the better book, raises questions about one
aspect of Bettelheim's life story after another, including his account of his
World War II experiences.

169 *"the worst torture":* Bruno Bettelheim, *The Informed Heart,* p. 119.

169 *"I felt pleased with myself":* Ibid., p. 126.

170 *"extreme situations":* See Bettelheim's essay "Individual and Mass Behavior in
Extreme Situations," included in *Surviving.*

170 *"a pied piper":* The description is Leon Eisenberg's, from his preface to a
collection of Kanner's papers entitled *Childhood Psychosis: Initial Studies and
New Insights,* p. xii.

170 *(He once wrote):* The essay, "The Ignored Lesson of Anne Frank," can be
found in *Surviving.*

171 *"Since 1938":* Kanner's essay was called "Autistic Disturbances of Affective
Contact." My page references below are to the essay as originally published. It
is perhaps easier to find reprinted in Kanner's *Childhood Psychosis.*

172 *"Every one of the children":* Kanner, "Autistic Disturbances of Affective Contact," p. 246.

172 *"a sack of flour":* Ibid., p. 243.

172 *"The father or mother":* Ibid., p. 247.

172 *"the wild boy of Aveyron":* This account is drawn from Uta Frith, *Autism,* and
Russ Rymer, *Genie.* For book-length accounts of this strange story, see Harlan
Lane's *The Wild Boy of Aveyron* or Roger Shattuck's *The Forbidden Experi-
ment.*

173 *"I am dismayed to see":* Russ Rymer, *Genie,* p. 66.

173 *"no sense of gratitude":* Uta Frith, *Autism,* p. 22.

173 *"Joanie is making a funny noise":* Oliver Sacks, *An Anthropologist on Mars,* p.
269. The student of autism is blessed with an abundance of excellent books,
Sacks's works notable among them. See also Sacks's essays on autism in *The
Man Who Mistook His Wife for a Hat.* Also excellent are Uta Frith's *Autism*
and *Autism and Asperger Syndrome.* Of a large number of memoirs by parents
of autistic children, my favorites are Clara Park's *The Siege,* Annabel Stehli's
The Sound of a Miracle, and Catherine Maurice's *Let Me Hear Your Voice.*
For first-person accounts of autism, see Temple Grandin's *Emergence: Labeled
Autistic* and *Thinking in Pictures,* and Donna Williams's *Nobody Nowhere*
and *Somebody Somewhere.* Grandin is the self-described "anthropologist on
Mars" of Sacks's book.

173 *"Oh, I am all right":* Sacks, *An Anthropologist on Mars,* p. 207.

173 *"Now I can tell":* Frith, *Autism and Asperger Syndrome,* p. 138.

173 *"obsessive desire":* Kanner, "Autistic Disturbances of Affective Contact," p. 245.

173 *One mother compiled:* Ruth Sullivan, "Autism: Definitions Past and Present,"
p. 7.

173 *Ian wept uncontrollably:* Russell Martin, *Out of Silence,* pp. 3–4.

174 *In San Diego:* Author interview with Gloria Rimland, April 9, 1996.

174 *Ian has watched the tape:* Martin, *Out of Silence,* p. 42.

174 *"A normal kid":* Author interview, May 17, 1996.

174 *"When we'd bring"*: Author interview, April 9, 1996.
174 *One mother remembers:* Stehli, *The Sound of a Miracle,* p. 21.
174 *"I could sit for hours"*: Grandin, *Thinking in Pictures,* p. 44.
174 *"a ray of sun"*: The observer was Itard, the Wild Boy's teacher, quoted in Seymour Sarason, *Psychological Problems in Mental Deficiency,* p. 324.
175 *"as one raindrop"*: Cited in Bernard Rimland, *Infantile Autism,* p. 17.
175 *When she brought her son:* Leo Kanner, "Early Infantile Autism, 1943–1955," in Kanner, *Childhood Psychosis,* p. 95.
175 *An autistic child:* Kanner, "Autistic Disturbances of Affective Contact," p. 237.
175 *"her face had lit up"*: Stehli, *The Sound of a Miracle,* p. 116.
175 *A woman named Ruth Sullivan:* Author interview, May 23, 1996.
176 *"simple, strong, universal"*: Sacks, *An Anthropologist on Mars,* p. 286.
176 *"The emotion circuit's"*: Ibid., p. 286.
176 *"It is not easy to evaluate"*: Kanner, "Autistic Disturbances of Affective Contact," p. 250.
176 *"The children of our group"*: Ibid., p. 248.
177 *"We must, then, assume"*: Ibid., p. 250.
177 *"The parents' behavior"*: Leo Kanner, "Problems of Nosology and Psychodynamics in Early Infantile Autism," in Kanner, *Childhood Psychosis,* p. 57.
177 *"sat down next to his mother"*: Ibid., p. 58.
177 *"Many of the fathers"*: Ibid.
177 *Kanner asked one father:* Ibid.
177 *"The children were"*: Ibid., p. 60.
178 *"Most of the patients"*: Ibid., p. 61.
178 *February 12, 1967:* This account is based on my interview with Annabel Stehli on May 7, 1996, and on her fine memoir *The Sound of a Miracle.*
179 *"Our studies concentrate"*: Bruno Bettelheim, "Where Self Begins," *New York Times Magazine,* Feb. 12, 1967, p. 65.
179 *"Our work demonstrates"*: Ibid., p. 71.
179 *"Things may go terribly"*: Ibid.
179 *"Foremost among the handful"*: *New York Times Book Review,* Feb. 26, 1967, p. 44.
179 *Autism is "a defense"*: Bruno Bettelheim, *The Empty Fortress,* p. 392n.

CHAPTER ELEVEN: *THE BUCHENWALD CONNECTION*

181 *My reactions to events:* Bruno Bettelheim, *A Home for the Heart,* p. 10.
181 *Their numbers would grow:* In *The Empty Fortress,* Bettelheim wrote that "the number of autistic children with whom we can work at any one time is relatively small because if we are to help them we can never have more than six to eight truly autistic children among our population of forty-five" (p. 94).
182 *"the result of the inhumanity"*: Bruno Bettelheim, "Feral Children and Autistic Children," p. 188. The essay can be found in *Freud's Vienna and Other Essays.*
182 *"a child who had been robbed"*: Bruno Bettelheim, "Joey: A Mechanical Boy," p. 117.
182 *"I have never seen a child"*: Bettelheim made this declaration in a letter to the editor in the May 1959 *Scientific American* (p. 16). He was replying to a letter from a doctor named Jacques May who had criticized Bettelheim for making statements that were "purely interpretative and cannot be proved" (p. 12). May was the father of autistic twins (though he made no mention of that fact in his letter); the year before, he had written a short but powerful book called *A*

Physician Looks at Psychiatry about his difficulties in finding help for his children. May was the first to write about autism from a parent's perspective; today there are dozens of such memoirs.

182 *"a 'hopeless' case":* Bettelheim, *A Home for the Heart,* p. 12. "Before our own children were born," Bettelheim wrote, "because of our fascination with child psychoanalysis which had just then begun to develop, my wife and I brought in a child who suffered from infantile autism (a 'hopeless' case) in order to find out whether the new discipline could help her." In *The Empty Fortress,* Bettelheim provided another version of the story that differed in one key, and puzzling, way. "From 1932 until March 1938 (the invasion of Austria)," he wrote, "I had living with me one, and for a few years two, autistic children" (p. 8). Both Richard Pollak and Nina Sutton, he a hostile biographer of Bettelheim and she an admiring one, agree that Bettelheim fabricated important parts of his autobiography. In particular, both biographers raise *three* serious questions about the claim quoted here. There was evidently one disturbed child, not two, living with the Bettelheims in the thirties; it is by no means clear that the young girl was autistic; and it appears that it was Bettelheim's wife who took care of the child, while he himself had almost nothing to do with her.

182 *She had been born:* Bettelheim tells Anna's story in *The Empty Fortress,* p. 7 and pp. 374–375.

182 *her story brought Bettelheim's:* Ibid., p. 7.

182 *"I had been unable":* Bettelheim, *A Home for the Heart,* p. 12.

183 *"The youngster who develops":* Bruno Bettelheim, "Schizophrenia as a Reaction to Extreme Situations," p. 116. The essay can be found in Bettelheim, *Surviving.*

183 *"The difference between the plight":* Ibid., p. 116.

183 *"taken on the hardest imaginable":* Robert Coles, "A Hero for Our Time," reprinted in *The Mind's Fate,* p. 138.

183 *"the child's parents may pose":* Ibid., p. 140.

184 *"Throughout this book":* Bettelheim, *The Empty Fortress,* p. 125.

184 *It is important to note:* Marian DeMyer, *Parents and Children in Autism,* p. xi.

184 *"These were beautiful":* Author interview, May 14, 1996.

184 *"Remember," Donnellan says:* Ibid.

185 *One autistic boy:* "Life in a Parallel World," *Newsweek,* May 13, 1996, p. 70.

185 *"Dangerous intersection":* Ruth Sullivan, "Rain Man and Joseph," in Eric Schopler and Gary Mesibov, eds., *High-Functioning Individuals with Autism,* p. 244.

185 *At age three:* Clara Park, *The Siege,* pp. 79–80.

185 *One famous pair:* By far the best article on the twins is Oliver Sacks's superb essay "The Twins," in *The Man Who Mistook His Wife for a Hat.* For photographs of the twins and an article that is better than one would guess from its title, see Dora Jane Hamblin, "They are 'Idiot Savants' — Wizards of the Calendar," *Life,* March 18, 1966. For a dry but detailed account, see also William Horwitz et al., "Identical Twin — 'Idiot Savants' — Calendar Calculators."

186 *They could not count:* Darold Treffert, *Extraordinary People: Understanding "Idiot Savants,"* p. 36.

186 *the simplest abstraction:* Horwitz et al., "Identical Twin–'Idiot Savants' — Calendar Calculators," p. 1078.

186 *Asked to multiply:* Hamblin, "They Are 'Idiot Savants' — Wizards of the Calendar."

186 *The psychiatrist David Viscott:* David Viscott, "A Musical Idiot Savant," pp. 494–515.

187 *"She puts excessive pressure":* J. Louise Despert, "Some Considerations Relating to the Genesis of Autistic Behavior in Children," p. 346.
187 *"Such interest as they have":* Leon Eisenberg, "The Fathers of Autistic Children," p. 722. Eisenberg's description of the fathers as "obsessive, detached, and humorless" is on p. 721.
187 *"scattered and fragmented":* Beata Rank, "Adaptation of the Psychoanalytic Technique for the Treatment of Young Children with Atypical Development," p. 136.
187 *"It has been suggested":* Michael J. A. Howe, *Fragments of Genius,* p. 67.
187 *The psychoanalyst Albert Cain:* Albert Cain, "Special 'Isolated' Abilities in Severely Psychotic Young Children," p. 145.
188 *"It's in my head":* Hamblin, "They Are 'Idiot Savants' — Wizards of the Calendar."
188 *She no longer:* Catherine Maurice, *Let Me Hear Your Voice,* pp. 40–41.
189 *"Convinced that her mother":* Bettelheim, *The Empty Fortress,* p. 163.
190 *"Peter was changed":* Ibid., p. 437.
190 *The couple had named:* "La Fillette au Moi Dormant," *Figaro-Magazine,* Sept. 21, 1991.
190 *"native habitat":* Jules Henry, *Pathways to Madness,* p. xv.
190 *"Every culture has to strive":* Ibid., p. 290.
190 *"The fact that parents":* Ribble made her comments as part of a discussion following the reading of a paper on autism by J. Louise Despert. See Despert, "Some Considerations Relating to the Genesis of Autistic Behavior in Children," pp. 347–348.
191 *"the tenuous relationship":* Rank, "Adaptation of the Psychoanalytic Technique for the Treatment of Young Children with Atypical Development," p. 136.
191 *"the sunshine which is radiated":* Ibid., p. 132.
191 *"the need to be a mother":* Ibid., pp. 131–132.
191 *"The passive child":* Ibid., p. 132.
192 *"The child has 'obeyed' ":* Henry, *Pathways to Madness,* p. 289.
192 *"to give the baby":* Maurice Green, "The Interpersonal Approach to Child Therapy," in Benjamin Wolman, ed., *Handbook of Child Psychoanalysis,* p. 532.
192 *"all very lonely":* Maurice Green and David Schecter, "Autistic and Symbiotic Disorders in Three Blind Children," p. 637.
192 *"There was little need":* Ibid., p. 640.
192 *"By excessive anticipation":* Tarlton Morrow and Earl Loomis, "Symbiotic Aspects of a Seven-Year-Old Psychotic," in Gerald Caplan, ed., *Emotional Problems of Early Childhood,* p. 341.
193 *"those who, on weighing":* Bettelheim, *The Empty Fortress,* p. 153.
193 *"The child longs":* Ibid., p. 248.
193 *they call themselves "you":* Leo Kanner, "Autistic Disturbances of Affective Contact," p. 244.
193 *When five-year-old Donald:* Ibid., p. 220.
193 *(Newsweek headlined):* *Newsweek,* March 27, 1967, p. 70.
193 *"Clearly the nonuse":* Bettelheim, *The Empty Fortress,* p. 244.
193 *"Elly knew who she was":* Park, *The Siege,* p. 206.

CHAPTER TWELVE: *THE SCIENTISTS*
194 *In saying this:* Nikolaas Tinbergen, "Ethology and Stress Diseases," p. 22.
194 *"Thousands of children":* Gertrude Samuels, "The Lost and Forgotten Children of Europe," *New York Times Magazine,* Oct. 24, 1948.

195 *"maternal deprivation"*: John Bowlby, *Maternal Care and Mental Health,* p. 11.

195 *the psychoanalyst René Spitz:* René Spitz, "Hospitalism: An Inquiry into the Genesis of Psychiatric Conditions in Early Childhood." Spitz's work is discussed in Diane Eyer's valuable *Mother-Infant Bonding: A Scientific Fiction.*

195 *"We did not smile"*: Wayne Dennis, "Infant Development Under Conditions of Restricted Practice and of Minimum Social Stimulation: A Preliminary Report," p. 150.

195 *"On day 192"*: Ibid., p. 151.

195 *"A large number"*: Ibid., pp. 156–157.

196 *What set the two:* Bowlby, *Maternal Care,* pp. 33–34.

196 *"Mother-love in infancy"*: Ibid., p.158.

196 *"Much emphasis has already"*: Ibid., p. 67.

196 *"The provision of constant attention"*: Ibid., p. 41.

196 *The list began:* Ibid., p. 73.

197 *Bowlby was "addicted"*: Robert Karen, "Becoming Attached," p. 44.

197 *"Konrad Lorenz noticed"*: Janet Malcolm, *Psychoanalysis: The Impossible Profession,* p. 158.

198 *In order to study fear:* Clara Mears Harlow, ed., *From Learning to Love: The Selected Papers of H. F. Harlow,* p. 328.

198 *"Depressed human beings"*: Stephen J. Suomi and Harry F. Harlow, "Apparatus Conceptualization for Psychopathological Research in Monkeys," p. 247. The photo of the cowering monkey is on p. 248.

198 *"the tunnel of terror"*: Ibid., pp. 248–249.

199 *"We have inadvertently produced"*: Harlow, *From Learning to Love,* p. 333.

199 *"The two monkeys sat staring"*: Ibid., p. xxxv.

199 *"a brooding, not a breeding"*: Ibid.

199 *He began with:* Ibid., p. xxxiii. The talk itself is reprinted in Harlow, *From Learning to Love,* pp. 101–120. Harlow's photographs of his handmade surrogate mothers appear on p. 106.

199 *this was, Harlow liked to say:* Ibid., p. xxxiii.

200 *"contact comfort"*: Ibid., p. 108. In Harlow's summary, "Man cannot live by milk alone" (p. 108).

200 *"A charming lady"*: Ibid.

200 *"characterized by coldness"*: Harry F. Harlow and William T. McKinney, Jr., "Nonhuman Primates and Psychoses," p. 371.

201 *"watching and wondering"*: Nikolaas Tinbergen, "Ethology and Stress Diseases," pp. 20–27. This article was Tinbergen's Nobel Prize acceptance speech.

201 *"To a trained observer"*: Ibid., pp. 22–23.

201 *"maternal, protective behavior"*: Ibid., p. 23.

201 *"willing to cooperate"*: Ibid.

201 *Tinbergen was a sophisticated man:* For a brief account of Tinbergen's life and work, see Ray Fuller, ed., *Seven Pioneers of Psychology.*

202 *Once, for example:* E. A. Tinbergen and N. Tinbergen, *Early Childhood Autism—An Ethological Approach,* pp. 19–20.

202 *"normal children can easily"*: Ibid., p. 21.

202 *"three semi-controlled situations"*: Ibid., p. 13.

202 *"a group of species"*: Ibid., p. 22.

202 *"this highly relevant work"*: Ibid.

202 *"motivational conflict"*: Ibid., p. 24.

202 "The core of the problem": Ibid., p. 34.

203 *"It would seem to make"*: Nikolaas Tinbergen and Elisabeth A. Tinbergen,

"Autistic" Children: New Hope for a Cure, p. 176. For critical examinations of Tinbergen's work, see Eric Schopler, "The Stress of Autism as Ethology," and Lorna Wing and Derek Ricks, "The Etiology of Childhood Autism: A Criticism of the Tinbergens' Ethological Theory."

CHAPTER THIRTEEN: *THE PARENTS*

204 *The parents believed:* Catherine Maurice, *Let Me Hear Your Voice,* p. 155.
204 *"I was made to feel":* Jacques M. May, *A Physician Looks at Psychiatry,* p. 40. May's fine book, which is out of print, is available in a photocopied version from the Autism Research Institute in San Diego.
205 *"I was carrying around":* Author interview, May 7, 1996.
206 *"You can have all kinds":* Author interview, May 20, 1996.
206 *Leo Kanner was too old:* This account is based on the author's interviews with Ruth Sullivan and Clara Park, who were in the audience at Kanner's talk, and on a transcript of Kanner's speech prepared by Sullivan and edited by Kanner. Sullivan kindly provided me with a copy of the transcript.
207 *"but because he* was *Leo Kanner":* Clara Park, personal communication.
207 "inborn autistic disturbances": Leo Kanner, "Autistic Disturbances of Affective Contact," p. 250.
207 *"the emotional significance":* Hilde Bruch, *Studies in Schizophrenia,* p. 12.
207 *"There is one type of child":* "The Child Is Father," *Time,* July 25, 1960, p. 78.
208 *"Let us, contemporary mothers":* Leo Kanner, *In Defense of Mothers,* p. 7.
208 *"weird words and phrases":* Ibid., p. 6.
208 *"atmosphere full of isms":* Ibid., p. 5.
208 *"a field of battle":* Leo Kanner, "Cultural Implications of Children's Behavior Problems," p. 358.
208 *"The mother continues":* Ibid., p. 358.
209 *"I have dwelt":* Leo Kanner, "Problems of Nosology and Psychodynamics in Early Infantile Autism," p. 61.
209 *"The coincidence of infantile":* Leo Kanner, "Infantile Autism and the Schizophrenias," reprinted in Leo Kanner, *Childhood Psychosis,* p. 134.
209 *"I had several long conversations":* Author interview, June 11, 1996.
209 *"I investigated all":* Author interview, May 22, 1996.
210 *"At a time when most":* Author interview, Dec. 15, 1995.
210 *"I think that despite himself":* Ibid.
210 *"analogous in every way":* Sigmund Freud, "Notes upon a Case of Obsessional Neurosis," SE, vol. 10, p. 206n.
210 *Even a close friend:* Bruno Bettelheim and Alvin Rosenfeld, *The Art of the Obvious,* pp. 4, 9.
210 *"he was a very decent man":* Author interview, May 22, 1996.
211 *"He was a sadistic":* Author interview, Dec. 15, 1995.
211 *"Bettelheim," he says flatly:* Author interview, May 17, 1996.
211 *"By pretending to have":* Bruno Bettelheim, "Master Teacher and Prodigious Pupil," in *Freud's Vienna and Other Essays,* p. 164.
212 *"As playing with blocks":* Bruno Bettelheim, "The Importance of Play," p. 45.
212 *"Altogether we have worked":* Bruno Bettelheim, *The Empty Fortress,* p. 413.
212 *Of those forty autistic children:* Ibid., p. 414.
212 *"The seventeen children":* Ibid., p. 415.
212 *"One of my former boys":* "World Without 'I,' " *Newsweek,* March 27, 1967, p. 71.
212 *"cured eighty-five percent":* Nina Sutton, *Bettelheim,* p. 374.

212 *"He told a tremendous lie"*: Author interview, May 17, 1996.

213 *"Bettelheim reported"*: Author interview, Dec. 15, 1995.

213 *"Almost overnight"*: Leo Kanner, "Autism and the Schizophrenias," reprinted in Kanner, *Childhood Psychosis*, p. 125.

213 *"truly autistic"*: Bettelheim, *The Empty Fortress*, p. 94.

213 "He *decided who was autistic"*: Author interview, May 22, 1996.

213 *"nobody knows how"*: Bettelheim and Rosenfeld, *The Art of the Obvious*, p. 120.

213 *"the Ford Foundation grant"*: Sutton, *Bettelheim*, p. 399.

214 *"Success in helping"*: Bettelheim's remark is from a manuscript version of *A Home for the Heart* that he gave a counselor at the Orthogenic School as a gift. The sentence does not appear in the published book, but is quoted in Sutton, *Bettelheim*, p. 449.

214 *"It was a protected, caring"*: Ekstein was quoted in the *New York Times* on March 14, 1990, in the story reporting Bettelheim's suicide.

214 *"Punishment teaches a child"*: Bruno Bettelheim, "Punishment versus Discipline," *The Atlantic Monthly*, Nov. 1985.

215 *"Since ven do ve hit"*: Tom Wallace Lyons, *The Pelican and After*, pp. 27–28.

215 *"He had discovered at Buchenwald"*: Sutton, *Bettelheim*, p. 380. On p. 383, she writes that "Dr. B was playing his role as a lightning rod."

216 *"We, too, have sometimes"*: Bruno Bettelheim, *Truants from Life*, pp. 478–479.

216 *"merely anxious or insecure"*: Ibid., p. 480.

216 *"It is not the maternal"*: Bettelheim, *The Empty Fortress*, p. 69.

216 *"I called Bruno"*: Author interview, May 22, 1996.

216 *"All my life"*: Sutton, *Bettelheim*, p. 305.

217 *"change of environment"*: Leo Kanner, *Child Psychiatry* (1948 ed.), p. 728. Bettelheim quotes Kanner approvingly in *Truants from Life*, p. 258.

217 *"Our own experience"*: Bettelheim, *Truants from Life*, p. 258.

217 *"As soon as we began"*: Bruno Bettelheim, "Schizophrenia as a Reaction to Extreme Circumstances," reprinted in *Surviving*, p. 119.

217 *To insure that parents*: Sutton, *Bettelheim*, p. 324.

217 *"We must protect"*: Bettelheim, "Schizophrenia as a Reaction to Extreme Circumstances," p. 122.

217 *"Trying to rehabilitate"*: Bettelheim, *The Empty Fortress*, p. 407.

CHAPTER FOURTEEN: *PARENT-BLAMING PUT TO THE TEST*

218 *From this observation*: Marian DeMyer et al., "Parental Practices and Innate Activity in Normal, Autistic, and Brain-Damaged Infants," p. 51.

218 *all such "irrelevant" courses*: Author interview, April 9, 1996.

218 *Bernard and Gloria Rimland's son*: This account is based on my interviews with Bernard, Gloria, and Mark Rimland on April 9, 1996, and on several follow-up interviews with Bernard Rimland alone.

224 *While he was working*: Nina Sutton, *Bettelheim*, p. 425.

225 *"Rimland, a psychologist"*: Bruno Bettelheim, *The Empty Fortress*, p. 433.

225 *"In the last decades"*: Bruno Bettelheim and Alvin Rosenfeld, *The Art of the Obvious*, p. 141.

226 *one autistic person in three*: Uta Frith, *Autism*, p. 69.

226 *The result, it turned out*: Marian K. DeMyer, "Research in Infantile Autism: A Strategy and its Results." The paper is reprinted in Anne Donnellan, ed.,

Classic Readings in Autism. For an overview of her own work and others', see Marian K. DeMyer et al., "Infantile Autism Reviewed: A Decade of Research."

226 *The parents of the autistic:* Ibid., p. 272.
226 *"Most of them were just":* Author interview, June 11, 1996.
226 *"If you give them items":* Ibid.
227 *80 percent of autistic children:* Marian K. DeMyer, *Parents and Children in Autism,* p. 128.
227 *"Kanner thought that":* Author interview, Dec. 15, 1995.
227 *"Neither DeMyer's findings":* Two recent studies of twins offer powerful support for the idea that autism has a genetic basis. See Bailey et al., "Autism as a Strongly Genetic Disorder: Evidence from a British Twin Study"; and LeCouteur et al., "A Broader Phenotype of Autism: The Clinical Spectrum of Twins."
227 *"In 1979," he boasted:* Rimland's proud declaration is from his afterword to Annabel Stehli's *Sound of a Miracle,* p. 222.

EPILOGUE: CURRENT THEORIES OF AUTISM

228 *"the 'islets' of abilities":* Frith, *Autism,* p. 91.
228 *"truly phenomenal memory":* Ibid., p. 95.
228 *Recite a random string:* Ibid., pp. 92–93.
229 *"makes no distinction":* Ibid., p. 147.
229 *A doll named Sally:* Ibid., p. 159.
229 *one actor looked inside:* Simon Baron-Cohen, *Mindblindness,* p. 77.
230 *"The same autistic child":* Frith, *Autism,* p. 176.
230 *" 'You married?' ":* Donna Williams, *Somebody Somewhere,* p. 172.
231 *If he is asked to hide:* Baron-Cohen, *Mindblindness,* pp. 77–78.
231 *("Everything over which"):* Donna Williams, *Nobody Nowhere,* p. 69.
231 *"I was always trying":* Paul McDonnell's description is from his afterword to his mother's memoir, *News from the Border.* The quoted passage is from p. 347.
231 *"A young autistic child":* Lorna Wing, *A Guide to Parents and Professionals,* p. 64.
231 *"I can tell":* Oliver Sacks, *An Anthropologist on Mars,* p. 270.
231 *"my emotions are simpler":* Temple Grandin, *Thinking in Pictures,* p. 89.
232 *"I can act social":* Ibid., p. 182.
232 *"I am not very good":* Williams, *Somebody Somewhere,* p. 201.
232 *"Please give me your hand":* Frith, *Autism,* p. 178.
232 *But Clara Park noted:* Clara Park, *The Siege,* p. 204.
233 *She learned the word "man":* Ibid., pp. 202, 212.
233 *"Jessy doesn't know":* Author interview, Jan. 14, 1997.

PART FIVE: OBSESSIVE-COMPULSIVE DISORDER

235 *Certainly this:* Sigmund Freud, "The Sense of Symptoms," SE, vol. 16, p. 259.

CHAPTER FIFTEEN: ENSLAVED BY DEMONS

237 *The man in charge:* Peter Brown and Pat Broeske, *Howard Hughes,* p. 312.
238 *"obtain a brand new knife":* Ibid., p. 261.
239 *Before I start to turn:* Steven Rasmussen and Jane Eisen, "Phenomenology

of OCD," in Joseph Zohar et al., eds., *The Psychobiology of Obsessive-Compulsive Disorder*, p. 28.

239 *One seven-year-old girl:* Judith Rapoport, *The Boy Who Couldn't Stop Washing*, p. 139.

239 *A woman with an obsessive:* Samuel M. Turner and Deborah C. Beidel, *Treating Obsessive-Compulsive Disorder*, pp. 9, 13.

239 *"I've learned never":* Rapoport, *The Boy Who Couldn't Stop Washing*, p. 187.

239 *a woman named Stacie Lewis:* "With Remedy in Hand, Drug Firms Get Ready to Popularize an Illness," *The Wall Street Journal*, April 5, 1994, p. A1.

239 *"What drives me":* Rapoport, *The Boy Who Couldn't Stop Washing*, p. 38.

240 *"From 1950 on":* Author interview, Sept. 18, 1996.

240 *Sal was a family man:* This account is based on the author's Sept. 18, 1996, interview with Rapoport and on her account in *The Boy Who Couldn't Stop Washing*.

241 *"to suffer secretly":* Rapoport, *The Boy Who Couldn't Stop Washing*, p. 70.

241 *(The professional basketball player):* Rick Reilly, "Quest for Perfection," *Sports Illustrated*, Nov. 15, 1993.

241 *"Sufferers from this illness":* Sigmund Freud, "Obsessive Acts and Religious Practices," SE, vol. 9, p. 119.

241 *"You know someone":* Author interview, Sept. 18, 1996.

242 *"kids who just woke up":* Rapoport, *The Boy Who Couldn't Stop Washing*, p. 72.

242 *Eighty-five percent of her patients:* Susan Swedo, Henrietta Leonard, and Judith Rapoport, "Childhood-Onset Obsessive-Compulsive Disorder," in Michael Jenike et al., eds., *Obsessive-Compulsive Disorders*, p. 30.

242 *Among Australian aborigines:* Author interview, June 26, 1997.

242 *"In rural Nigeria":* Ibid. The Israeli study Rapoport described is D. Greenberg and E. Witztum, "The Influence of Cultural Factors on Obsessive-Compulsive Disorder." See also D. Greenberg and E. Witztum, "Cultural Aspects of Obsessive-Compulsive Disorder"; M. Weissman, et al., "The Cross-National Epidemiology of Obsessive-Compulsive Disorder"; and A. Okasha et al., "Phenomenology of Obsessive-Compulsive Disorder: A Transcultural Study."

242 *In the early 1600s:* Michael MacDonald, *Mystical Bedlam*, p. 154.

243 *One two-year-old boy:* Rasmussen and Eisen, "Phenomenology of OCD," in Zohar et al., eds., *The Psychobiology of Obsessive-Compulsive Disorder*, p. 25.

243 *Robert, a graduate student:* Author interview, Nov. 19, 1993.

244 *"You say, 'Is the stove off?' ":* Jeffrey Schwartz, *Brain Lock*, p. 45.

244 *A thirty-two-year-old:* Rasmussen and Eisen, "Phenomenology of OCD," pp. 23–24.

CHAPTER SIXTEEN: *FREUD SPEAKS*

245 *In obsessive actions:* Sigmund Freud, "Obsessive Acts and Religious Practices," SE, vol. 9, p. 122.

245 *Even Emil Kraepelin:* Author interview with Judith Rapoport, Sept. 18, 1996.

245 *"A young married woman":* Padmal de Silva and Stanley Rachman, *Obsessive-Compulsive Disorder*, p. 16.

246 *"A woman kept washing":* Sigmund Freud, "Obsessions and Phobias," SE, vol. 3, p. 79.

246 *"unquestionably the most interesting":* Sigmund Freud, "Inhibitions, Symptoms, and Anxieties," SE, vol. 20, p. 113. Patrick Mahony discusses Freud's fascination with obsessiveness in *Freud and the Rat Man*, p. 20.

246 *"Obsessional neurosis is shown"*: Sigmund Freud, "The Sense of Symptoms," SE, vol. 16, pp. 258–259.
246 *He himself, he wrote:* William McGuire, ed., *The Freud/Jung Letters*, p. 82.
247 *"Oh, that's quite all right"*: Sigmund Freud, "Notes upon a Case of Obsessional Neurosis," SE, vol. 10, pp. 196–197.
247 *"The self-reproachful affect"*: Ibid., p. 198.
247 *"the sufferer from compulsions"*: Sigmund Freud, "Obsessive Acts and Religious Practices," SE, vol. 9, p. 123.
247 *"We can always find"*: Sigmund Freud, "Obsessions and Phobias," SE, vol. 3, p. 75.
248 *"a girl [who] reproached herself"*: Ibid., p. 76.
248 *"Several women complained"*: Ibid.
248 *"a woman [who] found herself"*: Ibid., pp. 77–78.
248 *Rituals were shaky defenses:* Sigmund Freud, "Obsessive Acts and Religious Practices," SE, vol. 9, p. 124.
248 *"The process of repression"*: Ibid.
249 *"In obsessive actions"*: Ibid., p. 122.
249 *"I could not help noticing"*: Sigmund Freud, "Notes upon a Case of Obsessional Neurosis," SE, vol. 10. Freud explores the meaning of "glejisamen" on p. 225 and pp. 280–281.
250 *Its kernel was obviously:* Sigmund Freud, "The Sense of Symptoms," SE, vol. 16, pp. 261–262.
250 *"led directly to the inmost"*: Ibid., p. 263.
250 *"We are publishing"*: Ronald Clark, *Freud: The Man and the Cause*, p. 417.
251 *The patient was nineteen:* This long story is in Sigmund Freud, "The Sense of Symptoms," SE, vol. 16, pp. 264–268.
252 *"Obsessional ideas are invariably"*: Sigmund Freud, "Further Remarks on the Neuropsychoses of Defense," SE, vol. 3, p. 169.
252 *"The connection between"*: Freud-Fliess, p. 66.
253 *"it would not surprise me"*: Sigmund Freud, "Notes upon a Case of Obsessional Neurosis," SE, vol. 10, p. 169.
253 *"Poets tell us"*: Ibid., p. 239.
253 fn *In a letter:* Gay, *Freud,* p. 264.
254 *"The doubt is in reality"*: Ibid., p. 241.
254 *"Compulsive orderliness"*: Karl Abraham, "A Short Study of the Development of the Libido," in his *Selected Papers,* p. 430.
255 *"noteworthy for a regular combination"*: Sigmund Freud, "Character and Anal Erotism," SE, vol. 9, p. 169.
255 *"as infants . . . seem"*: Ibid., p. 170.
255 *"the ancient civilizations"*: Ibid., p. 175.
255 *The artist, Karl Abraham noted:* The quotations in this paragraph are all from Karl Abraham, "Contributions to the Theory of the Anal Character," pp. 371, 385, in his *Selected Papers.* Ernest Jones writes to similar effect in "Anal-Erotic Character Traits," in his *Papers on Psycho-Analysis.* See especially p. 430.
255 *"An attack of diarrhea"*: Ruth Mack Brunswick, "A Supplement to Freud's 'History of an Infantile Neurosis.'" Brunswick's essay is reprinted in Muriel Gardiner, ed., *The Wolf-Man by the Wolf-Man.*
256 *Generosity, for example:* See, for example, Jones, "Anal-Erotic Character Traits," p. 433.
256 *Procrastination simply reenacted:* Jones, "Anal-Erotic Character Traits," pp. 415–416.
256 *"it is here for the first time"*: Sigmund Freud, "Introductory Lectures," SE, vol. 16, p. 315.

256 *And so the toilet is indeed:* Abraham, "Contributions to the Theory of the Anal Character," p. 375.

256 *"Obsessive and compulsive phenomena":* Leo Kanner, *Child Psychiatry* (4th ed.), p. 610.

256 *"an exceptional number of bookkeepers":* E. Fuller Torrey, *Freudian Fraud,* p. 221.

257 *"the fact that in clinical work":* Anna Freud, "Obsessional Neurosis," p. 253.

257 *"We have, of course":* Aaron Esman, "Psychoanalysis and General Psychiatry: Obsessive-Compulsive Disorder as Paradigm," p. 321.

258 *"It is precisely this sharpest difference":* Sigmund Freud, "Obsessive Actions and Religious Practices," SE, vol. 9, pp. 119–120.

258 *"[obsessive] neurosis":* Ibid., pp. 126–127.

258 *"moderately severe":* Sigmund Freud, "Notes upon a Case of Obsessional Neurosis," SE, vol. 10, p. 155.

258 *"Obsessional neurosis and hysteria":* Sigmund Freud, "The Sense of Symptoms," SE, vol. 16, p. 258.

258 *"We have found from psychoanalysis":* Ibid., p. 261.

259 *"I had an opportunity":* Sigmund Freud, "The Interpretation of Dreams," SE, vol. 4, p. 260.

259 *"a kind of magic":* Sigmund Freud, "The Question of Lay Analysis," SE, vol. 20, p. 187.

259 *"therapeutic exaggeration":* Patrick Mahony, *Freud and the Rat Man,* p. 85.

260 *"desperately wanted the appearance":* Ibid.

260 *And so he proclaimed success:* Ibid.

260 *"entirely incapacitated":* Sigmund Freud, "From the History of an Infantile Neurosis," SE, vol. 17, p. 7.

260 *"In a disproportionately short time":* Ibid., p. 11.

260 *"the most elaborate":* This is the judgment of James Strachey, the editor of the 24-volume *Standard Edition* of Freud. See SE, vol. 17, p. 3.

260 *Far from cured:* See Gardiner, *The Wolf-Man by the Wolf-Man,* or Karin Obholzer, *The Wolf-Man: Conversations with Freud's Patient—Sixty Years Later.* Obholzer is a journalist who found the Wolf-Man in Vienna in 1973, at age eighty-six, and gave him a chance to speak for himself. For a discussion of all of Freud's most famous cases, including the Wolf Man, see Frank Sulloway, "Reassessing Freud's Case Histories." Sulloway is a highly regarded historian of science whose 1979 opus *Freud, Biologist of the Mind* played a large role in inspiring a wave of reexaminations of Freud's thought. His article on Freud's case histories is short but essential.

260 *"Thanks to his analysis":* This is from Anna Freud's preface to Gardiner, ed., *The Wolf-Man by the Wolf-Man.*

260 *"his more disturbed periods":* Ibid., p. 360.

261 *"The analyst whom the Wolf-Man":* Ibid., p. 363.

261 *"That was the theory":* Obholzer, *The Wolf-Man,* p. 113.

261 *"In reality, the whole thing":* Ibid., pp. 171–172.

261 *"the truly complicated":* Mahony, *Freud and the Rat Man,* p. 84.

261 *"comparatively simple":* Muriel Hall, "Obsessive-Compulsive States in Childhood and Their Treatment," p. 55.

262 *A child who is by nature:* Ibid.

262 *"The average length of time":* Ibid., p. 56.

CHAPTER SEVENTEEN: *THE BIOLOGICAL EVIDENCE*

263 *These children were* catching: John Ratey, *Shadow Syndromes,* p. 318.
263 *"there is not a single":* Michael Jenike et al., eds., *Obsessive-Compulsive Disorders,* p. 101.
263 *Rapoport changed her mind:* Author interview, Sept. 18, 1996.
264 *About two-thirds:* Judith Rapoport, *The Boy Who Couldn't Stop Washing,* p. 104.
264 *Behavior therapy, too:* Lee Baer and William Minichiello, "Behavior Therapy for Obsessive-Compulsive Disorder," in Michael Jenike et al., eds., *Obsessive-Compulsive Disorder,* pp. 203–206.
264 *Only one in five:* Rapoport, *The Boy Who Couldn't Stop Washing,* p. 97.
265 *"Compulsive personalities don't usually":* Ibid., p. 182.
265 *Rapoport has treated boys:* Ibid., p. 98.
265 *Another psychiatrist describes:* Steven Rasmussen and Jane Eisen, "Phenomenology of OCD," in Joseph Zohar et al., eds., *The Psychobiology of Obsessive-Compulsive Disorder,* p. 38.
265 *He woke up:* Author interview, Sept. 18, 1996.
265 fn *A determined psychiatrist:* Breggin's remarks are from his *Toxic Psychiatry,* p. 263.
266 *"He often had, seemingly":* Lawrence McHenry, Jr., "Samuel Johnson's Tics and Gesticulations," p. 155.
266 *"had the character":* Ibid.
266 *"extraordinary gestures":* T. J. Murray, "Dr. Samuel Johnson's Movement Disorder," p. 1612.
266 *"another peculiarity":* Ibid.
266 *He never stepped in the cracks:* Ibid.
266 *Rapoport reports that:* Rapoport, *The Boy Who Couldn't Stop Washing,* p. 92.
267 *"The news that a completely":* Ratey, *Shadow Syndromes,* p. 318.
267 *Josh Brown caught his "cold":* This section is based on my interviews with Josh Brown and his mother, Tina Brown, on Nov. 30, 1993, and with his doctor, Susan Swedo, on Dec. 3, 1993. His story is told in more detail in Edward Dolnick, "Obsessed."
269 *Most drugs, Rapoport points out:* Rapoport, *The Boy Who Couldn't Stop Washing,* p. 102.
270 *Rapoport set up a study:* Judith Rapoport, "Treatment of Behavior Disorders in Animals."
271 *In monkeys at least:* Rapoport, *The Boy Who Couldn't Stop Washing,* p. 194.
271 *"no matter what":* Jeffrey Schwartz, *Brain Lock,* p. xxx.
272 *"she could have that":* Ibid., p. xxxiv.
272 *In all likelihood, what happens:* Ibid., p. 51.
272 *A woman named Sarah:* Author interview, Nov. 29, 1993.
273 *"every compulsion is":* George Weinberg, *Invisible Masters,* p. 78.
274 *"People," writes Pagels:* Elaine Pagels, *Adam, Eve, and the Serpent,* p. 146.
274 *"Psychology seems deeper":* Author interview, Sept. 18, 1996.

PART SIX: *CONCLUSION*

275 *Sometimes it is very difficult:* Virginia Axline, *Dibs in Search of Self,* p. 80.

CHAPTER EIGHTEEN: *PLACING THE BLAME*

277 *It's the easiest thing:* Author interview, Dec. 4, 1995.
277 *Before his depression hit:* This account of the Osheroff affair is based on
     Sandra Boodman, "The Mystery of Chestnut Lodge"; Darrell Sifford, "An
     Improper-Diagnosis Case that Changed Psychiatry"; Alan Stone, "The New
     Paradox of Medical Malpractice"; Gerald L. Klerman, "The Psychiatric Pa-
     tient's Right to Effective Treatment: Implications of *Osheroff v. Chestnut
     Lodge*"; and the debate in the letters column of the *American Journal of
     Psychiatry,* esp. April 1989, Jan. 1991, and March 1991.
279 *"Here's the bind":* Author interview, Dec. 15, 1995.
281 *Take Nancy Gibbons:* Joseph Wassersug, "None of the Physicians Could Find
     the Coin in Her Throat."
281 *Bonnie Burke's predicament:* "$97,500 Awarded in Psychiatric Malpractice
     Suit," *Los Angeles Times,* July 2, 1995, p. B1. See also Berton Roueché, "The
     Hoofbeats of a Zebra," for a discussion of a related case.
282 *The story of "David":* Irving Cooper, *The Victim Is Always the Same,* pp. 7,
     47–53.
283 *"The mother's personality":* René Spitz, *The First Year of Life: A Psychoana-
     lytic Study of Normal and Deviant Development of Object Relations.* Spitz is
     quoted in Barbara Ehrenreich and Deirdre English's fine book, *For Her Own
     Good* (p. 227). Their history of medical advice to women is excellent; the
     chapter entitled "Motherhood as Pathology" is especially valuable.
283 *"A child needs love":* Virginia Axline, *Dibs in Search of Self,* p. 166.
283 *"Most mothers do not murder":* Joseph Rheingold, *The Fear of Being a
     Woman: A Theory of Maternal Destructiveness,* p. 143.
283 *"We have gone a long way":* Edward Strecker, *Their Mothers' Sons,* p. 177.
284 *The practice ended only:* Robert E. Drake and Lloyd I. Sederer, "The Adverse
     Effects of Intensive Treatment of Chronic Schizophrenia," p. 313.
284 *"for everything and against anything":* Otto Bettmann, *A Pictorial History of
     Medicine.*
284 *"No other specialty blames illness":* Richard Hunter, "President's Address,"
     p. 359.
284 *"Badly treated families":* William S. Appleton, "Mistreatment of Patients' Fami-
     lies by Psychiatrists," p. 656.
285 *"People who read books":* Author interview, Dec. 4, 1995.
285 *If schizophrenia was caused:* The argument about stress in this paragraph and
     the next comes from Abram Hoffer and Humphry Osmond, *How to Live with
     Schizophrenia,* pp. 12–14.
285 *Almost no one did:* In 1959 two researchers at the University of Minnesota
     School of Medicine published a study comparing the families of 178 schizo-
     phrenic patients with those of a matched group of 150 psychologically normal
     people. They found essentially no differences between the parents in the two
     groups. See William Schofield and Lucy Balian, "A Comparative Study of the
     Personal Histories of Schizophrenic and Nonpsychiatric Patients."
286 *"The underlying assumption":* Miriam Siegler, Humphry Osmond, and Harriet
     Mann, "Laing's Models of Madness," in Robert Boyers and Robert Orrill, eds.,
     R. D. Laing and Anti-Psychiatry, pp. 136–137.
287 *"Where shall we find the evidence":* Peter Medawar, "Further Comments on
     Psychoanalysis," in Medawar, *Pluto's Republic,* p. 68.
288 *Until the mid-1940s:* The argument in this paragraph is drawn from Leon
     Eisenberg, "Past, Present and Future in Psychiatry: Personal Reflections." The

Medical Research Council paper was "Streptomycin Treatment for Pulmonary Tuberculosis."

288 *"The physician must go to the root":* Flanders Dunbar, *Mind and Body,* p. 37.

288 fn *The psychoanalyst Judd Marmor:* Judd Marmor, "Psychoanalytic Therapy as an Educational Process." Frank Cioffi cites Marmor's remarks in "Freud and the Idea of a Pseudo-Science," p. 514.

288 fn *This was a full:* Alan Gurney, *Below the Convergence: Voyages Toward Antarctica,* pp. 41–42.

289 *"The neutron did not come begging":* Seymour Kety, "The Academic Lecture: The Heuristic Aspect of Psychiatry," p. 385.

289 *"So far as the phenomena":* Henry Maudsley, *Mind and Body,* quoted in Daniel Rogers, *Motor Disorders in Psychiatry,* p. 1.

290 *"Although aspirin is well known":* Irving Gottesman, *Schizophrenia Genesis,* p. 9.

292 *Sorrow, he wrote to Princess Elisabeth:* L. J. Rather, *Mind and Body in Eighteenth Century Medicine,* p. 224n.

292 *("There are only two"):* Ibid., p. 200.

292 *take the use of placebos:* Walter Brown, "The Placebo Effect," explores the place of placebos in today's medicine in this *Scientific American* article.

292 *Favism, for example:* Brian MacMahon, "Gene-Environment Interaction in Human Disease," p. 394, in David Rosenthal and Seymour Kety, eds., *The Transmission of Schizophrenia.*

294 *"the most stupendous":* Peter Medawar, "Victims of Psychiatry," in Medawar, *Pluto's Republic,* p. 140.

294 *"something terrible happens":* Frost liked to offer his definition as a paraphrase of George Meredith's remark that "in tragic life no villain need be." Maryellen Walsh cites Frost's remark in her excellent book *Schizophrenia: Straight Talk for Family and Friends.*

Bibliography

Abraham, Hilda C., and Ernst L. Freud, eds. *A Psychoanalytic Dialogue: The Letters of Sigmund Freud and Karl Abraham, 1907–1926.* New York: Basic Books, 1965.

Abraham, Karl. *Selected Papers of Karl Abraham.* New York: Brunner/Mazel, 1927.

Alexander, Franz. *Psychoanalytic Pioneers.* New York: Basic Books, 1966.

———. *Psychosomatic Medicine.* New York: Norton, 1950.

Alexander, Franz, and Sheldon Selesnick. *The History of Psychiatry.* New York: Harper & Row, 1966.

Andreasen, Nancy. *The Broken Brain: The Biological Revolution in Psychiatry.* New York: Perennial Library, 1985.

———. *Schizophrenia: From Mind to Molecule.* Washington, D.C.: American Psychiatric Press, 1994.

Appleton, William S. "Mistreatment of Patients' Families by Psychiatrists." *American Journal of Psychiatry* 131, no. 6 (June 1974): 655–657.

Arieti, Silvano, ed. *American Handbook of Psychiatry.* New York: Basic Books, 1959.

———. *Interpretation of Schizophrenia.* New York: Robert Brunner, 1955.

———. *On Schizophrenia, Phobias, Depression, Psychotherapy, and the Farther Shores of Psychiatry.* New York: Brunner/Mazel, 1978.

———. *Understanding and Helping the Schizophrenic.* New York: Basic Books, 1979.

Axline, Virginia. *Dibs in Search of Self.* New York: Ballantine, 1967.

———. *Play Therapy.* Boston: Houghton Mifflin, 1947.

Ayd, Frank, and Barry Blackwell, eds. *Discoveries in Biological Psychiatry.* Philadelphia: J. B. Lippincott, 1970.

Bailey, Anthony, et al. "Autism as a Strongly Genetic Disorder: Evidence from a British Twin Study." *Psychological Medicine* 25 (1995): 63–78.

Bailey, Percival. "The Great Psychiatric Revolution." *American Journal of Psychiatry* 113 (Nov. 1956): 387–406.

Baron-Cohen, Simon. *Mindblindness.* Cambridge, Mass.: MIT Press, 1995.

Bateson, Catherine. *With a Daughter's Eye.* New York: Morrow, 1984.

Bateson, Gregory, ed. *Perceval's Narrative: A Patient's Account of his Psychosis, 1830–1832.* New York: Morrow, 1974.

Bellak, Leopold, ed. *Schizophrenia: A Review of the Syndrome.* New York: Logos Press, 1958.

Berger, Milton M., ed. *Beyond the Double Bind: Communication and Family Systems, Theories, and Techniques with Schizophrenics*. New York: Brunner/ Mazel, 1978.

Bettelheim, Bruno. *The Empty Fortress*. New York: Free Press, 1967.

———. *Freud's Vienna and Other Essays*. New York: Knopf, 1990.

———. *A Home for the Heart*. New York: Knopf, 1974.

———. "The Importance of Play." *Atlantic Monthly*, March 1987.

———. *The Informed Heart*. Glencoe, Ill.: Free Press, 1960.

———. "Joey: A Mechanical Boy." *Scientific American*, March 1959.

———. *Love Is Not Enough*. New York: Free Press, 1950.

———. "Punishment versus Discipline." *Atlantic Monthly*, Nov. 1985.

———. *Surviving and Other Essays*. New York: Knopf, 1979.

———. *Truants from Life*. New York: Free Press, 1955.

———. "Where Self Begins." *New York Times Magazine*, Feb. 12, 1967.

Bettelheim, Bruno, and Alvin Rosenfeld. *The Art of the Obvious*. New York: Knopf, 1993.

Bettmann, Otto. *A Pictorial History of Medicine*. Springfield, Ill.: Charles C. Thomas, 1956.

Blanton, Smiley. *Diary of My Analysis with Sigmund Freud*. New York: Hawthorn Books, 1971.

Blaser, Martin J. "The Bacteria Behind Ulcers." *Scientific American*, Feb. 1996.

Block, Jeanne, et al. "A Study of the Parents of Schizophrenic and Neurotic Children." *Psychiatry* 21 (1958): 387–397.

Bobrick, Benson. *Knotted Tongues: Stuttering in History and the Quest for a Cure*. New York: Kodansha, 1996.

Boodman, Sandra G. "The Mystery of Chestnut Lodge." *Washington Post Magazine*, Oct. 8, 1989.

Bookhammer, Robert, et al. "A Five-Year Clinical Follow-up Study of Schizophrenics Treated by Rosen's 'Direct Analysis' Compared with Controls." *American Journal of Psychiatry* 123, no. 5 (Nov. 1966): 602–604.

Bowlby, John. *Maternal Care and Mental Health*. Geneva: World Health Organization, 1951.

Boyer, L. Bryce, and Peter L. Giovacchini. *Psychoanalytic Treatment of Schizophrenic and Characterological Disorders*. New York: Science House, 1967.

Boyers, Robert, and Robert Orrill, eds. *R. D. Laing and Anti-Psychiatry*. New York: Perennial Library, 1971.

Brand, Millen. *Savage Sleep*. New York: Bantam, 1969.

Braslow, Joel T. "Effect of Therapeutic Innovation on Perception of Disease and the Doctor-Patient Relationship: A History of General Paralysis of the Insane and Malaria Fever Therapy, 1910–1950." *American Journal of Psychiatry* 152, no. 5 (May 1995): 660–665.

Breggin, Peter. *Toxic Psychiatry*. New York: St. Martin's, 1994.

Brome, Vincent. *Freud and His Disciples*. London: Caliban, 1984.

Brown, Bertram S. "The Life of Psychiatry." *American Journal of Psychiatry* 133, no. 5 (May 1976): 489–495.

Brown, Peter, and Pat Broeske. *Howard Hughes: The Untold Story*. New York: Dutton, 1996.

Brown, Walter A. "The Placebo Effect." *Scientific American*, Jan. 1998.

Bruch, Hilde. "Studies in Schizophrenia." *Acta Psychiatrica et Neurologica Scandinavica* 34, suppl. 130 (1959): 5–48.

Bullard, Dexter M., ed. *Psychoanalysis and Psychotherapy: Selected Papers of Frieda Fromm-Reichmann*. Chicago: University of Chicago Press, 1959.

Burke, Ross David. *When the Music's Over: My Journey into Schizophrenia.* New York: Plume, 1996.

Burston, Daniel. *The Wing of Madness: The Life and Work of R. D. Laing.* Cambridge, Mass.: Harvard University Press, 1996.

Burton, Arthur. "The Adoration of the Patient and Its Disillusionment." *American Journal of Psychoanalysis* 29, no. 2 (1969): 194–204.

———, ed. *Psychotherapy of the Psychoses.* New York: Basic Books, 1961.

Cain, Albert. "Special 'Isolated' Abilities in Severely Psychotic Young Children." *Psychiatry* 32 (1969): 137–149.

Caplan, Gerald, ed. *Emotional Problems of Early Childhood.* New York: Basic Books, 1955.

Chapman, A. H. *Harry Stack Sullivan: His Life and His Work.* New York: Putnam, 1976.

Chess, Stella. "The 'Blame the Mother' Ideology." *International Journal of Mental Health* 11: 95–107.

———. "Mal de Mère," *American Journal of Orthopsychiatry* 34 (1964): 613–614.

Cioffi, Frank. "The Cradle of Neurosis" (review of Jeffrey Masson's *Assault on Truth*). *Times Literary Supplement,* July 6, 1984.

———. "Freud and the Idea of a Pseudo-Science." In *Explanation in the Behavioural Sciences,* edited by Robert Borger and Frank Cioffi. Cambridge, Eng.: Cambridge University Press, 1970.

———. "Freud—New Myths to Replace the Old." *New Society,* Nov. 29, 1979.

———. "Psychoanalysis, Pseudo-Science, and Testability." In *Popper and the Human Sciences,* edited by Gregory Currie and Alan Musgrave. Dordrecht, Holland: M. Nijhoff, 1985.

———. "Wittgenstein's Freud." In Peter Winch, ed., *Studies in the Philosophy of Wittgenstein.* New York: Humanities Press, 1969.

Ciompi, Luc. *The Psyche and Schizophrenia.* Cambridge, Mass.: Harvard University Press, 1988.

Clark, Ronald. *Freud: The Man and the Cause.* New York: Random House, 1980.

Coleman, Mary, and Christopher Gillberg. *The Biology of the Autistic Syndromes.* New York: Cambridge University Press, 1992.

Coles, Robert. *The Mind's Fate.* Boston: Atlantic Monthly, 1975.

Cooper, Irving. *The Victim Is Always the Same.* New York: Harper & Row, 1973.

Corsini, Raymond, ed. *Handbook of Innovative Psychotherapies.* New York: Wiley, 1981.

Cranefield, Paul F. "Josef Breuer's Evaluation of his Contribution to Psycho-Analysis." *International Journal of Psycho-Analysis* 39 (1958): 319–322.

Crews, Frederick. *The Memory Wars.* New York: New York Review of Books, 1995.

———. *Skeptical Engagements.* New York: Oxford University Press, 1986.

Critchley, MacDonald. Review of *Great and Desperate Cures. New York Review of Books,* April 24, 1986.

Dawes, Robyn. *House of Cards.* New York: Free Press, 1996, paperback.

DeMyer, Marian. *Parents and Children in Autism.* Washington, D.C.: V. H. Winston, 1979.

———. "Research in Infantile Autism: A Strategy and Its Results." *Biological Psychiatry* 10 (1975): 433–452 (also in Donnellan, *Classic Readings in Autism*).

DeMyer, Marian K., Sandra Barton, and James A. Norton. "A Comparison of Adaptive, Verbal, and Motor Profiles of Psychotic and Non-Psychotic Subnormal Children." *Journal of Autism and Childhood Schizophrenia* 2, no. 4 (1972): 359–377.

DeMyer, Marian K., Joseph N. Hingtgen, and Roger K. Jackson. "Infantile Autism

Reviewed: A Decade of Research." *Schizophrenia Bulletin* 7, no. 3 (1981): 388–451.

DeMyer, Marian K., et al. "The Measured Intelligence of Autistic Children." *Journal of Autism and Childhood Schizophrenia* 4, no. 1 (1974): 42–60.

———. "Parental Practices and Innate Activity in Normal, Autistic, and Brain-Damaged Infants." *Journal of Autism and Childhood Schizophrenia* 2, no. 1 (1972): 49–66.

Dennis, Wayne. "Infant Development Under Conditions of Restricted Practice and of Minimum Social Stimulation: A Preliminary Report." *Journal of Genetic Psychology* 53 (1938): 149–158.

De Silva, Padmal, and Stanley Rachman. *Obsessive-Compulsive Disorder.* Oxford: Oxford University Press, 1992.

Despert, J. Louise. *The Emotionally Disturbed Child—Then and Now.* New York: Robert Brunner, 1965.

———. "Reflections on Early Infantile Autism." *Journal of Autism and Childhood Schizophrenia* 1, no. 4 (1971): 363–367.

———. *Schizophrenia in Children: Collected Papers.* New York: Robert Brunner, 1968.

———. "Some Considerations Relating to the Genesis of Autistic Behavior in Children." *American Journal of Orthopsychiatry* 21 (1951): 335–350.

Deveson, Anne. *Tell Me I'm Here.* New York: Penguin, 1991.

Dolnick, Edward. "Obsessed." *Health,* Sept. 1994.

Donnellan, Anne, ed. *Classic Readings in Autism.* New York: Teachers College Press, 1985.

Drake, Robert, and Lloyd Sederer. "The Adverse Effects of Intensive Treatment of Chronic Schizophrenia." *Comprehensive Psychiatry* 27, no. 4 (July–August, 1986): 313–326.

Dubos, René, and Jean Dubos. *The White Plague: Tuberculosis, Man, and Society.* London: Victor Gollancz, 1953.

Dufresne, Todd. "An Interview with Joseph Wortis." *Psychoanalytic Review* 83, no. 4 (Aug. 1996): 589–610.

Dunbar, Flanders. *Mind and Body: Psychosomatic Medicine.* New York: Random House, 1947.

Ehrenreich, Barbara, and Deirdre English. *For Her Own Good.* New York: Doubleday, 1978.

Eisenberg, Leon. "The Fathers of Autistic Children." *American Journal of Orthopsychiatry* 27 (1957): 715–724.

———. "Mindlessness and Brainlessness in Psychiatry." *British Journal of Psychiatry* 148 (1986): 497–508.

———. "Past, Present, and Future in Psychiatry: Personal Reflections." *Canadian Journal of Psychiatry* 42, no. 7 (Sept. 1997): 705–713.

———. "Seed or Soil: How Does Our Garden Grow?" *American Journal of Psychiatry* 153, no. 1 (Jan. 1996): 3–5.

———. "The Social Construction of the Human Brain." *American Journal of Psychiatry* 152, no. 11 (Nov. 1995): 1563–1575.

Ellenberger, Henri F. *History of the Unconscious.* New York: Basic Books, 1970, paperback.

English, O. Spurgeon. "Clinical Observations on Direct Analysis." *Comprehensive Psychiatry* 1 (1960): 154–163.

Esman, Aaron H. "Psychoanalysis and General Psychiatry: Obsessive-Compulsive Disorder as Paradigm." *Journal of the American Psychoanalytic Association* 37 (1989): 319–336.

Esterson, Allen. "Grunbaum's Tally Argument." *History of the Human Sciences* 9, no. 1 (Feb. 1996): 43–57.

———. "Jeffrey Masson and Freud's Seduction Theory: A New Fable Based on Old Myths." *History of the Human Sciences* 11, no. 1 (Feb. 1998): 1–28.

———. *Seductive Mirage.* Chicago: Open Court, 1993.

Eyer, Diane. *Motherguilt.* New York: Times Books, 1986.

———. *Mother-Infant Bonding: A Scientific Fiction.* New Haven, Conn.: Yale University Press, 1992.

Farrell, John. *Freud's Paranoid Quest.* New York: New York University Press, 1996.

Ferenczi, Sandór. "Psycho-Analytical Observations on Tic." *International Journal of Psycho-Analysis* 2, pt. 1 (March 1921): 1–30.

Fermi, Laura. *Illustrious Immigrants.* Chicago: University of Chicago Press, 1968.

Fine, Reuben. *A History of Psychoanalysis.* New York: Columbia University Press, 1979.

Fink, Max. "Meduna and the Origins of Convulsive Therapy." *American Journal of Psychiatry* 141, no. 9 (Sept. 1984): 1034–1041.

Freeman, Derek. *Margaret Mead and the Heretic.* New York: Penguin, 1996.

Freud, Anna. "Obsessional Neurosis: A Summary of Psychoanalytic Views." *International Journal of Psycho-Analysis* 47 (1966): 116–122. (Also in *The Writings of Anna Freud,* vol. 5.)

Freud, Ernst L., ed. *The Letters of Sigmund Freud.* New York: Basic Books, 1975, paperback.

Freud, Sigmund. *The Standard Edition of the Complete Psychological Works of Sigmund Freud.* Translated and edited by James Strachey. 24 vols. London: Hogarth Press, 1953–1974.

"Frieda Fromm-Reichmann: A Seminar in the History of Psychiatry." *Psychiatry* 45 (May 1982): 89–136. (This is a series of essays, by several authors, on Fromm-Reichmann's life and work.)

Friedman, Lawrence J. *Menninger: The Family and the Clinic.* New York: Knopf, 1990.

Frith, Uta. *Autism: Explaining the Enigma.* Cambridge, Mass.: Basil Blackwell, 1989.

———, ed. *Autism and Asperger Syndrome.* Cambridge, Eng.: Cambridge University Press, 1991.

Fromm, Eric. "The Oedipus Myth." *Scientific American,* Jan. 1949.

Fromm-Reichmann, Frieda. "Notes on the Development of Treatment of Schizophrenics by Psychoanalytic Psychotherapy." *Psychiatry* 11 (1948): 263–273.

———. *Principles of Intensive Psychotherapy.* Chicago: University of Chicago Press, 1960.

Fuller, Ray, ed. *Seven Pioneers of Psychology.* London: Routledge, 1995.

Gardiner, Muriel, ed. *The Wolf-Man by the Wolf-Man, with "The Case of the Wolf-Man" by Sigmund Freud and "A Supplement" by Ruth Mack Brunswick; foreword by Anna Freud.* New York: Basic Books, 1971.

Gardner, Martin. *Fads and Fallacies in the Name of Science.* New York: Dover, 1957.

Gay, Peter. *Freud: A Life for Our Time.* New York: Norton, 1988.

Gellner, Ernest. *The Psychoanalytic Movement: The Cunning of Unreason.* Evanston, Ill.: Northwestern University Press, 1996.

Gill, Brendan. "Dreamer and Healer." *New Yorker,* Oct. 10, 1953.

Gordon, James S. "Who Is Mad? Who Is Sane? R. D. Laing: In Search of a New Psychiatry." *Atlantic Monthly,* Jan. 1971.

Gottesman, Irving. "A Critical Review of Recent Adoption, Twin, and Family Studies of Schizophrenia: Behavioral Genetics Perspectives." *Schizophrenia Bulletin* 2, no. 3: 360–401. (This article is followed immediately by a critical commentary by Theodore Lidz, pp. 402–412.)

———. *Schizophrenia Genesis.* New York: W. H. Freeman, 1991.

Gottesman, Irving, and Aksel Bertelsen. "Confirming Unexpressed Genotypes for Schizophrenia—Risks in the Offspring of Fischer's Danish Identical and Fraternal Discordant Twins." *Archives of General Psychiatry* 46 (1989): 867–872.

Gottesman, Irving, and James Shields. "Schizophrenia Epigenesis: Past, Present, and Future." *Acta Psychiatrica Scandinavica* 90, suppl. 384 (1994): 26–33.

Grandin, Temple. *Emergence: Labeled Autistic.* Novato, Calif.: Arena Press, 1986.

———. *Thinking in Pictures.* New York: Doubleday, 1995.

Green, Maurice, and David Schecter. "Autistic and Symbiotic Disorders in Three Blind Children." *Psychiatric Quarterly* 31 (1957): 628–646.

Green, Vivian. *The Madness of Kings.* New York: St. Martin's, 1993.

Greenberg, D., and E. Witztum. "Cultural Aspects of Obsessive-Compulsive Disorder." In *Current Insights in Obsessive-Compulsive Disorder,* edited by Eric Hollander et al., Chichester, Eng.: Wiley, 1994.

———. "The Influence of Cultural Factors on Obsessive-Compulsive Disorder." *Israeli Journal of Psychiatry and Related Sciences* 31 (1994): 211–220.

Greenberg, Joanne. *I Never Promised You a Rose Garden.* New York: Holt, Rinehart & Winston, 1964.

Grinspoon, L., J. R. Ewalt, and R. I. Shader. *Schizophrenia: Pharmacotherapy and Psychotherapy.* Baltimore: Williams & Wilkins, 1972.

Grob, Gerald. "Origins of DSM-I: A Study in Appearance and Reality." *American Journal of Psychiatry* 148, no. 4 (April 1991): 421–431.

Groddeck, Georg. *The Book of the It.* New York: Vintage, 1961 (originally published in German in 1923).

Gross, Martin L. *The Psychological Society.* New York: Random House, 1978.

Grosskurth, Phyllis. *The Secret Ring.* Reading, Mass.: Addison-Wesley, 1991.

Gunderson, John, and Loren Mosher, eds. *Issues and Controversies in the Psychotherapy of Schizophrenia.* Northvale, N.J.: Jason Aronson, 1994.

Gurney, Alan. *Below the Convergence: Voyages Toward Antarctica.* New York: Norton, 1997.

Guze, Samuel. "Psychosomatic Medicine: A Critique." *Psychiatric Developments* 2, no. 1 (Spring 1984): 23–30.

———. *Why Psychiatry Is a Branch of Medicine.* New York: Oxford University Press, 1992.

Guze, Samuel B., and George E. Murphy. "An Empirical Approach to Psychotherapy: The Agnostic Position." *American Journal of Psychiatry* 120, no. 1 (July 1963): 53–57.

Hale, Nathan G. *Freud and the Americans: The Beginnings of Psychoanalysis in the United States, 1876–1917.* New York: Oxford University Press, 1971.

———. *The Rise and Crisis of Psychoanalysis in the United States: Freud and the Americans, 1917–1985.* New York: Oxford University Press, 1995.

Haley, Jay. *The Power Tactics of Jesus Christ and Other Essays.* Rockville, Md.: Triangle Press, 1986.

Hall, Muriel. "Obsessive-Compulsive States in Children and Their Treatment." *Archives of Disease in Childhood* 10 (1934): 49–59.

Hamblin, Dora Jane. "They are 'Idiot Savants'—Wizards of the Calendar." *Life,* March 18, 1966.

Harlow, Clara Mears, ed. *From Learning to Love: The Collected Papers of H. F. Harlow.* New York: Praeger, 1986.

Harlow, Harry F., and William T. McKinney. "Nonhuman Primates and Psychoses." *Journal of Autism and Childhood Schizophrenia* 1, no. 4 (1971): 368–375.

Harlow, Harry F., and Stephen J. Suomi. "Apparatus Conceptualization for Psychopathological Research in Monkeys." *Behavioral Research Methods and Instrumentation* 1, no. 7 (1969): 247–250.

Hatfield, Agnes B. Review of *Nadia: A Case of Extraordinary Drawing Ability in an Autistic Child*. In *Journal of Autism and Childhood Schizophrenia* 8, no. 4 (1978): 457–475.

Hecht, Ben. *Gaily, Gaily*. Garden City, N.Y.: Doubleday, 1963.

Hegarty, James D., et al. "One Hundred Years of Schizophrenia: A Meta-Analysis of the Outcome Literature." *American Journal of Psychiatry* 151, no. 10 (Oct. 1994): 1409–1416.

Henry, Jules. *Pathways to Madness*. New York: Vintage, 1973.

Heston, Leonard, and Duane Denney. "Interactions Between Early Life Experience and Biological Factors in Schizophrenia." In *The Transmission of Schizophrenia*, edited by Seymour Kety and David Rosenthal. Oxford, Eng.: Pergamon Press, 1968.

Hobson, J. Allan. *The Chemistry of Conscious States*. Boston: Little, Brown, 1994.

Hoffer, Abram, and Humphry Osmond. *How to Live with Schizophrenia*. New York: Citadel Press, 1992.

Hollander, Eric, ed. *Obsessive-Compulsive Related Disorders*. Washington, D.C.: American Psychiatric Press, 1993.

Horwitz, William. "Identical Twin — 'Idiot Savants' — Calendar Calculators." *American Journal of Psychiatry* 121 (1965): 1075–1079.

Horwitz, William, et al. "A Study of Cases of Schizophrenia Treated by 'Direct Analysis,'" *American Journal of Psychiatry* 114, no. 9 (March 1958): 780–783.

Howard, Jane. *Margaret Mead: A Life*. New York: Simon & Schuster, 1984.

Howe, Michael J. A. *Fragments of Genius*. London: Routledge, 1989.

Howells, John G., ed. *Modern Perspectives in World Psychiatry*. New York: Brunner/Mazel, 1971.

Hunter, Richard. "President's Address." *Proceedings of the Royal Society of Medicine* 66 (April 1973): 359–364.

Hunter, Richard, and Ida Macalpine. *George III and the Mad-Business*. London: Allen Lane, 1969.

———. *Three Hundred Years of Psychiatry: 1535–1860*. Hartsdale, N.Y.: Carlisle, 1982.

———, eds. and translators. *Memoirs of My Nervous Illness*, by Daniel Paul Schreber. Cambridge, Mass.: Harvard University Press, 1955.

Isaac, Rael Jean, and Virginia C. Armat. *Madness in the Streets: How Psychiatry and the Law Abandoned the Mentally Ill*. New York: Free Press, 1990.

Jackson, Don D. "A Note on the Importance of Trauma in the Genesis of Schizophrenia." *Psychiatry* 20 (1957): 181–184.

———. "The Transactional Viewpoint." *International Journal of Psychiatry* 4, no. 6 (Dec. 1967): 543–544.

———, ed. *The Etiology of Schizophrenia*. New York: Basic Books, 1960.

Jelliffe, Smith Ely. "The Parkinsonian Body Posture: Some Considerations on Unconscious Hostility." *Psychoanalytic Review* 27 (1940): 467–479.

Jenike, Michael; Lee Baer; and William E. Minichiello. *Obsessive-Compulsive Disorders: Theory and Management*. Chicago: Year Book Medical Publishers, 1990.

Jeste, Dilip V., et al. "Did Schizophrenia Exist Before the Eighteenth Century?" *Comprehensive Psychiatry* 26, no. 6 (Nov.–Dec. 1985): 493–503.

Jones, Anne Hudson. "Literature and Medicine: Narratives of Mental Illness." *Lancet* 350 (Aug. 2, 1997): 359–361.

Jones, Ernest. *The Life and Work of Sigmund Freud*. 3 vols. New York: Basic Books, 1953, 1955, 1957.

———. *Papers on Psycho-Analysis* London: Bailliere, Tindall, & Cox, 1950.

Jung, Carl. *Modern Man in Search of a Soul*. New York: Harcourt, Brace, 1950.

Kagan, Jerome. *Unstable Ideas*. Cambridge, Mass.: Harvard University Press, 1989.

Kanner, Leo. "Autistic Disturbances of Affective Contact." *Nervous Child* 2, no. 3 (April 1943): 217–250.

———. *Child Psychiatry*. Springfield, Ill.: Charles C. Thomas, 1948.

———. *Childhood Psychosis: Initial Studies and New Insights*. Washington, D.C.: V. H. Winston, 1973.

———. "Cultural Implications of Children's Behavior Problems." *Mental Hygiene* 25, no. 3 (July 1941): 353–362.

———. "Emotional Interference with Intellectual Functioning." *American Journal of Mental Deficiency* 56 (1952): 701–707.

———. *In Defense of Mothers*. Springfield, Ill.: Charles C. Thomas, 1941.

Kardiner, Abram. "Freud: The Man I Knew, the Scientist, and His Influence." In Benjamin Nelson, ed., *Freud and the Twentieth Century*. New York: Meridian, 1957.

Karen, Robert. "Becoming Attached." *Atlantic Monthly*, Feb. 1990.

Kaufmann, Walter. "Freud and the Tragic Virtues." *American Scholar* 29 (1960): 469–481.

Kazin, Alfred. "The Freudian Revolution Analyzed." *New York Times Magazine*, May 6, 1956.

Kety, Seymour. "Biochemical Theories of Schizophrenia." *Science* 129 (pt. 1, June 5, 1959: 1528–1532; pt. 2, June 12, 1959: 1590–1596).

———. "A Biologist Examines the Mind and Behavior." *Science* 132, no. 3443 (Dec. 23, 1960): 1861–1870.

———. "From Rationalization to Reason." *American Journal of Psychiatry* 131, no. 9 (Sept. 1974): 957–963.

———. "The Heuristic Aspect of Psychiatry." *American Journal of Psychiatry* 118 (Nov. 1961): 385–397.

———. "The Metamorphosis of a Psychobiologist." *Annual Review of Neuroscience* 2 (1979): 1–15.

———. "Studies Based on a Total Sample of Adopted Individuals and Their Relatives: Why They Were Necessary, What They Demonstrated and Failed to Demonstrate." *Schizophrenia Bulletin* 2, no. 3 (1976): 413–428.

Kety, Seymour, and Rosenthal, David, eds. *The Transmission of Schizophrenia*. Oxford, Eng.: Pergamon Press, 1968.

Kety, Seymour, et al. "Mental Illness in the Biological and Adoptive Relatives of Schizophrenic Adoptees: Replication of the Copenhagen Study in the Rest of Denmark." *Archives of General Psychiatry* 51 (June 1994): 442–455.

Klein, Donald. *Anxiety: New Research and Changing Concepts*. New York: Raven Press, 1981.

———. "Psychosocial Treatment of Schizophrenia, or Psychosocial Help for People with Schizophrenia?" *Schizophrenia Bulletin* 6, no. 1 (1980): 122–130.

Klein, Donald, and Paul Wender. *Mind, Mood, and Medicine*. New York: Farrar, Straus & Giroux, 1981.

Klerman, Gerald L. "The Psychiatric Patient's Right to Effective Treatment: Implications of *Osheroff v. Chestnut Lodge.*" *American Journal of Psychiatry* 147, no. 4 (April 1990): 409–418.

Kuhn, Thomas. *The Structure of Scientific Revolutions*. Chicago: University of Chicago Press, 1970.

Kysar, John E. "The Two Camps in Child Psychiatry: A Report from a Psychiatrist-Father of an Autistic and Retarded Son." *American Journal of Psychiatry* 125, no. 1 (July 1968): 1441–1447.

Laing, R. D. *Conversations with Adam and Natasha*. New York: Pantheon, 1977.

———. *The Divided Self*. New York: Penguin, 1990.

———. *The Politics of Experience*. New York: Pantheon, 1967.

Laing, R. D., and Aaron Esterson. *Sanity, Madness, and the Family*. New York: Basic Books, 1971.

Lane, Harlan. *The Wild Boy of Aveyron*. Cambridge, Mass.: Harvard University Press, 1976.

LeCouteur, Anne, et al. "A Broader Phenotype of Autism: The Clinical Spectrum in Twins." *Journal of Child Psychology and Psychiatry* 37 (1996): 785–801.

Levy, David. *Maternal Overprotection*. New York: Norton, 1943.

Levy, Robert I., and Roy Rapaport. "Gregory Bateson, 1904–1980." *American Anthropologist* 84 (1982): 379–394.

Lewontin, R. C., Steven Rose, and Leon Kamin. *Not in Our Genes: Biology, Ideology, and Human Nature*. New York: Pantheon, 1984.

Lidz, Theodore. *The Origin and Treatment of Schizophrenic Disorders*. Madison, Conn.: International Universities Press, 1990.

———. *The Person: His Development Throughout the Life Cycle*. New York: Basic Books, 1968.

———. "A Psychosocial Orientation to Schizophrenic Disorders." *Yale Journal of Biology and Medicine* 58 (1985): 209–217.

Lidz, Theodore, Stephen Fleck, and Alice Cornelison, eds. *Schizophrenia and the Family*. New York: International Universities Press, 1965.

Lifton, Robert Jay. *The Nazi Doctors*. New York: Basic Books, 1986.

Lyons, Tom Wallace. *The Pelican and After*. Richmond, Va.: Prescott, Durrell, 1983.

MacDonald, Michael. *Mystical Bedlam*. Cambridge, Eng.: Cambridge University Press, 1981.

MacDonald, Norma. "Living with Schizophrenia." *Canadian Medical Association Journal* 82 (Jan. 23, 1960): 218–221.

Macmillan, Malcolm. *Freud Evaluated*. Cambridge, Mass.: MIT Press, 1997.

Mahony, Patrick. *Freud and the Rat Man*. New Haven, Conn.: Yale University Press, 1986.

Malcolm, Janet. *In the Freud Archives*. New York: Knopf, 1984.

———. *Psychoanalysis: The Impossible Profession*. New York: Knopf, 1981.

Malcolm, Norman. *Ludwig Wittgenstein: A Memoir*. New York: Oxford University Press, 1984.

Malhi, Gin S., Paul K. Bridges, and Andrea L. Malizia. "Neurosurgery for Mental Disorders. A Clinical Perspective: Past, Present, and Future." *International Journal of Psychiatry in Clinical Practice* 1 (1997): 119–129.

Marshall, Barry, and J. Robin Warren. "Unidentified Bacilli in the Stomach of Patients with Gastritis and Peptic Ulceration." *Lancet*, no. 8390 (June 16, 1984): 1311–1315.

Martin, Russell. *Out of Silence*. New York: Henry Holt, 1994.

Masson, Jeffrey M. *Against Therapy*. New York: Atheneum, 1988.

———. *The Assault on Truth: Freud's Suppression of the Seduction Theory*. New York: Farrar, Straus & Giroux, 1984.

———, ed. *The Complete Letters of Sigmund Freud to Wilhelm Fliess, 1887–1904.* Cambridge, Mass.: Harvard University Press, 1985.

Maurice, Catherine. *Let Me Hear Your Voice.* New York: Knopf, 1993.

May, Jacques. *A Physician Looks at Psychiatry.* New York: John Day, 1958.

May, Philip R. A. "Schizophrenia: A Follow-up Study of the Results of Five Forms of Treatment." *Archives of General Psychiatry* 38 (July 1981): 776–784.

———. *Treatment of Schizophrenia: A Comparative Study of Five Treatment Methods.* New York: Science House, 1968.

McDonnell, Jane Taylor. *News from the Border.* New York: Ticknor & Fields, 1993.

McGuire, William, ed. *The Freud/Jung Letters.* Princeton, N.J.: Princeton University Press, 1974.

McHenry, Lawrence. "Samuel Johnson's Tics and Gesticulations." *Journal of the History of Medicine* 22 (April 1967): 152–168.

McHugh, Paul. "Psychiatric Misadventures." *American Scholar,* Autumn 1992.

———. "Psychotherapy Awry." *American Scholar,* Winter 1994.

Mead, Margaret. *Blackberry Winter: My Earlier Years.* New York: Morrow, 1972.

———. *Coming of Age in Samoa.* New York: Morrow, 1928.

Medawar, Peter. *Pluto's Republic.* Oxford: Oxford University Press, 1982.

Medical Research Council. "Streptomycin Treatment for Pulmonary Tuberculosis." *British Medical Journal* 2 (1948): 769.

Meng, Heinrich, and Ernst L. Freud, eds. *Psychoanalysis and Faith: The Letters of Sigmund Freud and Oskar Pfister.* London: Hogarth Press, 1963.

Menninger, Karl. "Death of a Prophet." *New Republic,* August 9, 1939.

———. "Hope." *American Journal of Psychiatry* 116 (Dec. 1959): 481–491.

———. *A Psychiatrist's World: The Selected Papers of Karl Menninger.* New York: Viking, 1959.

———. "Sigmund Freud." *The Nation,* Oct. 7, 1939.

———. *The Vital Balance.* New York: Viking, 1963.

Mitchell, Stephen A., and Margaret J. Black. *Freud and Beyond.* New York: Basic Books, 1995.

Monmaney, Terence. "Annals of Medicine: Marshall's Hunch." *New Yorker,* Sept. 20, 1993.

Montagu, M. F. Ashley. "Man—and Human Nature." *American Journal of Psychiatry* 112 (Dec. 1955): 401–410.

Mosher, Loren, and Lorenzo Burti. *Community Mental Health.* New York: Norton, 1994.

Mullahy, Patrick. "Harry Stack Sullivan's Theory of Schizophrenia." *International Journal of Psychiatry* 4, no. 6 (Dec. 1967): 492–521. (The entire issue is given over to this essay and replies to it.)

Mullan, Bob. *Mad to Be Normal: Conversations with R. D. Laing.* London: Free Association Books, 1995.

Murray, T. J. "Doctor Samuel Johnson's Abnormal Movements." In Arnold J. Friedhoff and Thomas N. Chase, eds., *Gilles de la Tourette Syndrome.* New York: Raven Press, 1982.

———. "Dr. Samuel Johnson's Movement Disorder." *British Medical Journal* 1 (1979): 1610–1614.

Neill, John. "Whatever Became of the Schizophrenogenic Mother?" *American Journal of Psychotherapy* 49, no. 4 (Oct. 1990): 499–505.

Niederland, W. G. "The 'Miracled-Up' World of Schreber's Childhood." *Psychoanalytic Study of the Child* 14 (1959): 383–413.

North, Carol S. *Welcome, Silence.* New York: Avon, 1989.

Obholzer, Karin. *The Wolf-Man.* New York: Continuum, 1982.

Okasha, A., et al. "Phenomenology of Obsessive-Compulsive Disorder: A Transcultural Study." *Comprehensive Psychiatry* 35 (1994): 191–197.

Osterkamp, Annemargret, and David Sands. "Early Feeding and Birth Difficulties in Childhood Schizophrenia: A Brief Study." *Journal of Genetic Psychology* 101 (1962): 363–366.

Owen, Michael J., and Peter McGuffin. "Genetics and Psychiatry." *British Journal of Psychiatry* 171 (1997): 201–202.

Pagels, Elaine. *Adam, Eve, and the Serpent.* New York: Random House, 1988.

Park, Clara. *The Siege.* Boston: Little, Brown, 1982.

Peck, Harris B., Ralph D. Rabinovitch, and Joseph B. Cramer. "A Treatment Program for Parents of Schizophrenic Children." *American Journal of Orthopsychiatry* 19 (1949): 592–598.

Perry, Helen Swick. *Psychiatrist of America: The Life of Harry Stack Sullivan.* Cambridge, Mass.: Harvard University Press, 1982.

Pollak, Richard. *The Creation of Dr. B.* New York: Simon & Schuster, 1997.

Pollin, William, James R. Stabenau, and Joe Tupin. "Family Studies with Identical Twins Discordant for Schizophrenia." *Psychiatry* 28, no. 1 (Feb. 1965): 60–78.

Porter, Roy. *Mind-Forg'd Manacles: A History of Madness in England.* Cambridge, Mass.: Harvard University Press, 1987.

———, ed. *The Faber Book of Madness.* London: Faber & Faber, 1991.

Poynton, Amanda M. "Current State of Psychosurgery." *British Journal of Hospital Medicine* 50, no. 7 (1993): 408–411.

Prasad, Ashoka Jahnavi, ed. *Biological Basis and Therapy of Neuroses.* Boca Raton, Fla.: CRC Press, 1988.

Prout, Curtis, and Mary Alice White. "A Controlled Study of Personality Relationships in Mothers of Schizophrenic Male Patients." *American Journal of Psychiatry* 107 (Oct. 1950): 251–256.

"Psychosurgery: Operation to Cure Sick Minds Turns Surgeon's Blade into an Instrument of Mental Therapy." *Life,* April 7, 1947.

"R. D. Laing: Interview," *Omni,* April 1988.

Rank, Beata. "Adaptation of the Psychoanalytic Technique for the Treatment of Young Children with Atypical Development." *American Journal of Orthopsychiatry* 19 (Jan. 1949): 130–139.

Rapoport, Judith. *The Boy Who Couldn't Stop Washing.* New York: Dutton, 1989.

———, ed. *Obsessive-Compulsive Disorder in Children and Adolescents.* Washington, D.C.: American Psychiatric Press, 1989.

———. "Treatment of Behavior Disorders in Animals." *American Journal of Psychiatry* 147, no. 9 (Sept. 1, 1990): 1249.

Ratey, John J., and Catherine Johnson. *Shadow Syndromes.* New York: Pantheon, 1997.

Rather, L. J. *Mind and Body in Eighteenth Century Medicine.* Berkeley, Calif.: University of California Press, 1965.

Reichard, Suzanne, and Carl Tillman. "Patterns of Parent-Child Relationships in Schizophrenia." *Psychiatry* 13 (1950): 247–257.

Reilly, Rick. "Quest for Perfection." *Sports Illustrated,* Nov. 15, 1993.

Restak, Richard. "Islands of Genius." *Science 82* (May 1982). (This excellent but short-lived magazine should not be confused with the journal *Science.* It can be found in large libraries, but note that its name — *Science 82, Science 83,* etc. — changed with each year.)

Rheingold, Joseph. *The Fear of Being a Woman: A Theory of Maternal Destructiveness.* New York: Grune & Stratton, 1964.

Rieff, Philip. *Freud: The Mind of the Moralist.* Chicago: University of Chicago Press, 1959.

Rimland, Bernard. *Infantile Autism.* New York: Appleton-Century-Crofts, 1964.

———. "Inside the Mind of the Autistic Savant." *Psychology Today,* Aug. 1978.

Roazen, Paul. *Brother Animal: The Story of Freud and Tausk.* New York: Knopf, 1969.

———. *Freud and His Followers.* New York: Knopf, 1975.

Rodgers, Joann. "Roots of Madness." *Science 82* (July–August 1982). (Please see the note with the Richard Restak citation.)

Rogers, Daniel. *Motor Disorder in Psychiatry: Towards a Neurological Psychiatry.* Chichester, Eng.: Wiley, 1992.

Ron, Maria, and Ian Harvey. "The Brain in Schizophrenia." *Journal of Neurology, Neurosurgery, and Psychiatry* 53 (1990): 725–726.

Rosen, John. *Direct Analysis: Selected Papers.* New York: Grune & Stratton, 1953.

Rosenthal, David, ed. *The Genain Quadruplets.* New York: Basic Books, 1963.

Rosenthal, Maurice J. "Psychosomatic Study of Infantile Eczema." *Pediatrics* 10 (1952): 581–592.

Roueché, Berton. "Annals of Medicine: The Hoofbeats of a Zebra." *New Yorker,* June 4, 1984.

Rutter, Michael. *The Qualities of Mothering: Maternal Deprivation Reassessed.* New York: Jason Aronson, 1972.

Rymer, Russ. *Genie.* New York: HarperPerennial, 1993.

Sacks, Oliver. *An Anthropologist on Mars.* New York: Knopf, 1995.

———. *The Man Who Mistook His Wife for a Hat.* New York: Perennial Library, 1987.

Sapolsky, Robert. "On the Role of Upholstery in Cardiovascular Physiology." *Discover,* Nov. 1997.

Sarason, Seymour. *Psychological Problems in Mental Deficiency.* New York: Harper & Brothers, 1953.

Sargant, William. *Battle for the Mind.* London: Heinemann, 1957.

Schachter, Stanley. "Non-Psychological Explanations of Behavior." In Leon Festinger, ed., *Retrospections on Social Psychology.* New York: Oxford University Press, 1980.

Schatzman, Morton. "Freud: Who Seduced Whom?" *New Scientist,* March 21, 1992.

———. "Paranoia or Persecution: The Case of Schreber." *International Journal of Psychiatry* 10, no. 3 (Sept. 1972): 53–78.

Schimek, Jean G. "Fact and Fantasy in the Seduction Theory: A Historical Review." *Journal of the American Psychoanalytic Association* 35 (1987): 937–965.

Schofield, William, and Lucy Balian. "A Comparative Study of the Personal Histories of Schizophrenic and Nonpsychiatric Patients." *Journal of Abnormal and Social Psychology* 59 (1959): 216–225.

Schopler, Eric. "Parents of Psychotic Children as Scapegoats." *Journal of Contemporary Psychotherapy* 4 (Winter 1971): 17–22 (also in Donnellan, *Classic Readings in Autism*).

———. "The Stress of Autism as Ethology." *Journal of Autism and Childhood Schizophrenia* 4, no. 3 (1974): 193–196.

Schopler, Eric, and Gary Mesibov, eds. *Autism in Adolescents and Adults.* New York: Plenum, 1983.

———. *High-Functioning Individuals with Autism.* New York: Plenum, 1992.

Schur, Max. *The Id and the Regulatory Principles of Mental Functioning.* London: Hogarth Press, 1967.

Schwartz, Jeffrey. *Brain Lock.* New York: Regan Books, 1996.

Searles, Harold. *Collected Papers on Schizophrenia and Related Subjects.* London: Hogarth Press, 1965.

———. *The Nonhuman Environment in Normal Development and in Schizophrenia.* New York: International Universities Press, 1960.

———. "The Schizophrenic Individual's Experience of His World." *Psychiatry* 30, no. 2 (May 1967): 119–131.

Sechehaye, Marguerite, ed. *Autobiography of a Schizophrenic Girl: The True Story of "Renée."* New York: Meridian, 1994 (1951).

Sedgwick, Peter. *Psycho Politics.* New York: Harper & Row, 1982.

Seeley, John R. "The Americanization of the Unconscious." *Atlantic Monthly,* July 1961.

Seligman, Martin E. P. *What You Can Change and What You Can't.* New York: Knopf, 1994.

Shapiro, Arthur K., and Elaine Shapiro. "Clinical Dangers of Psychological Theorizing." *Psychiatric Quarterly* 45 (1971): 159–171.

Shapiro, Arthur, et al. *Gilles de la Tourette Syndrome.* New York: Raven Press, 1978.

Shattuck, Roger. *The Forbidden Experiment.* New York: Farrar, Straus & Giroux, 1980.

Sheehan, Susan. *Is There No Place on Earth for Me?* Boston: Houghton Mifflin, 1982.

———. "The Last Days of Sylvia Frumkin." *New Yorker,* Feb. 20 and 27, 1995.

Shershow, John C., ed. *Schizophrenia: Science and Practice.* Cambridge, Mass.: Harvard University Press, 1978.

Shorter, Edward. *From Paralysis to Fatigue: A History of Psychosomatic Illness in the Modern Era.* New York: Free Press, 1992.

———. *A History of Psychiatry.* New York: Wiley, 1997.

Siegler, Miriam, and Humphry Osmond. *Models of Madness, Models of Medicine.* New York: Macmillan, 1974.

Siegler, Miriam; Humphry Osmond; and Harriet Mann. "Laing's Models of Madness." In *The Schizophrenia Syndrome: An Annual Review, 1971,* edited by Robert Cancro. New York: Brunner/Mazel.

Sifford, Darrell. "An Improper-Diagnosis Case That Changed Psychiatry." *Philadelphia Inquirer,* March 24, 1988.

Silvester, Christopher, ed. *The Norton Book of Interviews: An Anthology from 1859 to the Present Day.* New York: Norton, 1996.

Simon, Clea. *Mad House.* New York: Doubleday, 1997.

Slater, Lauren. *Welcome to My Country.* New York: Random House, 1996.

Snyder, Solomon H. *Madness and the Brain.* New York: McGraw-Hill, 1974.

Sommer, Robert, and Humphry Osmond. "A Bibliography of Mental Patients' Autobiographies, 1960–1982." *American Journal of Psychiatry* 140, no. 8 (August 1983): 1051–1054.

Sontag, Susan. *Illness as Metaphor.* New York: Vintage, 1979.

Sperling, Melitta. "The Neurotic Child and His Mother: A Psychoanalytic Study." *American Journal of Orthopsychiatry* 19 (1949): 351–364.

Spitz, René. *The First Year of Life: A Psychoanalytic Study of Normal and Deviant Development of Object Relations.* New York: International Universities Press, 1965.

————. "Hospitalism: An Inquiry into the Genesis of Psychiatric Conditions in Early Childhood." *Psychoanalytic Study of the Child* 1 (1945): 53–75.

Stannard, David. *Shrinking History.* New York: Oxford University Press, 1980.

Stanton, Alfred H., and Morris S. Schwartz. *The Mental Hospital.* New York: Basic Books, 1954.

Stehli, Annabel. *The Sound of a Miracle.* New York: Doubleday, 1991.

Stone, A. A. "The New Paradox of Psychiatric Malpractice." *New England Journal of Medicine* 311 (1984): 1384–1387.

Stone, Leo. "The Widening Scope of Indications for Psychoanalysis." *Journal of the American Psychoanalytic Association* 2, no. 4 (Oct. 1954): 567–594.

Storr, Anthony. *Freud.* New York: Oxford University Press, 1989.

Strecker, Edward. *Their Mothers' Sons.* Philadelphia: J. B. Lippincott, 1951.

Sullivan, Harry Stack. *Schizophrenia as a Human Process.* New York: Norton, 1974.

Sullivan, Ruth. "Rain Man and Joseph." In *High-Functioning Individuals with Autism,* edited by Eric Schopler and Gary Mesibov. New York: Plenum, 1983.

Sulloway, Frank. *Freud, Biologist of the Mind.* New York: Basic Books, 1979.

Sutton, Nina. *Bettelheim.* New York: Basic Books, 1996.

Swayze, Victor. "Frontal Leukotomy and Related Psychosurgical Procedures in the Era Before Antipsychotics (1935–1954): A Historical Overview." *American Journal of Psychiatry* 152, no. 4 (April 1995): 505–515.

Thompson, Clara. "Harry Stack Sullivan, the Man." *Psychiatry* 12, no. 4 (Nov. 1949): 435–437.

Tietze, Trude. "A Study of Mothers of Schizophrenic Patients." *Psychiatry* 12, no. 1 (Feb. 1949): 55–65.

Tinbergen, E. A., and N. Tinbergen. *"Autistic" Children: New Hope for a Cure.* London: George Allen & Unwin, 1983.

————. *Early Childhood Autism: An Ethological Approach.* Berlin: Parey, 1972.

Tinbergen, Nikolaas. "Ethology and Stress Diseases." *Science* 185 (July 5, 1974): 20–27.

Torrey, E. Fuller. *Freudian Fraud.* New York: HarperCollins, 1992.

————. *Surviving Schizophrenia: A Manual for Families, Consumers and Providers.* 3rd ed. New York: HarperPerennial, 1995.

Torrey, E. Fuller, et al. *Schizophrenia and Manic-Depressive Disorder.* New York: Basic Books, 1994.

Treffert, Darold. *Extraordinary People: Understanding "Idiot Savants."* New York: Harper & Row, 1989.

Trilling, Lionel, and Steven Marcus, eds. *The Life and Work of Sigmund Freud.* New York: Anchor, 1963.

Turner, Samuel M., and Deborah C. Beidel. *Treating Obsessive-Compulsive Disorder.* New York: Pergamon Press, 1988.

Valenstein, Elliot S. *Great and Desperate Cures.* New York: Basic Books, 1986.

Vaughan, Susan C. *The Talking Cure: The Science Behind Psychotherapy.* New York: Putnam, 1997.

Vertosick, Frank T. "Lobotomy's Back." *Discover,* Oct. 1997.

Victor, George. *The Riddle of Autism: A Psychological Analysis.* Northvale, N.J.: Jason Aronson, 1995.

Viscott, David. "A Musical Idiot Savant." *Psychiatry* 33, no. 4 (1970): 494–514.

Vonnegut, Mark. "Why I Want to Bite R. D. Laing." *Harper's,* April 1974.

Walsh, Maryellen. *Schizophrenia: Straight Talk for Family and Friends.* New York: Quill, 1985.

Wassersug, Joseph. "None of the Physicians Could Find the Coin in Her Throat." *American Medical News* 34, no. 20 (May 27, 1991).

Webster, Richard. *Why Freud Was Wrong.* New York: Basic Books, 1995.

Weigert, Edith. "In Memoriam: Frieda Fromm-Reichmann." *Psychiatry* 21 (Feb. 1958): 91–95.

Weiland, Hyman. "Considerations of the Development and Treatment of Autistic Childhood Psychosis." *Psychoanalytic Study of the Child* 16 (1961): 549–563.

Weinberg, George. *Invisible Masters: Compulsions and the Fear That Drives Them.* New York: Plume, 1995.

Weissman, M. M., et al. "The Cross-National Epidemiology of Obsessive-Compulsive Disorder." *Journal of Clinical Psychiatry* 55S (1994): 5–10.

Wender, Paul. "On Necessary and Sufficient Conditions in Psychiatric Explanation." *Archives of General Psychiatry* 16 (Jan. 1967): 41–47.

Wender, Paul H., et al. "Crossfostering: A Research Strategy for Clarifying the Role of Genetic and Experiential Factors in the Etiology of Schizophrenia." *Archives of General Psychiatry* 30 (Jan. 1974): 121–128.

Wender, Paul H., et al. "The Psychiatric Adjustment of the Adopting Parents of Schizophrenics." *American Journal of Psychiatry* 127, no. 8 (Feb. 1971): 53–58.

Williams, Donna. *Nobody Nowhere.* New York: Times Books, 1992.

———. *Somebody Somewhere.* New York: Times Books, 1994.

Wilson, Louise. *This Stranger, My Son.* New York: Putnam, 1968.

Wing, J. K. *Reasoning About Madness.* New York: Oxford University Press, 1978.

Wing, Lorna. *Autistic Children: A Guide for Parents.* New York: Brunner/Mazel, 1972.

Wing, Lorna, and Derek M. Ricks. "The Etiology of Childhood Autism: A Criticism of the Tinbergens' Ethological Theory." *Psychological Medicine* 6 (1976): 533–543.

Wing, Lorna, ed. *Early Childhood Autism.* Oxford, Eng.: Pergamon Press, 1976.

Wittels, Fritz. *Sigmund Freud.* New York: Dodd, Mead, 1924.

Wolman, Benjamin, ed. *Handbook of Child Psychoanalysis.* New York: Van Nostrand Reinhold, 1972.

Wolpe, Joseph, and Stanley Rachman. "Psychoanalytic 'Evidence': A Critique Based on Freud's Case of 'Little Hans.'" *Journal of Nervous and Mental Disease* 131 (1960).

Wortis, Joseph. "Fragments of a Freudian Analysis." *American Journal of Orthopsychiatry* 10, no. 4 (Oct. 1940): 843–849.

Wylie, Philip. *Generation of Vipers.* New York: Rinehart, 1942.

Zohar, Joseph; Thomas Insel; and Steven Rasmussen, eds. *The Psychobiology of Obsessive-Compulsive Disorder.* New York: Springer, 1991.

Acknowledgments

I N MANY WAYS, this book is a tribute to the dozens of parents of schizophrenic and autistic children who talked to me at great length, and at the cost of considerable emotional turmoil, about what they had endured through the years. Reluctant soldiers who found themselves serving in a lifelong war, they were heroes against their will. They were heroes nonetheless. But in the years that this book covers, they were doubly damned, first by fate and then by "healers" who accused them of driving their children mad. The outsider can hardly imagine the isolation they faced. It is a privilege to honor their accomplishment.

I found many of these parents with the help of the National Alliance for the Mentally Ill. This admirable organization, most of whose members have relatives with severe mental illness, was invaluable to me. I am grateful as well to the many scientists and psychiatrists who met with me and did their best to help me reconstruct a bygone intellectual world. Both those who disputed my thesis and those who supported it were generous with their time and their recollections. In addition, I sought advice and guidance of a more general sort from writers who have taken on related subjects. E. Fuller Torrey and Frederick Crews were especially helpful. At the outset of this project and at several points along the way, I turned to them for advice and navigational guidance.

This book rests on a solid foundation of work by renowned historians. In particular, I drew time and again on three especially valuable works of medical history: Edward Shorter's history of psychiatry, Nathan Hale's history of psychoanalysis, and Elliot Valenstein's history of psychosurgery. Those books are well known and widely available. For access to a host of far more obscure medical works, I am happy to acknowledge my debt to the National Library of Medicine. I spent the better part of two years burrowing through that almost limitless collection in search of ever more arcane books and articles. It should be noted, moreover, that my debt is figurative rather than literal, for the library remains gloriously free to all users.

Several readers helped me along the way. Some are editors by profession, others by inclination. For their labors with blue pencils, I'm grateful to Frederick Crews, Karel de Pauw, Anne Donnellan, Steven Flax, Ross Gelbspan, Arthur Golden, Stephen Golden, Holly Nixholm, Clara Park, Alfred Singer, Dinah Singer, and Susan West. Not content with editing, de Pauw, a psychiatrist and a voracious reader, took it upon himself to send me a steady stream of relevant but obscure texts.

One reader, Allen Esterson, deserves special thanks. We have never met. I wrote Esterson a fan letter after I read *Seductive Mirage*, his critique of Freud, and we began an e-mail correspondence that has grown beyond all reasonable bounds.

Esterson is a fair-minded, thoughtful, and scrupulous scholar; I have benefited enormously from our discussions.

I am deeply indebted as well to Kate Headline, researcher extraordinaire. She found the illustrations, often against long odds, reproduced in the text. For his zealous and resourceful pursuit of elusive documents, I am grateful to Andy Puente. I owe thanks to Corby Kummer, who steered me to my agent, Raphael Sagalyn. Rafe is a sophisticated reader and a loyal but levelheaded ally, and I relied on him heavily. At Simon & Schuster, I was the happy beneficiary of Roger Labrie's deft way with a manuscript. Fred Wiemer copyedited thoughtfully and meticulously. My greatest debt is to Alice Mayhew. She championed this project when it was barely shaped and helped nurture it as it grew. She is, to put it briefly, the editor that writers hope for.

I owe Ruth Holmberg special thanks. Many years ago, before I was properly embarked on a career, she suggested journalism, a notion that had never occurred to me. In that advice, and in countless ways, she has enriched my life. My wife, Lynn, has provided support and encouragement at every step of a long journey. She read and reread the manuscript as it evolved, edited it with a mix of kindness and ruthlessness, and improved it immensely. Her formidable editing skills are the least of the story. It would take a far greater writer than I am to find words to convey my devotion to her, and to our sons, Sam and Ben.

Index

Cromwell, Oliver, 9, 27
"Cultural Implications of Children's
Behavior Problems" (Kanner), 208

Dachau concentration camp, 169, 182–183
Dali, Salvador, 55n
Danton, Georges Jacques, 27
Darwin, Charles, 11, 27, 143
Darwin, Erasmus, 143
death, 26, 37–38, 96
    of patients, 37–38, 116, 146, 147
    purposefulness of, 25
death instinct, 28, 75
Delay, Jean, 151
delusions, 35, 87, 88–89, 91–92, 103, 105, 108–10, 112, 113–15, 151, 152
    direct analysis and, 108–9, 111–12
    of grandeur, 89n
DeMyer, Marian, 209, 226–27
Deniker, Pierre, 151
Denmark, 159, 163
Dennis, Wayne, 195–96
depression, 14, 15, 66, 77, 148, 151, 277
    antidepressant drug treatment for, 145, 149n, 263, 269, 277–78, 289, 291
    cingulotomy for, 149n
    electroshock therapy for, 145
    induced in monkeys, 198
    manic-, 14, 149n, 151n
    psychotherapy for, 277, 278
Depression, Great, 59, 67
Descartes, René, 292
Despert, J. Louise, 187, 188, 286–87
developmental disorders, 13, 125
diabetes, 68–69, 144, 155
    personality traits linked to, 69
direct analysis, 108–9, 111–12, 115
Discovery of the Unconscious (Ellenberger), 32
displacement, 14, 35, 247, 254
Divided Self, The (Laing), 133
dogs, 271
    obsessive-compulsive disorder in, 270
Donnellan, Anne, 184
doorway rituals, compulsive, 243, 266, 271

Dora case, 23–24, 36, 38, 40, 44, 48
double bind theory, 117, 119–23
    identification of, 166
    overabundant examples of, 165–66
    potential responses in, 120
doubts, obsessive-compulsive, 243–44, 253–54, 257, 271–72
Down's syndrome, 229
dreams, 23, 29n, 37, 44, 48, 65, 87, 93, 111, 260
    historical views of, 32
    importance of, 21–22
    symbolism in, 41, 250, 255
    wish-fulfillment in, 27–28, 33, 50, 250
drug addiction, 144
drug treatments, 150–53, 288, 289, 291
    serendipitous discovery of, 151n
    see also antidepressant drugs; antipsychotic drugs
Dryfoos, Jacqueline, 101–2
Dunbar, Helen Flanders, 68–70, 71, 288–89
dyspnea, symbolism of, 23–24
dystonia musculorum deformans, 282–283

Eckstein, Emma, case of, 44–47, 48
eczema, 69, 283
Eden Express, The (Vonnegut), 91
ego, 27
Ehrmann, Claudia, 116
Einstein, Albert, 27, 77
Eisenberg, Leon, 55, 61, 64–65, 187, 188, 210, 211, 213, 227, 279
Eisenbud, Jule, 109
Eisenhower, Dwight D., 57
Ekstein, Rudolf, 214
electroshock therapy, 64, 138, 144–45, 161, 284
Elisabeth of Bohemia, Princess, 292
Ellenberger, Henri, 32
Emotions and Bodily Changes (Dunbar), 68
Empty Fortress, The (Bettelheim), 179, 181, 183–84, 189, 205, 210, 212–213, 216, 217, 218, 225
England, 67, 89, 134n, 136
English, O. Spurgeon, 115

Printed in the United States
128474LV00002B/73/A